D1197661

POOR COLLINS

*His Life, His Art, and
His Influence*

POOR COLLINS

His Life, His Art, and His Influence

BY EDWARD GAY AINSWORTH JR.

ASSISTANT PROFESSOR OF ENGLISH
UNIVERSITY OF MISSOURI

ITHACA · NEW YORK
CORNELL UNIVERSITY PRESS

LONDON: HUMPHREY MILFORD
OXFORD UNIVERSITY PRESS
1937

PRINTED IN THE UNITED STATES OF AMERICA
THE COLLEGIATE PRESS, MENASHA, WISCONSIN

TO
MY FATHER AND MOTHER

PREFACE

THE PAGES on Collins which follow were really begun ten years ago when Professor Frederick Clarke Prescott awakened my interest in Collins in the class-room at Cornell University. Since that time Collins has fascinated me, and the conviction has grown with my growth that I should sometime write a study of his poetry. As I have taught his fine lyrics to my students at the University of Missouri, I have felt the need of some appreciative yet accurate commentary on his mind and art—a commentary to which my own enthusiastic students might care to turn. For their assistance in understanding poems which frequently cause difficulties I have in the text analyzed some of the odes in detail. I would not, however, put forward any of these interpretations dogmatically as final, for I feel with one of my finest teachers that it is dangerous to assign in prose too definite and exclusive a meaning to any poem. In writing I have tried as well to keep in mind those lovers of Collins who have approached him with a more mature and scholarly attitude.

Aside from Mr. Bronson's fine work on Collins in 1898, no American study of Collins has appeared in recent years, and I felt that my own researches added something to his study. Mr. Blunden's beautiful Haslewood Press edition of 1929, unfortunately a limited edition, stimulated my own enthusiasm and led me to follow up many of his suggestions more fully. Mr. Garrod's two studies of Collins in the same year challenged me and led me to weigh more carefully many of my own judgments, perhaps to temper my enthusiasms, perhaps to question again matters which had seemed clear to me although they puzzled him. The resulting study is, as was Mr. Garrod's, "something between an essay and a commentary."

I have tried to consider Collins from three aspects, distinct yet related. The first major division of the study attempts to see Collins as man and poet, to understand his mind and art as far as that is possible, to see what his limitations and his merits were. This has necessitated a brief restatement of essential biographical details, neither exhaustive nor original, but perhaps bringing together a number of small yet significant discoveries which have already appeared in print—discoveries which Mr. H. O. White, long acknowledged the foremost living authority on Collins, will undoubtedly supplement when his own long-awaited study of Collins appears. I have, however, rather followed the suggestion advanced long ago by M. Emile Montégut that the poems themselves constitute the best document we have concerning Collins, that in a sense they reveal his soul to us. In studying Collins's ideas of man, of nature, and of human life, I have endeavored to weigh justly yet cautiously the relation between the external facts of his life and the imaginative tissue of his work, showing as well as I can the characteristic qualities of his mind and art. The second major division of the book discusses the literary sources of Collins's poetry, the influences that stimulated his art and his expression. Here, too, it has been my aim to keep in the foreground the imaginative process itself, the use made of the source rather than the source itself. Convinced by such a study as Professor Lowes's *Road to Xanadu* that the imaginative process of the poet is the most fascinating side of his genius, I have purposely omitted, discussed summarily, or relegated to footnotes many minor suggestions of influence that have been noted by my predecessors. The third division of the work attempts to show anew and perhaps more specifically what M. Montégut suggested many years ago: that Collins enjoyed in the romantic age a "modest and amiable renown," that the major romantic poets recognized in Collins *"la molecule première, tout à fait irréductible et indivisible, de la poésie nouvelle qu'ils s'efforçaient de faire triompher."* Again I have been concerned with major figures for the most part. I have not attempted to trace the undoubted influence of Collins on every minor versifier who followed him. Rather I have been content to see how Collins touched the imagination of Wordsworth, of Byron, of Keats, and how significant his influence was, particularly at the time when the *Lyrical Ballads* were new and fresh. If in all of my study I have emphasized too sharply the romantic and imaginative sides of Collins's genius and influence, I have so erred because I feel that the point has not been sufficiently emphasized. The classical side of his genius and the coldly sculpturesque quality of his art have been stressed too sharply, I believe.

In a field where documents, testimonies, and articles are so few, I have, of necessity, resaid much that has already been printed or said. I have tried, whenever I could, to add something of my own to what I have used. In some cases I had independently worked out a problem myself before I was able to find the study of an earlier gleaner in the field; yet I have always checked my own observations with previous discoveries. Though I have sedulously attempted to acknowledge my exact indebtedness in the notes, I must here mention that I have drawn very largely on the work of Mr. Bronson, with whom I sometimes take issue; that I have read sympathetically the recent studies of Messrs. Edmund Blunden and H. W. Garrod; and that the researches of Messrs. H. O. White, Alan D. McKillop, and A. S. P. Woodhouse, which have appeared in the last ten years, have furnished the source or the basis for many of my conclusions.

I am grateful to the libraries of the University of Missouri and Cornell University and to the New York State Library for their courtesies in putting their facilities at my disposal. To the Newbury Library of Chicago, and the libraries of Yale University, Harvard University, and the University of Michigan I am indebted for the loan and use of books not here available. The Drexel Music Collection of the New York City Public Library was of particular assistance in helping me to find musical settings of the poems of Collins.

Many debts of a more personal nature are pleasant to record. My colleagues in the Department of English at the University of Missouri have given me friendly encouragement at every stage of my work. Dr. A. H. R. Fairchild and Dr. J. W. Rankin have read all or part of the manuscript and have made many helpful suggestions. To Dr. R. L. Ramsay I owe the source for one of the images in the *Ode on the Poetical Character* which I might otherwise have missed. Dr. H. M. Belden has given me unsparingly patient and judicious criticism and has imparted to me much of his enthusiasm for the literature of the eighteenth century. He has, too, aided me in many difficult matters of fact and interpretation. My deep appreciation is also due Dr. Walter Miller of the Department of Classics and Archaeology who painstakingly traced the classical suggestions in Collins's verse while recovering from a dangerous illness. My friends Dr. Gilbert M. Fess and H. McClure Young, M.D., have read the work critically; Dr. Helmut Rehder and Mr. Sam Bushman have patiently listened to the reading of much of the manuscript.

To many friends elsewhere I owe a debt of gratitude. My friend and former teacher, Professor F. C. Prescott of Cornell University, has been of inestimable assistance to me in kindly suggestion and counsel. Dr. Joseph Q. Adams of the Folger Shakespeare Library, Washington, D.C., once my teacher at Cornell University, has given me much friendly and scholarly advice. Besides making available to me his personal file of the *Scots Magazine,* Dr. Harold W. Thompson of the New York State College for Teachers at Albany has read all of the manuscript and has offered many a pointed suggestion, the more valuable because of my friendly association with him as a fellow-scholar and walking companion. Dr. John J. Elson, of George Washington University, Washington, D.C., has added to the sympathetic reading of the work the kindness of an intimate friend and fellow-student. Professor William Clyde De Vane has read the manuscript critically. Mr. Woodford Patterson has done many kind offices in helping to see the study through the press. Prof. Wilbur Gilman and Mr. Sam Davis have kindly assisted in reading the proof. And Miss Helen A. Fraser of Albany, N.Y., has given me much shrewd criticism and much cautious admonition. To my students, Mr. Robert J. Geist and Mr. Edwin J. Roeder, I owe a special debt. Both possessed their souls in patience during the trying process of typing the manuscript and both have given generously of that faith which is the true bond of relationship between student and teacher.

E. G. A., JR.

COLUMBIA, MISSOURI,
  MARCH 1, 1936.

CONTENTS

PART I

THE MIND AND ART OF COLLINS

I

COLLINS'S BRIEF HISTORY

We Poets in our youth begin in gladness;
But thereof come in the end despondency and madness.

So Wordsworth wrote of Chatterton and Burns and, he might have added, such was the fate of Collins. For of all the poets of his day Collins's promise was greatest and the tragedy of his life most pathetic. Yet too often has he been thought of as "poor Collins." The positive sides of his genius—his learning, his idealism, his imagination, now lofty, now delicate, his sensitiveness to nature, and his tender pity for man, his reaction to the stirring events of his own day—more than compensate for his tragic failures, for his unachieved aims. It is a fascinating task to try to understand his mind and his art, particularly because the testimonies about him are so few; it is, moreover, surprising to find that in the scant evidence we have left of him we can discover so much. Any study of a poet must necessarily consider the external events of his life, for they reveal something of the secret of his work, although, as a penetrating French critic observed long ago, the poems themselves constitute the best document we have concerning him. Particularly is this true of Collins, of whom his contemporaries left so slight a record.

For outside of the poems Collins has left us little account of himself. But two of his letters have to date been discovered; perhaps we have a prose essay of his. For the rest we have relatively little to reveal the man in his habit as he lived. No "character" of him appeared in his lifetime. Both the brief memoir in Fawkes and Woty's *Poetical Calendar,* reprinted in the *Gentleman's Magazine,* and the short life in Langhorne's edition of 1765 were written after his death; and Johnson's account of him in *The Lives of the Poets* came almost thirty years after the period of Johnson's friendship with him. The letters of his friends

Ragsdale and Gilbert White of Selborne were hazy reminiscences of a friendship obscured by time and separation. For the rest there are but occasional allusions to him in the letters and writings of the brothers Warton, in the letters of Mulso to Gilbert White, and in the correspondence of Johnson, supplemented by occasional comment about him in contemporary magazines. From these sources and from the painstaking search of his editors a shadowy and incomplete account of the facts of his life may be drawn. Each record adds something to the understanding of that inner world of imagination in which Collins most fully lived.

The poet was born at Chichester late in 1721, according to Johnson on Christmas Day. The Parish Register of the Subdeanery Church, otherwise St. Peter's the Great, records his baptism on January 1, 1721, Old Style (1722 N. S.). He was the son of William Collins, according to the register "Then Mayor of this City," and his wife Elizabeth. His father, a hatter of good reputation,[1] not the manufacturer of hats but the vender, according to Ragsdale,[2] lived in a genteel style at Chichester, numbering among his patrons Caryll, the friend of Pope.[3] He had, says Ragsdale, filled the office of Mayor more than once,

---

[1] Johnson, *Lives,* ed. G. B. Hill, III, 335.
[2] This and subsequent citations from Ragsdale are drawn from his letter to William Hymers of Oxford, dated July, 1783. Hymers was then collecting material for an edition of Collins. This with the letter of Thomas Warton to Hymers of about the same date was printed, after Hymers's death, in *The Reaper* (according to Dyce originally a part of *The York Chronicle*), from January, 1796–June, 1797. *The Reaper* was later privately reprinted in book form in 1798, though never published. Bronson notes that the letters of Warton and Ragsdale were reprinted in *The Gleaner*, edited by Nathan Drake (London, 1811, IV, 475-84). Ragsdale's letter, "shamefully mutilated" in *The Gleaner*, was correctly reprinted in *The Monthly Magazine*, vol. XXI, for July, 1806. The letter by Gilbert White, to which reference is made, is dated January 20, 1781. It appeared anonymously in the *Gentleman's Magazine* for January, 1781, signed "V." Moy Thomas prints it in the *Aldine Collins*, pp. xxxi-xxxiv, from the original manuscript addressed "For Mr. Urban. To the care of Mr. Newbury, at the Corner of St. Paul's Churchyard, London.", bearing the postmark "Alton." It is here (*Aldine Collins*, p. xxx) attributed to Gilbert White, "the celebrated author of the Natural History of Selborne.'" It had previously been attributed to White by "Scrutator," a correspondent of the *Gentleman's Magazine* for May, 1803 (vol. XCIII, pt. 1, p. 409). In the *Gentleman's Magazine* for February, 1781, p. 211, "Scrutator" had also identified Col. Martin as Collins's maternal uncle.
[3] *Aldine Collins,* p. xii.

according to Bronson in 1714 and in 1721, the year of the poet's birth.[4] The poet's mother, Elizabeth Martin of Southcott, near West Wittering, he had married on February 13, 1703, according to the parish register of Ernley. The poet was the youngest of three children. His sister Elizabeth was born in 1704, his second sister, Ann, in 1705. He was, then, much younger than the other children, born when his mother was about forty and his father about forty-seven, the child of their later years, a fact to which M. Montégut attributes with undue emphasis the instability of the poet's character. This difference in the ages of the children might also account for the later unsympathetic attitude of the sisters (particularly Ann) toward their gifted brother.

In his early youth he apparently attended the Prebendal School in Chichester, founded in the reign of Edward the Fourth.[5] Langhorne tells us[6] that Collins's father intended him for the service of the Church. With this view in mind he was admitted (in 1733) to Winchester College, according to the college register on January 19, "on the foundation," receiving his board, lodging, and tuition free.[7] The *Aldine Collins* gives an illuminating account of the years Collins spent there:

The scholars are formally elected; but the choice falls only upon such as have influence with the nominees, who are mostly clergymen. In this venerable institution, where the scholars on the foundation wear the dress prescribed by the rules of the founder, in which rejoicings over a holiday are sung in ancient Latin verse, and terms and phrases long fallen into disuse without its walls, are still the current talk of healthy boys, Collins remained seven years.[8]

Among his friends at Winchester were Joseph Warton, with whom his own interests were always closely associated, William Whitehead, later a minor poet and Poet Laureate, Hampton, the translator of Polybius, and the Reverend John Mulso, later the friend of Gilbert White of Selborne. At Winchester, too,

---

[4] The *Aldine Collins*, p. ix, says he was "thrice mayor."
[5] *Aldine Collins*, p. x.
[6] *Collins*, 1781, p. v.
[7] Bronson, xii. Cf. Johnson, *Lives*, III, 335: "He was in 1733 . . . admitted *Scholar* of Winchester College, where he was educated by Dr. Burton."
[8] *Aldine Collins*, p. x.

in the first year of his stay, he must have seen Pope, who visited the school in September, with his host Lord Peterborough, and proposed a subject for a prize poem.

Of his scholarship at Winchester there are two scant suggestions. Johnson records, possibly on the testimony of Warton, that his English exercises were better than his Latin. White, again on hearsay, for he did not know Collins until he came to Oxford, reports that he was "soon distinguished for his early proficiency and his turn for elegant composition." But he did begin to write poetry at an early date in his Wykehamite career. Tradition says that at the age of twelve he wrote a poem *On the Battle of the Schoolbooks,* suggested by Swift's *Battle of the Books,* one line of which survived:

> And every Gradus flapped his leathern wing.

The line is significant in itself. The phrase "leathern wing" comes from *A Midsummer Night's Dream,* testifying how early Collins had turned to Shakespeare; it was to reappear later in the texture of the *Ode to Evening.*[9]

During the Winchester period, too, Collins, in Johnson's phrase, "first courted the publick," by some verses *To a Lady Weeping,* published in the *Gentleman's Magazine* for October, 1739, under the title of *Sonnet.* It has since been concluded that although Johnson appended the verses as they appeared in *The Poetical Calendar,* 1763, vol. XII, to his life of the poet as Collins's first production, they are not by Collins.[10] But surely his are the verses labeled *Sonnet,* "When Phoebe formed

[9] This anonymous reminiscence appeared in *The European Magazine and London Review,* December, 1795, p. 377. Connected with the same period is the poem *On the Royal Nuptials* by William Collins, noted in the *Gentleman's Magazine* for March, 1734, in the register of books published for that month. Dyce sought for the poem in vain. Both Moy Thomas (*Aldine Collins,* p. xii) and Bronson (*Collins,* p. xiii) doubt that Collins could have written the poem at so early an age. Mr. Iolo A. Williams (*Seven Eighteenth Century Bibliographies,* 102-4) suggests that the poem was the work of one William Collier, who two years before had published a *Congratulatory Poem on his Majesty's Happy Return to England,* printed by the same printer. Mr. Williams considers "Collins" a misprint for "Collier."

[10] G. Birkbeck Hill attributes the verses to Dr. Swan (*Johnson's Letters,* II, 130; *Lives of the Poets,* III, 342). Dyce (*Poetical Works of William Collins,* p. 247) questions their authenticity. Bronson (*Collins,* p. 79) accepts them as genuine. They are not included in the Oxford Edition of Gray and Collins, edited by Christopher Stone and A. Lane Poole, 1917.

a Wanton Smile" which appeared in the *Gentleman's Magazine* for October of the same year, signed "Delicatulus," an admirable nom de plume for Collins. They form one of a group of three poems by Wykehamite poetasters. Wooll records in his *Memoirs of J. Warton,* p. 107, a signed memorandum in Dr. Warton's handwriting in a magazine (obviously the *Gentleman's*):

Sappho's Advice was written by me, then at Winchester School; the next by Tomkyns; and the sonnet by Collins.

Wooll reprints the three poems in his memoir and adds, p. 109, a criticism on them supposedly by Johnson in a letter to the editor of the *Gentleman's Magazine* for November, 1739. The criticism praises the poem of Collins:

The least, which is a favourite of mine, carries a force mixed with tenderness and an uncommon elevation.

If it be by Johnson it is more kindly than the comment he made on Collins's poetry in the *Lives* long afterwards. Moreover it notes in this early work that quality of tenderness always associated with the poet, and it is the first incident in what was later to ripen into a close friendship.

To the seven years at Winchester belong also two other more significant poems of Collins. The *Song. The Sentiments Borrowed from Shakespeare,* it is conjectured, was written in 1739.[11] The more typical qualities of the poet begin here to be

---

[11] *Aldine Collins,* p. 101, Oxford edn., p. 311. On the authenticity of this poem see McKillop, A.D., "A Poem in the Collins Canon," *MLN,* March, 1922, XXXVII, 181, which mentions that Beloe in *The Sexagenarian or the Recollections of a Literary Life,* London, 1817, I, 173-9, prints it as the work of Henry Headley. But see also Mr. McKillop's "Biographical Note on Collins," *MLN,* March, 1923, XXXVIII, 184-5, which cites a note in the *Gentleman's Magazine* for February, 1788, definitely attributing the authorship to Collins:

February 2

Mr. Urban,

    In turning over your magazine for May, 1765, I observed a copy of most elegant verses by Collins, which are not to be found in any edition of his poems. [Reference is, as Mr. McKillop points out, to *Verses Written on a Paper which contained a Piece of Bride Cake.*] The following lines are to the best of my knowledge in the same predicament, and I believe have never yet appeared in print.

Yours

J. C. C—T—O

This was the first printing of these verses. The poem also appeared in the *Public Advertiser* in 1788.

felt as well as his admiration for Shakespeare, shortly afterward to find expression in the *Epistle to Hanmer* in 1744. In the last part of his stay there, too, he came upon Salmon's *Modern History* and was influenced by the pastorals of Pope to write the *Persian Eclogues*. In his edition of Pope, Joseph Warton writes:

Mr. Collins wrote his Eclogues when he was about seventeen years old, at Winchester School, and as I well remember, had just been reading that volume of Salmon's *Modern History* which described Persia; which determined him to lay the scene of these pieces, as being productive of new images and sentiments.[12]

The same period of authorship is suggested in the title-page of one of the two copies of the 1742 edition preserved in the Dyce Library at South Kensington. The title-page bears the note "By Mr. Collins (written at Winchester School)." "This copy," Warton records on the back of the title-page, "Mr. Collins gave me . . . with his own Hands when I and my Brother visited Him for the last time at Chichester," an event possibly dated September, 1754, in a later letter of Thomas Warton. It is significant that even at Winchester Collins should have been interested in poetry "productive of new images and sentiments."

Collins's stay at Winchester was terminated in 1740. As Johnson records,[13] he stood first in the list of scholars to be received in succession at New College; but unhappily there was no vacancy—in Johnson's mind "the original misfortune of his life." The *Aldine Collins*[14] records the conditions of election to New College:

According to the custom of Winchester, each boy is superannuated on the first election day after he has attained the age of eighteen. On that day candidates from among the scholars undergo an examination, and their names are subsequently inscribed, in order of their degrees of proficiency, on a roll for admission to any vacancy that may occur during the succeeding year, at New College, Oxford.

An excerpt from the *Oxford University Calendar*, 1833, p. 207,[15] clarifies the relationship between New College and Win-

---

[12] Warton, *Pope*, 1797, I, 61.
[13] *Lives*, III, 334.
[14] *Aldine Collins*, p. xiv.
[15] Cited by G. B. Hill, Johnson, *Lives*, III, 335.

chester, which had a common foundation, and the method of selection employed:

The seventy Fellows and Scholars of New College are elected from the College of Winchester, where an election is held annually to supply the vacancies which may happen in the course of the ensuing year.

Collins stood first in the competitive examination, Joseph Warton was second, and Mulso third, according to Gilbert White's letter of 1781. As no vacancy ensued he remained at Winchester. Finally on March 21 he entered Queen's College, and matriculated the next day. The Register of Matriculations of Oxford records: "1739/40 Mar. 22. Coll. Reg. Gul: Collins 18 Gul: Fil: de Chichester in Com: Sussexiae. Gen: Fil." Johnson conjectures that his maintenance was probably scanty.[16] In July, 1741, he was elected a Demy of Magdalen College, supposedly through the influence of his cousin, Dr. William Payne, then a fellow of that college.[17] Bloxam's *Register of Magdalen College,* VI, 254, mentions Collins's election, but says nothing of his previous affiliation with Queen's:

Remaining still at Winchester he was elected in the summer of 1740, and placed first upon the roll for New College, but no vacancy occurring during the year he became superannuated. On July 29, 1741, he was admitted a Demy of Magdalen.

The *Magdalen College Register* records that on that date "were admitted Demies of Magdalen College, Thomas Vernon . . . and William Collins; the latter aged 19, from Chichester, Co. Sussex."

Collins found his college experience unsatisfactory. Like Wordsworth he may have felt that he was not of that age or of that hour. More probably his experience was like that of many a student of genius who rebels at the formality of the academic life and prefers to follow the desultory course in which his own interests lead him. Langhorne says[18] that during his residence at Queen's

---

[16] *Lives,* III, 334. On the duration of his stay at Queen's see *Ibid.,* III, 334; White's letter inaccurately states that "he remained a year or two."

[17] *Aldine Collins,* p. xv; article in *Gentleman's Magazine,* October, 1823, by "some contemporaries of Collins at Magdalen College."

[18] *Collins,* 1781, p. vi.

he was at once distinguished for genius and indolence; his exercises when he could be prevailed on to write, bearing the visible characteristics of both.

Gilbert White, who knew him at Oxford, records that

As he brought with him, for so the whole turn of his conversation discovered, too high an opinion of his school acquisitions, and a sovereign contempt for all academic studies and discipline, he never looked with any complacency on his situation in the university, but was always complaining of the dullness of a college life.

White's account reveals both the sharpness of the poet's mind and the restlessness and instability of his character, qualities accentuated in his maturer years. To this period belongs White's anecdote of Collins at Magdalen:

It happened one afternoon, at a tea visit, that several intelligent friends were assembled at his rooms, to enjoy each other's conversation, when in comes a member of a certain college [Hampton, who had been Collins's schoolfellow at Winchester], as remarkable at that time for his brutal disposition as for his good scholarship; who . . . was determined to quarrel; and, though no man said a word, lifted up his foot and kicked the tea-table and all of its contents to the other side of the room. Our poet, though of a warm temper, was so confounded at the unexpected downfall . . . that he took no notice of the aggressor, but getting up from his chair calmly, he began picking up the slices of bread and butter, and the fragments of his china, repeating very mildly,

> "Invenias etiam disjecti membra poetae."

The incident offers significant evidence that Collins was not a solitary, but in White's words a person "good natured and affable, warm in his friendships," however visionary his pursuits may have been. Collins's university life was strikingly like Wordsworth's; both developed a superficial and external intercourse with their fellows while their imaginative life matured and developed within. Yet Collins did not fail to profit by his studies, however desultory may have been his pursuit of them. He was one of Ascham's "quick wits." White speaks of him as possessed of "fine abilities, which, properly improved, must have raised him to the top of any profession." Johnson, too, praises his accomplishments. Collins was, he says "a man of extensive literature, and of vigorous faculties . . . [who] was acquainted not only with the learned tongues, but with the Italian, French, and Spanish languages."[19] In a letter of March 8, 1754, he again describes Collins as "versed in many languages" and in a note to his edition of Shakespeare,[20] he calls him "a man of uncommon learning and abilities." Johnson was unlikely to be extravagant in his praise of a man's intellectual attainments. But had he not spoken, the poems themselves would afford ample evidence of the poet's erudition, sometimes, it is true, inaccurately and carelessly displayed. At college, too, the flair for poetry he had shown at Winchester persisted. The *Persian Eclogues* were printed for J. Roberts in 1742. The ledger of Woodfall, the printer, records: "Mr. Andrew Millar, Dr. Dec. 10, 1741. *Persian Eclogues* 1½ shts; No. 500. Reprinting ½ sht."[21] Here appears for the first time in connection with Collins the name of Andrew Millar, who was later to be the publisher of the *Odes Descriptive and Allegoric*. At Oxford, too, Collins must have written the *Verses Humbly Address'd to Sir Thomas Hanmer* by "a gentleman of Oxford," which were published in 1743. The poem is dated Oxford, Dec. 3, 1743. Langhorne's comment on the occasion for it is pointed:

This poem was written by our Author at the University about the time when Sir Thomas Hanmer's pompous edition of Shakespeare was printed at Oxford. If it has not so much merit as the rest of his poems, it has still more than the subject deserves.

The Register of the University records that Collins had received his degree of B.A. on November 18, 1743, and it is possible that the epistle was calculated to secure the patronage of Hanmer, who had earlier been Speaker of the House of Commons, and might be influential. A second and revised edition of the *Epistle,* to which was added the *Dirge for Cymbeline,* appeared in the next year. Here for the first time the poet's name appears on a title-page.[22]

The future of the young poet was uncertain. He chafed at university life, yet he considered remaining seriously enough

---

[19] *Lives*, III, 337.
[20] Ed. G. Birkbeck Hill, VII, 358.
[21] *Notes and Queries*, 1st series, XI, 419.
[22] H. O. White, *TLS*, 1922, p. 109.

to stand for a fellowship, which, according to Ragsdale, "to his own mortification, he lost." *The Manners* possibly suggests his farewell to academic life and his desire to live in the world without. Shortly afterward (Johnson says about 1744) he suddenly left the University and came to London "a literary adventurer with many projects in his head, and very little money in his pocket." Exactly why he left the University is uncertain. It may have been because of his disappointment at losing the fellowship, which Ragsdale says he gave as his pretext. A less trustworthy account in the *Gentleman's Magazine* for October, 1823, suggests that "he offended his uncle, Dr. Payne, by refusing to pay attention to him and therefore left the university."[23] But Ragsdale hints further that

he had other reasons: he was in arrears to his bookseller, his tailor, and other tradesmen. But, I believe, a desire to partake of the dissipation and gaiety of London was his principal motive.

Gilbert White inclines to the same opinion. But Moy Thomas[24] conjectures that the illness of his mother, who died on July 6, 1744, was responsible for his departure. Or, as Mr. Blunden notes,[25] "he did not become a Fellow of Magdalen, it being necessary that Fellows should be clergymen, or exceptionally lawyers or physicians."

By his mother's death he obtained a share in the copyhold property in the Manor of Carkham, Sussex, secured by his mother's marriage settlement to her children. With this sum he may have gone to London to settle upon some profession, but with characteristic indecision he drifted about tasting of the pleasures which a great city offered, and the money must have been soon exhausted. He still continued to depend on the generosity of his uncle, Colonel Martin, who had supported him at the University, and who was at the time in Flanders. According to Ragsdale, he made periodical visits to Dr. Payne, who had the management of the Colonel's affairs and "had likewise a commission to supply the Collinses with small sums of money."

---

[23] "Observations on the Original Architecture of St. Mary Magdalen College, Oxford," in *Gentleman's Magazine*, October, 1823, CXXXIV, 334.
[24] *Aldine Collins*, p. xvi.
[25] *Poems of William Collins*, p. 11.

That he had thrown himself into the diversions of London life is evident from Ragsdale's account of his visit to his cousin Payne "gaily dressed, and with a feather in his hat." His Wyke-hamite friend, Mulso, writes to Gilbert White from Leeds Abbey near Maidstone, July 18, 1744:

I saw Collins in Town, he is entirely an Author, & hardly speaks out of Rule: I hope his Subscriptions go on well in Oxford: he told me that poor Hargrave was quite abandon'd, that he frequented Night Cellars . . .[26]

He was, then, in town by July of 1744 and had apparently already contemplated his *History of the Revival of Learning,* for which Ragsdale says he "printed proposals and took the first subscription money from many of his friends," stimulated perhaps by Mr. Payne's admonition after too frequent demands for money that "he must pursue some other line of life, for he was sure Colonel Martyn would be displeased with him. . . ." White recalls in his letter that he often met Collins in London and that "he lodged in a little house with a Miss Bundy, at the corner of King's-square-court, Soho." Mulso writes White from King's Square Court on October 8, 1744:

Collins is now my next neighbour. I breakfasted with him this morn-ing, & Capn. Hargrave play'd on ye Harpsichord, which He has not forgott quite so much as He has Himself.[27]

Collins was passionately fond of music and, as Mr. H. O. White conjectures,[28] the harpsichord may have proved the final attrac-tion which drew him to King's Square Court. "Capn. Hargrave," twice mentioned by Mulso in speaking of Collins, must have been one of his London companions; perhaps, as Mr. Blunden suggests, "Capn. Hargrave" was the "certain gentlewoman properly called Nell Burnet (but whose Nom de Guerre was Captain Hargrave)" mentioned in Gray's letter to Wharton, dated December 27, 1746.

Collins soon became a man about town. Following Ragsdale's testimony that he was an acceptable companion everywhere, we

[26] R. Holt-White, *Mulso's Letters to Gilbert White,* p. 3.
[27] *Ibid.,* 7.
[28] H. O. White, "William Collins and Miss Bundy," *RES,* 1930, pp. 437-442.

find him the friend of Johnson, the acquaintance of Doctors Armstrong, Barrowby, and Hill, noticed by the geniuses who frequented the Bedford and Slaughter's Coffee Houses. From this time too probably dates his friendship with Ragsdale. Attracted to the theatre he became the friend of Garrick and Foote, whose pieces he frequently criticized. Because of his friendship with Garrick he "had the liberty of the scenes and green-room where he made diverting observations on the vanity and false consequence of that class of people," a phrase suggestive not only of Collins's wit, but also indicative that he was trying to "catch the living manners" in the world outside the college cloisters—an indication substantiated by a postscript to his letter to Cooper several years later in which he comments wittily on the fortunes of actors at Covent Garden. It was perhaps at this time that he turned his thoughts toward the drama and planned several tragedies, though it may well have been later. But as Langhorne observes[29] he "proceeded so far towards a tragedy—as to become acquainted with the manager." Johnson records[30] that at this time he was frequently "doubtful of his dinner or trembling at a creditor." In spite of Johnson's affirmation that "his morals were pure, and his opinions pious," he must have had time for the temptations of London, though Johnson attributes his shortcomings to the long continuance of poverty and long association with fortuitous companions. With poverty and restlessness he tired his wit upon a thousand schemes and never fulfilled his vague resolves. The projected *Review of the Advancement of Learning from 1300 to 1521* is a case in point. Ragsdale and Mulso both say that he started subscriptions and published proposals for the project, but the work stood still soon after it was begun. His friends knew of the plan and apparently hoped that he would complete it. Johnson says of it:[31]

He published proposals for a History of the Revival of Learning; and I have heard him speak with great kindness of Leo the Tenth,

[29] *Life*, 1781, p. ix.
[30] *Lives*, III, 335.
[31] *Ibid.*, III, 335.

and with keen resentment of his tasteless successor. But probably not a page of his history was ever written.

The Wartons, who were somewhat associated with the venture, with which Thomas Warton's *History of English Poetry* was to be linked as part of a general history of the Revival of Letters in Europe,[32] mention it. Thomas Warton records in a note to Section XXXIII of the *History of English Poetry*:

He intended to write the *History of the Restoration of Learning under Leo the Tenth*, and with a view to that design, had collected many scarce books.

Gilbert White, too, mentions a proposal which Collins drew up for a "History of the Darker Ages," which probably refers to the same undertaking. And Mr. H. O. White[33] has recently discovered in *A Literary Journal* (I, i, Dec. 1744, Dublin, p. 226) among books deserving of mention: "*A Review of the Advancement of Learning from 1300 to 1521* by Wm. Collins, 4to." Although he did not then abandon the plan he soon turned his attention to other projects, perhaps stirred by the pinch of poverty.

Sometime before September 7, 1745, he had journeyed to Flanders to visit his uncle, Colonel Martin, for Mulso writes to White on that date:[34]

Collins has been some Time return'd from Flanders, in order to put on Ye Gown as I hear, & get a chaplaincy in a Regiment. Don't laugh, indeed I don't on these occasions. This will be ye second [Joseph Warton being the first] acquaintance of mine who becomes ye Thing he most derides.

With this visit is probably associated the account that his uncle "found him too indolent even for the army"; Col. Martin discovered that the poet's mind was fixed on letters and the improvement of his intellect. The account continues:

Returning therefore to England he applied, by the Colonel's desire, to Mr. Green who gave him a title to the curacy of Birdham, of which

---

[32] Wooll's *Warton*, p. 29.
[33] *RES*, 1927, p. 16.
[34] *Letters of Mulso*, p. 9.

Mr. Green was Rector, and letters of recommendation to the bishop (Doctor Mawson) then in London; with these and the necessary credentials he went to London; but he did not go to the bishop's, being dissuaded from the clerical office by Mr. Hardham, the to-bacconist.[35]

Hardham, a fellow-townsman of the poet, counted the pit for Garrick and was a friend of the actors.[36] He might well have encouraged Collins's attempts at drama. This interest in tragedy must have turned his attention to the *Poetics* of Aristotle, for about this time he first planned to write a translation with a large commentary. To this time too the odes on *Pity* and *Fear* may be assigned, for he was writing "now and then odes and other poems," according to Johnson. Ragsdale records:

To raise a present subsistence he set about writing his Odes; and, having a general invitation to my house, he frequently passed whole days there, which he employed in writing them, and as frequently burning what he had written, after reading them to me : many of them which pleased me, I struggled to preserve, but without effect; for pretending he would alter them, he got them from me, and thrust them into the fire.

Sometime between May, 1745, and June, 1746, he met Joseph Warton at the Guildford races, where a project of joint publication was agreed upon. Joseph Warton writes to his brother Thomas:

Collins met me in Surrey, at Guildford Races, when I wrote out for him my Odes, and he likewise communicated some of his to me : and being both in very high spirits we took courage, resolved to join our forces, and to publish them immediately. . . . You will see a very pretty one of Collins's, on the death of Colonel Ross before Tournay. It is addressed to a lady who was Ross's intimate acquaintance, and who by the way is Miss Bett Goddard. Collins is not to publish the Odes unless he gets ten guineas for them.[37]

The enthusiastic young poets apparently planned a joint volume which for its day was intended to reform English poetry

[35] Alexander Hay, *History of Chichester,* 1804, p. 527; *Aldine Collins,* p. xvii.
[36] *RES,* 1927, p. 13; *TLS,* 1929, p. 95. Hardham is mentioned again in Hay's *History of Chichester,* p. 376.
[37] Wooll, *Warton,* pp. 14-15. Mr. H. O. White, "Collins and Miss Bundy," *RES,* 1930, p. 440, dates the letter May, 1746.

as the *Lyrical Ballads* later attempted to do. Moreover, the letter mentions the *Ode on the Death of Colonel Ross* and hints that to Collins the volume of odes was intended to furnish a "present subsistence." According to the letter Collins stayed at Milford and then set out for London. A postscript in Mulso's letter to White from King's Square Court, May 28, 1746, shows that Collins was in need of money at that time:[38]

I can't help telling you, tho' 'tis a little uncharitable, that Collins appears in good cloathes & a wretched carcass, at all ye gay Places, tho' it was with ye utmost Difficulty that He scrap'd together 5 pound for Miss Bundy at whose suit He was arrested & whom by his own confession He never intended to pay. I don't believe He will tell ye Story in Verse, tho' some circumstances of his taking would be burlesque enough. The Bailiff introduc'd himself with 4 Gentlemen who came to drink Tea, & who all together could raise but one Guinea. The ἀναγνωρισις (a word He is fond of) was quite striking & ye catastrophe quite poetical & interesting.

As Mr. H. O. White points out[39] ἀναγνωρισις is the word Aristotle uses in the *Poetics* for Recognition. It may well signify that Collins was reading Aristotle in preparation for his own projected tragedies, or he may already have begun his translation of Aristotle. It is difficult to date Collins's work on this undertaking. Ragsdale indicates that he began it shortly after he had started his *History of the Revival of Learning*:

Both Dr. Johnson and Mr. Langhorne are mistaken when they say, the Translation of Aristotle was never begun: I know the contrary, for some progress was made in both, but most in the latter. . . . I one day reproached him with idleness; when, to convince me my censure was unjust, he showed me many sheets of his translation of Aristotle, which he said he had so fully employed himself about, as to prevent him calling on many of his friends so frequently as he used to do.

Johnson's account of the translation would seem to place it later, or perhaps Collins never entirely abandoned his work on it:

By degrees I gained his confidence; and one day was admitted to him when he was immured by a bailiff that was prowling in the

---

[38] *Letters of Mulso*, p. 14.
[39] *RES*, 1930, p. 441.

street. On this occasion recourse was had to the booksellers, who, on the credit of a translation of Aristotle's *Poeticks*, which he engaged to write with a large commentary, advanced as much money as enabled him to escape into the country. He shewed me the guineas safe in his hand. Soon afterwards his uncle, Mr. Martin, a lieutenant-colonel, left him about two thousand pounds. . . . The guineas were then repaid, and the translation neglected.

Col. Martin did not die until 1749, and that fact, together with Johnson's mention in his *Preface to the Preceptor*, 1748, of "a commentary upon Aristotle's Art of Poetry, with which the literature of this nation will be in a short time augmented,"[40] would date the occurrence later than that recorded in Mulso's letter. Collins apparently clashed with the bailiff on more than one occasion; and though Johnson's account would place the translation and commentary later than 1746 it may well have been begun by then, for Collins habitually clung to his projects— the proposed *Clarendon Review* and the *Review of the Advancement of Learning* are cases in point.

Shortly after the affair with the bailiff recorded in Mulso's letter the *Ode to a Lady*, which Collins had shown Joseph Warton at Guildford, was printed in Dodsley's *Museum*, June 7, 1746. By August he was again on the continent. Mulso writes to Gilbert White on August 1, 1746:[41]

I have just receiv'd a Letter from Collin's, dated Antwerp. He gives me a very descriptive Journal of his Travells thro' Holland to that Place, which He is in Raptures about, & promises a more Particular Account of : He is in high Spirits, tho' near ye French. He was just setting out for ye Army, which He says are in a poor way, & He met many wounded & sick Countreymen as He travell'd from Helvolt-Sluys.

That Collins had seen some of the horrors of war, though he did not participate in it, accounts in part for the vividness of his imagery in the odes *To Mercy* and *To Liberty*; moreover, in his visit to Holland he may have picked up first-hand the tradition of the stork which he records in a note to the *Ode to Liberty*. It is uncertain when he returned to England, but upon

[40] Johnson, *Works*, Ed. A. Murphy, 1816, II, 247.
[41] *Letters of Mulso*, p. 15.

his arrival he undoubtedly turned his attention to preparing his odes for publication. Through some change in the original plan made at Guildford, his odes were published separately from those of Joseph Warton, possibly because Collins held out for a fixed sum. Dodsley printed Warton's *Poems* in December, 1746, while Collins's *Odes* appeared, according to a notice in the *General Advertizer,* on December 20, 1746, printed for A. Millar, previously concerned with the appearance of the *Persian Eclogues.* They were, however, dated 1747, though Gray had read them by December 27, 1746. The ledger of Woodfall, the printer,[42] records:

> Mr. Andrew Millar, Dr. Dec. 15, 1746.
> Mr. Collins's *Odes,* 8 vo. No. 1000, 3½ shts.

The odes of Warton were well received, but those of Collins were scarcely noticed. However, the *Gentleman's Magazine* and the *Scots Magazine* for December, 1746, list both volumes among the new books. So sensitive was Collins to this neglect that, according to Langhorne,[43] "conceiving a just indignation against a blind and tasteless age", the poet "burnt the remaining copies with his own hands."

Yet in 1747 he turned to new projects and perhaps found new friends. At this time, or perhaps earlier, for Ragsdale's statement is indefinite, he

engaged with Mr. Manby, a bookseller on Ludgate Hill, to furnish him with some Lives for the Biographia Britannica, which Manby was then publishing. He showed me some of the lives in embryo; but I do not recollect that any of them came to perfection.

The *Scots Magazine* for March, 1745, announces among the new books for that date:

Biographia Britannica; or, the Lives of the most eminent persons. In numbers, 6 d. each.

Possibly Collins may have become associated with this venture shortly after it was projected. He was also projecting a *Clarendon*

---

[42] *Notes and Queries,* 1st series, XI, 419.
[43] *Life,* 1781, p. xi.

Review to be printed at the university press, under the conduct
and authority of the university[44] and in a letter of November
24, 1747, he writes to his friend John Gilbert Cooper concerning the "Friendly Examiner or Letters of Polémon and Philétus,"
perhaps in imitation of Shaftesbury's *Moralists,* which is composed of letters from Philocles to Polemon.[45] The conjecture
is plausible in view of Cooper's *Power of Harmony,* 1745, which
reveals the influence of Shaftesbury on his writing. Collins's
friendship with Cooper dates back at least to April 26, 1746,
when Cooper mentions him as "that wandering knight" in one
of his letters to Dodsley,[46] at a period when Cooper under the
pseudonym "Philaretes" was contributing to the *Museum.* But
at this time Cooper was without Collins's address—a time suspiciously close to Mulso's mention of his affair with the bailiffs
over rent due Miss Bundy, whose lodging he may have left.[47]
Collins may, as Mr. Page[48] and Mr. Meyerstein conjecture, have
been contributing essays to the *Museum.* The *Ode to a Lady*
appeared there during the year as did *A Song. Imitated from the
Midsummer Night's Dream of Shakespeare. Act II. Scene V.*
(August 16, 1746), which has lately been attributed to Collins.
Moreover, the *Ode Written in the Beginning of the Year 1746,*
the *Ode to a Lady,* and the *Ode to Evening* appeared in Dodsley's
Miscellany within the next two years.

Collins was apparently in Chichester in May. A note in *TLS,*
1933, p. 92, mentions two deeds dated May 1, 1747, bearing
the signatures of "Wm. Collins 1747" and his sisters Elizabeth
and Ann. The deeds relate to property in East Street, Chichester,
where the poet was born. Though his uncle, wounded in the
Battle of Val in Flanders, returned to live with Collins's sisters
in Chichester, the poet spent little time there. During this year
he was apparently much in the company of the poet Thomson
at Castle Inn, Richmond. It is uncertain how early the friendship began, but Thomson was in London in 1745 when his

[44] T. Warton, *Letter to Hymers,* 1781.
[45] This explanation of the title of the letters seems as plausible as that
suggested by Mr. H. O. White, *RES,* 1927, p. 15.
[46] E. H. W. Meyerstein, "A Hitherto Unpublished Letter of William Collins," *London Mercury,* Dec. 1924, pp. 169-174.
[47] E. Blunden, "Collins and Dodsley's 'Museum,' " *TLS,* 1935, p. 501.
[48] *TLS,* 1935, p. 448.

Tancred and Sigismunda was presented with Garrick in the rôle of Tancred.[49] The acquaintance between the two poets might have been made through their common acquaintance with Garrick, Quin, and Armstrong. Ragsdale, a neighbor of Thomson at Richmond, might have presented his friend, or A. Millar, who was Thomson's printer as well as Collins's, may have introduced them. At any rate Collins was part of that company which was associated in the Castle of Indolence. He must through Thomson have known Lyttleton, then in favor with Frederick, Prince of Wales, who was something of a patron of poets. Through David Mallet, whose *Amyntor and Theodora* appeared in 1747, and through Thomson he must have been acquainted with the voyages of Martin Martin.[50] Collins introduced Joseph Warton to Thomson, according to a note in Warton's edition of Pope:

Thomson was well acquainted with the Greek tragedies, on which I heard him talk learnedly, when I was introduced to him by Mr. W. Collins.[51]

To Collins Thomson also confided that he took the first hint of writing his *Seasons* from the titles of Pope's four *Pastorals*.[52] Though Lyttleton had secured pensions for Mallet and Thomson,[53] he quarreled with the Prince of Wales and the pensions of those poets were withdrawn, so that Collins could entertain no hope of a similar favor. Finally in 1748 Thomson died of fever on August 27 and was buried in the church at Richmond. The gay life of the Castle of Indolence was over. Murdoch, Thomson's first biographer, records:

Only one gentleman, Mr. Collins, who had lived some time at Richmond, but forsook it when Mr. Thomson died, wrote an Ode to his Memory. This, for the dirge-like melancholy it breathes, and the warmth of affection that seems to have dictated it, we shall subjoin to the present account.[54]

---

[49] Johnson, *Lives,* III, 293; Davies, *Garrick,* I, 85.
[50] Collins may possibly have read the excerpt from Martin's *Description of the Western Islands of Scotland* which appeared in the *Gentleman's Magazine,* 1747, XVII, 469-71.
[51] J. Warton, *Pope's Works,* IV, 10n.
[52] *Pope's Works,* I, 115.
[53] Johnson, *Lives,* III, 448.
[54] *The Seasons,* with *Life of the Author* by Patrick Murdoch, N.Y. 1802, p. xxvii.

The ode was printed (in 1749) by Manby, for whom Collins had earlier undertaken to write memoirs for the *Biographia Britannica*. It is noted among the new books in the *Gentleman's Magazine* and in the *Scots Magazine* for June, 1749.

The years 1749 and 1750 represent the last period of Collins's poetic development before the coming of the mental disease which clouded the last nine years of his life. In April, 1749, his uncle, Col. Martin, died; his death is recorded in the *Gentleman's Magazine* for April of that year. Johnson says[55] that his uncle "left him about two thousand pounds; a sum which Collins could scarcely think exhaustible, and which he did not live to exhaust." His struggles with poverty and bailiffs were over and he should have been able to bring his many projects to completion. Recollecting in his prosperity that Millar had been a loser by his odes, he desired Millar to balance the account, "declaring he himself would make good the deficiency; the bookseller readily acquiesced in the proposal; and gave up to Collins the remainder of the impression, which the generous, resentful Bard immediately consigned to the flames."[56] At the same time he apparently repaid the guineas advanced on his translation of Aristotle and neglected the project.[57] Yet before the year was over his poetry was slightly recognized. In October the *Song From Shakespeare's Cymbeline* was reprinted in the *Gentleman's Magazine*, badly mutilated, perhaps by Cave, the proprietor.[58] Nor had he entirely neglected the muse, for during this year he became acquainted with John Home, the author of *Douglas*, and probably wrote the *Ode on the Popular Superstitions of the Highlands of Scotland*. And at the end of the year he must have written the lost *Epistle to the Editor of Fairfax his Translation of Tasso*, advertised in the *Whitehall Evening Post*, February 1-3, 1750.[59]

[55] *Lives*, III, 337.
[56] *Monthly Review*, XXXII, 294.
[57] *Lives*, III, 335.
[58] Nichols, *Literary Anecdotes*, London, 1812, V, 53. On the same point Mr. Blunden cites Hawkin's *Life of Johnson*, 1787, p. 48. As a possible instance of his growing recognition as a poet see the doubtful testimony in Barrett's *Guide to Chichester*, Chichester, n.d., p. 17: "As a poet, his 'Odes [sic] on the Passions,' though it sold for only £10, established his reputation as a lyrist of high order."
[59] McKillop, "Lost Poem by Collins," *TLS*, 1928, p. 965.

The circumstances of the composition of the *Ode on the Popular Superstitions* are significant. Home came to London late in 1749[60] to interest English patrons in his *Agis*. He indicates in a letter to Alexander Carlyle, later responsible for presenting Collins's ode before the Royal Society of Edinburgh, that the English were unreceptive to his drama, although he mentions that he has met "some charming fellows amongst them, Oxonians that were republicans," one of whom may have been Collins.[61] Collins's acquaintance with Home is mentioned in Carlyle's letter to Alex. Fraser Tytler, Esq., preserved in the *Transactions of the Royal Society of Edinburgh* for 1788:

Mr. Collins and Mr. Home had been made acquainted by *Mr. John Barrow*, (the cordial youth mentioned in the first stanza), who had been, for sometime, at the University of Edinburgh; had been a volunteer, along with *Mr. Home* in the year 1746; had been taken prisoner with him at the battle of Falkirk, and had escaped together with him and five or six other gentlemen from the Castle of Down. *Mr. Barrow* resided in 1749 at Winchester, where *Mr. Collins* and *Mr. Home* were, for a week or two, together on a visit. Mr. Barrow was paymaster in America in the war that commenced in 1756, and died in that country.

Home told Carlyle that the *Ode on the Popular Superstitions* had been addressed to him by *Mr. Collins*, on his leaving London in the year 1749 : that it was hastily composed and incorrect; but that he would one day find leisure to look it over with care.

At about the same time Collins was at work on the *Epistle to the Editor of Fairfax his Translation*. A fourth edition of Fairfax's *Tasso* appeared in October, 1749, at about the time of Collins's acquaintance with Home. There are certain definite parallels between the two poems on which Collins was then working: both are verse epistles, and the passage on Tasso in stanza XII of the *Ode on the Popular Superstitions* is ample proof of Collins's interest in the translation at that time.[62]

[60] *Works*, 1822, I, 35.
[61] Garrod, *TLS*, 1929, p. 624.
[62] Mr. Garrod has recently added to our knowledge of the "cordial youth," Barrow (*TLS*, 1929, p. 624). Barrow, according to Henry Mackenzie, was "a young English student." Home introduced him to Lord Bute to whom, according to Ferguson, he owed the office of paymaster. Mr. Garrod further adds (*TLS*, 1929, p. 668), citing from Home's *History of the Rebellion of*

In 1750 Collins was still in London, for Thomas Warton mentions in the letter to Hymers that he often saw him there. At that time he was still cherishing the project of his "intended history of the Revival of Learning" of which, says Warton, he had finished a Preliminary Dissertation, and proposed to Warton the scheme of the *Clarendon Review* of which he had already written to John Gilbert Cooper in 1747. At this time, Collins proposed to "overcome the dislike of a particular Body of Jealous Literati" by having its publication sponsored by the university.[63] The *General Advertiser* for March 27, 1750, sets the date of the appearance of the *Epistle to the Editor of Fairfax* for "Saturday next," but no trace of the poem has yet been found.

In the summer of 1750 Collins was honored at Oxford when Dr. William Hayes, Professor of Music at the university, set *The Passions* to music. From a copy of this edition of the poem in the library of Worcester College, Mr. H. O. White discovered[64] that the ode was "Performed at the Theatre in Oxford, July 2, 1750." The ode is split into Arias, Recitatives, and Choruses, to fit the musical setting. A different ending, written by the Earl of Lichfield, Vice-Chancellor of the University, interrupts line 93 of the ode, and with Recitative, Air, and Chorus brings it to a lame and impotent conclusion. Collins was not present at the performance and did not learn of it until some time later from one of his friends at Winchester.

Late in the year he was at Chichester, possibly to attend the wedding of his sister, Elizabeth, to Lieutenant Nathaniel Tanner, an officer who had fought with Col. Martin in all his campaigns and who had been wounded at Fontenoy.[65] From Chichester he wrote to Hayes at Oxford on November 8 thanking Hayes for the honor done him at the university in the summer, requesting that a copy or two of the ode (as printed at Oxford) be sent to Winchester to one Mr. Clarke, possibly a Wykehamite

---

1745, that his name was Thomas, not John, that he was "a student of physic at the University of Edinburgh" and that at the affair of Doune Castle he was "the only Englishman in the company."

[63] H. O. White, *RES*, 1927, p. 16.

[64] *RES*, 1927, p. 19.

[65] *Aldine Collins*, p. xxix.

schoolfellow, and asking also for the musical score of the ode. Mr. H. O. White infers[66] that his friends at Winchester were contemplating a public performance of *The Passions* at the school there in anticipation of which the ode, with Lichfield's conclusion, was specially printed at Winchester. This special printing is noted in Mr. Iolo A. Williams's *Seven Eighteenth Century Bibliographies,* which dates the pamphlet conjecturally about 1750 and notes that "the poem is divided into two parts and is marked off into arias, recitations, etc." In the same letter Collins mentions another ode on music now lost:

Inform me by a line, if you should think one of my better judgment acceptable. In such case I could send you one written on a nobler subject; and which, tho' I have been persuaded to bring it forth in London, I think more calculated for an audience in the University. The subject is the Music of the Grecian Theatre; in which I have, I hope naturally, introduced the various characters with which the chorus was concerned, as Oedipus, Medea, Electra, Orestes, etc., etc. The composition, too, is probably more correct as I have chosen the ancient tragedies for my models and only copied the most affecting passages in them.[67]

The rest of Collins's brief history is concerned with his madness. Always high-strung and visionary, able to plan great undertakings, but irresolute and unable to concentrate, he was now seized by a malady both mental and physical. On the physical side it took the form of debility and weakness; on the mental side it manifested itself in depression of mind, with alternate periods of mental clarity and total derangement. Johnson places the beginning of his illness shortly after the death of his uncle, but from Thomas Warton's letter his stay in London in 1750 was "before his illness." Warton gives the first hint of its appearance at Easter, 1751:

About Easter, the next year, I was in London; when, being given over and supposed to be dying, he desired to see me, that he might take his last leave of me; but he grew better; and in the summer he sent me a letter on some private business, which I have now by me, dated Chichester, June 9, 1751, written in fine hand, and without the least symptom of a disordered or debilitated understanding.

[66] *RES,* 1927, p. 21.
[67] The letter was first printed in Seward's *Supplement to Anecdotes of Some Distinguished Persons,* London, 1797, p. 123.

These periods of mental and physical instability continued, and by 1754 they had become more violently pronounced. He endeavored by travel and by seeking old friends to throw them off, but in vain. Ragsdale records that

When his health and faculties began to decline, he went to France, and after to Bath, in hope his health might be restored, but without success.

He does not date the visit, but it must have been before 1754, or at least early in that year. On this point Johnson says:

These clouds which he perceived gathering on his intellects he endeavoured to disperse by travel and passed into France; but found himself constrained to yield to his malady and returned.

Johnson adds an anecdote which is the last mention we have of Johnson's seeing him:

After his return from France the writer of this character paid him a visit at Islington, where he was waiting for his sister, whom he had directed to meet him: there was then nothing of disorder discernible in his mind by any but himself, but he had withdrawn from study, and travelled with no other book than an English Testament, such as children carry to the school; when his friend took it into his hand, out of curiosity to see what companion a Man of Letters had chosen, "I have but one book," said Collins, "but that is the best."

Johnson tells us that "he was for some time confined in a house of Lunaticks," which Ragsdale identifies as McDonald's Madhouse at Chelsea. Both Johnson and Ragsdale agree that he was afterwards retired to the care of his sister. Johnson's letter to Thomas Warton of March 8, 1754, would indicate that he had been confined early in that year:

But how little can we venture to exult in any intellectual powers or literary attainments, when we consider the condition of poor Collins. . . . This busy and forcible mind is now under the government of those, who lately could not have been able to comprehend the least and most narrow of his designs. What do you hear of him? are there hopes of his recovery? or is he to pass the remainder of his life in misery and degradation? perhaps, with complete consciousness of his calamity.[68]

---

[68] It is difficult to place the date of Collins's visit to France and Johnson's meeting with him after his return. From Johnson's comment that "there was then nothing of disorder discernible in his mind" and the mention of his

But he did not, as Ragsdale says, soon sink into a deplorable state of idiotism. Thomas Warton and his brother visited him in September of 1754 at Chichester, where he was living with his sister, Ann, now Mrs. Sempill. (His sister Elizabeth had died in Scotland in 1754.) Warton writes:

The first day he was in high spirits at intervals, but exerted himself so much that he could not see us the second.

On this occasion he showed them the "Ode to Mr. John Home, on his leaving England for Scotland" with which the Wartons were impressed. He also showed them

another ode, of two or three four-lined stanzas, called the the Bell of Arragon; on the tradition that, anciently, just before a King of Spain died, the great bell of the cathedral of Sarragossa, in Arragon, tolled spontaneously. It began thus:—

> The bell of Arragon, they say,
> Spontaneous speaks the fatal day, &c.[68a]

Soon afterwards were these lines:

> Whatever dark aëreal power,
> Commissioned, haunts the gloomy tower.

The last stanza consisted of a moral transition to his own death and knell, which he called "some simpler bell."

In November, 1754, he came to Oxford for change of air and amusement and remained a month. Thomas Warton saw him then and mentions:

I saw him frequently, but he was so weak and low, that he could not bear conversation. Once he walked from his lodgings, opposite Christ Church, to Trinity College, but supported by his servant.

On November 28, 1754, Johnson wrote to Warton expressing solicitude for Collins. Boswell records in a note on Johnson's letter:

---

sister, it might have occurred after his incarceration in the madhouse. But Ragsdale puts the visit to France before his confinement, and Thomas Warton mentions that the illness had begun in 1751. While with equal certainty either position is tenable it would seem that the visit to France occurred before the malady increased in violence. Johnson's reference to "those, who lately could not have been able to comprehend the least and most narrow of his designs" might with equal certainty refer to the keepers of the madhouse or, as Mr. Blunden suggests, to his sister Ann.

[68a] The Bell of Arragon was completed by Nathaniel Drake. See his Mornings in Spring, London, 1828, II, 387-8.

Collins (the poet) was at this time at Oxford, on a visit to Mr. Warton; but labouring under the most deplorable langour of body and dejection of mind.

Johnson wrote to Warton again on December 24, 1754:

Poor dear Collins! Let me know whether you think it would give him pleasure if I should write to him. I have often been near his *state,* and therefore have it in great commiseration.

With this visit, too, may have been associated the reminiscence in White's letter that he saw Collins at Oxford

under Merton wall, in a very affecting situation, struggling, and conveyed by force, in the arms of two or three men, towards the parish of St. Clement, in which was a house that took in such unhappy objects.

Perhaps this occurrence prompted Johnson's December letter. It is, however, possible that the poet made several visits to Oxford. In his letter to Hymers, Warton mentions Collins's visit to Oxford *before* the September visit of the brothers to Chichester, though the reminiscence may be inaccurate.

From this time until his death in 1759 the poet was apparently closely confined to Chichester. He dropped out of his circle of friends in London. Johnson remembered him with tenderness in 1756 when he wrote to Thomas Warton on April 9:

What becomes of poor dear Collins? I wrote him a letter which he never answered. I suppose writing is very troublesome to him. That man is no common loss. The moralists all talk of the uncertainty of fortune, and the transitoriness of beauty: but it is yet more dreadful to consider that the powers of the mind are equally liable to change, that the understanding may make its appearance and depart, that it may blaze and expire.

But the last years were not entirely clouded. Thomas Warton visited him at least twice. On one occasion Collins told him that he had found a source for *The Tempest*;[69] on another occasion "not many months before his death," Collins showed him a rare work of Skelton.[70] In his lucid intervals he labored on

[69] *History of English Poetry*, Section LX.
[70] *Ibid.*, Section XXXIII, footnote.

his *Review of the Advancement of Learning.* Thomas Warton tells in the letter to Hymers that

Collins had finished a Preliminary Dissertation to be prefixed to his History of the Restoration of Learning, and that it was written with great judgment, precision, and knowledge of the subject.

This, however, may have been the work noted in *A Literary Journal* in 1744. Yet Joseph Warton speaks hopefully of the work in 1756 in his *Essay on the Genius and Writings of Pope*:

Concerning the particular encouragement given by Leo X to polite literature and the fine arts, I forbear to enlarge because a friend of mine is at present engaged in writing The History of the Age of Leo X.[71]

In the same work appears a fragment of an *Ode on the Use and Abuse of Poetry,* suspiciously like the work of Collins—perhaps one of the "few fragments" of odes, containing "traces of high imagery" which Collins gave Joseph Warton on his visit to Chichester in 1754. And in spite of his contempt for the *Persian Eclogues,* which he called "Irish Eclogues," and his mortification that they found more readers and admirers than his odes, they were reprinted in January, 1757, with the title of *Oriental Eclogues,* evidently corrected and altered by the poet's own hand. Sometime during these last years he was visited by William Smith of Chichester, afterwards Treasurer of the Ordnance, who had formerly been Collins's schoolfellow at Winchester. Though "in a deplorable state of mind" Collins remembered soberly a melancholy dream which he had communicated to Smith at Winchester.

Two more traditional accounts piece out the picture of the last years. Thomas Warton apparently attended his funeral in 1759, for he recounts an anecdote, half-pathetic and half-amusing, from the Rev. Mr. Shenton, Vicar of St. Andrew's at Chichester, by whom Collins was buried:

Walking in my vicarial garden one Sunday evening, during Collins's last illness, I heard a female (the servant, I suppose) reading the Bible in his chambers. Mr. Collins had been accustomed to rave much and make great moanings; but while she was reading, or rather at-

[71] J. Warton, *Essay on the Genius and Writings of Pope,* ed. 1806, I, 182.

tempting to read, he was not only silent but attentive likewise, correcting her mistakes, which indeed were very frequent, through the whole of the twenty-seventh chapter of Genesis.

Dyce quotes further a doubtful account from a manuscript note of Mr. T. Park relating to Ann Collins, who later married the Rev. Mr. Durnford of Chichester. She

evinced so outrageous an aversion to her brother because he squandered or gave away to the boys in the cloisters whatever money he had, that she destroyed, in a paroxysm of resentment, all his papers and whatever remained of his enthusiasm for poetry so far as she could.[72]

When he died in her arms on June 12, 1759,[73] his fame as a poet was but beginning; Goldsmith had mentioned him kindly in the *State of Polite Learning in Europe* shortly before. His death passed unnoticed. His sad history closes with the entry in the parish register of burials for the year 1759:

June 15, William Collins, Gent.

[72] Dyce's *Collins*, p. 39.
[73] Her death is recorded in the Register of the *Gentleman's Magazine* for November, 1789, the source for the detail. The date of the poet's death is there erroneously given as 1756.

II

COLLINS AND THE ARTS

THE BRIEF history of Collins gives only glimpses of a fascinating personality and reveals only a few of the qualities that were his. Much of it, seen through the reminiscent haze of the years, obscures the sharpness of the pictures of the poet himself. Yet if one hold with Ruskin that much of the man's life, at least the best of it, is inseparable from his work and that the author's work is, "in his small human way and with whatever degree of true inspiration is in him, his inscription, or scripture," one may turn to the few poems that Collins has left us and discover something of his beliefs, his mind, and his art as they are therein revealed.

Collins's period of poetic development is brief, extending at most over the ten years from 1739 to 1749. Yet one is cognizant of a progress in his art; one watches a crystallization of his poetic power toward an individual manner of expression, and one senses the poet's conscious searching for his own best field of endeavor. At the same time one learns of his aims and interests, which give some insight into the richness of his mind, the possibilities of his genius, and the quality of his imagination. Conventional as they are in form and substance, the *Persian Eclogues*, the *Epistle to Hanmer,* and the early lyrics are significant, for in them appear in imperfect form some of the ideas and poetic images that are later to be perfected in the *Odes Descriptive and Allegoric.* They reveal as well Collins's early allegiance to the conventions of a poetic school from which he was shortly to break away. The twelve *Odes Descriptive and Allegoric* of 1746 show a fuller development of Collins's power. That some of them are well-nigh perfect, while others fall far short of perfection, only makes the rapidity of the poet's development the more remarkable and hints that, fine as it was, it was still incomplete. At least four of the odes—the *Ode to Eve-*

ning, the *Ode written in the beginning of the Year 1746,* the *Ode on the Poetical Character,* and *The Passions*—represent the best work of which Collins was then capable. All of them offer a fascinating approach to the ideas and images which absorbed the poet. For the rest the *Ode on the Death of Mr. Thomson* and the *Ode on the Popular Superstitions* are more than merely reminiscent of the odes of 1746; they reveal a further development of the poet's art and imagination.

The few extant poems richly suggest the endowment of their poet. They give glimpses of a sensitive and poetic temperament, of a cultivated scholar, albeit sometimes a careless one. The golden realms of books he had travelled much for his years, and so erudite was he, yet so enthusiastic, that his odes are full of reminiscences of his reading. Johnson tells us how busy and forcible his mind was, and one has only to read his odes to learn how deeply they bear the impress of what he had read. Versed in the learned tongues and following Pindar in his desire to be "a worthy servant of the Nine," he was also devoted to the English classics. Milton and Shakespeare he desired to emulate. Like Keats he combined a love of the classical with a taste for the riches of Elizabethan poetry—Spenser and Drayton and Fairfax's *Tasso* with their color and richness touched him. Yet, a man of his own age, he found much to admire in Pope and Thomson. And with an enthusiasm for Jonson's comedies of the humors went an appreciation of the novelists of his own day. LeSage he mentions appreciatively, and he must have read Fielding with pleasure. Like Scott he was interested in the pageantry of history, and there is ample evidence, besides his own projected ventures in the field of history, that he had delved into recondite bits of historical tradition and folk-lore. With a passion for collecting black-letter books went an absorbing interest in the lives and manners of simple folk in the far-off Hebrides, the fascinating province of books of travel.

The poet's literary preferences, then, were those of a scholar and an antiquarian—a curious mixture of the classical and the romantic, the popular and the erudite. His reading in the classics and in the poets of his day helped to impart that finished and polished quality which marks his best odes; his fondness for the great Elizabethans and his store of information in the quaint and remote realms of tradition and popular lore gave the definitely romantic cast to much of his expression.

The drama, particularly tragedy, the arts of music, painting, and sculpture also contributed much to the development of Collins's taste and genius as a poet, for he was of a finely sensitive and artistic nature as well as by temperament a scholar. Most significant, perhaps, is the influence of the drama upon his poetry and his ideas. In his adventurous years in London when he "had the liberty of the scenes and green-room," he came to know the theatre and the actors and to be interested in the stage and its requirements. It is significant that the emblem on the title-page of *Odes on Several Descriptive and Allegoric Subjects* represents at the top the heads of Tragedy and Pastoral and beneath a lyre and Pan-pipes in a wreath of laurel, oak-leaf, corn, and berries—an indication, perhaps, of the fields of poetry in which he desired to excel or the examples he hoped in his poetry to emulate.[1]

Equally indicative of his aspiration is his appeal in the *Ode to Fear*, an appeal stated again in the conclusion of the *Ode to Pity*:

> O Thou whose Spirit most possest
> The sacred Seat of *Shakespear's* Breast!
> By all that from thy Prophet broke, . . .
> Hither again thy Fury deal,
> Teach me but once like Him to feel:
> His *Cypress Wreath* my Meed decree.[2]

Though he planned several tragedies he finished none. Perhaps he failed, as Campbell suggests,[3] because his mind "had a passion for the visionary and remote forms of imagination too strong

---

[1] In his letter to Hayes, speaking of his *Ode on the Music of the Grecian Theatre*, he says:

"The composition, too, is probably more correct, as I have chosen the ancient Tragedies for my models, and only copied the most affecting passages in them."

[2] Quotations from the poetry of Collins follow the text of the Oxford edition of *Gray and Collins Poetical Works*, edited by Christopher Stone and A. Lane Poole, Oxford, 1917.

[3] *Specimens of the British Poets*, V, 311.

and exclusive for the general purposes of the drama." But many passages in his poetry show the effect the drama had on his expression. That the passages come almost equally from Shakespeare and from the classical dramatists indicates that here as elsewhere in his verse "Graecia's graceful Orders" join with the Gothic design of a later day. Perhaps because of his interest in history the pomp and pageantry of the drama impressed him from the time of the *Epistle to Hanmer,* where he mentions how the Muse

>Graced with noblest Pomp her earliest Stage,

to the writing of the *Ode on the Popular Superstitions,* where

>The shadowy kings of Banquo's fated line,
>Through the dark cave in gleamy pageant past.

In several striking passages from his own poetry Collins reveals how that pageantry which he admired in dramatic representation had carried over to his own pictures. In discussing the historical plays of Shakespeare in the *Epistle to Hanmer* he presents a moving show of the English kings:

>Wak'd at his Call I view, with glad Surprize,
>Majestic Forms of mighty Monarchs rise.
>There *Henry's* Trumpets spread their loud Alarms,
>And laurel'd Conquest waits her Hero's Arms.
>Here gentler *Edward* claims a pitying Sigh,
>Scarce born to Honours and so soon to die!

Again in the *Ode on the Popular Superstitions* there are the pageant-like processions of

>Old Runic bards . . .
>With uncouth lyres, in many-coloured vest,
>Their matted hair with boughs fantastic crown'd:

of the "mighty kings of three fair realms," who "at midnight's solemn hour"

>stalk with sov'reign power
>In pageant robes, and wreath'd with sheeny gold,
>And on their twilight tombs aerial council hold;

and of the "shadowy kings of Banquo's fated line," a procession drawn from drama itself. Similarly the train of Fear in the *Ode to Fear* stalks with dramatic tread, and there is something essentially suggestive of the stage in *The Passions*—as Mrs. Barbauld says of it[4], "its beauties are brought out by recitation."

In the great writers of tragedy he found, too, a truth to nature and a realistic and feeling portrayal of human passion. In the *Epistle to Hanmer* he shows how

> Preserv'd thro' Time, the speaking Scenes impart
> Each changeful Wish of *Phaedra's* tortur'd Heart:
> Or paint the Curse, that mark'd the *Theban's* Reign,
> A Bed incestuous, and a Father slain.

His tribute to Shakespeare in the same poem praises his skill in holding the mirror up to nature:

> Drawn by his Pen, our ruder Passions stand
> Th' unrivall'd Picture of his early Hand.

But he is not unaware that imagination must be part of the playwright's gift. Shakespeare's fancy, he reminds us, could call us to the magic world of *A Midsummer Night's Dream* and *The Tempest,* to

> the rural Grove;
> Where Swains contented own the quiet Scene,
> And twilight Fairies tread the circled Green.

Collins is cognizant, too, as the *Ode on the Popular Superstitions* shows, that in soberer mood, "in musing hour," Shakespeare's imagination described the "wayward sisters" in *Macbeth* and dressed the magic scene with their terrors. A poet who "delighted to rove through the meanders of enchantment," Collins found a kindred spirit in Shakespeare; both poets loved to deal with the delicate and the horrible in the unreal world of the imagination. With the perception of the poet Collins insists, in an almost Aristotelian judgment, that this fairy world is the dramatist's province, that scenes like these

> which, daring to depart
> From sober truth, are still to nature true,
> And call forth fresh delight to fancy's view.

[4] *Critical Essay*, 1797 edn., p. xli. Cf. Dickens, *Great Expectations*, chapter VII (Ed. J. M. Dent, 1907, pp. 39-40):

The odes abound, too, with scenes which suggest the realistic and dramatic manner of a stage representation, where characters live, move, and have their being while the poet is spectator. Typical instances are two descriptions from the *Epistle to Hanmer* of scenes from the tragedies of Shakespeare, which Collins might have seen performed on the London stage as he describes them. The first, from *Julius Caesar,* presents Marc Antony:

> And see, where *Anthony* in tears approv'd,
> Guards the pale relics of the chief he lov'd:
> O'er the cold corse the warrior seems to bend,
> Deep sunk in grief, and mourns his murder'd friend!
> Still as they press, he calls on all around,
> Lifts the torn robe, and points the bleeding wound.[5]

The second, representing *Coriolanus,* while not substantially true to Shakespeare's spirit in the play, may describe the scene as Collins saw it acted, for as Campbell points out,[6] "Shakespeare's *Coriolanus* was never acted genuinely from 1660 to 1820:"

> But who is he, whose brows exalted bear
> A wrath impatient, and a fiercer air?
> Awake to all that injur'd worth can feel,
> On his own Rome he turns th' avenging steel.
> Yet shall not War's insatiate fury fall,
> (So heav'n ordains it) on the destin'd wall.
> See the fond mother 'midst the plaintive train
> Hung on his knees, and prostrate on the plain!
> Touch'd to the soul, in vain he strives to hide

"There was a fiction that Mr. Wopsle 'examined' the scholars, once a quarter. What he did on those occasions was to . . . give us Mark Antony's oration over the body of Caesar. This was always followed by Collin's [sic] Ode on the Passions, wherein I particularly venerated Mr. Wopsle as Revenge, throwing his blood-stained sword in thunder down, and taking the war-denouncing trumpet with a withering look. It was not with me then, as it was in later life, when I fell into the society of the Passions, and compared them with Collins and Wopsle, rather to the disadvantage of both gentlemen."
Cf. also Byron, *Letters and Journals* (ed. Prothero, London, 1902) I, 27-8. Among the Harrow School Public Speeches for June 6, 1805 and July 4, 1805 was Collins's *Ode to the Passions* [sic] recited by Byron's schoolfellow, Locke.
[5] *Epistle to Hanmer,* 112-120. This passage is taken from the variant reading followed in Dodsley's *Collection,* 1755, IV, 64-70. It is accepted as the preferred reading by Langhorne, Dyce, Bronson, and Mr. Blunden.
[6] *Mrs. Siddons,* 1834, II, 154.

The son's affection, in the Roman's pride:
O'er all the man conflicting passions rise,
Rage grasps his sword, while *Pity* melts the eyes.[7]

A scene in the epode of the *Ode to Fear* has the same dramatic quality:

Wrapt in thy cloudy Veil the *Incestuous Queen,*
Sigh'd the sad Call her Son and Husband hear'd,
When once alone it broke the silent Scene,
And He the Wretch of *Thebes* no more appear'd.

The description of Fear in the strophe of the ode is intensely dramatic, though it does not represent an actual figure from the drama as do the other instances cited:

Ah *Fear!* Ah frantic *Fear!*
I see, I see Thee near.
I know thy hurried Step, thy haggard Eye!

It is at least worth noting that most of the scenes in the odes which suggest the drama rouse the pity or the fear of the poet and of the spectator.

Closely allied with Collins's interest in tragedy is his pre-occupation with the *Poetics* of Aristotle. Through the odes dealing with the drama run a number of Aristotelian concepts. The Aristotelian theory of the effect of tragedy on the spectator is several times definitely suggested. In the *Epistle to Hanmer* the reaction of the audience to the spectacle of "Phaedra's tortured Heart" has some of the implications of Aristotle's doctrine of catharsis:

With kind concern our pitying eyes o'erflow,
Trace the sad tale, and own another's woe.

Collins's invocation to Shakespeare in the same poem attributes to him the same power over the poet's own emotions:

O more than all in pow'rful genius blest,
Come, take thine empire o'er the willing breast!

---

[7] *Epistle to Hanmer,* 121-132. This is again Dodsley's variant. The description of Volumnia in the original version is more strikingly dramatic, but conveys the situation in the scene even less in the spirit of Shakespeare:

Till, slow-advancing o'er the tented Plain,
In sable Weeds, appear the Kindred-train:
The frantic Mother leads their wild Despair,
Beats her swoln Breast, and rends her silver Hair.

Whate'er the wounds this youthful heart shall feel,
Thy songs support me, and thy morals heal!

The moving power of tragedy, principally through the effect
of pity, is again suggested in the *Ode to Pity* when Collins pays
tribute to the tragedies of Otway:

Wild *Arun* too has heard thy Strains,
And Echo, 'midst my native Plains,
Been sooth'd by *Pity's* Lute.

Again in the *Ode on the Popular Superstitions of the Highlands
of Scotland* Collins anticipates the effect of Home's tragedies
on the emotions of his friends:

those soft friends, whose hearts, some future day,
Shall melt, perhaps, to hear thy tragic song.

In the *Ode to Fear* there is an allusion to the Aristotelian concept of the joint influence of pity and fear on the emotions of
the spectator:

O *Fear,* I know Thee by my throbbing Heart,
Thy with'ring Pow'r inspir'd each mournful Line,
Tho' gentle *Pity* claim her mingled Part,
Yet all the Thunders of the Scene are thine!

It is noteworthy that, while in Collins's poetry images of horror
conducive to fear are so strikingly numerous, he should also
be regarded as the bard "who touched the tenderest notes of
Pity's lyre." In a sense his interest in tragedy may have turned
his imagination and feeling to the contemplation of these
qualities.

By the sister arts of painting, sculpture, and music, Collins
was moved more subtly than by the drama. In his edition of the
poet, Dyce, pp. 39-40, quotes a manuscript note by T. Park,
Esquire, in his copy of Collins which testifies that Collins
attempted drawing as well as poetry:

Mr. Hayley told me, when I visited him at Eartham, that he had
obtained from her (Collins's sister) a *small drawing* by Collins;
but it possessed no other value than as a memorial that the bard had
attempted to handle the pencil as well as the pen.

Collins apparently attained to fair skill in drawing, particularly emblems suggestive of Greek sculpture. Mr. Blunden[8] conjectures that Collins sketched the emblem for the 1746 edition of the *Odes,* though the name of the engraver is given on the title-page; and in the letter to John Gilbert Cooper, Collins draws the design for a medallion for the "Friendly Examiner or Letters of Polémon and Philétus" to appear in the proposed *Clarendon Review.* He says:

You found by my last that I propos'd the more literary papers should fall under the name of Polémon, and the more lusory or comic under that of Philéthus. In order to hint this at the head of the Paper I shall have a medallion engrav'd of two elegant Heads *á l'antique* thus (Don't you think 'em *á l'antique?*) over the lower part of the necks of which there shall be a veil thrown, from under which a little Art shall appear writing on a Roman scroll, & a Satyr either in contrast holding up another, or writing on part of the same, or suppose the veil to be upheld by Friendship, who may at the same time point to the Relievo of the medallion while she discovers the ornaments of the base by supporting the veil.

The design is reminiscent of the same symbolic and almost statuesque quality found in the odes. The lines at the beginning of the strophe in the *Ode to Mercy* offer one instance of the point:

O thou, who sit'st a smiling Bride
By *Valour's* arm'd and awful Side,
Gentlest of Sky-born Forms, and best ador'd:
Who oft with Songs, divine to hear,
Win'st from his fatal Grasp the Spear,
And hid'st in Wreaths of Flow'rs his bloodless Sword!

On the passage, Mrs. Barbauld[9] comments:

The maxim of Horace, *ut pictura poesis,* may be strictly applied to the first stanza of the *Ode to Mercy;* for the figures and attitudes are delineated so perfectly, that a painter has nothing left to do but to transfer it to the canvas.

A second example is in the *Ode on the Death of Colonel Ross,* where

[8] *Poems of William Collins,* p. 14.
[9] *Critical Essay,* p. xxvi.

> lost to all his former Mirth,
> *Britannia's* Genius bends to Earth,
>   And mourns the fatal Day:
> While stain'd with Blood he strives to tear
> Unseemly from his Sea-green Hair
>   The Wreaths of cheerful *May*.

Collins apparently believed with Sidney that poetry should be a speaking picture, for there are several parallels drawn between the art of the poet and that of the painter—a parallelism more significant when one considers that Collins's odes were to be "descriptive." In the *Epistle to Hanmer* Shakespeare is compared to the painter:

> Drawn by his Pen, our ruder Passions stand
> Th' unrivall'd Picture of his early Hand.

There follows a description of how the scenes in Shakespeare might live in painting as they live on the stage:

> Methinks ev'n now I view some free design,
> Where breathing Nature lives in ev'ry line:
> Chaste and subdu'd the modest lights decay,
> Steal into shades, and mildly melt away.[10]

The passage is significant, for it reveals the kind of painting which touched Collins; moreover, the last two lines of the passage almost epitomize Collins's own picture painting in the *Ode to Evening*. The same harmony of painting and drama is suggested again in stanza six of the *Ode to Pity,* which Mrs. Barbauld says[11] alludes to a plan for a gallery of paintings to illustrate Shakespeare. After describing the adornment of the temple to Pity, which with Fancy's aid he will build in his thoughts, Collins draws a striking parallel between tragedy and the pictorial art:

> There Picture's Toils shall well relate,
> How Chance, or hard involving Fate,
>   O'er mortal Bliss prevail:
> The Buskin'd Muse shall near her stand,
> And sighing prompt her tender Hand,
>   With each disastrous Tale.

[10] The Dodsley version is here followed.
[11] *Critical Essay*, p. ix.

That the concept was not original with Collins his note on the passage in the *Epistle to Hanmer* indicates. He was referring to Spence's *Essay on Mr. Pope's Odyssey in Five Dialogues,* 1737, where a similar sentiment is expressed:

And certainly what makes so beautiful a figure in the finest poets might deserve the imitation of the best painters. . . . If our Shakespeare can give us the struggles of Passions in the breast of Coriolanus, Wall might trace the same, and speak them as well with his pencil.[12]

Yet Collins seems to have applied the statement to his own practice, for he refers to the parallelism several times in his odes. In the *Ode on the Death of Colonel Ross,* for example, the poet speaks of the "pictur'd Glories" he has paid in honor of the dead, though he fears they may be "weak to soothe so soft an Heart" as that of the Colonel's lady. And in the *Ode on the Popular Superstitions* Collins encourages Home to treat in verse the copious subjects that should prompt the poet to write:

> Thou need'st but take the pencil to thy hand,
> And paint what all believe who own thy genial land.

When one remembers that the *Ode to Evening* has been compared in spirit to the paintings of Poussin, Claude, and Corot,[13] one feels that in the best of his poetry he applied the relationship between the arts that he had sensed and appreciated.

Collins had no Elgin marbles to inspire him as did Keats. Yet one feels that the simplicity and proportion of the best Greek sculpture subtly infused itself into his poetry. His verse is, as Gosse has said, clearly-cut and direct, marble pure. The perfect line and form of *How Sleep the Brave* exemplifies it. And in the *Ode to Liberty,* though he is there describing a

---

[12] *An Essay on Mr. Pope's Odessey in Five Dialogues,* by Mr. Spence, Professor of Poetry in the University of Oxford, London, 1737, p. 81. (Cited in Bronson, p. 95.) The reference to Spence offers an interesting insight into the workings of Collins's mind. The description of Coriolanus in the *Epistle to Hanmer* follows shortly after Collins's note on Spence, in which Coriolanus is mentioned. Moreover, Collins may have remembered in this connection some of the vivid picture painting which he found in Sidney's *Arcadia,* which Dyce suggests he had read.

[13] Nathaniel Drake, *Literary Hours,* Sudbury, 1798, p. 391. Cf. Gosse, *History of English Literature, Eighteenth Century,* pp. 231-5.

broken statue symbolic of Rome's fallen glory after the Gothic invasions, its once fine symmetry is still felt:

> How *Rome,* before thy weeping Face,
> With heaviest Sound, a Giant-statue, fell,
> Push'd by a wild and artless Race,
> From off its wide ambitious Base,
> When Time his Northern Sons of Spoil awoke,
>   And all the blended Work of Strength and Grace,
>   With many a rude repeated Stroke,
> And many a barb'rous Yell, to thousand Fragments broke.

The concept of its former perfection developed in the epode shows even more definitely Collins's appreciation of the sculpturesque:

> Still 'midst the scatter'd States around,
> Some Remnants of Her Strength were found;
> They saw by what escap'd the Storm,
> How wond'rous rose her perfect Form;
> How in the great the labour'd Whole,
> Each mighty Master pour'd his Soul!

And again in the second epode of the same poem, in describing the new temple that Liberty will erect in England, Collins recognizes the majesty and grace of Greek architecture:

> Ev'n now before his favor'd Eyes,
> In *Gothic* Pride it seems to rise!
> Yet *Graecia's* graceful Orders join
> Majestic thro' the mix'd Design.[14]

Gilbert White tells us in his letter to the *Gentleman's Magazine,* 1781, that Collins was passionately fond of music. That he listened to the harpsichord played by the dissolute Captain Hargrave when he lodged with Miss Bundy, that he attended the opera in London, that he was keenly interested in the musical setting of his ode on *The Passions,* and that he apparently knew

---

[14] Closely related to Collins's interest in the architectural and sculpturesque is his fondness for the image of shrines at which he would pay the service of votary—the Temple to Pity which he would build her (*Ode to Pity,* 25-30); the Roman shrine deserted by Simplicity (*Ode to Simplicity,* 40); the "vaulted Shrine" of the Almighty (*Ode on the Poetical Character,* 33); the shrine and altar and the roseate bower of Mercy (*Ode to Mercy,* 11-14, 25); the beauteous model and inmost altar of Liberty's temple (*Ode to Liberty,* 113-130); the tomb to the dead soldier (*Ode to a Lady,* 19-24); the sullen shrines of war (*Ode to Peace,* 9); and the pale shrine of the departed poet (*Ode on the Death of Mr. Thomson,* 26).

Dr. John Worgan, organist at Vauxhall,[15] substantiate the point. Though Collins's poetry reveals no particularly technical knowledge of music, he shows some appreciation for it in the *Odes Descriptive and Allegoric,* a feeling growing perhaps from his sensitiveness to sound itself. Though he seems to prefer some softened strain, the tone of Pity's lute, or the delicate sound of the airy harp of Aeolus, he describes with equal skill the martial effect of trumpet, fife, and bugle, or the sound of some rude choral dirge. And in *The Passions* he appreciates the requirements of an ode written for music almost as thoroughly as did Dryden in *A Song for St. Cecilia's Day.* That he was attempting an *Ode on the Music of the Grecian Theatre,* as the letter to Dr. Hayes informs us, argues not only a reasonable familiarity with music, but furnishes further evidence of that relation of the arts which he had already felt in the *Epistle to Hanmer,* where music is linked with painting and drama— a relation which was closer in the days of Greek tragedy than in Collins's own. The concluding part of *The Passions* expresses that kinship which Collins felt perhaps was even stronger between music and poetry than between painting and poetry; in the passage, too, is the poet's oft-expressed wish for a revival of the arts which droop in the laggard age in which he lives, Handel to the contrary notwithstanding:[16]

[15] H. O. White, *RES,* 1927, p. 21. See also "Memoir of Dr. Worgan," *Quarterly Musical Magazine and Review,* 1823, V, 122:

> It is not impossible that his youthful intimacy
> with poor Collins inspired the couplet:
> 'Arise as in that elder Time, Warm, Energic,
> Chaste, Sublime.'

John Worgan succeeded his brother James at Vauxhall in 1751. Doubtful evidence on the same point is the *Ode on the Late Taste in Music* attributed to Collins in *The Muses' Library* edition of the *Poems of Johnson, Goldsmith, Gray, and Collins,* 1905, and in the earlier *British Poets* series (Boston, Houghton Mifflin, N.D., p. xxxviii), where it is attributed to him "from the coincidence between Collins's love of, and addresses to, Music, his residence at Oxford, and from internal evidence." It is, however, thoroughly unlike Collins and at best resembles his manner even in the *Persian Eclogues* or the *Epistle to Hanmer* but slightly. It is not printed in any standard edition of his poems.

[16] Collins was undoubtedly condemning contemporary taste for the Italian opera, which still flourished despite the attacks of Addison and Gay and which was later to draw the criticism of Burns. For a similar view cf. *Ode to Simplicity,* 42, and *On the Late Taste in Music,* attributed to Collins.

O *Music,* Sphere-descended Maid,
Friend of Pleasure, *Wisdom's* Aid,
Why, Goddess, why to us deny'd?
Lay'st Thou thy antient Lyre aside?
As in that lov'd *Athenian* Bow'r,
You learn'd an all-commanding Pow'r,

. . . .

Arise as in that elder Time,
Warm, Energic, Chaste, Sublime!
Thy wonders in that God-like Age,
Fill thy recording *Sister's* Page—
'Tis said, and I believe the Tale,
Thy humblest *Reed* could more prevail,
Had more of Strength, diviner Rage,
Than all which charms this laggard Age,
Ev'n all at once together found,
Caecilia's mingled World of Sound—
O bid our vain Endeavors cease,
Revive the just Designs of *Greece,*
Return in all thy simple State!
Confirm the Tales Her Sons relate![17]

[17] Music is called "Sphere-descended Maid." For a similar concept of the divine origin of music see *Ode on the Poetical Character,* 25-38; *Ode to Peace,* 10-12.

III

NATURE

COLLINS thought, too, "of man, of nature, and of human life," though his experience of them was neither as perceptive nor as sympathetic as that of Wordsworth, or even of Cowper, to whom he is more closely akin. Yet he saw nature more definitely and more sympathetically than most of his commentators have said. There is frequently an Arcadian flavor to his descriptions of nature, for he was always fond of the pastoral manner, and he never entirely outgrew the influence of Pope's generalized description so evident in the *Persian Eclogues* in spite of Collins's freshness and delicacy of treatment. Though he was writing in a day when landscape-painters in verse like Thomson and John Dyer were carrying on the pastoral tradition of Milton, which Collins himself followed to a degree, something of his own visionary spirit and his sensitive awareness of the sights and sounds of nature touched and refined his pictures, softened them, and harmonized them. Even conventional descriptive phrases seem transmuted as his imagination grows— a change that becomes evident as one follows his brief development from the *Persian Eclogues* to the *Ode on the Popular Superstitions*. Individual details in his pictures of nature suggest the photographic minuteness of Cowper's landscape painting, but the shadowy and imaginative quality with which he blends and harmonizes the details makes the effect essentially his own.[1] And closely allied with his actual picture of nature, one often senses the presence of a fanciful personified figure, a presiding genius over the scene—almost Greek in its suggestion, like a character from some myth.

The *Persian Eclogues,* modeled so closely after the prevailing

[1] If Gilbert White's description of Collins's "grey eyes, so very weak at times as hardly to bear a candle in the room" be reliable, it may help to account for the shadowy quality of his descriptions of nature.

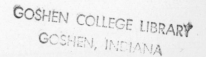

taste in pastoral, are naturally somewhat conventional or bookish in their descriptions of nature. He employs much of the generalized scenery so characteristic of Pope. "Limpid springs," "verdant vales," "flow'ry valleys," "sylvan scenes," "shady groves," "wanton gales," "breezy mountains" are among the stock descriptive phrases. Some of the less conventional pictures, drawn from his reading in Salmon's *Modern History*, are calculated to furnish the exotic atmosphere one would expect in poems purporting in Collins's fiction to be the work of "one Abdallah, a native of Tauris." These pictures are invested with something of the delicate perceptiveness of the poet, and, appropriately enough for an oriental study, appeal to the sense of smell as well as to the world of eye and ear. Two passages from the *Third Eclogue* illustrate the blending of the conventional or the bookish with the poet's own sensitiveness. The first is the setting for the eclogue:

> In *Georgia's* Land, where *Tefflis'* Tow'rs are seen,
> In distant View along the level Green,
> While Ev'ning Dews enrich the glitt'ring Glade,
> And the tall Forests cast a longer Shade,
> Amidst the Maids of *Zagen's* peaceful Grove,
> *Emyra* sung the pleasing Cares of Love.[2]

A second passage modeled closely from a passage in Salmon has also a suggestion of Milton's *L'Allegro:*

> Deep in the Grove beneath the secret Shade,
> A various Wreath of od'rous Flow'rs she made.
> Gay-motley'd Pinks and sweet Junquils she chose,
> The Violet-blue, that on the Moss-bank grows;
> All-sweet to Sense, the flaunting Rose was there;
> The finish'd Chaplet well-adorn'd her Hair.

[2] Lines 5-6 added in the Edition of 1757 (called *Oriental Eclogues*) show the poet's growing sensitiveness:

> What time 'tis sweet o'er fields of rice to stray,
> Or scent the breathing maize at setting day;

The lines are, however, subjected to the critical strictures of a reviewer in *The Quarterly* for 1826, XXXII, 15-16: "Had Collins been better informed . . . we should not have to lament some blots in his exquisite oriental eclogues; he would have hardly applied to any hour, as an appropriate pleasure 'o'er fields of rice to stray,' but would have been sensible that to wade through a rice-field is a most laborious and wearisome occupation, at whatever period of the day. . . ."

In spite of the conventional quality of the descriptions the aspects of nature which were to appeal most to Collins are represented here, and all of them suggest the taste and character of the poet. He alludes most frequently to the secret shade or the shady grove—indicative of his own love for retirement and solitude. And the spell of darkening vale and fairy valley begins first to be felt in the eclogues. Here, too, Collins's love of wandering rivers is first evident, as well as his peculiar sensitiveness to the murmur of distant streams and to the howling of storm winds. Further in keeping with Collins's retiring nature, these scenes have the enchantment that distance lends them.[3]

The descriptions of nature in the odes are less conventional than those in the *Persian Eclogues,* and over all of them there is "a glamour of the imagination." They represent nature viewed at the twilight hour, when to the mind of the visionary she is most shadowy and most enchanting; or she is viewed from a distance so that her more realistic aspects are softened. Or some wholly fanciful and visionary scene is clothed with "the light that never was on land or sea." If nature is represented in her harsher moods, as in the description of storms and of the sea, a kind of imaginative terror aroused by the scene takes it from the real. Collins did not see nature so sharply as did some of his contemporaries like John Dyer, or even Gray, but certain aspects of her beauty or her grandeur appealed to him, and to these few images he returned again and again with a growing sense of their charm.

Collins's favorite view of nature is at twilight—a broad sweep of valley is seen from a distance with one or two prominent details or groups of details harmonized by the indefiniteness of the time—suggestive, too, of a delicate fairyland by the subtle allusion to fairy creatures dimly made part of the scene. The spell of "silent Eve" is first felt in the third of the eclogues:

[3] As a typical instance cf. *Ode on the Popular Superstitions:*
> All hail, ye scenes that 'oer my soul prevail,
> Ye————friths and lakes, which, far away, . . .
>   . . . at distance, hail!

Here is the romantic poet's fondness for a far-off country; and in the passage is a rephrasing of a fine image in *The Passions.*

> In distant View along the level Green,
> While Ev'ning Dews enrich the glitt'ring Glade.

In the *Epistle to Hanmer* the same effect is developed. When epitomizing the comedies of Shakespeare, Collins describes how charmed by wild-winged Fancy the soul is content to rove with humbler nature:

> Where Swains contented own the quiet Scene,
> And twilight Fairies tread the circled Green:
> Drest by her [Fancy's] Hand, the Woods and Vallies smile,
> And Spring diffusive decks th' *enchanted Isle.*

Here is the germ of the mood in the *Ode to Evening* as well as the suggestion of one of the delicate images of the *Ode Written in the Beginning of the Year 1746.* There is the further indication here that part of Collins's love of the fanciful in nature came from his appreciation of the fairyland of *A Midsummer Night's Dream* and the enchanted island of *The Tempest.* In the *Ode to Simplicity* appears again the mood of "evening Musings slow." In *Song. The Sentiments borrowed from Shakespeare* the favorite scene is again pictured—"the lowland hamlets," the "dewy turf," "the bell of peace." These sights and sounds which haunt the poet suggest the quiet melancholy of the youth's death and they are touched and softened by the "twilight hour" when he was buried. The same spell of evening and quiet fancy is felt in the *Song from Shakespeare's Cymbeline,* where the peace of the "grassy tomb" and the "quiet grove" is deepened by the suggestion:

> The female fays shall haunt the green,
> And dress thy grave with pearly dew,

and the further quiet and unobtrusive account of the red-breast's kindly aid at "ev'ning hours." So often does Collins associate the scenery of the evening time with the lament for one dearly beloved and lately dead that to the hushed pensiveness of the time there is almost always added a note of tender melancholy, felt even when it is not directly expressed. Even in the description of the "luckless swain" in the *Ode on the Popular Superstitions* the mention of the "smoking hamlet" and the "dim hill

uprising near" heightens the pity and tragic horror that the
incident arouses in the poet. The *Ode on the Death of Mr.
Thomson* best illustrates the harmony between the twilight hour
and the sense of vague sadness and tender pity the poet so
often associates with that time. The sound of the Aeolian harp,
swelling at a distance, the hushed suspending of the dashing
oar, the softened view of the whitening spire, the gliding sail,
the pale shrine glimmering near, the green hill, and the cold
turf, all suggest the quiet sadness and subdued tenderness of the
poet; but best of all is the delicate sense of the enchantment of
the twilight time expressed in the fine image.:

> And see, the fairy valleys fade,
> Dun Night has veil'd the solemn view!

The combined effect of the mood and of the details suggests
the earlier use of the same mood and tone in the *Ode to Evening,*
of which in many phrases the *Ode on the Death of Mr. Thomson* is reminiscent.

All of the *Ode to Evening,* with the possible exception of
the last three stanzas (though they, too, are closely enough in
harmony with the mood of the time), shows the poet's skill
in selecting details from the world of eye and ear appropriate
to the vague and shadowy hour. The cloudy skirts of the sun
"o'erhang his wavy Bed"; the "Brede ethereal" creates the
fanciful and other-worldly atmosphere of which everything in
the picture partakes. The weak-eyed bat, the beetle, the hamlets brown, the pilgrim, all suggest the homely and simple
rusticity of the scene touched and transformed by the magic
of the hour. The twilight path, the darkening vale, the folding star, the sheety lake, the lone heath, the time-hallowed pile,
the upland fallows grey, the dim-discovered spires are softened
and blended and subdued to fit the musing mood of the poet;
all partake of the spell that the twilight casts over the simple
landscape. The hut on the mountain's side—the "sylvan Shed"
—emphasizes the retirement of the poet's own temperament.
The whole landscape study is done in subdued colors of browns
and grays and whites—all suggestive of that transition which
comes as the dewy fingers of evening draw "the gradual dusky

Veil" over the scene, half misty in the driving rain.[4] There is no attempt to fit the details of landscape into a finished photographic picture such as Cowper sometimes gives us in *The Task;* rather the poet selects those aspects of the scene which best harmonize with the time itself or which respond most fully to the genial influence of evening. Whatever completeness there is in the picture comes from the effective fusing of the details selected into the twilight softness of the poet's mood.

Part of the effectiveness of the picture of nature comes, too, from the poet's blending of the visual aspects of the scene with the sounds of nature most harmonious with the evening time. Most of the sounds are subdued, monotonous, or intermittent, and serve adequately to emphasize the essential silence so appropriate to the twilight and to the quiet musing mood of the poet. That they are, for the most part, faint and distant as well, further enhances their effect. All are in the "softened Strain" of the poet's own song; all steal upon the ear. The sound of "solemn Springs," and "dying Gales," the monotony of "the short shrill Shriek" of the bat and the "small but sullen Horn" of the beetle harmonize with the hushed air and the stillness of evening. And blending most into the quiet pensiveness of the scene, showing that essential harmony of sight, sound, and feeling in the poem, is the note of the simple bell which in its very tone has something of the melancholy solemnity of the time.[5] But perhaps the most subtle touch is the poet's mention of the "chill blust'ring Winds or driving Rain," which appeals to both sound and sight, perhaps, too, to the sense of touch, and emphasizes the whole musing and retired mood by suggesting its contrast. At such a time the poet must be content to look out upon the landscape and find his favorite scenes in nature enhanced by distance, instead of being a participant in their charm.

[4] This passage harks back to the *Song from Shakespeare's Cymbeline,* 18-19:
When howling winds and beating rain,
In tempests shake the sylvan cell.

[5] So sensitive a critic as Mr. Blunden feels the suggestion of the evening bell in the sound of "While *now* the bright-hair'd Sun," "*Now* Air is hushed," and "*Now* teach me." Is it not also suggested in "solemn Springs"?

The sense of magic and delicate enchantment is also enhanced
by Collins's weaving into the actual scene the shadowy forms
of the Goddess of Evening and her attendant spirits, the fanciful creatures of English folk-lore found in the pages of Shakespeare. To Collins as to the Greeks, from whom he is never
far away, nature is alive with airy beings. While her presence
is suggested rather than described, Collins applies to Evening
epithets which harmonize and blend her attributes with the
sights and sounds she has touched with her spell. In accord
with the hushed stillness of nature, she is chaste, modest, and
meek, a nymph reserved, a maid composed, a calm votaress.
Her shadowy car is attended by the fragrant Hours and Elves,
"Who slept in Flow'rs the day," by "many a Nymph who
wreaths her Brows with Sedge," suggestive of the sober melancholy time, and by the "pensive Pleasures sweet." Her place
as a presiding genius over the sights and sounds of evening
is made more fitting by such phrases as "*thy* dark'ning Vale,"
"*thy* folding Star," "*thy* own solemn Springs." These things of
nature are her own dear and familiar possessions dedicated to
her service, and all feel her gentlest influence. And it is this
goddess at whose shrine the poet would worship with a votive
hymn, for her spell, her quiet calm, and her harmonizing power
over all of the aspects of nature associated with her sway sym-
bolize, in a sense, the poet's own best-loved mood and most
intimately touch his own temper. Under her influence alone can
he "breathe some soften'd Strain"; only in her presence can he
muse slowly and deeply. Her return is genial to his spirit, for
she is a loved friend. He feels her gentlest influence, for hers
is to him a favorite name. She is at once distinct from the nature
which responds to her, and a part of it. Spring's showers bathe
her breathing tresses; Summer "sports beneath her ling'ring
Light"; sallow Autumn fills her lap with leaves; Winter affrights her shrinking train and rudely rends her robes. The Seasons themselves are, like Evening, at once personified and
described. Each descriptive picture of the season itself is subtly
identified with the shadowy figure which represents Spring or
Summer. This skillful blending of pictured fact and suggested

fancy marks the peculiar effectiveness of Collins's presentation of nature, and makes the *Ode to Evening* a masterpiece.[6]

This same blending of the real and the imaginative associates several of Collins's other poems with the *Ode to Evening*. The fine passage in the *Ode on the Death of Colonel Ross:*

> Blest Youth, regardful of thy Doom,
> Aërial Hands shall build thy Tomb,
> With shadowy Trophies crown'd:

[6] Collins's sensitiveness to the harmony and fitness of his images is well illustrated in the revisions he made in the *Ode to Evening*. He changed "brawling Springs" (l. 2) to "solemn Springs" with a fine sense of the greater harmony of the latter. Wordsworth, we know, felt that the first version was inharmonious. In the last line of the ode the change of "love" to "hymn" helps to emphasize the spell of the goddess and Collins's feeling that this poem is a votive offering at her shrine. One cannot, however, feel that the change of line 49 from the first reading, "So long regardful of thy quiet Rule," to "So long sure-found beneath the sylvan Shed" is an equally felicitous alteration. The most significant and effective change he made in lines 29-32. The original version read:

> Then let me rove some wild and heathy Scene,
> Or find some Ruin 'midst its dreary Dells,
> Whose Walls more awful nod
> By thy religious Gleams.

This was changed to:

> Then lead, calm Vot'ress, where some sheety lake
> Cheers the lone heath, or some time hallow'd pile,
> Or up-land fallows grey
> Reflect its last cool gleam.

The second version is far more in harmony with the simple pastoral imagery of the rest than the first version with its suggestion of "Gothic" melancholy. Over the exact meaning of the last line of this version there has been too much needless quibbling. The "its" refers to the "shadowy Car" of evening (l. 28). The image in the stanza is a common enough natural phenomenon—the lingering light of the evening sky reflected on a quiet body of water after sunset. Ker in his essay, "Romantic Fallacies" (*The Art of Poetry,* 1923, pp. 86-7) has described it best: "There is the fresh vision and understanding of the effect of the surface of water in twilight, when all the land round it is dark, and in place of the conventional ruin that 'nods,' there is the old building, church or castle, dimly seen as part of the evening light along with the large bulging hillside." Legouis's suggested emendation of "thy" for "its" would be unnecessary. (See A. MacDonald, *TLS,* 22 March, 1928, where Legouis's note to his translation of the ode in Ritchie and Morris's *Manual of French Composition* is quoted. See also O. Elton, *Survey of English Literature,* 1730-80, II, 306.) And Mr. Garrod's suggested reading of "light's last cool Gleam" (*TLS,* 1928, p. 188; *Collins,* pp. 48-51) might clarify the picture, but suggests rather that in spite of his insistence on the letter rather than the spirit of the passage, he has seen something of what Ker has seen. For other suggested readings of the passage see: J. R. MacPhail, *TLS,* 1928, p. 221; Margaret Bourke, *TLS,* 1928, p. 243; John Sparrow, *TLS,* 1928, p. 272; Takeshi Saito, "Collins and Keats," *TLS,* 1930, p. 991.

is reminiscent of the atmosphere of the *Ode to Evening,* though it only suggests it. Yet the suggestion is stronger when one remembers that one version of the lines reads:

> O'er him, whose doom thy virtues grieve,
> Aërial forms shall sit at eve
> And bend the pensive head![7]

Again the images in *Ode Written in the Beginning of the Year 1746:*

> By Fairy Hands their Knell is rung,
> By Forms unseen their Dirge is sung;

seem only appropriate to the evening time, recalling as they do not only the "simple Bell" and "gradual dusky Veil" of the *Ode to Evening,* but also the "bell of peace" and the "twilight hour" of *Song. The Sentiments from Shakespeare* and as well the unfinished fragment, *The Bell of Arragon,* with its mention of "some simpler Bell," the knell for the poet's own death.

Two other descriptions of nature in the odes illustrate Collins's ability to portray and emphasize the imaginative and symbolic aspects of a scene; both are farther away from reality than the landscape of the *Ode to Evening.* The first passage, the tribute to Milton in the *Ode on the Poetical Character,* presents a purely symbolic description of nature; yet it is composed of many of Collins's characteristic images:

> High on some Cliff, to Heav'n up-pil'd,
> Of rude Access, of Prospect wild,
> Where, tangled round the jealous Steep,
> Strange Shades o'erbrow the Valleys deep,
> And holy *Genii* guard the Rock,
> Its Gloomes embrown, its Springs unlock,

---

[7] They are so given in Dodsley's *Collection,* 1765 (first edition, 1748), and in Bell's *Poets of Great Britain,* 1781, which follows Langhorne's edition of 1765. There are both a recollection of the *Ode to Evening* and an anticipation of the present form in the stanza as it appeared in Dodsley's *Museum,* 1746:

> Ev'n now, regardful of his Doom,
> Applauding *Honour* haunts his Tomb,
>   With shadowy Trophies crown'd:
> Whilst *Freedom's* Form beside her roves
> Majestic thro' the twilight Groves,
>   And calls her Heroes round.

> While on its rich ambitious Head,
> An *Eden,* like his own, lies spread.
> I view that Oak, the fancied Glades among,
> By which as *Milton* lay, His Ev'ning Ear,
> From many a Cloud that drop'd Ethereal Dew,
> Nigh spher'd in Heav'n its native Strains could hear:
> On which that ancient Trump he reach'd was hung.

The poet's favorite descriptive effects are here: the valleys, the glades, the springs, the evening hour, the glooms embrowned. Yet all are touched by the power of his imagination. Closely allied to the scene itself are the "strange Shades" and the "holy Genii," who here serve to heighten the awe and grandeur of the whole and to emphasize the solitary and divine inspiration that Collins attributed to Milton. The description of "an Eden like his own" on the top of inaccessible and rugged cliffs symbolizes at once the heavenly heights to which Milton's genius had aspired and the difficulty of attaining to them or of emulating his power. The whole description of "the inspiring Bow'rs" is loftily imaginative, yet it is akin in its essence to the other pictures Collins has drawn.[8]

The description of pale Melancholy in *The Passions* represents again an ideal scene, the details of which harmonize with the fanciful character there personified. For her environment is as appropriate to her spell and influence as are the haunts of Evening to that goddess. That Melancholy is the only Passion honored with a finished descriptive setting suggests that Collins felt her power as he did the genial influence of Evening:

> With Eyes up-rais'd, as one inspir'd,
> Pale *Melancholy* sate retir'd,
> And from her wild sequester'd Seat,
> In Notes by Distance made more sweet,
> Pour'd thro' the mellow *Horn* her pensive Soul:
> And dashing soft from Rocks around,
> Bubbling Runnels join'd the Sound;
> Thro' Glades and Glooms the mingled Measure stole,
> Or o'er some haunted Stream with fond Delay,
> Round an holy Calm diffusing,

---

[8] Perhaps Collins here had in mind the old idea that the terrestrial paradise is on an inaccessible mountain top as it is pictured in *Purgatorio,* cantos xxvii and xxviii. Cf. Lane Cooper, *Mod. Phil.,* III, 327 ff.

Love of Peace, and lonely Musing,
In hollow Murmurs died away.

Like Evening, Melancholy is revealed more by her attributes than by her actual appearance. She, like Evening, is "retir'd," "pensive"; she inspires, as does Evening, "holy Calm" "Love of Peace," and "lonely Musing." She, too, is congenial to the poet, for she is "as one inspir'd." And the description, like that in the *Ode to Evening,* is concerned only with those sights and sounds most fitting to the goddess. The "sequester'd Seat," the "Glades and Glooms" are appropriate to her pensiveness, her loneliness, and her retirement. The subdued sounds of the "Notes by Distance made more sweet," the softness of the "bubbling Runnels," and the harmonious blending of the two; the sense of lonely mystery in the "haunted Stream," the dying away of the "hollow Murmurs," show that fine blending of details so effective in the *Ode to Evening.* In that this deals with a wholly fanciful scene it is closest to the passage in the *Ode on the Poetical Character,* which it also resembles in descriptive detail. The echoes and suggestions of Milton in this passage in *The Passions* show that Collins's ideal poet was never far from his mind.

Collins seems to have been interested in nature in a topographical sense, too, perhaps because of his familiarity with Drayton's *Poly-Olbion,* perhaps because of his reading in Spenser and the historians. He frequently speaks of rivers, particularly those with which some historical event is associated, though he undoubtedly found some pleasure in visualizing a wandering stream like the Arun, by which he apparently loved to muse. Even the *Persian Eclogues* give some evidence of the point. His moralizing shepherd, Selim, sits by Tigris' wandering waves, to teach his useful lesson to the fair and young. The fugitives in the *Fourth Eclogue* lament that since the Turkish invasions the Persian virgins no longer rove by Sargis' banks. But most often the poet associates with the river some historical or literary tradition. In the *Epistle to Hanmer* and in the *Ode to Pity* he describes the Ilissus as a haunt associated with Greek tragedy; in the *Ode to Simplicity* the wavy sweep of Cephisus was the first home of Simplicity. In like manner the Arno is associated with the Provençal love poetry; the Arun suggests Otway; and the Yarrow recalls the balladry of the North. In his elegiac poems the dead friend is buried near a murmuring river or is appropriately mourned by the spirits of the river associated with his fame. For example, in his allusion in *The Manners* to the supposed death of LeSage he speaks of

> Him, whom *Seine's* blue Nymphs deplore,
> In watchet Weeds on *Gallia's* Shore.

In two instances, the grave of the dead friend for whom the poet mourns is close to a river. In the *Ode on the Death of Colonel Ross* that soldier's grave is "by rapid Scheld's descending Wave." And the Woodland Pilgrim in the *Ode on the Death of Mr. Thomson* is buried near the stealing wave of the Thames, so closely associated with the later years of Thomson's life. In this last passage Collins has imparted in small degree something of that reminiscent sadness in visiting the old haunts hallowed by memories of friendship felt so much more strongly in Arnold's *Thyrsis*.

In his fascination with the wilder and stormier aspects of nature Collins almost anticipates Gray's enthusiasm for the Alps and the rude magnificence of the Grand Chartreuse.[9] In his descriptions of the sea, generalized though they are, he precedes Macpherson's *Ossian* and Beattie's *Minstrel* in appreciating its power. These pictures have not the reminiscent and pensive softness of the landscape in the *Ode to Evening,* but make an awesome appeal to the sense of fear and horror. Such is the effect of his sharp picture in the antistrophe of the *Ode to Fear:*

> Or, in some hollow'd Seat,
> 'Gainst which the big Waves beat,
> Hear drowning Sea-men's Cries in Tempests brought!

The same tone marks the description in the *Ode to Liberty* of the preternatural storm which swept away the passage between France and England; here as in the very different picture in the

[9] See *Journal*, Sept. 17, 1739; Letter to Mrs. Dorothy Gray, Oct. 13, 1739; Letter to Richard West, Nov. 17, 1739 N.S.

Ode to Evening the activities of nature are associated with the presence of airy beings:

> To the Blown *Baltic* then, they say,
> The wild Waves found another way,
> Where *Orcas* howls, his wolfish Mountains rounding;
> Till all the banded West at once 'gan rise,
> A wide wild Storm ev'n Nature's self confounding,
> With'ring her Giant Sons with strange uncouth Surprise.
> This pillar'd Earth so firm and wide,
> By Winds and inward Labors torn,
> In Thunders dread was push'd aside,
> And down the should'ring Billows born.

Collins seems to have been particularly sensitive, too, to the sound of storm-winds. He was as alive to harsh and terrifying sounds as to the soft and harmonious murmur of limpid springs. The descriptions of "chill blust'ring Winds" and "Winter yelling thro' the troublous Air" of the *Ode to Evening,* the "howling wind and beating rain" of the *Song from Shakespeare's Cymbeline* show that he was sensitive to these harsh sounds particularly because they were so dissonant to the quiet and retirement he loved so well; possibly, too, because they aroused in him a sense of terror and fear akin to that which he felt in the spectacle of tragedy.

IV

MAN

IN UNDERSTANDING of and insight into human character the poetry of Collins is notably deficient. A poet exposed to the hardships of poverty in London as was Collins, and acquainted with the life and manners of the city, where he was an agreeable companion everywhere and a genial friend of both scholars and actors, might be expected to write more feelingly of men. But Collins did not. His limitations in this respect arose partly from the very restrictions he had set upon himself, partly from the retiring and visionary side of his character. That he chose to write odes which were descriptive and allegorical rather than personal kept him from dealing directly with men, though many of his odes show that he was not unaware of their basic emotions. That several of the odes are concerned with contemporary events and that two of them lament the death of friends argues some awareness of and sympathy with human suffering. His desire to emulate those who had most studied men shows a realization of his own deficiency. But he had chosen the imaginative and, to a degree, the conventional manner of expressing himself, and he did not rise above his self-imposed restrictions. Adhering to the pastoral tradition, he never departed widely from the impersonal attitude toward the humble man of whom Thomson and Ramsay had already shown understanding. Nor did he have the melancholy and sympathetic kinship that Gray felt for men in his *Elegy Written in a Country Churchyard*. Yet in his way he expressed as much tenderness and pity for them as his own introspective and visionary temper and his artistic limitations would allow.

Collins's poetic treatment of humble man shows at once his aloofness from him and his adherence to the pastoral tradition. His shepherds and shepherdesses in the *Persian Eclogues* for all their oriental environment are purely the conventional characters of the artificial pastoral such as Pope had written. While there is some delicacy of touch in portraying their manners, particularly in the charming *Third Eclogue,* there is only a literary attempt to gain verisimilitude. In the *Epistle to Hanmer* there is merely conventional and casual mention of the "shepherd Swains." And though in the *Ode to Simplicity* and at the beginning of the *Ode to Evening* he declares his intention of becoming a pastoral poet, he does not show any great sympathy for those who he hopes will be his audience:

> I only seek to find thy temp'rate Vale:
> Where oft my Reed might sound
> To Maids and Shepherds round,
> And all thy Sons, O *Nature,* learn my Tale.

In the *Ode on the Death of Colonel Ross* humble man serves but as a part of the pastoral setting of Ross's grave. Collins is still aloof from him:

> That sacred Spot the Village Hind
> With ev'ry sweetest Turf shall bind,
> And Peace protect the Shade.

Again in the *Ode on the Death of Mr. Thomson* the country folk play only a conventional part in the tribute to the dead poet:

> The genial meads assign'd to bless
> Thy life, shall mourn thy early doom;
> Their hinds, and shepherd-girls shall dress
> With simple hands thy rural tomb.

Even in Collins's two most tender and delicate poems in the pastoral manner, *Song. The Sentiments Borrowed from Shakespeare* and *Song from Shakespeare's Cymbeline,* the coldness of his picture of the country-folk is marked. In the first, Damon and Lucy are the names of a conventional shepherd and shepherdess; the sentiment, too, is characteristic of many a pastoral elegy. The second poem again employs the favorite image. The country-folk deck the tomb of the departed with flowers, but they are not more than artistic parts of a picture:

> To fair Fidele's grassy tomb
>   Soft maids and village hinds shall bring
> Each op'ning sweet, of earliest bloom,
>   And rifle all the breathing Spring.

In the *Ode on the Popular Superstitions* Collins approaches
closest to a sympathetic picture of the actual life of the humble
man, but even here there is some detachment. His advice to
Home shows something of this almost patronizing attitude:

> Nor thou, though learn'd his homelier thoughts neglect;
>   Let thy sweet muse the rural faith sustain.

The poem pictures detail after detail of the rustic life, but
Collins seems far more concerned with their appropriateness
for poetic treatment than with their revelation of the loves and
hates of men. Moreover, almost all of his pictures are derivative,
not the product of first-hand observation. The conventional
pastoral note is still present in such a passage as this, which has
the familiar scene described in the *Ode on the Death of Mr.
Thomson* and the *Song from Shakespeare's Cymbeline* flavored
with an element of folk-lore:

> Whether thou bid'st the well-taught hind repeat
>   The choral dirge that mourns some chieftain brave,
> When ev'ry shrieking maid her bosom beat,
>   And strew'd with choisest herbs his scented grave.

The two most extensive accounts of humble man in the poem are
derivative, the first obviously from Thomson's *Winter,* the second from Collins's reading in Martin's *Voyage to St. Kilda.* The
first passage is the longest study of humble man that Collins
made and the closest he comes to a realistic treatment of him:

> Ah, luckless swain, o'er all unblest indeed!
>   Whom late bewilder'd in the dank, dark fen,
> Far from his flocks and smoking hamlet then!
>   To that sad spot ——————:
> On him enrag'd, the fiend, in angry mood,
>   Shall never look with pity's kind concern,
> But instant, furious, raise the whelming flood   110
>   O'er its drown'd bank, forbidding all return.
> Or, if he meditate his wish'd escape
>   To some dim hill that seems uprising near,
> To his faint eye the grim and grisly shape,

In all its terrors clad, shall wild appear.
Meantime, the wat'ry surge shall around him rise,
  Pour'd sudden forth from ev'ry swelling source.
What now remains but tears and hopeless sighs?
  His fear-shook limbs have lost their youthly force,
And down the waves he floats, a pale and breathless corse.

For him, in vain, his anxious wife shall wait,   121
  Or wander forth to meet him on his way;
For him, in vain, at to-fall of the day,
  His babes shall linger at th' unclosing gate![1]
Ah, ne'er shall he return! Alone, if night
  Her travell'd limbs in broken slumbers steep,
With dropping willows drest, his mournful sprite
  Shall visit sad, perchance her silent sleep:
Then he, perhaps, with moist and wat'ry hand,
  Shall fondly seem to press her shudd'ring cheek   130
And with his blue swoln face before her stand,
  And, shiv'ring cold, these piteous accents speak:
Pursue, dear wife, thy daily toils pursue
  At dawn or dusk, industrious as before;
Nor e'er of me one hapless thought renew,
  While I lie welt'ring on the ozier'd shore,
Drown'd by the KAELPIE'S wrath, nor e'er shall aid thee more!

Though Collins does feel "pity's kind concern" for the luckless swain, he has not come to view his tragic fate and the grief of his bereaved family with the deeper sympathy that Gray was to feel when he wrote a similar passage in the *Elegy*. Rather Collins treats of the horrible and fearful aspects of the scene, with the terrors of the water Kaelpie and the gruesome spectacle of the returned spirit with moist and watery hand and blue-swoln cheek, as well as the fear and horror of the sleeping wife to whom he speaks words of tender consolation. The poet is most

---

[1] Compare Dryden, *Annus Mirabilis*, 1666, stanza xxxiv:
      This careful husband had been long away
    Whom his chaste wife and little children mourn,
    Who on their fingers learned to tell the day
      On which their father promised to return.

The image goes back, however, to Lucretius, *De Rerum Natura*, III, 894 ff. Horace has a resembling passage in *Epode II*, 39 ff. It is something of a literary convention. Cf. Gray, *Elegy Written in a Country Churchyard*, 21-24; Burns, *Cotter's Saturday Night*, 19-26; Arnold, *Balder Dead*, I, 274-325.

concerned with the supernatural elements of the scene; his sympathy with the suffering of humble man is subdued and secondary. Here his pity is subordinated to his sense of fear.

The description of the virtuous race who inhabit the island of St. Kilda is almost entirely drawn from Collins's reading of a passage in Martin, possibly too from his remembrance of Mallet's account of them in *Amyntor and Theodora,* which in turn goes back to Martin for its source. Though he carefully omits some of the more cheerful aspects of it, he paints the desolate and limited environment, with its bleak rocks and rugged cliffs bounded by the wintry main, as he had found it described. For the rest he is impressed by the unusual aspects of the peoples' lives, how

> With sparing temp'rance, at the needful time,
> They drain the sainted spring, or, hunger-prest,
> Along th' Atlantic rock undreading climb,
> And of its eggs despoil the Solan's nest.

With a sentiment suspiciously reminiscent of an earlier passage in the *Persian Eclogues* he finds in these remote people what so many of his contemporaries sought to find in turning to a far-off and colorful past, natural chivalry and blameless manners:

> Thus blest in primal innocence they live,
> Suffic'd and happy with that frugal fare
> Which tasteful toil and hourly danger give.

But this is idealization, rather than a sympathetic approach to their experience.[2]

---

[2] Typical of Collins's interest in the color and fascination of a past age is his frequent allusion to the Druids, who not only represented to him a simple and virtuous people, but appealed also to his antiquarian taste and to his love of the weird and strange. See, for example, the second epode of the *Ode to Liberty,* where the Druid rites are thus described:

> Then too, 'tis said, an hoary Pile,
> 'Midst the green Navel of our Isle,
> Thy Shrine in some religious Wood,
> O Soul-enforcing Goddess stood!
> There oft the painted Native's Feet,
> Were wont thy Form celestial meet.

That this passage immediately follows the description of Mona shows something of Collins's associative process. Langhorne says naïvely in his com-

In his interest in peasant lore and folk tradition, Collins
approaches closest to sympathy with the humble man. These
themes appealed as well to his visionary nature as to his love
of the antiquarian and traditional. His attitude towards these
country beliefs is like that of Milton in *L'Allegro* and *Il Penseroso,* which are undoubtedly the sources for some of them. He
is the cultivated observer, not the sympathetic participant—*rusti-
cans sed non rusticus.* Especially is he fascinated by those traditions which deal with the supernatural, and in most instances,
the tragical or horrible aspects of it. As Johnson puts it, "He
loved fairies, genii, giants, and monsters; he delighted to rove
through the meanders of enchantment." But he was not insensitive to the delicate and fanciful in fairy-lore; surely his *Stanzas
Written on a Paper, which Contained a Piece of Bride-Cake* show
an airy fancy which approaches in charm the most delicate
passages in *The Rape of the Lock.* There are touches of this delicacy, too, in the descriptions of the *Ode to Evening* and in *How
Sleep the Brave,* where fairy forms are subtly blended into the
mood and spell of the poems. But in the *Ode to Fear* and in the
Ode on the Popular Superstitions Collins's fondness for the simple folk-lore is most evident, and there are traces of it in the
Song from Shakespeare's Cymbeline. The passage in the *Ode to
Fear* is concerned with the tradition regarding the "thrice-
hallowed Eve," perhaps Hallowe'en, perhaps the Eve of St.

---

ment on the ode (ed. 1781, p. 166): "Mona is properly the Roman name of
the isle of Anglesey, *anciently so famous for its Druids;* but sometimes, as in
this place, it is given to the Isle of Man. Both those isles still retain much
of the genius of superstition, and are now the only places where there is
the least chance of finding a Fairy." See also the appropriate use made of
"Druid" in *Ode on the Death of Mr. Thomson;* it not only pays a fitting
tribute to the dead poet of nature, but adds something to the magic spell of
the whole. A third instance is the account in the *Ode on the Popular Superstitions* of the old Runic bards, "with uncouth lyres," "Their matted hair
with boughs fantastic crown'd." In the *Essay on the Genius and Writings of
Pope,* I, 355, Joseph Warton writes: "I have frequently wondered that our
modern writers have made so little use of the druidical times, and the traditions
of the old bards, which afford fruitful subjects of the most genuine poetry,
with respect both to imagery and sentiment." And again, *ibid.,* I, 357, "What
pictures would a writer of the fancy of Theocritus have drawn from the
scenes and stories of the Isle of Angelsey!" Had he forgotten Collins's use
of these traditions in the *Ode to Liberty,* or had he possibly suggested the
theme to Collins?

Mark's, or, as Scott suggests, St. John's Eve. The folk-belief impresses the poet most because of the fear and terror that it inspires in him when he contemplates it imaginatively, though he knows that it is but a popular tradition. He addresses Fear, half-credulous, half-terrified:

> And lest thou meet my blasted View,
> Hold each strange Tale devoutly true;
> Ne'er be I found, by Thee o'eraw'd,
> In that thrice-hallow'd Eve abroad,
> When Ghosts, as Cottage-Maids believe,
> Their pebbled Beds permitted leave,
> And *Gobblins* haunt from Fire, or Fen,
> Or Mine, or Flood, the Walks of Men!

The same imaginative terror is suggested in the *Song from Shakespeare's Cymbeline:*

> No wailing ghost shall dare appear
>   To vex with shrieks this quiet grove:

and again in:

> No wither'd witch shall here be seen,
> No goblins lead their nightly crew.

Ghosts, witches, and goblins, the terrifying creatures of folk-lore, strike his imagination most, possibly because of his own sensitiveness to the horrible as well as to the delicate.

The folk-imagery of the *Ode on the Popular Superstitions* is more extensive and more commonplace. There is Collins's fascination with the delicate and enchanting aspects of fairy lore in his description of the fairy people who meet "beneath each birken shade, on mead or hill." A homelier sort of rustic lore furnishes the description of the brownies to whom the trim lass allots the cream bowl. In the account of how the sick ewe and heart-smit heifer are struck by the arrows of the malignant elves, in the description of the hideous spells of the "wizzard seer" of Sky, in the mention of "second sight," and in the fearful story of the Kaelpie Collins has caught that underlying suggestion of malignant influence and uncanny terror that marks so many folk-tales of the supernatural. Yet in all of Collins's allusions to the stories of popular tradition one feels their appeal to his imagination far more than to his sympathies. In his treatment of the popular superstitions he anticipates the more understanding presentation of these same traditional themes in Burns's *Address to the Deil;*[3] neither Collins nor Home could be as intimate and as familiar in treating these beliefs as the simple ploughman who had grown up with them. Nor could either enter into the traditions of the Highlanders as thoroughly and spiritedly as Scott was soon to do in *The Lady of the Lake* and in many a fine lyric besides.

[3] Contrast, for instance, Burns's treatment of the water kaelpie and the will-of-the-wisp, 67-78.

V

CONTEMPORARY EVENTS

OF MEN in his own day Collins had little to say directly. He was not oblivious, however, of the events that were passing. He had twice been in Flanders and had seen the sick and the wounded, if he did not witness actual fighting. At least five of the odes grow directly or indirectly out of the political and martial struggles of the times. So sensitive and retiring a person as Collins must have been terrified by the thoughts of war or rebellion, if one judges by the vividness of his imagery in dealing with it. Yet he was a patriot and an Englishman, and one of his finest poems is a perfect tribute to those who have fallen in their country's service. The War of the Austrian Succession with the courageous struggle and hard defeat of the English at Fontenoy, the rebellion of Bonny Prince Charles with the battles of Preston Pans and Falkirk, the fear of a French invasion, the panic of Black Friday, the defeat of the Pretender at Culloden made the years 1745 and 1746 stirring times. A poet with Collins's interest in history must naturally have been moved by the rebellion of the Highlanders, the popular admiration for Cumberland, and the fate of the Scotch rebels, Balmerino and Kilmarnock, events of which Horace Walpole has left us a colorful record in his letters.[1] But Collins has left us no intimate account of how the events moved him or touched him personally, such a record, for example, as Wordsworth gives us in *The Prelude*. He is, rather, content to refer to them allegorically and to allude to persons and events indirectly. Behind the veil of the allegory, however, one can sense the poet's own reaction to the moving pageant of history before his eyes.

[1] Bronson cites the letter of May 24, 1745, as testimonial of the bravery of the Duke of Cumberland at Fontenoy; the letter of April 25, 1746, is proof of his popularity after Culloden, which did not survive his prosecution of the rebels. Walpole observes, August 1, 1746, that he "has not so much of Caesar after a victory, as in gaining it," and notes the nickname of "The Butcher" that was fastened on him.

The War of the Austrian Succession and the gallant courage of the English at Fontenoy he commemorated directly in the *Ode to a Lady on the Death of Colonel Ross,* lamenting the death of an intimate friend of Miss Goddard, whom tradition says Collins himself had loved. If this be true, the poem is a generous gesture of sympathy on the poet's part, but more than that, it represents his tribute to a brave soldier and shows his patriotism.[2] The statement, "written May 1745," appended to the title in Dodsley's *Miscellany* indicates further that it was written while the event was fresh in the poet's mind and in contemporary interest. The whole ode is full of tender and reserved grief for the dead youth and of delicate sympathy for the soft heart of the mourning maiden; it is colored too by reminiscent suggestions of the battle itself and of England's heroic tradition. In the first stanza allusion is made to the "fatal Day" of the battle. The further suggestion of the time when it occurred, too joyous a season for so tragic an event, is vividly phrased at the end of the same stanza when Britannia's Genius is represented:

> While stain'd with Blood he strives to tear
> Unseemly from his Sea-green Hair
> The Wreaths of chearful *May.*

The third stanza names the place of the battle and the burial spot of the fallen youth, albeit inaccurately: "by *rapid* Scheld's descending Wave."[3] The fifth stanza, appropriately enough,

[2] Verse 49 of the ode originally read "If drawn by all a lover's art" (according to T. Warton, in *Reaper,* No. 26), which would substantiate the tradition, and perhaps indicate Collins's delicacy of feeling in changing the line to "If, weak to soothe so soft an heart." This second reading also appears in Langhorne's edition, 1765. For further details on the point see Joseph Warton's letter to Thomas Warton cited in Wooll's *Warton,* pp. 14-15. See also Thomas Warton's letter to Hymers: "I had lately his first manuscript of the Ode on the Death of Colonel Ross with many interlineations and alterations. The lady to whom this ode is addressed was Miss Elizabeth Goddard, who then lived at or near Harting, in Sussex." Seward's *Supplement to Anecdotes of Some Distinguished Persons,* London, 1797, p. 125, records that he loved a lady who did not return his passion. It is said that she was his elder by a day, and that he wittily remarked, with a reference to his unhappy love-suit, that he came into the world "a day after the fair." As a source of the phrase, cf. Etherege, *The Man of Mode,* III, i, 41. A slightly different version of the anecdote appears in *The European Magazine* for October, 1795.

[3] Compare Goldsmith's *Traveller,* 2, "or by the *lazy* Scheld."

represents old Edward's sons feeling again for Britain's wrongs, and wishing once more to take arms to avenge the defeat at Fontenoy. The reference to Cressy is apt, too, for at that battle four hundred years before, the English had defeated the French by such courageous conduct as the soldiers had recently exhibited at Fontenoy, although in both encounters the odds were strongly against them. As the ode appeared in Dodsley's *Museum* in 1746 and in Dodsley's *Collection* there was no direct allusion to the Forty-Five, but in the *Odes Descriptive and Allegoric*, 1746, two stanzas deal with the rebellion and the admiration Collins must have felt at that time for the Duke of Cumberland. Distraught and sunk in deep despair, impatient Freedom awaits the restoration of peace and the end of the rebellion which the Duke, mentioned by name, shall bring about:

> Ne'er shall she leave that lowly Ground,
> Till Notes of Triumph bursting round
>   Proclaim her Reign restor'd:
> Till *William* seek the sad Retreat,
> And bleeding at her sacred Feet,
>   Present the sated Sword.

The inserted stanzas obviously detract from the unity of a piece supposed to assuage the grief of a lady.[4]

But from the sentiment and spirit of the *Ode to a Lady* came Collins's most perfect tribute to the heroic dead of his country, the ode familiarly called *Ode Written in the Beginning of the Year 1746*. As Mrs. Barbauld has said,[5] the little dirge bears the same relation to the earlier ode "which an elegant vignette bears to an engraving of full size." As the poem appears in Dodsley's *Collection*, where it follows the *Ode to a Lady*, it has the subtitle "Written in the Same Year," which would make its resemblance to the previous ode more direct. The title in Langhorne's edition of the poet, 1765, and in Bell's *Poets*, 1781, *Written in the Year 1746*, suggests a later composition and perhaps indicates

---

[4] Langhorne, however, protests at their omission: "It is needless to observe that this ode is replete with harmony, spirit, and pathos: and there surely appears no reason why the seventh and eighth stanzas should be omitted in that copy printed in Dodsley's Collection of Poems." See J. Langhorne, *Poetical Works of William Collins*, London, 1765, p. 167.

[5] *Critical Essay*, p. xxvi.

ow deeply the Forty-Five had stirred him. But Collins's own title in the *Odes Descriptive and Allegoric,* the title by which he ode is familiarly known, seems most appropriate to it.[6]

It seems logical to infer, as several commentators on Collins have done,[7] that the *Ode Written in the Beginning of the Year 746* grew directly out of the earlier *Ode to a Lady.* In imagery, one, and theme the second ode is a more perfect rendition of he earlier one. In the first ode Collins was expressing a tender nd sympathetic pity for the lady whose soldier lover had died ighting. It is a tribute to an individual who died in a famous attle, and it praises the patriotism and honor of one soldier who ought courageously at Fontenoy. The second ode, still full of ity and tenderness, does honor to all brave soldiers who have lied in the service of their country. It seems natural to suppose rom the reminiscences of the earlier ode that Collins is looking ack to Fontenoy; yet he must surely, too, have been thinking of he courageous fighting of English soldiers in the struggle gainst the Pretender in 1745 and at the beginning of 1746. he lines:

> When *Spring,* with dewy Fingers cold,
> Returns to deck their hallow'd Mold,

est place its time of composition and yet refer back to the *Ode o a Lady,* which was written in "chearful May." For all the inest effects of the *Ode to a Lady* have been concentrated and lended into perfect expression in the second poem. The suggestion of the spring, the presence of Fancy and of the delicate, ërial forms who preside over the tomb, the hallowed grave of he dead soldier, and the figures of Honour and Freedom are ll in the first poem. But in the *Ode Written in the Beginning f the Year 1746* Collins has selected and ordered his pictures

[6] See Bronson's discussion of the problem, *Poems of William Collins,* pp. 03-4. His conjecture is that the ode seems to have been occasioned by a articular and recent battle and suggests Falkirk, by reason of its date, as the robable battle. In view of the composition of the *Ode to a Lady* at the me of the battle of Fontenoy this conjecture seems reasonable; yet there s nothing specific in the poem as there is in the *Ode to a Lady* to make it ecessarily refer to a definite occasion. Langhorne's comment (*Poems of Col-ns,* p. 161) links it directly with the rebellion.

[7] See, e.g., Garrod, *Collins,* pp. 79-82; J. M. Murry, *Countries of the Mind,* "The Poetry of William Collins," pp. 79-100.

more finely. He has condensed the substance of two stanzas c the *Ode to a Lady* into four lines, reminiscent of the earlie poem, yet distinct and individual because of the new perfectio he has attained. In the *Ode to a Lady* we find:

> By rapid *Scheld's* descending Wave
> His Country's Vows shall bless the Grave,
>   Where'er the Youth is laid:
> That sacred Spot the Village Hind
> With ev'ry sweetest Turf shall bind,
>   And Peace protect the Shade.

> Blest Youth, regardful of thy Doom,
> Aërial Hands shall build thy Tomb,
>   With shadowy Trophies crown'd:
> Whilst *Honor* bath'd in Tears shall rove
> To sigh thy Name thro' ev'ry Grove,
>   And call his Heros round.

This is transformed into:

> By Fairy Hands their Knell is rung,
> By Forms unseen their Dirge is sung;
> There *Honour* comes, a Pilgrim grey,
> To bless the Turf that wraps their Clay.

The picture of Freedom in the second ode is also softened. Th scene of violent grief in the first ode is tempered in the secon in keeping with the note of subdued and quiet sorrow whic runs through the poem. Again the single phrase "hallow' Mold" sums up the whole substance of the third stanza of th *Ode to a Lady*. For Collins, then, contemporary situation coul best be treated suggestively and imaginatively. He was move deeply enough by the events of 1745 to write about them, bu he was touched by them as the poet could feel them, in a broa sympathy with their effect on men.

In three other odes, the *Ode to Mercy*, the *Ode to Peac* and the *Ode to Liberty*, Collins is also moved by the events c his day, though he does not attain to such felicitous expressio The first two of these odes and, to a degree, the third are cor cerned with the propitious outcome of the rebellion. Langhorn says of the first that it was written "to excite sentiments of con passion in favor of those unhappy and deluded wretches who became a sacrifice to publick justice."[8] The reference is obviously to Balmerino and Kilmarnock, about whose trial and execution here was so much popular interest. Moreover, an allusion to the Duke of Cumberland and to his valor in the rebellion is made in the lines where Mercy is represented

> amidst the deathful Field,
> By Godlike Chiefs alone beheld,

though it seems inept in view of Cumberland's treatment of the Scots after the rebellion. In retrospect the terror that was felt in England at the threatened approach of the Pretender's fleet is vividly recalled in the lines:

> When he whom ev'n our Joys provoke,
> The *Fiend of Nature* join'd his Yoke,
> And rush'd in Wrath to make our Isle his Prey;
> Thy Form, from out thy sweet Abode,
> O'ertook Him on his blasted Road,
> And stop'd his Wheels, and look'd his Rage away.

There is, perhaps, too, in the last lines an allusion to the destruction of the Pretender's fleet by a storm. In the concluding lines of the ode there is a plea that in the fate of the rebels mercy temper justice.

The *Ode to Peace* expresses the relief that the poet and all of England felt in the restoration of peace after the rebellion, although England did not cease to participate in the War of the Austrian Succession. The imagery of the ode suggests entirely the events of the rebellion. Such lines as:

> When *War,* by Vultures drawn from far
> To *Britain* bent his Iron Car
> And bad his Storms arise!

are reminiscent of the threatened invasion by the Pretender. This is suggested again in:

> And, while around her Ports rejoice.

But the ode has also a staunchly English and patriotic tone. The British Lion is represented as ready to own the holier reign of Peace. It must, however, be Peace wed with warlike Honour

---

[8] *Poems of Collins,* 1765, p. 161.

—an echo of praise for the courage of England's soldiers at Fontenoy and in the Forty-Five.

The *Ode to Liberty*, too, seems to arise spiritedly enough from England's martial exploits and their successful conclusion. That it ends much as does the *Ode to Peace* argues that it, too, regards the events of the rebellion and of the continental wars in retrospect and makes a proud boast of the insular independence of the "western Isle." The stirring introductory passage is full of patriotic suggestion of the response of England's soldiery to the military crises of the time. The allusion in the first antistrophe to the separation of England and France and to the wide, wild storm may well be a veiled reminiscence of recent events, and the concluding passage, like that at the end of the *Ode to Peace,* suggests the restoration of Concord and honorable Peace as well as declaring that Liberty, like Peace, is a peculiar possession of Britain:

> Now sooth Her, to her blissful Train
> Blithe *Concord's* social form to gain:
> *Concord,* whose Myrtle Wand can steep
> Ev'n *Anger's* blood-shot Eyes in Sleep:
> Before whose breathing Bosom's Balm,
> *Rage* drops his Steel, and Storms grow calm;
> Her let our Sires and Matrons hoar
> Welcome to *Britain's* ravag'd Shore,
> Our Youths, enamour'd of the Fair,
> Play with the Tangles of her Hair,
>
> . . . .
>
> O how supremely art thou blest,
> Thou, Lady, Thou shalt rule the West!

The other odes, too, contain passages suggestive in their imagery of the sharpness with which war and its terrors had struck the imagination of the poet. The description of part of the train of Fear in the *Ode to Fear* suggests the horrors of war, particularly because of the resemblance in imagery to the first stanza of the antistrophe of the *Ode to Mercy:*[9]

---

[9] Does this passage throw some light on Collins's conception of the Fiend of Nature in the *Ode to Mercy,* the significance of which has been much disputed? On the point, however, see also *Paradise Lost,* IV, 970 ff., which may have suggested the image to Collins. See also Pindar, *Second Pythian* 10-12.

> And those, the Fiends, who near allied,
> O'er Nature's Wounds, and Wrecks preside;
> Whilst *Vengeance,* in the lurid Air,
> Lifts her red Arm, expos'd and bare.

An equally suggestive description is the account of Revenge in *The Passions:*

> *Revenge* impatient rose,
> He threw his blood-stain'd Sword in Thunder down,
> And with a with'ring Look,
> The War-denouncing Trumpet took,
> And blew a Blast so loud and dread,
> Were ne'er Prophetic Sounds so full of Woe.
> And ever and anon he beat
> The doubling Drum with furious Heat.

And in the *Ode on the Popular Superstitions* there is the same fascination with war in the passage describing

> some sounding tale of war's alarms;
> When at the bugle's call, with fire and steel,
> The sturdy clans pour'd forth their bony swarms,
> And hostile brothers met to prove each other's arms.[10]

From Collins's feeling for England and his interest in the stirring happenings of the day came his most ambitious patriotic

---

[10] In this connection one should not omit the fourth of the *Persian Eclogues* in which the theme is the terrors of war. Had Collins certainly written the lines on "Preston's fight," "sad Falkirk," and "pale, red Culloden" and the praise of "illustrious William" as they are given in the anonymous edition of the *Ode on the Popular Superstitions,* they would furnish additional evidence of his absorption with the events of the rebellion. Mr. Blunden, *Poems of William Collins,* p. 175, is inclined to believe that the stanzas are genuine and not the work of the anonymous London editor on the ground that: "Its historical enthusiasms could only have been produced when the Forty-Five was still recent, and are exactly in Collins's character. The clumsy defects of phrase are also evidences of transcription and not correction." But see Bronson's careful argument, *Poems of Collins,* pp. 121-132, which seems more conclusive. On the point, too, see *Memoirs of Francis Horner,* 1843, II, 276, where the anonymous edition is described as the work of "a very low northern littérateur. . . . The editions were a forgery of his own, of which he boasted to Mackintosh." The language and tone of the passage certainly are inferior to that of the rest of the poem. And as Mr. Bernbaum observes, *Guide and Anthology of Romanticism,* II, 445, the stanza is a digression from the chief theme, out of tune with it, and not a very happy topic to touch upon in a poem addressed to a Scotch friend, since the Highlanders had sympathized with the Pretender and would obviously not appreciate a panegyric on "Illustrious William." For further evidence see appendix, pp. 322-3.

poem—the *Ode to Liberty,* which anticipates in its sweep and power the later panegyrics of Coleridge, Shelley, and Byron. But unlike the poet's other patriotic odes the *Ode to Liberty* gives an elaborate and eloquent account of the power of freedom (or liberty, for Collins uses the two interchangeably) as an inspiring force in the history of nations since classical times. Though the outcome of the recent wars may have originally turned Collins's mind to the theme, his own love of history and his pride in England colored his treatment of it. The spirited and vigorous note of patriotism is struck at the beginning of the first strophe. The first six lines recall the glory of Sparta's warlike youth, of old dear to applauding freedom. Lines 7-12 are parallel to lines 1-6 in that they cite a specific instance of the heroism of Athenian youths in striking for liberty—the story of Harmodius and Aristogiton who slew Hipparchus near the temple called Leocorium as he was marshaling the Panathenaic procession. The "fragment of Alcaeus" in Collins's note is the direct source of the story, and if the allusion in lines 9-12:

> At *Wisdom's* Shrine a-while its Flame concealing,
> (What Place so fit to seal a Deed renown'd?)
> Till she her brightest Lightnings round revealing,
> It leap'd in Glory forth, and dealt her prompted Wound!

be obscure, its meaning seems clear from Thucydides' account of the event:

They and the other conspirators had already laid their preparations, but were waiting for the festival of the great Panathenaea when the citizens who took part in the procession assembled in arms; for to wear arms on any other day would have aroused suspicion. They found Hipparchus near the Leocorium, as it was called, and then and there falling upon him with all the blind fury, one of an injured lover, the other of a man smarting under an insult, they smote and slew him.[11]

Both instances are recalled to the poet by the victorious conclusion of England's wars in 1745-6. The invocation "Who shall

[11] Thucydides, V, 54-6 (Tr. Jowett, Oxford, 1881, I, 446-9). The story is also mentioned in Herodotus, V, 56; Polybius, V, 1311; Diodorus, X, 16; and, of course, in the "fragment of Alcaeus."

awake the Spartan Fife," 1, and the reference[12] to the "New Alcaeus," 7, indicate that the events which have just passed are as worthy of celebration in poetry as were those sung by the Spartan poet, perhaps bold Tyrtaeus, or by the poet of Athens. Lines 13-16 substantiate the point: Collins himself is the New Alcaeus. The "feeling Hour" is the time when, made enthusiastic by the recent victories, the poet traces the progress of liberty to its final abode in England. Lines 17-25 describe the fall of the Roman Empire and its dissolution at the hands of "the Northern Sons of Spoil," the barbarians. The first strophe, then, gives instances of the power of Liberty or Freedom in ancient Greece, both at Athens and Sparta, and traces the fall of the Roman state, once a symbol of liberty. The giant-statue of Rome, a blended work of strength and grace, was the work of Liberty's hand—in a somewhat Platonic sense a Divine Idea or pattern of Liberty shadowed forth in earthly form, a concept to which Collins returns in the second epode, 100-112, where it is treated more directly.

The first epode, continuing directly with the theme of the strophe, traces the survival of Liberty, or rather the Idea of it represented in the Roman Empire, from Roman times through the Middle Ages to Collins's day, in all of the countries of Europe which were once parts of Rome. The substance of the epode is difficult to disentangle, for Collins weaves two ideas almost inextricably together as he does also in the epode of the *Ode on the Poetical Character*. The first idea is, briefly, that wherever the least fragment of the broken statue remained some remnant of Rome's power was left and some trace of Liberty's spell was felt. The states around, scattered by the storm of the barbarian invasions, saw in the fragments of the statue, the blended work of strength and grace, some remnants of the strength of Rome. From the least[13] of those parts they were

---

[12] Collins had earlier referred to the "Sword, in Myrtles drest." Cf. *Eclogue* III, 67-8:

Or wreathe . . .
The Lover's Myrtle, with the Warrior's Crown.

[13] Mr. Garrod (*Collins*, pp. 88-9) is unable to find a meaning for "the least," 26, and conjectures that "the" is "a mere blunder for 'she' (i.e. Rome)." But obviously "fragment" is understood.

able to understand how wondrous had been the perfect form of the statue, how every Master of Rome had contributed to the Whole. A part of the Roman ideal of Liberty was preserved in sunny Florence, until the family of the Medici quenched her flame. Another humbler relic of it was preserved in jealous Pisa. In small Marino, in Venice, in Genoa, some trace of Roman Liberty was kept alive in the Italian city states. Wild Helvetia, once a Roman province, had also been a haunt of Liberty, for here the daring Archer, the favored of Liberty, had driven out the ravening Eagle, obviously a reference to William Tell who drove out the tyrants under the Hapsburg Eagle. Holland's willowed meads have also sheltered Liberty, and last of all Liberty has come to England's shores. The second idea of the epode goes back to the first strophe and is, in a sense, carried throughout the poem. The poet, himself the New Alcaeus, courts Liberty to return to Britain, by rehearsing the progress of her influence. He strikes the ennobling strings louder in praise of Venice. Then, 60-64, he concludes the epode with the idea that Liberty has been moved by the incantation of his verse to return. One holier name need be mentioned to complete the perfect spell to summon up the goddess—that is the name of *Britain.*

The antistrophe and the concluding second epode trace the influence of Liberty in Britain and boast that Britain is her last and permanent home. The most spirited and powerful section of the antistrophe, 64-79, describes the wide, wild storm which brought about the "blest Divorce" of England and France. Britain with the little Isles, Mona and Wight, which make up a laughing train of attendants to her sovereign pride, was separated from France by Liberty herself that she might make the vales of England her last abode, a proud boast of England's insular independence. The second epode traces the influence of Liberty in England just as the first epode showed the progress of Liberty after the fall of the Roman Empire. In Druid times the shrine of Liberty was deep in some religious wood of Britain where the painted native saw the celestial form of the goddess just as in Roman days it was revealed in the "blended work of

Strength and Grace," the Roman state.[14] But the shrine of Liberty was destroyed either by the fiery-tressed Dane or by the Roman invader. Yet the poet's insight reveals that the "beauteous Model" of the Temple of Liberty still remains in Heaven, a divine Archetype of the earthly shrine, guarded by the warlike Chiefs of Albion's story and the Druids, the first priests of Liberty.[15] Then in a fine frenzy the poet calls up the magic fabric. He reconstructs the temple in imagination as he had built the Temple of Pity in his thoughts in an earlier ode. A fine combination of Gothic pride and Grecia's grace,[16] majestically adorned with sphere-found gems,[17] its walls graven with the fame of Albion, it unites the classical and the romantic. He calls upon Liberty's attendant train to come with her, he urges Britain's sires and matrons to welcome her and Britain's youth to love her that she may rule the West, her last, her blest abode. The poem ends on a note of exulting triumph that Britain is preserved a land of liberty. It is suggestive that the strophe and first epode deal with the classical concept of Liberty while the antistrophe and second epode present the Gothic or romantic concept of it. In the poet's reconstructed temple of Liberty the best elements

[14] This passage is perhaps an echo of Dryden, *Astraea Redux*, 46-8:

> They owned a lawless savage liberty,
> Like that our painted ancestors so prized,
> Ere Empire's arts their breasts had civilized.

[15] Lines 107-8 of the ode:

> There happier than in Islands blest,
> Or Bow'rs by Spring or *Hebe* drest,

seem to refer back to the "fragment of Alcaeus" (Moore's translation):

> Yet, loved Harmodius, thou'rt undying;
>   Still midst the brave and free,
> In isles, o'er ocean lying,
>   Thy home shall ever be.

Albion's chiefs and the Druids who preserved Liberty in a later day are happier "amidst the bright pavilion'd Plains" than are Harmodius and Aristogiton, also defenders of Liberty, in the Islands of the Blest.

[16] Cf. *Epistle to Hanmer*, 47-8:

> The beauteous Union must appear at length,
> Of Tuscan Fancy, and Athenian Strength.

[17] Cf. Milton, *University Carrier*, II, 5-6:

> Made of sphear-metal, never to decay
> Untill his revolution was at stay.

of "Gothic Pride" and "Græcia's graceful Orders" are to be combined—a combination that marks the imaginative pattern of the *Ode to Fear* and the *Ode to Evening* as well.

Rich in Collins's knowledge of history, especially indicative of his interest in the Italian republics, full of his love of antiquarian lore and druidical tradition, the poem is still a patriotic panegyric in honor of England's triumph and the end of the rebellion. Though Collins's concept of Liberty is as spiritual and visionary as his ideal of the Poetical Character or his appreciation of evening, the ode is as noble and enthusiastic in its expression of patriotism as Thomson's *Rule, Britannia,* which it resembles in theme, though it falls short in energy and succinctness. The longest of the odes, it shows most spiritedly the influence of the War of the Austrian Succession and the Rebellion upon the poet's imagination.

VI

ASPIRATIONS AND SHORTCOMINGS

W HILE THE stirring times in which he lived colored the theme and the imagery of his poetry, Collins was singularly reserved in the expression of his personal feeling. This reticence in dealing more directly with the emotions marks his treatment of every subject in which the passions play a part. Of love as a theme he speaks either conventionally as he does in the *Persian Eclogues* and in *When Phoebe form'd a wanton Smile,* or slightingly as he does in the *Epistle to Hanmer* and the *Ode to Simplicity,* or, in the *Stanzas written on a Paper which Contained a Piece of Bride-Cake,* in the language of graceful and delicate compliment. As both Mrs. Barbauld and Langhorne have observed, Love is not fully described in *The Passions* and plays but a minor part there. Of friendship he has spoken more feelingly in the *Ode on the Death of Mr. Thomson* and in the *Ode on the Popular Superstitions,* but Mr. Garrod[1] has censured the coldness of his sentiment in the former of these. Of death he has written frequently, but like Emily Brontë's, his descriptions emphasize the coldness of death and the grave; his meditations have not the human sympathy of Gray's. One cannot say of his sentiments on the grave, as Johnson said of Gray's expression in the *Elegy,* that they "abound with images which find a mirrour in every mind, and with sentiments to which every bosom returns an echo."[2] Collins has enthusiasm for Liberty, for poetry as a divinely inspired gift, for the folklore of the Highlands of Scotland; but he has not passion. Dr. Johnson said rightly that "while he was intent upon description he did not sufficiently cultivate sentiment."[3] It seems only just to the poet to suggest that he made no attempt to express

[1] *Collins,* pp. 107-11.
[2] *Lives of the Poets,* III, 441.
[3] *Ibid.,* III, 338.

feeling more deeply than he had experienced it. He was, after all, but twenty-five when he wrote the *Odes*. Moreover, his visionary enthusiasm led him to prefer in his poetry a world of his own creating to the "world which is the world of all of us." His retiring disposition kept him from the intimate and varied experience of life which brings the insight of a Browning or a Shakespeare. Possibly the literary fashion of his day, surely not conducive to the expression of deep feeling, restricted him. Most significant of all, however sensitive he may have been, his personality was perhaps not yet strong enough or deep enough to sound either the depth or the tumult of the soul. It is to his credit that he felt his need. Yet in the poems in which he senses his limitation, he neglects the most obvious means of remedying it. He prefers always a visionary approach to life to a realistic facing of it. Or perhaps he is groping for the means of fulfilling it. In the *Ode to Pity* he calls upon that goddess to help him in his writing of tragedy. He would take refuge in the temple he has built to her in his mind:

> There let me oft, retir'd by Day,
> In Dreams of Passion melt away,
> Allow'd with Thee to dwell.

But when he would feel Pity's spell he must be in retirement from the world; he would dream of passion rather than experience it. Again in the *Ode to Fear,* contemplating Shakespeare's power, he cries to Fear:

> Hither again thy Fury deal,
> Teach me but once like Him to feel.

And he comes closest to feeling deeply when Fear's spell is upon him. Or he addresses Simplicity:

> I only seek to find thy temp'rate Vale:
> Where oft my Reed might sound
> To Maids and Shepherds round,
> And all thy Sons, O *Nature,* learn my Tale.

Here is again expressed a craving to feel so that he may move men, yet an aloofness from those whom he would have learn his tale.

The Manners affords the most illuminating study of Collins's sense of his own limitation as a poet and illustrates, too, his failure to remedy it when the opportunity offered. The ode may, as Langhorne conjectures, have been written when Collins left Oxford, or as Mr. Blunden remarks,[4] "Not less probably, it is an imaginative adieu to philosophical reading, even Aristotle's Poetics, and a welcome to the romances and novels of the age." None the less it is something like *L'Allegro* and *Il Penseroso* rolled into one; Collins, during the mood of the poem, is bidding farewell to the world of the visionary and the philosopher, and turning to the world of reality, hoping thereby to learn the power to feel. Yet the highly imaginative passages describing the world of fancy he would leave behind are finer than those conjuring up the pleasures of the world to which he is turning. It is not a wholehearted choice, although it is a hopeful one. The first passage of the poem, 1-12, bids a slightly reluctant farewell to "the dim-discovered Tracts of Mind," to the "magic Shores" of philosophy, even to the "dreams of Passion" of the *Ode to Pity,* to the "Fairy Field" of such endeavor. Collins is, then, renouncing for the moment both the speculations of philosophical study and the world of fancy and vision which was to absorb him in such odes as the *Ode to Pity* and *Ode on the Poetical Character,* the world "from Action's Paths retir'd." A second passage, 13-18, bids farewell to the haunts of learning, or perhaps by the allusion to the Porch, the olive, and Plato, to the precincts of philosophy in general. A third passage, 19-30, turns to the world of reality, welcomes Observance as a guide, and commends the "quick uncheated Sight" of such a guide. It speaks of "life's wide Prospects," of mingling with men and of learning

> To read in Man the native Heart,

knowledge of which can come only

> From Nature as she lives around:
> And gazing oft her Mirror true,
> By turns each shifting Image view!

[4] *Poems of William Collins,* p. 173.

Though this experience of the world may "reverse the Lessons taught before," the poet is still drawn by the spell of dreaming in Art's enchanted school. Yet one feels that the poet hopes to profit by his experience of the world. To Collins it seems that this widens the range of his poetry, however much the spell of the visionary world colors the imagery. Retiring from the world of manners

> As *Fancy* breathes her potent Spell

the poet finds that his observation of the manners has added to the themes which he can treat in his verse. For now the pageant quaint and the motley mask of the countless manners pass before the musing eyes of Fancy. Satire and humor are to be added to the poet's themes. One remembers his diverting observations on the foibles and manners of the greenroom. Collins's invocation to Humour:

> Me too amidst thy Band admit,
> There where the young-eyed healthful *Wit,*
>
> . . . .
>
> In Laughter loos'd attends thy Side!

resembles his addresses to Pity and to Fear; he would find the power to feel through whatever medium he may. Of the passage following, 60-74, Mrs. Barbauld remarks,[5] "When he speaks of studying the manners he has only laid down his *Plato* to take up *Gil Blas*." This is obviously a misinterpretation of the intent of the passage. As a whole it is an invocation to "boon Nature" to teach him, by observing the realistic side of life, as Le Sage and Cervantes have done, to feel more deeply:

> O Nature boon, from whom proceed
> Each forceful Thought, each prompted Deed;
> If but from Thee I hope to feel,
> On all my Heart imprint thy Seal!

The passage may indicate, as Mr. Blunden suggests, Collins's turn from philosophical reading to the lighter novels of his day. Or, more probably, it suggests that Collins had turned to reading such realistic literature as a supplement to his own actual ex-

---

[5] *Critical Essay*, p. xxxv.

perience of the world, possibly with the desire to emulate the skill of these writers in understanding human nature. The last passage of the poem argues the abandonment of philosophy and of vicarious experience for an actual excursion into the world of reality:

> Let some retreating Cynic find,
> Those oft-turn'd Scrolls I leave behind,
> The *Sports* and I this Hour agree,
> To rove thy Scene-full World with Thee!

From Ragsdale's testimony in his letter that Collins quitted Oxford from "a desire to partake of the dissipation and gaiety of London," from his account of Collins's call on his cousin Payne "gaily dressed and with a feather in his hat," from Ragsdale's further mention of his frequenting the Bedford and Slaughter's Coffee-houses, and "his liberty of the scenes and the green room," one concludes that Collins did follow in the sportive train of mirth and was not devoid of either wit or perception in observing "the Scene-full World." Yet the poem represents only a realization of a defect and the remedy, not an actual reformation. In the poem itself he employs the same allegorical and descriptive manner characteristic of the other odes. And with the possible exception of the *Ode on the Popular Superstitions,* Collins made no use of his observations of "the Scene-full World" or his penetration in reading "the native Heart of Man." Even in that poem the experience is vicarious. Nor did he learn to feel much more deeply, unless one allow that in the *Ode on the Death of Mr. Thomson* he did so. He never came to view the sceneful world with the minuteness and understanding of a later poet who could describe

> The Man who slices lemons into drink,
> The coffee-roaster's brasier, and the boys
> That volunteer to help him turn its winch.

One must, however, credit him with having realized his own defect. Had he lived longer and had insanity not clouded his mind he might have triumphed over it.

In speaking of his failure, one must not overlook his achievement. He did feel for men tenderly and sensitively, though he always expressed himself with restraint. Though not a poem of violent grief, his *Ode on the Death of Mr. Thomson* is a beautiful and finely tender expression of pity and sorrow. Even here we must remember Tennyson's counsel that:

> words, like Nature, half reveal
> And half conceal the soul within.

The *Ode to a Lady* and *Ode Written in the Beginning of the Year 1746* are exquisitely phrased expressions of sympathy for those who have been bereaved by war, and tender and patriotic tributes to those who have fallen. And in the *Ode to Liberty* there is a fine fervor of patriotism. But were one to epitomize his feeling for men most aptly it would be in Wordsworth's observation concerning him. The poet who more deeply felt for man understood both the greatness and the weakness of his predecessor when he wrote of him in *Remembrance of Collins* as the poet who

> Could find no refuge from distress
> But in the milder grief of pity.

VII

ARS POETICA

B OTH THE substance and the manner of the *Odes,* however, with their defects and their merits, grow out of Collins's own concept of the sort of poetry he should write. Furthermore, they reflect his own notion of the poet and the poetic imagination. He felt concerning the poetry of his day much as did Blake at a slightly later time when he wrote *To the Muses:*

> How have you left the ancient love
> That bards of old enjoyed in you!
> The languid strings do scarcely move,
> The sound is forced, the notes are few.

With the Wartons he intended to become an innovator, to find a new charm in poetry which his "laggard Age" had missed. If one except an essay "On the Essential Excellencies in Poetry," recently ascribed to Collins by Mr. Frederick Page,[1] he has left no theory of poetry of his own. But Joseph Warton, with whom Collins was so closely associated and whose ideas he shared, has definitely enunciated his own standards of poetry, to which, judged by his practice in his poems, Collins also subscribed. In the *Essay on the Genius and Writings of Pope,* III, 54, Warton clearly defines the type of poetry to which both he and Collins had earlier turned: the descriptive and allegorical. In a sense it is a criticism of the age as well as an apologia for his own practice of a few years before:

If it be a true observation, that for a poet to write happily and well, he must have seen and felt what he describes, and must draw from living models alone; and if modern times, from their luxury and refinement afford not manners that will bear to be described; it will then follow, that those species of poetry bid fairest to succeed at present, which treat of things, not men; which deliver doctrines, not display events. Of this sort is didactic and descriptive poetry.

[1] *TLS,* 1935, p. 448.

The passage reflects ideas that Collins himself had thought and expressed. The futility of attempting any great art in his own degenerate day he had deplored in the odes to *Pity* and *Simplicity* in the *Ode on the Poetical Character,* and in *The Passions.* The need of drawing from life he had felt in *The Manners.* He had admired Shakespeare's skill in that art in the *Epistle to Hanmer* and in the *Ode to Fear.* Though he did not frequently write didactic verse, he, too, had turned to descriptive poetry. Since he and Joseph Warton were so closely associated, it is but natural to conclude that the beliefs of one poet influenced the other. But in the preface to the *Odes on Various Subjects* of Joseph Warton there is a more conclusive statement of the purpose both Joseph Warton and Collins hoped that their poetry would accomplish. Joseph Warton's letter to his brother, Tom Warton, May, 1746 makes it clear that when Collins met him at the Guildford races the two closely enough agreed in their purposes to consider publishing their odes jointly. The project of joint publication fell through and the odes of the two poets were published separately. But the Preface to Joseph Warton's volume also describes Collins's poetry adequately and, as Mr. Garrod conjectures, would have served as introduction to the work of both poets if the original plan had been followed. The Preface reads:

The public has been so accustomed of late to didactic poetry alone and essays on moral subjects, that any work where the imagination is much indulged, will perhaps not be relished or regarded. The author, therefore, of these pieces is in some pain, lest certain austere critics should think them too fanciful or descriptive. But he is convinced that the fashion of moralizing in verse has been carried too far, and as he looks upon invention and imagination to be the chief faculties of a poet, so he will be happy if the following Odes may be looked upon as an attempt to bring back poetry into its right channel.

Collins's greatest powers lie in fanciful and imaginative themes and after the *Persian Eclogues* there is little moralizing in his poetry. Under the influence of his association with Joseph Warton, then, Collins consciously limited himself to subjects descriptive and allegorical, albeit highly imaginative.

In the odes we find reflected not only Collins's concept of the poet and his function, but also his idea of the poetic imagination. Although he has expressed them directly and finely for himself, these ideas are to a large degree derivative and were shared by Collins's contemporaries. The concept was in many respects, it is true, not new or peculiar to his age. The true poet, as Collins and his contemporaries viewed him, was divinely inspired. Poetry was the product of a rapt enthusiasm, an ecstatic or visionary glow which the poet felt in composing and which he imparted to his readers. Imagination, ecstatic vision, was granted to a few of the great poets like Shakespeare and Milton; the true poet was a Maker, as Sidney and his contemporaries had regarded him.[2] While taste and simplicity were necessary adjuncts to creation, imagination was primary; the poet must first be "enthusiastic" and so stimulate feeling in his readers.

The concept is not entirely foreign to Pope himself. In spite of his dictum in *An Essay on Criticism:*

> 'Tis more to guide than spur the Muses' steed;
> Restrain his fury, than provoke his speed;
> The winged courser, like a generous horse,
> Shows most true mettle when you check his course,

he had written in *Windsor Forest:*

> Ye sacred Nine! that all my soul possess,
> Whose raptures fire me, and whose visions bless,
> Bear me, oh bear me to sequester'd scenes,
> The bowery mazes and surrounding greens.

That he felt Homer was such an inspired poet, we know from his commentaries on Homer. In the *Preface to the Iliad,* after having attributed to Homer the greatest invention of any writer, he says,

> It is to the strength of this amazing invention we are to attribute that unequalled fire and rapture, which is so forcible in Homer, that no man of a true poetical spirit is master of himself when he reads him.

Again, though he qualifies his enthusiasm, he admits:

[2] In "Collins and the Creative Imagination," *Studies in English,* University of Toronto, 1931, pp. 59-130, Mr. A. S. P. Woodhouse has shown the relationship of Collins's conception of the creative imagination to that commonly held in Renaissance criticism.

Exact disposition, just thought, correct elocution, polished numbers, may be found in a thousand; but this poetical fire, this *vivida vis animi* in a very few. Even in works where all these are imperfect or neglected, this can overpower criticism, and make us admire even while we disapprove. Nay, where this appears, though attended with absurdities, it brightens all the rubbish about it, till we see nothing but its own splendor. . . . In Milton it glows like a furnace kept up to an uncommon ardour by the force of art: in Shakespeare it strikes before we are aware, like an accidental fire from Heaven; but in Homer, and in him only, it burns everywhere clearly, and everywhere irresistibly.

A similar opinion of Homer is implied in Pope's *Postcript to the Odyssey,* and again in his letter to Bridges, 1708:

. . . for the distinguishing excellences of Homer, are, by the consent of the best critics of all nations, first in the manners . . . and then in that rapture and fire which carries you away with that wonderful force that no man who has a true poetical spirit is master of himself while he reads him.[3]

More sharply, too, the same concept of the poetic inspiration is enunciated in Thomson's *Seasons.* From at least three passages might have come part of the concept and part of the imagery of the *Ode on the Poetical Character,* though Thomson's source, like that of Collins, is Milton. In *Summer,* 15-20, Thomson addresses Inspiration:

> Come, Inspiration! from thy hermit-seat,
> By mortal seldom found: may fancy dare,
> From thy fixed serious eye and raptured glance
> Shot on surrounding Heaven, to steal one look
> Creative of the poet, every power
> Exalting to an ecstasy of soul.

A second passage, *Summer,* 518-28, strongly suggests the picture of Milton in the antistrophe of the *Ode on the Poetical Character:*

> Still let me pierce into the midnight depth
> Of yonder grove, of wildest largest growth,

---

[3] Elwin-Courthope, *Pope,* VI, 12-13. For a similar conception of the poetic inspiration see Shaftesbury, *Letter Concerning Enthusiasm* (*Characteristics of Men, Manners, and Opinions,* Ed. J. M. Robertson, London, 1900, I, 36) and *Advice to an Author* (*ibid.,* I, 135-6), where the poet is called "indeed a second Maker; a just Prometheus under Jove." It is significant, too, that "enthusiast," as Collins and his contemporaries use the word, has a more favorable connotation than that Dryden (also Shaftesbury) applies to it.

That, forming high in air a woodland quire,
Nods o'er the mount beneath. At every step,
Solemn and slow the shadows blacker fall,
And all is awful listening gloom around.
These are the haunts of meditation, these
The scenes where ancient bards the inspiring breath
Ecstatic felt, and, from this world retired,
Conversed with angels and immortal forms.

And again in *Autumn,* 1030-36, the setting and mood of the
same passage in Collins is suggested:

Oh! bear me then to vast embowering shades,
To twilight groves, and visionary vales,
To weeping grottoes, and prophetic glooms;
Where angel forms athwart the solemn dusk,
Tremendous, sweep, or seem to sweep along;
And voices more than human, through the void
Deep sounding, seize the enthusiastic ear.

In all three passages Thomson regards poetic inspiration as an
ecstatic communion with a heavenly source of power, an insight
which raises the poet out of himself and reveals to him a new
heaven and a new earth. In all three excerpts, too, this communion comes about in solitude, in twilight groves, in visionary
vales, and in prophetic glooms.

It is evident from both their critical and poetical works that
Collins's friends, the Wartons, held this general view. Several
excerpts from the poetry of Thomas Warton bear testimony to
his belief in this prevailing concept of the poet. In an ode called
Morning, written in 1745, this picture of the poet is first given:

The pensive poet thro' the green-wood steals,
Or treads the willow'd marge of murmuring brook,
Or climbs the steep ascent of airy hills;
There sits him down beneath a branching oak
Where various scenes and prospects wide below,
Still teach his musing mind with fancies high to glow.

In the *Ode Sent to a Friend,* 1750, the ideal Bard is more clearly
delineated:

For lo! the Bard who rapture found
In every rural sight or sound;
Whose genius warm, and judgment chaste,
No charm of genuine nature pass'd;

> Who felt the Muses' purest fires,
> Far from thy favour'd haunt retires:
> Who peopled all thy vocal bowers
> With shadowy shapes, and airy powers.[4]

Both in his critical writing and in his poetry Joseph Warton has a similar view. In the Dedication to the *Essay on the Genius and Writings of Pope* he defines the true poet and his imaginative power:

It is a creative and glowing imagination, "acer spiritus ac vis" and that alone, that can stamp a writer with this exalted and very uncommon character which so few possess and of which so few can properly judge.

In the essay itself he makes a distinction between the "man of rhymes" and "the genuine poet, of a lively and plastic imagination, the true MAKER or CREATOR," a distinction which, to be sure, he owed to Pope. And the concluding part of his *Ode to Fancy* so closely resembles some passages of Collins that it might almost represent Collins's opinion of the matter:

> At every season let my ear
> Thy solemn whispers, Fancy, hear.
> O warm, enthusiastic maid,
> Without thy powerful, vital aid,
> That breathes an energy divine,
> That gives a soul to every line,
> Ne'er may I strive with lips profane
> To utter an unhallow'd strain,
> Nor dare to touch the sacred string
> Save when with smiles thou bid'st me sing.

After a tribute to Shakespeare, "Fancy's darling," Warton voices a hope that some inspired poet in his day will again rouse men by his poetry; perhaps, as Mr. Garrod[5] suggests, Warton thought of Collins, or of himself, as such a poet:

> O queen of numbers, once again
> Animate some chosen swain,

[4] The concept persists in his later poetry. The *Ode on the Approach of Summer* speaks of Fancy portraying "her kindred visions bright" to the poet. A passage in the *Ode on his Majesty's Birthday*, written many years later, praises the Fancy of Spenser and is reminiscent of Collins's *Ode on the Poetical Character*. For a similar concept see also Warton's *Sonnet to Mr. Gray*.

[5] *Collins*, p. 105.

> Who, fill'd with unexhausted fire,
> May boldly smite the sounding lyre,
> Who with some new, unequall'd song,
> May rise above the rhyming throng,
> O'er all our list'ning passions reign,
> O'erwhelm our souls with joy and pain;
> With terror shake, and pity move,
> Rouse with revenge, or melt with love.

Warton's aspirations resemble Collins's hopes for his own poetry as he expresses them in the odes to *Pity* and *Fear* and especially in *The Passions,* of which Warton's whole passage is strongly suggestive. A third passage echoes the same hope for a fusion of romantic enthusiasm and Greek simplicity and restraint that Collins had voiced in the *Epistle to Hanmer,* in the *Ode to Simplicity,* in *The Passions,* and in the *Ode to Liberty,* and that he had exemplified in the *Ode to Fear* and the *Ode to Evening:*

> Teach him to scorn with frigid art
> Feebly to touch th' unraptur'd heart;
> Like lightning, let his mighty verse
> The bosom's inmost foldings pierce;
> With native beauties win applause,
> Beyond cold critics' studied laws;
> O let each Muse's fame increase!
> O bid Britannia rival Greece![6]

Nor was this concept of the poet held only by Collins and the Wartons. Gray's descriptions of Shakespeare and of Milton in *The Progress of Poesy* suggest the same idea. In the *Stanzas to Mr. Bentley,* too, Gray expresses a similar feeling, with a judgment on the "laggard Age" in which he writes, that echoes the conclusion to Collins's *Ode on the Poetical Character:*

> But not to one in this benighted age
> Is that diviner inspiration giv'n,
> That burns in Shakespeare's or in Milton's page,
> The pomp and prodigality of Heav'n.

---

[6] The whole concept was, in fact, a reaction against the literary standards of the age of Pope. In *The Enthusiast* Warton asks,

> What are the lays of artful Addison,
> Coldly correct, to Shakespear's warblings wild?

To Warton, Addison is the man of rhymes; Shakespeare is the true Maker.

It appears, too, in the work of Mark Akenside, who in taste and imagination, was somewhat akin to Collins. In *The Pleasures of the Imagination* he writes:

> . . . for fruitless is the attempt
> By dull obedience and by creeping toil
> Obscure to conquer the severe ascent
> Of high Parnassus. Nature's kindling breath
> Must fire the chosen genius; Nature's hand
> Must string his nerves, and imp his eagle-wings
> Impatient at the painful steep, to soar
> High as the summit; there to breathe at large
> Ethereal air, with bards and sages old,
> Immortal sons of praise.

And in the *Ode to Francis Earl of Huntingdon,* 1747, he asserts the need of "enthusiasm" in a poet:

> But thou, O faithful to thy fame,
> The Muse's law did'st rightly know;
> That who would animate his lays,
> And other minds to virtue raise,
> Must feel his own with all her spirit glow.

Further evidence of the new taste in poetry at the time when Collins published the odes is the essay in Dodsley's *Museum,* July 4, 1747, "On the Essential Excellencies of Poetry," recently claimed for Collins by Mr. Frederick Page.[7] Whether or no Collins wrote it, the essay enunciates principles which he shared. The thesis of the piece is: "there is something in poetry supernatural or divine." This divinity imparts to the writings of Spenser, Shakespeare, and Milton "a Perfection . . . much superior to the Times in which they lived." The essayist continues:

I shall at present insist on one Argument only . . . that there is something peculiarly luminous in the poetic Genius, and it is this. There is nothing that gives us so clear a Notion of the Divinity as his Power of Creating. . . . Yet this very power of Creating, tho' in a very weak and remote Degree, seems to be communicated to the Poet, and we cannot without amazement behold the effects of it in some of the best Performances both of the Antients and the Moderns.

---

[7] *TLS,* 1935, p. 448. Mr. Page is not, however, the first to discover the relation of the essay to Collins. Mr. A. S. P. Woodhouse, "Collins and the Creative Imagination," *University of Toronto Studies,* 1931, associates the essay with Collins, though he does not attribute the authorship of it to the poet.

An instance of the poet's creative power is found in "The Fairy World of Spenser" which "may be stiled imaginary, but still there is a kind of Reality in it. . . . We may say the same thing of the Magic of Shakespeare." The reality comes, says the essayist, from the pleasure we have in conceiving and apprehending the poet's power in dealing with scenes or ideas frankly supernatural. And this pleasure may arise as well from the contemplation of the terrible and hideous as from the beautiful.

The power of Milton's genius in this imaginative creating, the critic feels, surpasses that of any other poet:

It is this great, this divine Power that distinguishes true Poets from mere versifiers; the latter only copy Nature, and that but faintly; the former surpass Nature and transcend her. Therefore it is no Compliment, but a bare Piece of Justice done to Milton, when we not only compare him to Homer and Virgil, but even prefer him to both those Great Poets; because his Genius evidently appears to have been superior to theirs by the frequent Proofs he gives us of that Power which constitutes a sublime Genius, and which as it is more conspicuous in him than in any other Poet, obliges us to own him the greatest of Poets, for the same Reason that we own those to be Poets that he has excelled.

Reacting in part against the critical standards of the Augustans, the critic admits that "while Accuracy and Correctness are without doubt Advantages which add to the Beauty of Performances in which they are found . . . they are not essentials." The essay concludes with a panegyric on Mallet's *Amyntor and Theodora*, which had recently appeared, and praises particularly its imaginative representation of the island of St. Kilda:

The last new Poem that has made such an impression on me is the Hermit, which I have heard, is the Work of the ingenious *Mr. Mallet*. In this Poem, there is not only Elegance and Variety, fine Sentiments and lofty Expression, but the essential Qualities of a Poet indisputably appear. His imagination is not only warm and sprightly, but pregnant and sublime; his Pictures are equally majestic and striking; they are, in themselves, great and noble, and they are executed with a force equal to the Height and Dignity of the Design. Hence it is that we see, in his Performance, that great Poetic Perfection which is at once so excellent and so rare; I mean, the rendering satisfactory and pleasing those Images which, in their own nature, are apt to affect the Mind in a very different Manner. The little barren Island of St. Kilda, which, in the Prose Description of a very accurate and sensible Author, makes but a very indifferent, though at the same time a new and strange Figure as it is described by him, appears not only surprising, but the surprise is also accompanied with Pleasure. It appears the Scene of that affecting Story, which is the subject of his Poem, and is so united therewith, that we cannot help seeing the whole at one View, and retaining, after one has read the Piece, a clear and distinct Notion, and which is more, a pleasant and satisfactory Remembrance of a Place that, otherwise would be thought scarce worthy of finding Room in our Memory, or if retained there, must owe its Station to its singularity. But such is the Force of Poesy, such the Power of a Great Genius, that even Nature is changed and heightened in his Hands, and the Smallest Things become considerable, if he thinks fit to celebrate or describe them; Ithaca, in that case, becomes Greece, and *Kilda,* the smallest of the British Isles, is consecrated by a like Genius, to Immortality.

Mr. Page has pointed out a number of striking resemblances between the essayist's opinions and the known views of Collins: the concept of the poet as a genius with a creative power in a degree resembling that of the Creator's power and the praise of Milton as the greatest of poets, suggests the *Ode on the Poetical Character,* which had appeared in print a few months before; the justification of poets who in portraying a fairy world "are still to nature true" anticipates the *Ode on the Popular Superstitions* as does the enthusiastic account of the island of St. Kilda, which was to absorb the poet's own imagination in stanza IX of the ode; the suggestions of the *Ode to Simplicity* and the *Epistle to Hanmer* evident in the essay, and the imaginative fascination of the horrible exemplified in the *Ode to Fear,* are additional bits of evidence. Mr. E. H. W. Meyerstein adds the further point[8] that the phrase in the essay "there is something peculiarly luminous in the poetic Genius" suggests "Truth in sunny Vest array'd" and "the rich-hair'd Youth of Morn," lines 45 and 39 of the *Ode on the Poetical Character.* To these suggestions it may be added: that Shakespeare, Milton, and Spenser were Collins's favorites, that in the *Ode on the Popular Superstitions* Spenser's fairy world and Shakespeare's magic are considered together, as scenes which "daring to depart From sober truth are still to nature true," and that the essayist's account of the poet's power

[8] *TLS,* 1935, p. 477.

over his reader's imagination is essentially that which Collins expresses. Moreover, there is the praise of both the classical poets and the poets of romantic fancy—a harmony which Collins's own poetry strove to attain; and in the panegyric on St. Kilda the author is commending for imaginative treatment the themes of "simple sure effect" Collins was later to urge Home to describe. At the time the essay appeared both Collins and Mallet were in Thomson's circle at Richmond, and if Collins did not write the piece, it was composed by one who shared his views and knew his poetry[9]—again an evidence that in critical theory Collins was a poet of his day.

[9] Some evidence negating Collins's authorship may be suggested. As Mr. Blunden has noted (*TLS,* 1935, p. 501) "the period which produced Dodsley's *Museum* was rather apt to dominate individuality and critical positions and expressions then were shared by not a few writers." The preceding pages of this study have indicated that Thomson (who had also mentioned St. Kilda in *The Seasons*), Akenside (then editor of the *Museum* and, according to Mr. Blunden, formally undertaking to write a fortnightly essay), and the Wartons, among others, shared Collins's views. Moreover, some of the criticism is commonplace: that poetic inspiration is supernatural or divine and that the poet is a "Second Maker" had already been enunciated by Shaftesbury; the praise of Milton might have come from any of the school of imitators of *Il Penseroso,* as might the admiration of Shakespeare and Spenser, to whom both the Wartons were devoted. The distinction between "true poets and mere versifiers" goes back, in that age, at least to Pope and is reiterated in Joseph Warton's *Essay on the Genius and Writings of Pope* (1756).

Thomas Warton in *Observations on the Fairy Queen of Spenser,* 1754, II, 268, praises the power in romances "to rouse and invigorate all the powers of the imagination; to store the fancy with those sublime and alarming images which poetry best delights to display." If the essay be by Collins it shows conclusively that his own theory of poetry partook of the general enthusiasm for imagination and insight in poetry that was developing in the years between 1725 and 1770. The treatment of the terrible and horrible and the world of fancy was frequently justified in that age—Addison had dealt with it and at a slightly later date it was discussed by Bishop Hurd (1762) in *Letters on Chivalry and Romance,* Letter VI.

A word might be said on Mr. Meyerstein's suggestions about Collins's contribution to the *Museum* (*TLS,* 1935, p. 477). The essay on *Milton's Muse,* June 7, 1746, signed J. C., has the sentence: "See with what Beauty and Dignity this Sovereign Sapience appears in Spenser's description of her, in his *Hymn of Heavenly Beauty.*" As I shall show in my discussion of the *Ode on the Poetical Character* Spenser's *Hymn* was one of the sources; this may be a further hint of Collins's authorship. It may or may not be significant that on the same date the *Ode to a Lady* appeared; at least Collins was then a contributor. On Saturday, August 16, 1746, *A Song, Imitated from the Midsummer Night's Dream of Shakespeare, Act II, Scene V,* recently attributed to Collins, appeared in the *Museum.* At a slightly earlier date the *Museum* printed "Prologue & Epilogue to *Venice Preserv'd*" (May 10, 1746)

At any rate Collins was close enough to the Wartons and interested enough in the prevailing ideas of his day to share their feeling in the matter, and of this his odes give evidence. To him also the act of poetic composition is "enthusiastic," spontaneous, and ecstatic. In the *Epistle to Hanmer* he says of Shakespeare's work:

> There ev'ry thought the poet's warmth may raise,
> There native music dwells in all the lays.

In the *Ode to Pity,* too, he speaks of retiring into the Temple of Pity:

> There let me oft, retir'd by Day,
> In Dreams of Passion melt away,
>   Allow'd with Thee to dwell:
> There waste the mournful Lamp of Night,
> Till, Virgin, thou again delight,
>   To hear a *British* Shell.

Retirement and visionary contemplation are essential to poetic composition. This he feels even in *The Manners* when the real world is the source of his inspiration, for he retires to the thoughtful cell when the powerful spell of Fancy is upon him. And though in the *Ode to Simplicity* he insists that Simplicity must inspire the poet's work, however blest with taste and genius, he does not minimize the necessity of inspiration:

> Tho' Taste, tho' GENIUS bless,
>   TO SOME DIVINE EXCESS,
> Faints the cold Work till Thou inspire the whole;
>   What each, what all supply,
>   May court, may charm our Eye,
> Thou, only Thou, can'st raise the MEETING SOUL!

With his contemporaries Collins feels, too, that poetry must be more than inspiring to the poet. It must evoke a feeling response in those who read—the poet "must raise a wild Enthusiast Heat" in all who come to his poetry. Hence in the *Ode on the Popular Superstitions* he urges Home to treat of rustic themes:

---

and *An Ode to the People of Great Britain* (May 24, 1746) both of which Mr. Blunden includes in his Haslewood Press edition as "Poems of Doubtful Authenticity." Through his friendship with Cooper and his earlier relation with Dodsley in the printing of the second edition of the *Epistle to Hanmer,* 1744, Collins may have become a frequent contributor.

Let thy sweet muse the rural faith sustain;
  These are the themes of simple, sure effect,
That add new conquests to her boundless reign,
And fill, with double force, her HEART-COMMANDING STRAIN.

He praises the same power in Tasso, to whom Collins responds
almost as Pope did to Homer:

How have I sat, when pip'd the pensive wind,
  To hear his harp, by British FAIRFAX strung. . . .
Hence, at each sound, imagination glows;
  Hence his warm lay with softest sweetness flows:
Melting it flows, pure, num'rous, strong and clear,
And fills th' impassion'd heart, and wins th' harmonious ear.

In poetry Collins felt the same emotional stimulus that he attributes to the power of music over the Passions in *The Passions:*

By turns they felt the glowing Mind,
Disturb'd, delighted, rais'd, refin'd.
Till once, 'tis said, when all were fir'd,
Fill'd with Fury, rapt, inspir'd,
From the supporting Myrtles round,
They snatch'd her Instruments of Sound,
And as they oft had heard a-part
Sweet Lessons of her forceful Art
Each, for Madness rul'd the Hour,
Would prove his own expressive Pow'r.

He aspired to express his own passion and by his poetry to move
others to feel as he had himself been touched by the poets whom
he most admired. But in the *Ode on the Poetical Character,* in
which he embodies the prevailing idea of poetical inspiration
more imaginatively and enthusiastically than any of his contemporaries, he best expresses his concept of the imagination. As
the title suggests, he tells, too, whom he considers to be the
"poetical character," the true poet. He pays tribute to two of his
favorite poets, Spenser and Milton, and voices his own faint hope
of himself becoming such a poet. In the poem, too, he comes
closest to attaining to his own ideal, for in no other ode does he
achieve so ecstatic and glowing an imaginative power. He begins by a finely appreciative tribute to "that gifted Bard," Spenser, and his Elfin Queen. Though there is some confusion in
detail, he alludes to the magic girdle described in the Fourth

Book of the *Faerie Queene,* which (Collins says) Amoret alone could wear at the tourney because only she had the requisite virtue of "chaste love and wivehood true." The gift of poetry is to Collins such a magic girdle; it is the cest of amplest power, true and full poetic inspiration which is granted to few of the choicest spirits, perhaps to but one. Fancy or Divine Imagination bestows such power only on the worthiest. That Collins should call this Fancy "to me divinest Name" shows only how deeply he was absorbed by the desire to be a poet and how devoutly he was a worshipper at the shrine of Fancy. The gift of poetry is of divine origin, for the cest, symbolic of poetry, is "prepar'd and bath'd in Heaven." Fancy, who bestows it, is also divine, the handmaiden of the Almighty. The favored poet who merits the gift is such a Maker as Collins and the Wartons had conceived him to be. For Fancy

> To few the God-like Gift assigns,
>   To gird their blest prophetic Loins,
> And gaze her Visions wild, and feel unmix'd her Flame!

Such a poet is divinely favored. He is both poet and prophet. His poetic power is ecstatic and visionary; and he feels deeply the enthusiastic warmth that true imagination imparts. Having defined the ideal poet in the strophe of the ode, Collins turns in the epode to the creation of the gift of poetry itself, the magic Band, showing by the account of its origin how divine and precious it is. Though the imagery is shadowy and symbolic it is finely inspired and nobly ecstatic. For the epode blends together two myth-like conceits—the weaving of the magic band "prepar'd and bath'd in Heaven," the gift of poetry, and the birth of the true poet for whom it is destined. The true poet, or the Poetical Character, is the child of the union of the Almighty (Thought) and Fancy, born full-grown on the very day when the world was created. The conception and birth of the poet, "the rich-hair'd Youth of Morn," is simultaneous with the magic weaving of the girdle which Fancy, his mother, allots to him. Collins weaves the two themes together inextricably. After all, the two are inseparable, for the girdle of poetry would be useless were there no poet to wear it. Yet, for the sake of clarity, each conceit should be examined separately to discover the implications therein. The epode reads in part:

> The Band, as Fairy Legends say,   23
> Was wove on that creating Day,
> When He, who call'd with Thought to Birth   25
> Yon tented Sky, this laughing Earth,
> And drest with Springs, and Forests tall,
> And pour'd the Main engirting all,
> Long by the lov'd *Enthusiast* woo'd,
> Himself in some Diviner Mood,   30
> Retiring, sate with her alone,
> And plac'd her in his Saphire Throne,
> The whiles, the vaulted Shrine around,
> Seraphic Wires were heard to sound,
> Now sublimest Triumph swelling,   35
> Now on Love and Mercy dwelling;
> And she, from out the veiling cloud,
> Breath'd her magic Notes aloud:
> And Thou, Thou rich-hair'd Youth of Morn,
> And all thy subject Life was born!   40
> The dang'rous Passions kept aloof,
> Far from the sainted growing Woof:
> But near it sate Ecstatic *Wonder,*
> List'ning the deep applauding Thunder:
> And *Truth,* in sunny Vest array'd,   45
> By whose the Tarsel's Eyes were made;
> All the shad'wy Tribes of *Mind,*
> In braided Dance their Murmurs join'd,
> And all the bright uncounted *Pow'rs*
> Who feed on Heav'n's ambrosial Flow'rs.   50

Lines 23-25 begin the description of the weaving of the Band of poetry on the day when the Almighty created the world. Poetry, then, is coeval with creation. Lines 25-40, however, describe the parentage and birth of the Poetical Character. In these lines the weaving of the girdle is not mentioned, but one has a shadowy sense of its simultaneous creation. Lines 41-50 return to the description of the "sainted growing Woof." The description of the Poet's birth is particularly rich in symbolic suggestion and implication. While it is almost oriental, at least Greek, in its anthropomorphism, in its suggestiveness it is not far from the account of the parentage of Melancholy which Milton gives in

Il Penseroso. The Almighty, who "with *Thought*" brought the world to birth, retired with Fancy, the "lov'd Enthusiast," placed her on his sapphire throne in heaven, and in "some diviner Mood" created the poet, born from the union of Thought and of Fancy, breathing her "magic Notes" aloud. Fancy herself is conceived as a handmaiden to God. She existed before the creation of the world as did the Almighty. Her relation to the Almighty and to the poet and his "subject Life" seems peculiarly akin to the picture of Sapience which Spenser presents in his *Hymne of Heavenly Beautie,* of which the whole passage in Collins is strongly reminiscent.[10] Or perhaps Collins recalled *Proverbs,* VIII, 29-31:

> When He marked out the foundations of earth,
>   Then I was by Him
>   As a master workman;
>   And I was daily His delight,
>   Sporting always before Him,
>   Sporting in His habitable earth,
> And my delight was with the sons of men.[11]

That the retirement of the Almighty with Fancy is in "some diviner Mood" may well argue that Collins felt that the creation of the poet, the union of Thought and Fancy, was a more divine act than the birth of the world, the result only of Thought. In this connection one must remember that Fancy was, to Collins, "divinest Name." Several implications must be drawn from the

---

[10] M. Pierre Legouis in a brief article in *Revue Anglo-Americaine,* December, 1930, "Les Amours de Dieu chez Collins et Milton," suggests that the source of the conceit is *Paradise Lost,* VII, 8-12, and two prose passages from the *Tetrachordon,* which he assumes Collins was too indolent to have read. The resemblance to stanzas 27-38 of *An Hymne of Heavenly Beautie,* which was called to my attention by my colleague, Dr. H. M. Belden, seems to me far closer to Collins. The abode of Sapience in the bosom of the Almighty, the description of the Almighty's throne, the relationship of Sapience to the world of the Almighty's creation, are suggestive of parallel details in Collins. And compare especially lines 225-231 of *An Hymne of Heavenly Beautie* with lines 51-54 of *Ode on the Poetical Character.*

[11] As another possible source for the relation of Fancy to the Almighty, cf. Milton's invocation to the Heavenly Muse, *P.L.,* I, 19-22:

> . . . Thou from the first
> Wast present, and, with mighty wings outspread,
> Dove-like sat'st brooding on the vast Abyss,
> And mad'st it pregnant: . . .

myth: First, the poet is of divine parentage, a creation of the divine mind as is nature. Second, the true poet is a fine union of Thought and Fancy, truly "Fancy's child." Third, he is coëval with the world and it is subject to him; he is, as Browning says, "Earth's essential king."[12] The whole myth is a glorified treatment of that concept of the poet and of poetry that was so popular with Collins's contemporaries, but in the presentation of it he infinitely surpassed any of them in imaginative power.

At line 41 Collins returns to his first conceit, the preparation of the magic girdle of poetry destined for the Poetical Character. It actually symbolizes and describes the substance and nature of poetry, an art as magic and intangible as the girdle which represents it. The "dang'rous Passions" keep aloof from the growing web, but near it sit Ecstatic Wonder and Truth, clear-eyed and bright. The shadowy tribes of mind and the bright uncounted powers of Heaven join their murmurs in "braided dance." The whole rhythm and the intangible quality of the passage suggest such an exalted symbolism as one meets in the *Paradiso* of Dante. But in the symbols the poet is defining the province of poetry. Poetry does not arouse or stir the dangerous passions, for it is untainted with evil. It does rouse ecstatic wonder, and it teaches truth seen sharply and radiantly. It is a fine harmony of living ideas, "the shad'wy tribes of Mind," woven together by the poet, with the perfect rhythm of a finely executed dance. It deals, too, with divine and heavenly things. In this last idea one sees a recurrence of the imagery of the first myth; poetry, like the poet, is a rhythmic harmony of Thought and Fancy, but also it is a

---

[12] Lines 39-40 have been the subject of considerable controversy. Mrs. Barbauld considered the "rich-hair'd Youth of Morn" to represent the sun. Bronson (*Poems of Collins,* p. 102), follows her with the observation, "cf. the Greek conception of the youthful Apollo god of the sun" and a parallel citation from *F.Q.,* I, v, 2, 7-9. But Apollo was also the god of poetry. And in view of lines 25-28 of the ode, the interpretation of "the rich-hair'd Youth" as the sun would make an inartistic redundancy. And, after all, Collins is primarily discussing the Poetical Character, not the creation of the world. Mr. Garrod (*Collins,* p. 69) gives the more logical view that he is the Poet, though one hardly needs his emendation to line 40 for the sense. In this interpretation he is followed by Mr. Blunden (*Poems of William Collins,* p. 168), who speaks of "Collins's vision of the Creator, Thought, wedding Fancy, and begetting the Poetical Character." However, it is unwise to be too dogmatic in interpreting such cloudy symbolism; perhaps either interpretation is tenable.

blending of the human and the divine.[13] Small wonder, then, that Collins should add after so exalted a concept of the poet and poetry:

> Where is the Bard, whose Soul can now
> Its high presuming Hopes avow?

He feels his aspirations far too high and his powers far too weak to hope that he can be such a poet. The epode ends by referring again with fine unity of concept to the magic Band:

> Where He who thinks, with Rapture blind,
> This hallow'd Work for Him design'd?

No poet, however blinded with enthusiasm for his high calling, could deem himself worthy of "this hallow'd Work," the Cest, the magic Band of poetry. The antistrophe carries the idea of the ode to its logical conclusion. It describes Collins's ideal poet, Milton, who was to Collins a true embodiment of the Poetical Character, and it repeats his own aspirations to be such a poet, though he feels them vain in his admiration of his ideal. The first thirteen lines give a finely symbolic picture of the dignity and divinity of Milton's poetry, in the image of the lofty cliff "to Heav'n up-pil'd," guarded by holy Genii. The rude and wild prospect of the precipice and the presence of the strange shades suggest the awesome quality Collins felt in such a genius as Milton possessed. Milton's poetry, it is implied, was inspired divinely; in evening contemplation he was touched by heavenly visitation and, as Collins's ideal should be, was raised himself to an ecstatic vision of heaven.[14] The oak tree by which Milton lay,

---

[13] For a similar concept of the divine nature of Poetic Inspiration, cf. *Ode to Liberty,* 101-4:

> Yet still, if Truth those Beams infuse,
> Which guide at once, and charm the Muse,
> Beyond yon braided Clouds that lie,
> Paving the light-embroider'd Sky.

[14] As a source of line 61 of the ode, "On which that ancient Trump he reach'd was hung," cf. *Exodus,* xix, 16: "And it came to pass on the third day in the morning that there were thunders and lightnings, and a thick cloud upon the mount, and the voice of the trumpet exceeding loud. . . ." The biblical passage with its allusion to Mount Sinai is in keeping with the exalted imagery of Collins's poem. Milton, like Moses, is a divinely inspired prophet. The biblical tone of the ode is marked by such suggestive expressions as "To gird their blest prophetic Loins," 21, and the account of the "creating Day" in the epode, as well as the picture of Eden in the antistrophe—not unusual in a poet who later had but one Book and that the best.

though reminiscent of the "accustomed oak" of *Il Penseroso,* may well be the Tree of Poetry, as Mr. Blunden suggests.[15] The lines of the ode which follow are particularly in accord with Collins's reaction to a dream which he recounted to his schoolfellow, Smith:

He was observed one morning to be particularly depressed and melancholy. Being pressed to disclose the cause, he at last said it was in consequence of a dream. . . . He said he dreamed that he was walking in the fields where there was a lofty tree; that he climbed it; and when he had nearly reached the top, a great branch, upon which he had got, failed with him, and let him fall to the ground. This account caused more ridicule; and he was asked how he could possibly be affected by this common consequence of a schoolboy adventure, when he did not pretend, even in imagination and sleep, to have received any hurt. He replied that the tree was the Tree of Poetry.

That Collins wished deeply to follow Milton's footsteps, but that he felt he was doomed to failure because the task was too great and the time out of joint is evident from the concluding lines of the ode:

> Thither oft his Glory greeting,
> From *Waller's* Myrtle Shades retreating,
> With many a Vow from Hope's aspiring Tongue,
> My trembling Feet his guiding Steps pursue;
> In vain—Such Bliss to One alone,
> Of all the Sons of Soul was known,
> And Heav'n, and *Fancy,* kindred Pow'rs,
> Have now o'erturn'd th' inspiring Bow'rs,
> Or curtain'd close such Scene from ev'ry future View.

The reverence for Milton, Collins's avowed master, is as significant as his reaction against Waller in showing Collins a poet of his time. But equally marked is Collins's own feeling that such a vision of Heaven as Milton was granted and such Fancy (which by Collins's own myth in the epode is divine) as Milton possessed are shut from himself and from the poets of his "laggard Age."

---

[15] *Poems of William Collins,* p. 27. It is interesting to note in connection with the passage that the oak tree at Dodona was sacred to Jupiter. From the rustling of its leaves the future was predicted. The prophetic power of the poet may be subtly suggested by the choice of the oak tree.

In these last lines Collins asserts that to Milton alone was the Cest of Poetry granted, thereby carrying through the whole poem the conceit which he had borrowed from the *Faerie Queene* at the beginning. Yet he seems also by his admiration for Spenser and his obvious allusion to his work through the poem to imply that he, too, was a true poet. And from his discussion of Shakespeare in other poems one is tempted to believe that had not the exigencies of his conceit and his excessive admiration for Milton prevented he would have included him also as a worthy possessor of the magic girdle; for the invocation at the end of the *Ode to Fear* describes Shakespeare in terms similar to those applied to Milton in the *Ode on the Poetical Character:*

> O THOU WHOSE SPIRIT MOST POSSEST
> THE SACRED SEAT OF *Shakespear's* BREAST!
> BY ALL THAT FROM THY PROPHET BROKE,
> IN THY DIVINE EMOTIONS SPOKE:
> HITHER AGAIN THY FURY DEAL,
> Teach me but once like Him to feel.

In one of the versions of the *Epistle to Hanmer,* too, Shakespeare is regarded as "Fancy's child":

> Long slighted *Fancy,* with a Mother's Care,
> Wept o'er his Works, and felt the last Despair.
> Torn from her Head, she saw the Roses fall,
> By all deserted, tho' admir'd by all.
> "And oh! she cried, shall Science still resign
> "Whate'er is Nature's and whate'er is mine?
> "Shall *Taste* and *Art,* but shew a cold Regard,
> "And scornful Pride reject th' unletter'd Bard?
> "Ye myrtled Nymphs, who own my gentle Reign,
> "Tune the sweet Lyre, and grace my airy Train!
> "If, where ye rove, your searching Eyes have known
> "One perfect Mind, which Judgment calls its own:
> "There ev'ry Breast its fondest Hopes must bend,
> "And every Muse with Tears await her Friend."

Fancy is suggested as weeping "with a Mother's Care" over Shakespeare's works, and in Shakespeare she finds "One perfect Mind, which Judgment calls its own."[16] Surely, too, the epithet

---

[16] Though the sense is here obscure Collins could hardly have been so fulsomely humble as to mean Sir Thomas Hanmer as the "One perfect Mind, which Judgment calls its own."

"Fancy-blest," applied to Alcaeus in the later *Ode to Liberty,* bears something of the same connotation.

The concept of Fancy drawn in the *Ode on the Poetical Character* is followed consistently in the other poems. Almost always she stands for the Poetical Imagination, that intermediary power by which the poet comes into communication with the shadowy and visionary world of which Collins delights to write. In some instances Collins admits that it is an illusory world, an escape from the real world, yet he loves it. Such a world he finds in the fanciful comedies of Shakespeare:

> Where'er we turn, BY FANCY CHARM'D, we find
> Some sweet Illusion of the cheated Mind.

In the *Ode to Fear,* too, Fancy is the intermediary by which the shadowy, unknown world of the supernatural, the province of Fear, is revealed:

> Thou, to whom the World unknown
> With all its shadowy Shapes is shown;
> Who see'st appall'd th' unreal Scene,
> WHILE FANCY LIFTS THE VEIL BETWEEN:
> Ah *Fear!* Ah frantic *Fear!*
> I see, I see Thee near.

Fancy, too, must aid Pity when the Poet would build Pity's Temple in his mind:

> Come, *Pity,* come, BY FANCY'S AID,
> Ev'n now my Thoughts, relenting Maid,
> Thy Temple's Pride design.

And in *The Manners,* Fancy has a part with Reason, Science, and Pride in revealing "the dim-discover'd Tracts of Mind," "the Magic Shores," and the "Fairy Field" from which Collins would retreat; yet she still breathes her potent spell when he turns to interpret the real world. Surely, too, the world of superstition and tradition which Collins pictures in the *Ode on the Popular Superstitions* is "Fancy's land." And Fancy is appropriately present in the "sylvan Shed" of the *Ode to Evening* among the "pensive Pleasures sweet," for her power is felt in that poem as strongly as in any of Collins[17]—that, too, is Fancy's land.

[17] Other instances are: *The Passions,* 104, "Devote to Virtue, *Fancy,* Art"; *On the Death of Mr. Thomson,* 27, "With Him, Sweet Bard, may *fancy*

Simplicity, Collins feels, is closely allied with Fancy. For Simplicity is also taught in the school of Nature. She is Sister to Truth. Fancy is her child or the child of pleasure—imagination springs from clear vision or from joy, as Coleridge was later to feel. Simplicity is sister to Truth and nurses in Fancy the powers of song—"Numbers warmly pure and sweetly strong." The poet must have simplicity to proportion and shape his work. For simplicity is akin to both Truth and Fancy. True imagination conceives things directly and simply; it is ordered and clearly formed. Collins's invocation to Simplicity, then, is like his addresses to Pity and to Fear. He would feel her power, too, in his work:

> O Sister meek of Truth,
> To my admiring Youth,
> Thy sober Aid and native Charms infuse!
> The Flow'rs that sweetest breathe,
> Tho' Beauty cull'd the Wreath,
> Still ask thy Hand to range their order'd Hues.

To this fine and clear-cut order Collins aspired to shape his poetry, to fuse with imaginative power a perfection of line, and to form a true harmony of the romantic and the classical. In the *Ode to Evening* and the *Ode Written in the Beginning of the Year 1746* he succeeded perfectly. Yet one senses such a fine orderliness, too, in the *Ode to Simplicity* itself, and in the proportion of the Pindaric odes where a lofty imaginative theme is shaped and restrained by a well-ordered metrical structure.

---

die"; in the *Ode written at the Beginning of the Year 1746*, 5-6; "She there shall dress a sweeter Sod, Than *Fancy's* Feet have ever trod."

VIII

QUALITIES "DESCRIPTIVE AND ALLEGORIC"

A SSOCIATED with Collins's concept of Fancy and his idea of
the subject-matter of poetry is his treatment of "allegory,"
or more directly, his use of personification, surely part of "invention and imagination" which Collins, with Joseph Warton,
felt to be "the chief faculties of a poet." Collins's treatment of
his personifications is one of the most characteristic qualities of
his poetry, at once one of his merits and one of his faults, and
especially indicative, too, of the poetical traditions which he
followed. It relates him, in a sense, to the Spenserian revivalists
like Thomson and Shenstone, although his personified figures
resemble more the mythological figures of Milton's *L'Allegro*
and *Il Penseroso*. And in some instances one is reminded that the
spell of Pope and the Augustan age was not entirely dissipated
when Collins was writing.

In most of the odes the major personified figure is shadowy,
and, instead of being directly described, is suggested more by its
influence. There is relatively little in Collins of that sharp, colorful, and picturesque delineation of a virtue or vice so characteristic of Spenser. Instead, Collins employs a few descriptive epithets appropriate to the figure described and subordinates these
to the effect which the personified quality produces on the poet
or the reader. And since Pity, Fear, Fancy, Peace, Mercy, and
Simplicity are part of that visionary world to which Evening belongs, the descriptions are, appropriately enough, shadowy and
vague, the presence of these god-like figures being more often
felt than fully seen. Most of the descriptive details are adjectival,
in the form of suggestive epithets. So in the *Ode to Pity,* the address to Pity begins by an apostrophe and invocation to that Goddess,

>   the Friend of Man assign'd,
>   With balmy Hands his Wounds to bind,
>   And charm his frantic Woe.

But the actual descriptive touches are brief. Pity is further invoked:

> Long, *Pity*, let the Nations view
> Thy sky-worn Robes of tend'rest Blue,
> And Eyes of dewy Light!

Attributes appropriate to her are the soothing lute, the myrtles, the retired cell, and the soft notes of turtle doves. She is further fittingly called "relenting Maid"; to her Collins would dedicate a temple, ornamented by pictures representing the great scenes from tragedy. But that is all. She is a shadowy figure, her presence and power suggested by her influence on *"Pella's* Bard" and "gentlest *Otway."* In the *Ode to Simplicity,* too, the figure of Simplicity is more suggested by appropriate details than described. In form the ode follows that of the *Ode to Pity.* It begins with an apostrophe[1] to the divine power addressed, "O Thou by *Nature* taught." It then invokes the goddess in the names of those places and things dearest to her, suggestive of those who best have served her:

> By all the honey'd Store
> On *Hybla's* Thymy Shore,

and

> By old *Cephisus* deep,

and then concludes with the poet's request for her favor. The goddess herself is again described by a few phrases suggestive of the quality she represents. She is a "chaste unboastful Nymph," a "Sister meek of Truth." The poet would have her "sober Aid." Her appearance is but briefly mentioned. She is

> a decent Maid
> In *Attic* Robe array'd.

Her haunts, like those of Evening, are in keeping with the quality she represents. For Simplicity dwells in the seclusion of a pastoral environment, on mountains wild, in green retreat, or in temperate vale. She flees from lands where Freedom and Spontaneity

---

[1] This use of apostrophe becomes almost a formula with Collins. Five of the odes—those to *Pity, Fear, Simplicity, Mercy,* and *Peace*—begin with "Thou" or "O Thou."

have died. Again, the actual description of the figure of Simplicity is suggested by her attributes rather than sharply drawn.

The figure of Peace, too, in the *Ode to Peace* is but slightly described. And in the *Ode to Liberty* no direct attempt is made to describe the presiding goddess. One learns that Liberty is to make her last abode in the vales of Britain. She is called "Soul-enforcing Goddess." Her inmost altar or shrine is described, as is her "blissful Train" of attendant qualities, and she is invoked at the end of both epodes. Collins devotes himself more directly to describing the progress of Liberty and her influence. In the *Ode to Mercy* and in the *Ode to Fear,* however, Collins describes the personified figure more vividly, possibly because the qualities he presented were more sharply associated with his own temperament, or possibly because the attributes personified lend themselves more effectively to descriptive representation. In the *Ode to Mercy* that goddess is described by her actions more than by her appearance. She is apostrophized as "Gentlest of Sky-born Forms, and best ador'd," but for the most part, she is presented through deeds suitable to the quality she represents. She is the bride of Valour, for Mercy is never apart from deeds of heroism —the bravest are the tenderest. She wins the spear of war from Valour and hides his bloodless sword in wreaths of flowers. With bared bosom she pleads for the fallen soldier on the field of battle. She leaves her heavenly abode and drives back the chariot and sable steeds of the Fiend of Nature, War. She is made alive by her activity, although there is something of that static and posed quality so characteristic of the personified figures of Spenser in her appearance.

In the *Ode to Fear* the appearance of the goddess is more fully described, yet even she is shadowy and vaguely drawn, for fear is in essence vague and uncertain. Fear herself is appalled at the shadowy shapes of the unreal world she haunts. She is frantic, madly wild. Her step is hurried, her eyes haggard. She starts and flies disordered. She is accompanied by a ghostly train of monsters. Her own fright moves the poet. He identifies his own emotion and terror with the goddess, the mad nymph, who embodies it. Yet even Fear is shadowy and unsubstantial. There is not that sharp and realistic painting that one finds in the allegorical figures of the Elizabethans. One cannot visualize Collins's Fear as clearly as one can see the figure of Dread in Sackville's Induction to *The Mirror for Magistrates:*

> Next saw we Dread, all trembling how he shook,
> With foot uncertain proffered here and there;
> Benumbed of speech, and with a ghastly look
> Searched every place, all pale and dead for fear,
> His cap borne up with staring of his hair,
>   Stoined and amazed at his owne shade for dread,
>   And fearing greater dangers than was need.

Yet in Collins one senses the power of Fear, nameless, vague, and disquieting by the very shadow-scantness of the picture. In all of the odes considered, with the possible exception of the *Ode to Mercy,* Collins's descriptions of his allegorical figures are diffuse and suggestive rather than sharp and concentrated.

In *The Passions,* Collins makes his most extensive use of the personified figure. In this ode the Passions form a pageant-like procession somewhat like the parade of the Seven Deadly Sins in the first book of *The Faerie Queene.* But all of the Passions are not presented with equal clarity and effectiveness. There is a certain dramatic quality in the way in which the various Passions try their turn at the instruments of Music, carried away to madness by her power over them. And there is an obvious attempt at contrast in the order in which they try their skill. Fear hesitatingly tries first and is followed by Anger. Despair appropriately succeeds Anger, and, again for contrast, Despair is followed by Hope. Then Revenge and Jealousy change the tempo of the ode. Finally Melancholy is succeeded by Chearfulness; the mood of *Il Penseroso* gives way to that of *L'Allegro.* Last, Joy and his train bring the pageant to a close in a kind of Bacchic revel. But Collins varies his method of delineating the figures, with the result that some of the Passions are presented more vividly and effectively than others. The description of Fear is brief. That he was "bewilder'd" and "back recoil'd" at the sound he had made tells his actions, but only vaguely suggests his appearance. The succeeding account of Anger is of the same length, yet it is sharper. The description of Anger's "Eyes on

Fire" vividly represents his appearance, but he is made real by his actions—his rushing forward, his striking the lyre in one rude clash, his sweeping the strings with hurried hand. Except for the one adjective "wan," Despair is not described at all; Collins gives only the effect of his music. Hope, too, is hardly described. Again Collins is more concerned with the influence of her playing. In the picture of Revenge, Collins comes close to the Elizabethan manner of allegory painting. Both the actions and appearance of Revenge are described, and the music he evokes is harmonious with the passion he represents. Revenge is "impatient"; he throws "his blood-stain'd Sword in Thunder down." He frowns, his look is withering, his appearance wild—"each strain'd Ball of Sight" seems "bursting from his Head." He beats the drum "with furious Heat"; he blows a loud, dread blast on the trumpet. But Jealousy, who follows him in the procession, is not described at all and, instead of the appearance of Melancholy, her appropriate haunt is described and her influence is suggested. One learns only that she is pale and pensive and that she sits "with Eyes up-rais'd." Chearfulness, who is described next, resembles most the pictorial figure so frequently found in Spenser. She might well be Belphoebe as she appears in the second book of the *Faerie Queene*. She is presented entirely by means of details of external appearance, though the description is more concentrated than one finds in Spenser:

> But O how alter'd was its sprightlier Tone!
> When *Chearfulness,* a Nymph of healthiest Hue,
>   Her Bow a-cross her Shoulder flung,
>   Her Buskins gem'd with Morning Dew,
> Blew an inspiring Air, that Dale and Thicket rung.

Joy, who comes last in the procession, is hardly described at all. Rather Collins builds up the spirit of his influence, for the passage is the most pulsating and spirited part of the ode. Collins is not, then, consistent in his manner of personifying the major Passions in the ode, nor does he seem to have intended to make them of equal importance, for the space he allots to describing each Passion varies without any definite plan. To Fear, Anger, Despair, and Jealousy he allows four lines each. The descriptions of Melancholy, Revenge, and Chearfulness are of nearly equal length, all treated more fully than those of the earlier Passions. To the description of Joy he gives the greatest number of lines. Yet there seems to be no set plan in the procedure. One feels that he described Melancholy and Revenge so well because they were figures to which he was particularly sensitive. One is surprised that he should have treated his favorite Pity in but two lines, and Fear, by which he was so haunted, in but four lines, and that he should have made that passion male, instead of female as in the *Ode to Fear*. But since the poem is an irregular ode in the manner of Dryden's *Alexander's Feast,* one cannot reasonably expect the fine proportioning that the more exacting structure of the Pindaric ode would have required of him.

Personification was almost second nature to Collins; moreover, his odes were to be descriptive. In addition to his portrayal of the major personified figures in each of the odes addressed to them, he is fond of creating a series of minor figures, some of them drawn by a distinctive phrase or two. These are at once indicative of the poet's manner of expression and of his imaginative acuteness. Sometimes, after the Miltonic manner in *L'Allegro* and *Il Penseroso,* these minor figures are part of the train of virtues attendant upon the major quality personified. Even in the early *Persian Eclogues* Chastity appears attended by Faith, Meekness, Pity, Love. In the *Epistle to Hanmer* Fancy has her "airy Train" of myrtled nymphs. Fear, too, has a ghastly train of monsters attendant upon her—Danger, Vengeance and a Thousand Shapeless Phantoms—finely symbolic of the causes that rouse fear in the mind. In the *Ode to Liberty* a blissful train of the virtues attendant upon Liberty is presented, Concord among them. Peace, too, is accompanied by a "beamy Train," and in *The Manners,* truly in the spirit of *L'Allegro,* there is the band of Humour and the attendant "Young-eyed healthful Wit, with Jewels in his crispèd Hair." Nor must one forget the delicate train of elves and nymphs who attend the shadowy car of Evening in that ode. Too numerous to mention are all of the personified figures presented briefly and sharply in a meaningful phrase or two. There is the figure of Danger in the *Ode to Fear:*

> *Danger,* whose Limbs of Giant Mold
> What mortal Eye can fix'd behold?

an almost Blake-like form conjuring up to the imagination the
enormity and the terror of danger itself. In *Ode Written at the
Beginning of the Year 1746,* Honour, a pilgrim grey, and Freedom, a weeping hermit, are each finely drawn by a single suggestive phrase. Part of the allegro tempo of the passage descriptive
of Joy in *The Passions* is suggested in the rhythm of the dance
in which Love and Mirth are joined:

> While as his flying Fingers kiss'd the Strings,
> LOVE fram'd with *Mirth,* a gay fantastic Round,
> Loose were Her Tresses seen, her Zone unbound,

a joyous dance suggestive of that "braided Dance" in the *Ode
on the Poetical Character.* So sharply and suggestively drawn,
too, are *"Distress* with Dagger keen" in the *Ode to Pity,* and Observance in *The Manners,* "Youth of the quick uncheated Sight."

Yet all of Collins's personifications are not so imaginatively
presented. He was a poet of his day and owed some allegiance to
Pope. In some instances the personification amounts to no more
than the presence of a capital letter. The address to Music at the
end of *The Passions:*

> Where is thy native simple Heart,
> Devote to Virtue, Fancy, Art?

is an instance in point. But Collins sins less frequently in using
this colorless personification than do most of his contemporaries,
and the number of instances becomes increasingly smaller when
one leaves the *Persian Eclogues* and the *Epistle to Hanmer* behind.

IX

FAILURES AND ACHIEVEMENTS

THE POETRY of Collins is small in quantity, but it reveals clearly the potentialities and powers of its author and gives some insight into his elusive personality, to which there are all too few clues. One wishes he had written more, but the very paucity of his work makes what there is doubly precious. The tragedy of his small achievement is the more poignant when one realizes that, like Coleridge, he had the possibility of accomplishing so much. For with a well-stored mind and a fine imagination went an insuperable indolence, abetted by a visionary disposition which could plan great achievements and begin them, but which hampered the actual power of clothing fine thoughts in finer expression. Whether or no Thomson was describing his friend in one of the stanzas of *The Castle of Indolence,* as Mr. Garrod has already observed, the description fits Collins as we know him and, if it refers to him, shows a penetrating understanding of his failure:

> For oft the heavenly fire, that lay concealed
> Amongst the sleeping embers, mounted fast,
> And all its native light anew revealed.
> Oft as he traversed the cerulean field,
> And marked the clouds that drove before the wind,
> Ten thousand glorious systems would he build,
> Ten thousand great ideas filled his mind;
> But with the clouds they fled, and left no trace behind.

The tragedy is that there were traces left behind, hints of the great ideas and promises of the glorious systems. The translation of Aristotle's *Poetics,* the memoirs for the *Biographia Britannica,* the projected history of the age of Leo X went unfinished, perhaps not more than sketchily begun, perhaps only planned. Yet the odes bear tantalizing traces of Collins's critical abilities and his latent power as an antiquarian, a historian, and a scholar. The *Ode to Evening,* the *Ode on the Poetical Character,*

The Passions, and the *Ode Written in the Beginning of the Year 1746,* almost perfect though they are, give only glimpses of a fine creative power, brief flashes of that "heavenly fire" of which Thomson speaks. The rest melted away in dreams of passion, never articulated. What the natural indolence of the dreamer did not do to hamper their expression, the clouds of madness did.

One must be cognizant, however, of what the few poems which are left contribute positively to an understanding of their poet. They give brief and shadowy glimpses of a mind well-stored with the treasures of classical literature, striving to attain to the poetical ideal that Shakespeare, Spenser, and Milton had set for him to follow. They reveal a scholar who was fond of historical tradition, and who was, at the same time, an enthusiastic student of popular literature and folk-lore. They reveal a sensitive soul, who preferred to withdraw from the world and to live instead in a world of his own creating, peopled with airy beings, shadowy forms, at times delicate and fanciful, at times fearful and horrible. Yet he could find in the real world of nature, in the solitary charm of an evening landscape or the moving grandeur of a powerful storm, some of the enchanting spell or some of the horror and terror that filled his visionary kingdom of the mind. And through his own sensitive spirit, he could feel a tender and gentle pity for the fortunes of men in a world from which he had substantially withdrawn and a patriotic enthusiasm for the struggles of his country from which he stayed aloof. He strove besides to attain to a fine poetic ideal, and at times, in pensive and quiet mood or in a fervor of poetic enthusiasm, he did achieve almost perfect expression of his ideal—a fine and subtle blending of romantic fancy with a clear-cut and simple purity of classical form. Faults and deficiencies he had, it is true, but few poets, except Keats, had achieved so much in twenty-five short years; and in the remaining years of his creative life he developed even more remarkably. If one regrets that he has left so little, one has the consoling observation of Mrs. Barbauld, sometimes one of his most penetrating critics, that "Posterity has done him justice, and assigned him an honourable rank among those of our poets who are more distinguished by excellence than by bulk."[1]

[1] *Critical Essay,* p. xlix.

PART II
SOURCES AND INFLUENCES

INTRODUCTORY NOTE

FOR A young man of twenty-five Collins had read widely by the time he wrote the *Odes Descriptive and Allegoric*. Not yet original enough in poetic experience to cleave out a style of his own, he turned to his favorite poets for inspiration, for imagery, and for suggestive phrase. Yet he culled choice phrases from many gardens and out of old fields came a new and fresh bloom—a cultivated flower, the product of a careful grafting and budding. To the classical writers whom he loved, to Shakespeare and the great Elizabethans, to Milton, to Dryden, and to Pope, he turned with reminiscent fondness. And he was influenced as well by the circle of poets of which he was himself a part, sharing their ideas and sometimes transcending them in imaginative vision. There is a fascination apart from the pleasure of mere scholarly analysis in finding how closely and how fully the substance of his poetry comes from the world of books. For few writers owe so many of their ideas and so much of their phrasing to other poets. Yet Collins weaves the phrase or the image so skillfully into the pattern of his verse that it becomes, in a sense, his own, and the pleasure of recognizing it is twofold. One turns with a reminiscent pleasure to the original that it recalls and finds an added satisfaction in discovering how skillfully by something of the poet's alchemy Collins has made it part of his own imaginative experience.

I

THE CLASSICS

TRAINED in an age when the classical studies flourished, Collins came early to have a love for the literature and the traditions of Greece and Rome. More than any of his contemporaries, save Gray, he was passionately devoted to the Greek spirit—in poetry, in drama, and in music. And, like Pope and the Queen Anne wits, he found a scholarly pleasure in the poetry of Horace and Virgil. Even a casual examination of his volumes of verse with their mottoes from Pindar and Virgil, and their scholarly notes quoting excerpts from Sophocles and from Callimachus, reveals his classical tastes. The "beautiful fragment of Alcaeus" (since attributed to Callistratus) from the Greek *Anthology* furnishes the theme for the *Ode to Liberty;* and the *Ode written at the Beginning of the Year 1746* has the clean-cut and marble-pure finish of the epitaphs of Simonides in the Greek *Anthology.* Though there are a number of classical echoes in the poetry of Collins, his debt is more directly one of spirit and of form; he had turned to the past to bring new vitality and fresh inspiration to the poetry of his laggard age.

Collins's favorite Greek poets were Homer and Pindar. Had he written nothing else than the concluding passage of the *Epistle to Hanmer,* his admiration for Homer would be evident:

> So spread o'er *Greece,* th' harmonious Whole unknown,
> Ev'n *Homer's* Numbers charm'd by Parts alone.
> Their own *Ulysses* scarce had wander'd more,
> By Winds and Water cast on ev'ry Shore:
> When, rais'd by Fate, some former *Hanmer* join'd
> Each beauteous image of the tuneful mind.[1]

Occasional echoes of the phrasing of both the *Iliad* and the *Odyssey* scattered through the poems show that he remembered the

---

[1] The reading of the Dodsley version, "Each beauteous image of the boundless Mind," is better here. The Platonic concept of "the harmonious Whole" and "Each beauteous Image of the boundless Mind" stated in the passage, Collins was later to weave into the pattern of the *Ode to Liberty.*

Homeric idiom. Though they are possibly stock phrases in the
poetry of the age in which Collins wrote, they are none the less
interesting. Such expressions in the *Persian Eclogues* as:

> The sultry sun had gain'd the MIDDLE SKY,[2]

or

> THRICE HAPPY THEY, the wise contented Poor,[3]

are typical. A phrase or two in the *Ode to Liberty* also go back
to a Homeric original:

> The Youths, whose Locks divinely spreading,
> Like vernal Hyacinths in sullen Hue,

lines 3-4, recalls *Odyssey*, VI, 230-1:

> κὰδ δὲ κάρητος
> οὔλας ἧκε κόμας, ὑακινθίνῳ ἄνθει ὁμοίας.

And 'green Navel,' 90, suggests *Odyssey*, I, 50:

> ὅθι τ' ὀμφαλός ἐστι θαλάσσης.

In the *Ode on the Poetical Character*, too, the splendid description of the creation of the world with the main engirting all possibly owes something to the account of the shield of Achilles,
Iliad, XVIII, especially 607-8.[4] And perhaps Collins's elabora-
tion of the Girdle of Poetry owed something to Homer's account
of the Cestus of Aphrodite described in *Iliad*, XIV, 197-221.
These are but "faint Homeric echoes," it is true, but they testify
that Collins, like Keats, had breathed the pure serene of Homer's
world.

To Pindar Collins owed a greater debt. The motto to the *Odes
Descriptive and Allegoric* is drawn from Pindar's *Ninth Olympian*, 80-3:

> Would I could find me words as I move
> onward as a bearer of good gifts in the

[2] *Eclogue II*, 7, cf. *Iliad*, VIII, 68: ἦμος δ' ἠέλιος μέσον οὐρανὸν
ἀμφιβεβήκειν. Cf. *Odyssey*, IV, 400; XVI, 777.
[3] *Eclogue II*, 65, cf. *Odyssey*, V, 306: τρὶς μάκαρες. Cf. *Odyssey*, VI, 154;
see also *Aeneid*, I, 94.
[4] But for the source of the phrase "the Main engirting all," cf. *Iliad*,
XIII, 43; *Odyssey*, I, 68; *Odyssey*, XXV, 68; *Horace*, Epode XVI, 41,
"Oceanus circumvagus."

Muses' car; would I might be attended by
daring and by all-embracing Power.[5]

The motto epitomizes Collins's own aspirations to write poetry
in the best classical tradition and voices as well his craving for
poetic power expressed in the odes themselves. Several of his
odes he modeled consciously after Pindar's structure, though he
altered the position of the epode. Some of them have the archi-
tectonic structure of Pindar's own odes, but Collins does not
attain to Pindar's all-embracing power. In several of the poems of
Collins, moreover, there are suggestions of the imagery of Pindar.
In the antistrophe of the *Ode on the Poetical Character,* 58,
"Strange Shades o'er-brow the Valleys deep," echoes the second
antistrophe of Pindar's *First Pythian,* 29-30:

> Grant, grant, we may find grace with thee,
> O Zeus, that hauntest that mount, that
> forefront of a fruitful land . . . .[6]

Again the strophe of the *Ode to Mercy,* 4-6:

> Who oft with Songs, divine to hear,
> Win'st from his fatal Grasp the Spear,
> And hid'st in Wreaths of Flow'rs his bloodless Sword!

resembles the first antistrophe of the *First Pythian,* 10-12:

> For even the stern god of war setteth aside
> his rude spears so keen, and warmeth
> his heart in deep repose; and thy shafts
> of music soothe even the minds of the deities.[7]

The same passage from Pindar colors the antistrophe of the *Ode
to Mercy,* 14-19, when Mercy stops the Fiend of Nature on
his "blasted Road" and looks his rage away. Perhaps, too, the
account of the "wide, wild Storm," 75-8 of the *Ode to Lib-*

---

[5] Translation Sandys (London: Heinemann, 1915), p. 103:

> εἴην εὑρησιεπὴς ἀναγεῖσθαι
> πρόσφορος ἐν Μοισᾶν δίφρῳ·
> τόλμα δὲ καὶ ἀμφιλαφὴς δύναμις
> ἕσποιτο.

[6] *Op. cit.,* pp. 156-7: εἴη, Ζεῦ, τὶν εἴη ἀνδάνειν, | ὃς τοῦτ' ἐφέπεις ὄρος,
εὐκάρποιο γαίας μέτωπον, τοῦ μὲν ἐπωνυμίαν. . . .

[7] *Op. cit.,* pp. 154-5: . . . καί γὰρ βιατὰς Ἄρης, | τραχεῖαν ἄνευθε
λιπὼν | . . . φρένας,

erty, goes back to the same ode of Pindar, where in the second strophe, 20-6, the devastating power of Etna is pictured.[8] The description of the "bright pavilion'd Plains," where the beauteous Model of Liberty is still preserved, 101-112, owes something to Pindar's *Second Olympian,* the fourth antistrophe of which describes the Islands of the Blest. In structural device Collins followed Pindar; frequently, too, he remembered some of the passages of power in the odes of his great master.

By the Greek tragedians Collins was also impressed. Had he completed a tragedy of his own it might have been modeled, like his projected ode on music, after the Greeks. In the *Epistle to Hanmer* he alludes to the *Hippolytus* of Euripides. Both the *Ode to Pity* and the *Ode to Fear* breathe the spirit of Greek tragedy. The invocation to "Pella's Bard," lines 7-9 of the *Ode to Pity,* Collins explains in a footnote, refers to "Euripides, of whom Aristotle pronounces on a comparison of him with Sophocles, that he was the greater master of the tender passions."[9] The scholarly notes of the *Ode to Fear* mention the *Electra* of Sophocles, the source of "that rav'ning Brood of Fate," line 22 of the ode. The epode mentions in successive stanzas Aeschylus and Sophocles, and alludes directly to the *Oedipus Coloneus* in the text of the poem and in a footnote to the passage. Yet Collins was inaccurate in asserting that in this play Sophocles had "left a-while o'er Hybla's Dews to rove," to trace "the baleful Grove" of the Furies at Colonus; the *Oedipus Coloneus* has much of the grace and sweetness that earned Sophocles the name of "Attic bee." Lines 38-41 of the epode purport to describe the action of a part of the play:

> Wrapt in Thy cloudy Veil the *Incestuous Queen*
> Sigh'd the sad Call her Son and Husband hear'd,
> When once alone it broke the silent Scene,
> And He the Wretch of *Thebes* no more appear'd.

[8] Cf. also Horace, *Odes,* III, iv.

[9] Collins has not read Aristotle aright. Aristotle says, Chapter 13 of the *Poetics* (Translation Lane Cooper, p. 43): "Euripides, even if his procedure be faulty in every other respect [as some maintain], is yet, through the unhappy ending, certainly the most tragic of poets on the stage." There is no direct comparison with Sophocles.

The passage in *Oedipus Coloneus*, 1619-25, is the Messenger's account of Oedipus' parting from his children at the call of the Zeus Chthonius:

> On such wise, close-clinging to each other,
> Sire and daughters sobbed and wept. But
> when they had made an end of wailing, and
> the sound went up no more, there was a
> stillness; and suddenly a voice of one who
> cried aloud to him, so that the hair of all
> stood up on their heads for sudden fear,
> and they were afraid. For the god called
> him with many callings and manifold:
> "Oedipus, Oedipus, why delay we to go?
> Thou tarriest too long." [10]

The scene is, as Collins says, a powerful example of the mingling of Fear's withering power with gentle pity. But he had confused the details of it: Jocasta is not mentioned in the passage; the sad call was that of a god, whose summons "broke the silent Scene," not "once alone," but many times. With his characteristic desire to mingle the classical and the romantic, Collins devotes the entire epode to classical tragedy and assigns the antistrophe to the more romantic tragedy of Shakespeare. In the *Ode to Simplicity*, too, the influence of Greek tragedy is still present. Stanza 3 alludes in its invocation to "the honey'd Store" of Hybla, her "Blooms and mingled Murmurs"—again a tribute to the sweetness and grace of the poetry of Sophocles. Collins notes on the line "Sooth'd sweetly sad Electra's Poet's Ear":

> The ἀηδών, or Nightingale, for which Sophocles
> seems to have entertained a peculiar Fondness.

The allusion is, he tells us, to the *Electra* of Sophocles (though Milton in the phrase Collins is here echoing refers to Euripides). But perhaps in this and the following stanza of the ode Collins remembered again the *Oedipus Coloneus*. Lines 13-20 of Collins's ode read:

> By all the honey'd Store
> On *Hybla's* Thymy Shore,

[10] Jebb's translation, Cambridge, 1889, p. 251. The Greek passage begins: τοιαῦτ' ἐπ' ἀλλήλοισιν ἀμφικείμενοι. . . .

By all her Blooms, and mingled Murmurs dear,
  By Her, whose Love-born Woe
  In Ev'ning Musings slow
Sooth'd sweetly sad *Electra's* Poet's Ear:

  By old *Cephisus* deep
  Who spread his wavy Sweep
  In warbled Wand'rings round thy green Retreat . . .

The first strophe and first antistrophe of the ode beginning
εὐίππου, ξένε τᾶσδε χώρας. . . , lines 668-693 of *Oedipus Coloneus,* are particularly close in spirit and detail:

Stranger, in this land of goodly steeds thou hast come to earth's
fairest home, even to our white Colonus; where the nightingale, a
constant guest, trills her clear note in the covert of green glades. . . .
   And, fed of heavenly dew, the Narcissus blooms morn by morn
with fair clusters . . . and the crocus blooms with golden beam.
Nor fail the sleepless founts where the waters of Cephissus wander,
but each day with stainless tide he moveth over the plains of the
land's swelling bosom, for the giving of quick increase; nor hath
the Muses' quire abhorred the place. . . .[11]

But with this ode the spell of Greek tragedy ceases to be felt in
the poet's verse; the romantic fancies of the *Ode on the Popular
Superstitions of the Highlands* are culled from fresh fields and
pastures new, no longer from "*Hybla's* Thymy Shore."

Among the Latin poets, Virgil and Horace were Collins's favorites. Twice he chooses mottoes for his poems from Virgil.
The motto of the *Persian Eclogues*

   —Ubi primus equis Oriens adflavit anhelis,

comes from Virgil's *Georgics,* I, 250, an appropriate tribute to
the earlier pastoral poet. The motto of the *Ode Occasion'd by the
Death of Mr. Thomson,* again from the pastorals of Virgil, pays
fitting tribute to the Woodland Pilgrim, the dead poet of *The
Seasons.* It is chosen from the fifth eclogue of Virgil's *Bucolics,*
a funeral song on Daphnis the dead shepherd, lines 74 and 75,
to which is added the last half of line 52:

Haec tibi semper erunt, & cum solennia Vota reddemus Nymphis,
& cum lustrabimus Agros.—Amavit nos quoque Daphnis.

[11] Translation Jebb, *op. cit.,* pp. 116-117.

In the *Persian Eclogues* and the *Epistle to Hanmer* the reminiscences of Virgil are marked; there are few traces of the Virgilian phrase in the later poems. In the *First Eclogue,* 51:

> Lost to our fields, FOR SO THE FATES ORDAIN

is an echo of a characteristic Virgilian phrase:

> Sic fata ferebant.[12]

Again the *Third Eclogue,* 4:

> And the tall forests cast a longer Shade,

virtually translates *Bucolics, Eclogue I,* 84:

> Maioresque cadunt altis de montibus umbrae.

Twice in the *Fourth Eclogue* there are suggestions of Virgil. Line 28 of the eclogue:

> Droops its fair Honours to the conqu'ring Flame

recalls *Georgics, II,* 404:

> Frigidus et silvis aquilo decussit honorem.

Lines 71-2 of the same eclogue:

> He said; when loud along the Vale was heard
> A shriller Shriek, and nearer Fires appear'd:

follow *Aeneid, II,* 705-6:

> Dixerat ille; et jam per moenia clarior ignis
> Auditur, propiusque aestus incendia volvunt.[13]

Twice in the *Epistle to Hanmer* Collins alludes to the *Aeneid.* Lines 87-8:

> The Time shall come when *Glo'ster's* Heart shall bleed,
> In Life's last Hours, with Horror of the Deed:

the poet himself owns in a footnote are from Virgil, though he quotes the lines incorrectly:

> Tempus erit Turno, magno cum optaverit emptum
> Intactum Pallanta, etc. VIRG.—C.[14]

[12] *Aeneid,* II, 34; IX, 135; cf. also II, 433; IV, 614; XI, 112.
[13] In the couplet of Collins appears "shriller Shriek" later to be part of the diction of the *Ode to Evening.* "Shriek" is a favorite word in Collins; cf.: *Ode on the Popular Superstitions,* 46; *Song from Shakespeare's Cymbeline,* 6.
[14] The passage cited is *Aeneid,* X, 503:

> Turno tempus erit magno cum optaverit emptum
> intactum Pallanta. . .

Again the allusion in line 137:

> Those Sibyl-Leaves, the Sport of ev'ry Wind

is drawn from *Aeneid, III,* 448-51:

> verum eadem, verso tenuis cum cardine ventus
> impulit et teneras turbavit ianua frondes,
> numquam deinde cavo volitantia prendere saxo
> nec revocare situs aut iungere carmina curat.[15]

Except in the motto to the *Ode Occasion'd by the Death of Mr. Thomson* Collins takes no other significant suggestion from the poetry of Virgil.[16]

There are also occasional echoes of the poetry of Horace in the phrasing of the early poems and the odes. Most of them are such slight reminiscences as would be recalled to any poet as steeped in the classics as was Collins; many of the recollections are probably purely accidental. Instances in the *Persian Eclogues* are relatively numerous. Line 37 of the *Second Eclogue:*

> Full oft we tempt the Land, and oft the Sea,

follows *Odes, III,* iv, 29-32:

> libens
> insanientem navita Bosporum
> temptabo et urentis harenas
> litoris Assyrii viator.

Line 8 of the *Third Eclogue:*

> Emyra sang the pleasing Cares of Love

is drawn from *Epode II,* 37:

> quas amor curas habet.

Line 48 of the *Fourth Eclogue:*

> With Ease alluring and with Plenty blest

suggests *Odes, I,* xvii, 15:

> copia
> manabit ad plenum benigno
> ruris honorum opulta cornu.[17]

---

[15] Cf. also *Aeneid,* VI, 74-5.

[16] Compare, however, *Ode to Simplicity,* 52-4, with *Bucolics, Eclogue I,* 2. The correspondence may well be accidental.

[17] Cf. *Carm. Saec.,* 59; *Epode XVI,* 41.

At least one line in the *Epistle to Hanmer* is Horatian in origin; line 14:

> When wintry Winds deform the plenteous Year

comes from *Odes,* II, x, 15:

> Informis hiemes reducit Iuppiter.

One significant reminiscence of Horace occurs in the later poems. Line 21 of the *Ode to Fear:*

> Lifts her red Arm, expos'd and bare,

goes back to *Odes,* I, ii, 2-4:

> . . . rubente
> dextera sacras iaculatus arces
> terruit urbem.[18]

The flavor of the classics pervades the poetry of Collins from the beginning. It is most obvious in the early poems in the heroic couplet where it may well be part of the influence of Pope, then Collins's poetic master. It is marked, too, in those odes prompted by Collins's devotion to the writers of Greek tragedy—the odes to *Pity,* to *Fear,* and to *Simplicity.* And Pindar is an ever-present source of inspiration. In the later odes, with the exception of *To Liberty,* Collins borrows less directly from the classical writers, and the influence becomes one of spirit rather than of letter. Yet in his allegiance to Milton he is still following the classical tradition, for Milton's poetry is informed with the classical phrase and the classical spirit. But the poet's most significant debt is his recognition of the finish and clear-cut precision of the best classical writing. Pindar and Sophocles taught him, in the words of a later poet:

> O Poet, then, forbear
> The loosely-sandaled verse,

---

[18] But cf. also *P.L.,* II, 174:

> Arm again his red right arm to plague us.

Some less direct suggestions of Horace occur in the other poems: with the account of "Kilda's race," *Pop. Super.,* stanza ix, cf. *Odes,* III, xxiv, 9 ff.; with the legend of Cytherea, *Sonnet,* stanza 2, *On a Piece of Bride-Cake,* stanzas 3-4, cf. *Odes,* I, xxx, 1 ff.; with the account of the "luckless swain," *Pop. Super.,* 122-4, cf. *Epode II,* 39 ff. and *Odes,* I, xii, 42 ff. But as possible parallels for the passage see also Ovid, *Metamorphoses,* IX, 654-8, and Lucretius, III, 894 ff.; cf. also *Iliad,* V, 150, 409; XVII, 207; XVII, 59, 440.

Choose rather thou to wear
  The buskin—straight and terse;

Leave to the tiro's hand
  The limp and shapeless style;
See that thy form demand
  The labor of the file.[19]

[19] Several minor classical parallels might be cited: *Eclogue II*, 25: "Green Delights," cf. Euripides, *Bacchae*, ll. 866-7; *Eclogue II*, 51, "What if the Lion in his Rage I meet?" cf. Catullus, XLV, 6-7:
> Solus in Libya Indiaque tosta
> Caesio veniam obvius leoni.

Ode to Mercy, 1-13, cf. Statius, *Thebais*, III, 261-5. Nor should one omit the influence of the Idylls of Theocritus from which the second of the *Persian Eclogues* derives its form.

II

MILTON

BY FAR THE most significant influence on Collins's verse is the poetry of Milton. His interest in Milton coincides with the vogue for imitating the Miltonic manner current in his day—a fashion that had begun at least as far back as 1726 and extended well down to 1770. Imitations of the verse form and substance of *L'Allegro* and *Il Penseroso* flourished—Thomas Warton's *First of April* and *On the Approach of Summer* and Joseph Warton's *Ode to Fancy* are instances, to mention but a few. Following the fashion set by Thomson's *Seasons* such poems as Dyer's *Fleece* and Phillips's *Cyder* copied the blank verse and the diction of *Paradise Lost*. And the unrhymed lyric, imitating Milton's crude experiment in that form in his translation of the "Pyrrha Ode" from the first book of Horace, flourished in Collins's day. This form, apparently revived by Thomas Warton the Elder in his *Ode to Taste,* was to be used by both his sons as well as by many a minor poet. Sharing as he did the critical notions and the literary tastes of his friends the Wartons and Thomson, Collins naturally turned to Milton, and he paid to his avowed master a finer tribute than any of his contemporaries. Collins's debt to Milton was great, yet he was more than a mere pick-purse of another's wit. He turned for inspiration and suggestion to the verse form, to the diction, and to the substance of *L'Allegro* and *Il Penseroso,* and, following the practice of the Wartons, he wrote one unrhymed lyric in the stanza of the "Pyrrha Ode" admittedly the most perfect of the poems in that form. But his poetry shows also a remarkable familiarity with the other minor poems of Milton. There are reminiscent phrases from *Comus,* from *Lycidas,* from the ode *On the Morning of Christ's Nativity,* and from one of the sonnets. And though he wrote no poetry in blank verse, Collins frequently echoes the imagery and diction of *Paradise Lost* and *Paradise Regained* in his poems; occasionally, too, he draws a phrase or a suggestion from *Samson Agonistes*. His verse is well-nigh saturated with the Miltonic idiom.

Collins was influenced by Milton in several ways. His first debt is one of form and structure. More important is his use of images drawn directly from a passage in Milton: in several instances a single image suggests a Miltonic original, in some cases the whole of an ode represents a skilful combination of ideas drawn from Milton. Finally, he uses the Miltonic idiom so extensively that his poems constantly echo the phrases of Milton, frequently without conscious reference to the context of a passage in Milton where the word or phrase occurs. To pursue the guiding steps of his master was with Collins a mark of literary distinction. He felt, perhaps, that to write in the manner of Milton was a greater achievement than finding a style of his own.

In his adherence to the verse forms and structural patterns of Milton, Collins was less slavishly imitative than most of his contemporaries. In his use of the unrhymed lyric stanza of the "Pyrrha Ode" he found a new beauty and effectiveness in a form which his master had handled woodenly at best; the *Ode to Evening* infinitely surpasses Milton's translation. Though the stanza form he employed in the *Ode to Simplicity* was consciously imitated from that of the ode *On the Morning of Christ's Nativity*, Collins modified it by omitting the last two lines of Milton's stanza. The octosyllabic couplet of *L'Allegro* and *Il Penseroso* Collins tried frequently, but except for *The Manners*, he did not use it throughout a poem. Even in *The Manners*, he departs from Milton's practice of beginning with a ten-line invocation. He does, however, employ the tetrameter again in his strophe and the antistrophe of the *Ode to Fear*, although lines 5 and 6 of each part are trimeter and lines 7 and 8 are pentameter, perhaps in imitation of Milton's practice in the invocation to each of the minor poems.[1] Again the epode of the *Ode on the Poetical Character* is in octosyllabic couplets and the strophe and antis-

---

[1] Milton, however, alternates trimeter and pentameter lines in the invocation. Collins arranges them in couplets.

trophe of the ode, though irregular, begin with four couplets in tetrameter. In the *Ode Written in the Beginning of the Year 1746,* each of the two stanzas is composed of three octosyllabic couplets. Both epodes of the *Ode to Liberty* employ the same meter; and in *The Passions,* in form an irregular or English ode, the first sixteen and the last twenty-four lines are also arranged in octosyllabic couplets. While, it is true, the tetrameter had been used consistently by poets from Milton's time to Collins's, it seems reasonable to suppose that his fondness for Milton prompted his frequent use of it.

Collins also imitated the structural characteristics of *L'Allegro* and *Il Penseroso,* and frequently appropriated or modified a phrase from them. The influence is not so strong as one might reasonably expect; yet Collins's borrowings from the two companion pieces are significant enough to require examination.

The structural formula of the two poems, which Milton himself perhaps owed to the classics, is well-defined. Each begins by banishing what Mr. Havens in his careful study of the poems[2] calls an "execrated quality" with the term "hence" and later welcomes the desired quality with "come" or a similarly appropriate greeting. Each personified figure is attended by a "train" of related personifications. Each ends with the author's associating himself in the train of the quality whose virtues he has extolled. And each is full of mythology, which frequently reveals the parentage of the personified figure described, a parentage appropriate to the qualities it represents.

Even in the first of the *Persian Eclogues,* which resembles the pastoral manner of Pope far more than that of Milton, Collins shows some evidence of his fondness for *L'Allegro* and *Il Penseroso.* Modesty is invoked with the familiar "Come," and her train of attendant virtues is described. The *Ode to Pity* begins with the invocation "Thou," and in the fifth stanza, Pity is

---

[2] In his monumental *Influence of Milton on English Poetry.* In that work, pp. 453-7, he has discussed the influence of *L'Allegro* and *Il Penseroso* on the poetry of Collins. He has not, however, treated the problem so thoroughly in detail as it deserves to be presented, possibly because the enormous amount of material which he has compiled on the influence of the *Minor Poems* would not permit him to devote further space to Collins.

invoked with the familiar "Come." The phrase "Allow'd with Thee to dwell" in the last stanza of the ode is reminiscent of "And I with thee will choose to live," the concluding formula of *Il Penseroso*. The *Ode to Fear* is even more closely in the pattern of *Il Penseroso* with its invocation, its description of the train of Fear, and the concluding lines of the strophe:

> Who, *Fear*, this ghastly Train can see,
> And look not madly wild, like Thee?

which echo again the conclusion of *Il Penseroso*. In the antistrophe the invocation "Mad Nymph" and the concluding formula:

> His *Cypress Wreath* my Meed decree,
> And I, O *Fear*, will dwell with Thee!

are in the same tradition. The *Ode on the Poetical Character* employs none of the structural formulae of the Miltonic poems, but the fanciful account of the parentage of the Poetical Character in the epode is at least reminiscent of the parentage of Melancholy in *Il Penseroso*. In the *Ode to Liberty*, too, the conclusion to the first epode:

> Hail Nymph, ador'd by *Britain*, Hail!

is reminiscent of:

> But hail, thou Goddess sage and holy,
> Hail, divinest Melancholy!

In the second epode the description of the blissful train of Liberty and the concluding line:

> Thou, Lady, Thou shalt rule the West!

are also like the manner of *L'Allegro* and *Il Penseroso*. There is a trace of the same influence in the invocations to the Goddess of Evening; and in the last stanza of that ode:

> So long, regardful of thy quiet Rule,
> Shall *Fancy, Friendship, Science,* smiling *Peace,*
> Thy gentlest Influence own,
> And love thy fav'rite name!

there is again a suggestion of the concluding formula of the two Miltonic poems. There is something of the same implication in the apostrophe to Music to return to Britain in *The Passions*. But it is in *The Manners* that Collins most consistently follows the structural formula of *L'Allegro* and *Il Penseroso*. The ode begins by banishing the "execrated qualities" with "Farewell" instead of "Hence," implying perhaps a reluctance on Collins's part that is not felt in Milton. Then follows the invocation to the desired quality, Observance, and as in *L'Allegro* and *Il Penseroso,* a list of the pleasures to be gained from association with that personified figure:

> To read in Man the native Heart,
> To learn, where Science sure is found.

Collins's invocation to Humour reminds one of Milton's invocation to Mirth in *L'Allegro,* and the appeal "Me too amidst thy Band admit" is almost an echo of "Mirth, admit me of thy crew." There follows a description of the train of Humour, which is closely akin to the crew of Mirth in *L'Allegro*. The appeal to "Nature boon":

> If but from Thee I hope to feel,

and the concluding lines:

> The *Sports* and I this Hour agree,
> To rove thy Scene-full World with Thee!

again repeat the concluding formula of *L'Allegro* and *Il Penseroso* with the difference that in Collins the choice is made while in Milton it is still conditional.

In view of the popular vogue of these two poems, it is surprising to find few direct verbal borrowings in the poetry of Collins. More often he weaves some reminiscence of the phrasing of *L'Allegro* or *Il Penseroso* into an expression of his own, a practice he apparently followed in all of his extensive borrowings from his favorite poets. A number of the phrases in Collins may, however, be counted as directly taken from the companion poems themselves. Examples are found in such phrases as:

> With Truth she wedded in the SECRET GROVE (*Pen.* 28-9)
> Desponding Meekness with her DOWN-CAST Eyes (*Pen.* 43)

in the early *Persian Eclogues*. In the *Ode to Simplicity,* too, one finds such reminiscent expressions as "decent Maid" (*Pen.* 35) and "meeting Soul" (*All.* 138). In the *Ode on the Poetical Character* "jealous Steep" (*All.* 6) is a direct borrowing. Similar reminiscences are found in the "Lydian Measure" (*All.* 136) of the *Ode to Liberty*, and in the "haunted Stream" (*All.* 130), the abode of Melancholy, in *The Passions*. Again the epithet "bright-hair'd" which Collins uses in the *Ode to Evening* comes from *Il Penseroso*, 23.

More often, however, Collins modifies the Miltonic phrase, though not sufficiently to destroy the resemblance. Such a phrase as "scepter'd pall" (*Pen.* 98) Collins renders "trailing Pall" in the *Ode to Simplicity*. Similarly the "uncouth cell" of *L'Allegro* becomes "haunted Cell" in the *Ode to Fear*. Two particularly pertinent instances of Collins's transforming power occur in the *Ode to Evening*. The phrases "upland Fallows gray" and "Hamlets brown" represent a transposition of two phrases in *L'Allegro*, "russet lawns and fallows gray" (*All.* 72) and "upland hamlets" (*All.* 92).[3] And in the *Ode on the Poetical Character*, "solemn Turney" is a modification of *Il Penseroso*, 115-17:

> And if aught else great bards beside
> In sage and SOLEMN tunes have sung
> Of TURNEYS . . .

The two poems were often the source of some of the imagery of Collin's poems. There are suggestions of *L'Allegro* in the third of the *Persian Eclogues;* the description of "Pale Melancholy" in *The Passions* is reminiscent of the figure of Melancholy in *Il Penseroso;* and the folk-lore of the peasantry in the *Ode on the Popular Superstitions* is drawn in part from *L'Allegro.* The spirit of *Il Penseroso* breathes in the antistrophe of the *Ode on the Poetical Character* in the description of Milton himself:

[3] For other instances of the same sort of modification of phrases still definitely suggestive of the original see the following: *Pity*, "mournful Lamp of Night" (*Pen.* 85); *Pity*, "buskin'd Muse" (*Pen.* 102); *Passions*, "a gay fantastic Round" (*All.* 34); *Mr. Thomson*, "to breezy lawn" (*All.* 71); *Popular Superstitions*, "There each trim lass . . . jocund notes" (*All.* 86, *All.* 94); *Popular Superstitions*, "smoking hamlet" (*All.* 92); *Popular Superstitions*, "some dim hill" (*All.* 55); *Song. "Young Damon,"* "lowland hamlets" (*All.* 92); *Song. Cymbeline*, "howling winds" (*Pen.* 126); *Persian Eclogues*, III, "Deep in the Grove . . . Shade" (*Pen.* 28-9); *Persian Eclogues*, III, "The Violet-blue . . . grows" (*All.* 21); *Manners*, "In Pageant quaint, in motley Mask" (*All.* 128); *ibid.*, "The Comic Sock that binds thy Feet" (*All.* 132); *ibid.*, "In Laughter loos'd attends thy Side" (*All.* 32).

> I view that Oak, the fancied Glades among,
> By which as *Milton* lay, his Ev'ning Ear,
> From many a Cloud that drop'd Ethereal Dew,
> Nigh spher'd in Heav'n its native Strains could hear:

which suggests in detail and spirit the passage in *Il Penseroso*, 59-64:

> While Cynthia checks her dragon yoke
> Gently o'er THE ACCUSTOMED OAK:
> Sweet bird, that shun'st the noise of folly,
> Most musical, most melancholy!
> Thee, chauntress, oft the woods among,
> I woo to hear thy EVEN-SONG,

as well as lines 165-6:

> Dissolve me into ecstasies,
> AND BRING ALL HEAVEN BEFORE MINE EYES.

Though Collins imitated Milton in the manner of his friends and contemporaries he was strong enough to draw the line between mere copy work and the genuinely poetic use of his favorite poetry. More striking than Collins's relatively small use of the two most popular of Milton's minor poems is the extent to which he was familiar with and indebted to the Miltonic idiom as it is represented in the other minor poems, particularly *Comus, Lycidas,* and *On the Morning of Christ's Nativity,* and in the major poems, *Paradise Lost, Paradise Regained,* and *Samson Agonistes.*[4]

To Collins *Comus* and *Lycidas* were as significant as the companion poems *L'Allegro* and *Il Penseroso.* In his admiration for them he showed a greater appreciation of Milton than most of his contemporaries. From the early *Persian Eclogues* to the *Ode on the Popular Superstitions* there are numerous verbal echoes of the two poems, and in some of the odes Collins's imagination was stimulated by the spirit of them. Hence it is not surprising that the folk-lore in the antistrophe of the *Ode to Fear* should come in part from *Comus,* nor that in the *Ode to Liberty* part of the spell of the remote and the traditional history of Britain

---

[4] The appendix gives a complete list of the verbal echoes and suggestions of Miltonic idiom in the poems of Collins as well as a full list of Miltonic words which Collins has employed without conscious reference to a specific passage in Milton.

so marked in *Comus* should color Collins's poem. And the fantastic round of "Joy's ecstatic Trial" in *The Passions* has something of the mad abandon of Comus and his crew in Milton's masque. In *Lycidas,* too, Collins found something of the magic of the far-off Hebrides; he sensed as well that brooding and tragic sadness that marks part of Milton's elegy. The mood of romantic strangeness which Milton found in Mona, Collins caught in the *Ode to Liberty.* The elegiac tone of *Lycidas* influences the *Ode on the Death of Mr. Thomson,* but it is in the *Ode on the Popular Superstitions* that the spell of *Lycidas* works most strongly on Collins's imagination.

Like the *Ode to Liberty,* the *Ode on the Popular Superstitions of the Highlands of Scotland* is inspired by Collins's reading and illustrates his interest in the remote and the traditional. In the earlier poem Collins was stimulated by Milton's treatment of these themes in *Comus* and *Lycidas;* in the later poem he recalls Milton's treatment of folk-lore in *L'Allegro* and his fondness for old forgotten far-off things in *Lycidas.* Over the more tragic part of the ode broods the sad recognition of the malignant forces in nature, so powerful in the lives of men, which Milton had expressed in *Lycidas.* Hence the poem is rich in Miltonic diction and image, for Milton had, like Shakespeare and Spenser, found the stuff of romance in the legend of the north country and in the spell of the far-off Hebrides. If stanza II of the ode, 18-35, is in the spirit of *L'Allegro* with its mention of the Brownies, the trim lass, and the cream bowl, much more of the poem is in the spirit of *Lycidas.* Collins's mention of "Old Runic Bards," 41, recalls *Lycidas,* 54:

> Where your old bards, the famous Druids lie.

Again the account of the shrieking maid, 47, who "strew'd with choicest herbs" the scented grave of her chieftain recalls *Lycidas,* 151:

> To strew the laureate Herse where Lycid lies

and the lines preceding it. Some of the fascination of the far-off and the enchanted found in *Lycidas,* 55:

> where Deva spreads her wizard stream

is transmitted to line 54 of the ode where

> In SKY's lone isle the gifted wizzard seer

has the power of second-sight. And in the account of the death of the luckless swain, stanzas VII and VIII of the ode, the brooding sorrow arising from the inevitable influence of fate so strongly felt in *Lycidas* is carried over in the suggestive diction of the ode.

> Ah, luckless swain, o'er all unblest indeed!

line 104 of the ode, echoes *Lycidas, 92*:

> What hard mishap hath doom'd this gentle swain?

The cruelty of the malignant forces of nature to man felt in lines 108-11 suggests in *Lycidas* the fate of the perfidious Bark built in the eclipse, and the phrase "whelming flood," 110, echoes "whelming tide," *Lycidas*, 157, making the parallelism in spirit stronger. Again the account of the luckless swain's death, 119-20:

> His fear-shook limbs have lost their youthly force,
> And down the waves he floats a pale and breathless corse,

and his words when as a *revenant* he speaks to his bereaved wife, 136:

> While I lie weltering on the osier'd shore,

show how thoroughly Collins had *Lycidas* in mind. They echo *Lycidas*, 12-13:

> He must not float upon his watry bier
> Unwept, and welter to the parching wind.

And the sad inevitability of the event felt in line 118:

> What now remains but tears and hopeless sighs?

echoes *Lycidas*, 57:

> Had ye bin there—for what could that have done?

The spell of the remote and traditional in *Lycidas* is suggested again in lines 139-41 of the *Ode:*

> Thy muse may, like those feath'ry tribes which spring
> From their rude rocks, extend her skirting wing
> Round the moist marge of each cold Hebrid isle.

For in one of the finest passages in *Lycidas,* 154-62, Milton had felt the fascination of the "stormy Hebrides," and his phrase "moist vows," *Lycidas,* 159, might have suggested "moist marge" to Collins. Collins's use of *Lycidas* is in a sense a tribute to Milton, who did not disdain to "let his sweet muse the rural faith sustain."

A number of images in the odes are drawn from a Miltonic original; frequently the substance of Collins's ode is informed with the spirit of the passage in Milton from which it is drawn. Hence lines 60-63 of the *Ode to Fear:*

> When Ghosts, as Cottage-Maids believe,
> Their pebbled Beds permitted leave,
> And Gobblins haunt from Fire, or Fen,
> Or Mine, or Flood, the Walks of Men,

follow the diction of *Comus,* 432-6:

> Some say no evil thing that walks by night
> In fog, or fire, by lake or moorish fen,
> Blew meager Hag, or stubborn unlaid ghost
> That breaks his magick chains at curfew time
> No goblin or swart faery of the mine . . .

It carries as well some of the eerie spirit of the Miltonic passage.

In several instances Collins turned to the ode *On the Morning of Christ's Nativity* for a suggestive image or a personification. The description of Britannia's Genius mourning the fatal day of the engagement at Fontenoy, lines 2-6 of the *Ode on the Death of Colonel Ross,* especially the passage:

> While stain'd with Blood he strives to tear
> Unseemly from his Sea-green Hair
>   The Wreaths of chearful *May;*

is drawn from lines 186-7 of the *Nativity Ode:*

> The parting Genius is with sighing sent,
> With flowre-inwoven Tresses torn.

Again the figure of Peace in Collins's ode to that goddess resembles the description of Peace in the ode *On the Morning of Christ's Nativity,* although Collins's portrait is less adequate than Milton's. Both pictures are also somewhat conventional. Collins's description:

O Thou, who bad'st thy Turtles bear
Swift from his Grasp thy golden Hair,
    And sought'st thy native Skies:
When *War*, by Vultures drawn from far,
To *Britain* bent his Iron Car,
    And bad his Storms arise,[5]

is far less complete than Milton's *Nativity Ode,* 54-62, which it
resembles:

But he her fears to cease,
Sent down the meek-ey'd Peace,
She crown'd with Olive Green came softly sliding
    Down through the turning Sphear
    His ready Harbinger
With Turtle wing the amorous clouds dividing,
And waving wide her mirtle wand,
She strikes a universall Peace through Sea and Land.

Actually the stanza in Milton seems to embrace the whole
thought of the *Ode to Peace.* The parallel is made closer by the
phrase "turning Spheres," 10, a direct echo of "turning Sphear,"
line 48 of the *Nativity Ode.* The *Ode to Mercy,* too, draws much
of its substance and some of its imagery from Milton. In stanza
XV of the *Ode on the Morning of Christ's Nativity* Mercy is
described seated between Truth and Justice, and like them, returning to men upon Christ's advent. Collins follows the conceit
in part in the first lines of his ode by describing Mercy who sits
as a smiling bride of Valour; and at the end of the ode she is
mentioned with Justice. There seems to be a further suggestion of
Milton in the antistrophe, 14-20, where Mercy stops the wheels
of the chariot of the Fiend of Nature "whom ev'n our Joys provoke" as he rushes to make the Isle of Britain his prey. The image
suggests the episode in *P.L.* IV, 970 ff., where Satan, called the
Fiend (line 1013), provoked by the joys he has seen in the
Garden of Eden, is prevented from working his will upon Adam
and Eve by the Angelic squadron. The parallel seems closer because of the resemblance to the diction of the antistrophe of the
Ode to Mercy of two passages of the account in *Paradise Lost.*
Lines 975-6 of *P.L.,* IV, read:

[5] Dyce, p. 176, cites as a source for the passage Jonson's *Every Man out
of his Humour.*

Used to the YOAK, drawst his TRIUMPHANT WHEEL
In progress through the ROAD of Heav'n star-pav'd.

The passage in the *Ode to Mercy* reads:

When he whom ev'n our Joys provoke,
The *Fiend of Nature* join'd his YOKE,
And rush'd in Wrath to make our Isle his Prey;
Thy Form, from out thy sweet Abode,
O'ertook Him on his blasted ROAD,
And stop'd his WHEELS, and look'd his Rage away.

Again lines 897-8 of *P.L.,* IV:

let him surer BARR
HIS IRON GATES . . .

suggests "Where *Justice* BARS HER IRON TOW'R" in the ode, 24. Similar borrowings from specific passages in Milton color the imagery of *The Passions* and the *Ode on the Popular Superstitions.*[6]

Milton's diction Collins followed consistently. Though the *Ode to Peace* and the *Ode on the Death of Colonel Ross* have relatively few words drawn from Milton, *The Manners, The Passions,* and the odes *To Pity, To Fear,* and *To Simplicity* are predominantly Miltonic in diction. In short, Collins had made Milton's vocabulary his own, and in many instances he used Milton's word without consciously associating it with a given passage in the poet's work. Moreover, he employed words which have the flavor of the Miltonic idiom, though they do not appear in his poetry. Compounds like "fiery-tressed," "heav'n-left," "light-embroider'd," "time-hallow'd," "oak-crown'd," and "chast-eye'd" suggest Milton's influence, as do such words as "upthrows," "unclosing," and "undreading."

In at least two of the odes, the *Ode on the Poetical Character* and the *Ode to Evening,* and to a lesser degree in the *Ode to Liberty,* Milton's influence is felt throughout the poem—in atmosphere and tone, in suggestive imagery, and in the use of the Miltonic idiom. So typically do these poems represent Collins's assimilation of the suggestions he drew from Milton into his own imaginative pattern that they deserve detailed examination.

[6] A full list of these parallels is given in the appendix.

The *Ode on the Poetical Character* is fully and thoroughly Miltonic in substance, in imagery, and in diction. This is but appropriate in a poem which pays so lofty a tribute to Milton, and it is significant that in the poem in which Collins approaches closest to the "grand style" of Milton much of the imagery should suggest the Miltonic dignity and sublimity of *Paradise Lost* as well as the imaginative richness of the minor poems. Throughout the poem the suggestion of Milton is present and shows Collins's power to weave the images of his master into his own imaginative concept, paying him thereby the double tribute of inspiration and imitation. The first Miltonic suggestion, "love-darting Eye," line 8,[7] is more than a mere verbal echo of *Comus,* 753. It fits by suggestion as an integral part of the conceit of the girdle which only true beauty free of blot may wear, for it is a part of Comus's speech to the Lady extolling the power and use of earthly beauty. But the epode describing the birth of the Poetical Character and the weaving of the magic girdle of poetry is in itself a harmoniously woven texture of Miltonic images and phrases. The description of the joyful day of creation, 26-7, when God with Thought called to birth

> Yon tented Sky, this laughing Earth,
> And drest with Springs, and Forests tall,

has something of the spirit of *Paradise Lost,* VIII, 273-5:

> Thou Sun . . . faire Light
> And thou enlight'nd Earth, so fresh and gay,
> Ye Hills and Dales, ye Rivers, Woods, and Plaines.

Again the account of the union of Thought and Fancy, 30-8:

> Himself in some Diviner Mood,
> Retiring, sate with her alone,
> And plac'd her on his SAPHIRE THRONE,
> The whiles, the vaulted Shrine around,
> SERAPHIC WIRES were heard to sound,
> Now sublimest Triumph swelling,
> Now on Love and Mercy Dwelling;

is suggestive of two passages in Milton, resembling the first, from *At a Solemn Musick,* 3-14, more closely in spirit and diction:

[7] After "solemn Turney," 7, from *Il Penseroso,* 117.

> And to our high-raised phantasie present,
> That undisturbed Song of pure content,
> As sung before the SAPHIRE-COLOURED throne
> To him that sits thereon
> With saintly shout, and solemn Jubily,
> Where the bright Seraphim in burning row
> Their loud up-lifted Angel trumpets blow,
> And the Cherubick host in thousand quires
> Touch their immortal Harps of GOLDEN WIRES.

The second passage, *P.L.*, VI, 757-9, however, describes a "chrystal firmament" and a "saphir throne" and perhaps adds to the suggestion of Collins's source for the passage. The fancy of the "veiling Cloud" about the throne of the Almighty, although Biblical in tone, may be drawn from one of two Miltonic passages. *P.L.* III, 376-82, which describes the throne of the Almighty:

> Amidst the glorious brightness where thou sit'st
> Thron'd inaccessible, but when thou shad'st
> The full blaze of thy beams, and through a cloud
> Drawn round about thee like a radiant shrine, . . .
> . . . that brightest Seraphim
> Approach not, but with both wings veil their eyes,

seems the closer, but *P.L.*, VI, 28-9:

> . . . a voice
> From midst a golden cloud thus milde was heard

furnishes the suggestion for the image of Fancy breathing her magic notes aloud in line 38 of the ode. The phrase "the deep applauding Thunder," 44, suggesting as its does the presence of the "veiling Cloud" resembles Milton's paraphrase of Psalm LXXXI, 29-30:

> I answered thee in thunder deep
> With clouds encompass'd round.

The account of the "braided Dance" of the "shadowy Tribes of Mind" and "the bright uncounted Pow'rs Who feed on Heav'n's ambrosial Flow'rs," 47-50, is also drawn from a favorite Miltonic image, the mystical dance of the planets about the sun, described in *P.L.*, V, 178-80, and VIII, 122-5; or perhaps it

resembles the "mystical dance" of the angels about the Sacred
Hill, described in *P.L.*, V, 619-20. It is significant that Collins
has here woven the Miltonic concept into a finely original
image of his own. Incidentally the adjective "braided" is Miltonic, too, occurring in *P.L.*, IV, 349.

The symbolic account of Milton in the antistrophe of the ode
is also full of Milton's own imagery. The description 55-60:

> High on some Cliff, to Heav'n up-pil'd,
> Of rude Access, of Prospect wild,
> Where, tangled round the jealous Steep,
> Strange Shades o'erbrow the Valleys deep,
> And holy *Genii* guard the Rock,
> Its Gloomes embrown, its Springs unlock,
> While on its rich ambitious Head
> An *Eden,* like his own, lies spread,

is consciously or unconsciously an Eden like Milton's own, for
it is drawn closely after his description of Eden, *P.L.*, IV, 133-
42:

> So on he fares, and to the border comes
> Of Eden, where delicious Paradise,
> Now nearer, crowns with her enclosure green,
> As with a rural mound the champain head
> Of a steep wilderness, whose hairie sides
> With thicket overgrown, grotesque and wilde
> Access denied; and overhead up grew
> Insuperable hight of loftiest shade,
> Cedar, and Pine, and Firr, and branching Palm
> A Silvan Scene, and as the ranks ascend
> Shade above shade, a woodie Theatre
> Of stateliest view. Yet higher than their tops
> The verdurous wall of Paradise up sprung.[8]

Interwoven into Collins's description come suggestions of other
Miltonic phrases. "Tangled round the jealous Steep" suggests a
line in the *Nativity Ode,* 188, "the Nymphs in twilight shade of
tangled thickets mourn." "Embrown," 60, and "unlock," 60,
are also in the Miltonic idiom, occurring in *P.L.*, IV, 246, and
P.L., II, 852, respectively. "Rude" (*C.* 352) and "Access" (see
passage quoted), 56; "jealous" (*P.L.*, X, 478; *All.* 6), 57, also

[8] Compare also as a possible source *Arcades,* 42-83.

give a thoroughly Miltonic flavor to the descriptive passage which is intended as a tribute to that poet and a symbol of his achievement.

A further description in the antistrophe owes something in spirit to a passage in *Paradise Lost*. The picture of Milton drinking heavenly inspiration as he lies under the oak, 63-5:

> His Ev'ning Ear,
> From many a cloud that drop'd Ethereal Dew,
> Nigh spher'd in Heav'n its native Strains could hear:

especially in view of lines 55-60 of the ode, seems suggested by *P.L.,* IV, 680-8:

> how often from the steep
> Of echoing Hill or Thicket have we heard
> Celestial voices . . .
> With Heav'nly touch of instrumental sounds
> In full harmonic number join'd, their songs
> Divide the night and lift our thoughts to Heaven.

Finally the phrase "curtain'd close" in the last line of the ode seems to be a modification of "close-curtained," *Comus,* 554.

Moreover, apart from its relation to specific passages in his poetry, the diction throughout the poem suggests Milton. Words like "aright," 2, "God-like," 20, "Ecstatic," 43, are favorites in Milton as are compounds like "unrival'd," 5, "unblest," 13, "unmix'd," 22 (See *P.L.,* VI, 742), or participial adjectives like "loath'd," 13, "vaulted," 33, "sainted," 42, "hallow'd," 54, and "spher'd," 66 (*Comus,* 2-4). Miltonic compounds like "o'er-brow," 58 (not however found in Milton), also suggest the influence of the master-poet. The *Ode on the Poetical Character* is, then, in every respect a tribute to Milton: Collins literally, as he says in the ode, pursues his guiding steps. But the greatest tribute to his master lies in Collins's own imaginative power, which here reached a height and a sublimity not unworthy of Milton himself.

The *Ode to Evening,* too, abounds with reminiscences of Milton. The stanza form, the imagery, and the diction of the poem are all suggestive. Yet it is a tribute to Collins that in a poem so largely derivative as this one, the freshness of the ex-

perience, the mood of the poem, the imaginative power of its
poet are all enhanced by these suggestions of another poet's impressions of the spell of evening. Mr. Blunden has finely described the effect Collins secures by this embroidery of phrases
from other poets, phrases which have passed through a rich and
strange distillation in Collins's own imagination, yet are reminiscent of the poet who first shaped them. He says:

Besides the immediate object of this delight, Collins by allusion
recalls and honours the previous poets of evening, as Milton,
Fletcher, Shakespeare, and Spenser. He has felt, through their fancy
as through his own, that the *dramatis personæ* of Evening may be
in themselves widely different but are all made of one importance
by the fantasy of the time.[9]

Collins's achievement lies in the pleasure that these reminiscences of other poets add to a sensitive reader's imaginative
enjoyment of the poem. Collins owed most to Milton in his
allusions to evening. Knowing and admiring Milton as he did,
he could not have been insensitive to the fine pictures of evening
in *Il Penseroso,* in *Comus,* and in *Paradise Lost,* nor could he
have forgotten the spell of the pastoral atmosphere in *L'Allegro*
and in *Lycidas.* Hence the suggestions of Milton begin with the
poem itself and are felt to the end of it.

The stanza form, the unrhymed lyric stanza that Milton had
used in the translation of Horace's "Pyrrha Ode," admirably
suits the purpose of the poet, and in the use of it he has surpassed the performance of his master. One line fuses and blends
into another, one stanza melts into another as the impressions
of evening fuse and blend together. The absence of rhyme allows
many an opportunity for subtle sound effects secured by asso-
nance, by alliteration, and by rich use of tone color and onomat-
apoeia. The form of the poem, then, is as Miltonic as its substance.

The mood and spirit of Collins's poem might almost be said
to have developed from two passages in *Paradise Lost.* Lines
598-9 of Book IV:

[9] *Poems of William Collins,* p. 171.

> Now came still Evening on, and Twilight gray
> Had in her sober Liverie all things clad

suggest not only the setting and tone of the poem, but almost furnish the hint for the shadowy figure of Evening herself. Lines 646-7 of the same book:

> sweet the coming on
> Of Grateful Evening milde . . .

hymn the "genial loved Return" of the goddess as does Collins. But the reminiscences of Milton are more direct and sharp than this. The first line:

> If ought of OATEN STOP, or PASTORAL Song,

is almost an echo of *Comus,* 345:

> Or sound of PASTORAL REED with OATEN STOPS,

and strikes the keynote of the poem. The *Ode to Evening* is, like *Comus* and *Lycidas,* in the pastoral tradition. Lines 5-8 subtly suggest the imagery and diction of Milton:

> while now the BRIGHT HAIR'D Sun
> Sits in yon western Tent, whose cloudy SKIRTS,
> With BREDE ETHEREAL wove,
> O'er-hang his wavy Bed.

"Bright hair'd" is a direct echo of *Il Penseroso,* 23. The image in the next two lines suggests *P.L.,* IV, 592-7, especially:

> The Clouds that on his Western Throne attend.

Again "skirts" is familiarly associated in Milton with clouds, as in *P.L.,* V, 187:

> . . . till the sun paint your FLEECY SKIRTS

or in *P.L.,* XI, 878:

> The fluid SKIRTS of that same watrie cloud.

Further, "Brede" (in Milton "Braid") and "ethereal" are also favorite words in Milton. Again in lines 11 and 12 of the ode there is an image from Milton though there is a suggestion of Shakespeare in it too. The phrase:

> Or where the Beetle WINDS
> His small but sullen HORN,

ɔrings to mind *Lycidas,* 28:

> What time the gray-flie WINDS her sultry HORN.

Again the phrase "Maid compos'd," 15, uses the adjective as Milton employs it in *P.L.,* XII, 596, and in *P.R.,* II, 108. "Un-seemly," 18, also lends a Miltonic flavor to the passage. Lines 21-8 of the ode represent a fine weaving of Miltonic idiom and Miltonic mythology. "Thy folding Star," 21, recalls *Comus,* 93:

> The STAR that bids the shepherd FOLD.

"Paly Circlet," 22, suggests *P.L.,* V, 169, "bright circlet." The "warning Lamp," 22, recalls *P.L.,* VIII, 519-20:

> and bid haste the evening Starr
> On his Hill top, to light the bridal Lamp.

And the whole spirit of the passage suggests the *Ode on the Morning of Christ's Nativity,* 240-2:

> Heavn's youngest teemed star
> Hath fixt her polisht Car
> Her sleeping Lord with Handmaid Lamp attending.

There is, too, a hint of the sober mood of *Lycidas* in "many a Nymph who wreaths her Brows with Sedge," 25, suggesting as it does the "bonnet sedge" of *Lycidas,* 105. The weaving of Miltonic phrase and atmosphere in the passage cannot but build up by suggestion the sense of awe and quiet devotion so frequently felt in Milton's own descriptions of evening, deeply appropriate to the "softened Strain" in which Collins would hymn the favorite name of the goddess. The fine description, lines 29-32:

> Then lead, calm Vot'ress, where some sheety Lake,
> Cheers the lone heath, or some time-hallow'd pile,
> Or up-land fallows grey,

is again an embroidery of Miltonic phrase. For the epithet "calm Vot'ress," 29, associated with Evening comes directly from *Comus,* 188-9:

> . . . the gray-hooded EEV'N
> Like a sad VOTARIST in Palmer's Weed.

The "upland fallows," 31, is from *L'Allegro*, 72. The next two lines of the ode, 33-4:

> But when chill blust'ring winds, or driving rain,
> Forbid my willing feet, . . .

represent again a fine weaving of Miltonic phrases. "Chill blust'ring winds" comes directly from *P.L.*, II, 286, "the sound of blustering winds"; "willing feet" occurs in *P.L.*, III, 73. The rest of the ode, has the suggestion of Milton, though except for "Hamlets brown," 37 (*All.*, 92) the borrowings are not so direct. But "dusky," 40, "breathing," 42, "sallow," 45, are favorite Miltonic adjectives, and "sylvan Shed," 49, owes something to "silvan Lodge," *P.L.*, V, 376. "Time-hallow'd," 30, "dim-discover'd," 37, and "rose-lip'd," 50, are compounds in the Miltonic manner. Yet in spite of the abundance of suggestions from Milton one feels that they are so subtly woven into the poet's own imaginative experience that they are used instinctively and appropriately. They are so much part of the poet that they almost cease to touch us out of their context.

The *Ode to Liberty*, too, is full of suggestions drawn from Milton, particularly from *Comus* and from *Lycidas*. The first fine image in the poem, lines 3-5, describing the youths

> whose Locks divinely spreading,
> Like vernal Hyacinths in sullen Hue,
> At once the Breath of Fear and Virtue shedding,

owes something to Milton, though it has many other possible sources. It suggests the description of Adam in *P.L.*, IV, 300 ff.:

> Hyacintin Locks
> Round from his parted forelock manly hung
> Clustring. . . .

though equally plausible is the suggestion which Mr. Bronson quotes from the Colchester edition of Collins, 1796:

On ceremonious occasions the Spartans used to adorn their heads with hyacinthine chaplets. (See Theocritus, Idyl 18.) This custom probably suggested the comparison.[10]

---

[10] Bronson, *Poems of William Collins*, p. 105. Compare also *Comus*, 105-6. Mr. Blunden, *Poems of Collins*, p. 168, quotes an illuminating passage from "a schoolbook known to Collins" that the privileges of Sparta's soldiers were

While the diction of the rest of the strophe and first epode is suggestively Miltonic, there is no direct image drawn from Milton. Line 42:

> Strike, louder strike th' ennobling Strings

does, however, suggest *Lycidas,* 17:

> Begin, and somewhat loudly sweep the string.

"Lydian Measure," 47, is, of course, directly from *L'Allegro.* But in the antistrophe and the second epode both imagery and diction become strikingly suggestive of Milton. Several details in the description of the "wide wild Storm" which separated the coast of France from England are drawn from passages in Milton. The account, 73-5:

> Till all the BANDED WEST at once 'gan rise,
> A wide wild Storm ev'n Nature's self confounding,
> With'ring her Giant Sons with strange uncouth Surprise,

seems to be a composite picture drawn from two passages in Milton. "Banded West" has always remained unexplained, although it has in it the implication of the influence of those malignant airy beings of which Collins was so fond. But Collins might have had in mind the passage in *Paradise Lost,* Book VI, which describes the rebellion of Satan and the war in Heaven. In this connection lines 78-86 of Book VI are particularly pertinent:

> at last
> FAR IN THE HORIZON OF THE NORTH appeer'd
> From skirt to skirt a fierie Region, stretcht
> In battailous aspect. . . .
> The BANDED Powers of Satan hasting on
> With furious expedition.

Considering that the preternatural combat which shakes heaven's foundations immediately follows this passage, the implication is obvious. In *Paradise Lost,* the malignant powers of Satan banded in the North of Heaven caused a tremendous upheaval. In Collins's poem the malignant powers of the air (of which Satan is

"to have costly Arms, and fine Cloaths, and frequently perfume their Hair." But the phrasing of the passage is suggestively Miltonic. "Divinely," "vernal," and "sullen" are all favorite words in Milton. See also *Odyssey,* VI, 230-1.

prince) banded in the West and caused a preternatural storm which shook Earth to its foundations.[11] And though such an antiquarian as Collins must have read in many an old historian of the giant race in prehistoric Britain, he might very naturally have remembered reading in the first book of Milton's *History of Britain* the words of Diana, who appeared in a vision to Brutus sleeping before her altar:

> Brutus, far to the West in th' Ocean wide
> Beyond the Realm of Gaul, a land there lies,
> Sea-girt it lies, where giants dwelt of old.

Moreover, the diction of the whole passage in the ode has a Miltonic flavor—"confounding," "with'ring," and "uncouth" are all found in *Paradise Lost;* "Giant Sons" comes directly from *P.L.,* I, 778. The passage following, 76 to the end of the antistrophe, is an embroidery of Miltonic phrase and image. The description of the upheaval caused by the storm:

> This pillar'd Earth so firm and wide,
>   By Winds and inward Labors torn,
> In Thunders dread was push'd aside,
>   And down the should'ring Billows born,

suggests the confusion caused by the war in Heaven in Book VI of *Paradise Lost.* But "this PILLAR'D Earth so firm and wide" seems to come from *P.R.,* IV, 455:

> As dangerous to the PILLAR'D FRAME OF HEAVEN
> Or to the Earth's dark basis underneath,

although "the PILLAR'D firmament" occurs also in *Comus,* 598. *P.L.,* X, 664-7, seems, too, a possible source for the whole passage from 70-9:

> To the Winds they set
> Thir corners, when with bluster to confound
> Sea, Aire, and Shoar, the Thunder when to rowle
> With terror through the dark Aereal Halls,

[11] Mr. Woodhouse makes the plausible suggestion that Collins was influenced in the passage by his reading in Thomas Nash. See "Collins and the Creative Imagination," Univ. of Toronto *Studies in English,* p. 105. For a similar indication of the malignant power of the West cf. *Ode on the Popular Superstitions,* 146.

though it directly embodies the imagery only of lines 77-8. "Inward" (used in a similar sense in *P.L.*, VI, 861) and "should'ring" (*P.R.*, II, 462) are used in a Miltonic sense.

An account of the formation of the islands of Mona and Wight follows the description of the wide wild storm. This passage is richly suggestive of *Comus* and *Lycidas,* for in both of these poems there is an atmosphere of the remote and traditional. The passage, 80-4 of the *Ode to Liberty:*

> And see, like Gems, her laughing Train,
>   The little Isles on ev'ry side,
> *Mona,* once hid from those who search the Main,
> Where thousand Elfin Shapes abide,
> And *Wight* who checks the west'ring Tide,

is again a composite of Miltonic images. The first two lines almost directly echo *Comus,* 21-3:

> all the SEA-GIRT ILES
> That like to rich and various gems inlay
> The unadorned bosom of the deep.

The parallel becomes closer when one considers that Milton is probably referring to the same islands in *Comus.* Though the next three lines are undoubtedly drawn from Collins's wealth of reading in such books as Camden's *Britannia* and diverse other histories and books of tradition, he must surely have remembered Milton's reference to Mona, *Lycidas,* 65, for two lines later he mentions:

> Wight who checks the WEST'RING Tide

in which "west'ring" is directly borrowed from *Lycidas,* 84.

The second epode begins with a description of the shrine of Liberty which in Druid days was in Albion's isle. The first four lines, 89-92 of the poem, suggest the haunt of Comus and the sylvan atmosphere of Milton's poem:

> Then, too, 'tis said, an hoary Pile
> 'Midst the green NAVEL of our Isle,
> Thy Shrine in some religious WOOD,
> O Soul-enforcing Goddess stood.

The suggestion is reinforced by line 90, which comes directly from *Comus,* 520:

> Within the NAVIL of this hideous WOOD.[12]

The rest of the second epode is full of Miltonic words: "infuse," 101, "braided," 103, "paving," 104, "pavilion'd," 105 (a direct suggestion of *P.L.,* XI, 215), "consorted,"[13] 111, "fabric," 116, "mold," 123, "emblaze," 124, "grav'd," 127, are all found in Milton and are used as Milton employs them. Several compounds, which do not occur in Milton, suggest the poet's imitation of Miltonic diction. Instances are: "fiery-tressed," 97, "heav'n-left," 99, "light-embroider'd," 104, and "sphere-found," 117. Finally lines 139-40 directly echo a passage in *Lycidas,* though the image in Collins has been considered infelicitous.[14] Surely the lines:

> Our Youths, enamour'd of the Fair,
> Play with the TANGLES of her HAIR,

closely resemble *Lycidas,* 68-9:

> To sport with Amaryllis in the shade,
> Or with the TANGLES of Neaera's HAIR.

But one should remember in this connection the lines in Lovelace's *To Althea from Prison:*

> While I lie TANGLED in her HAIR,
> And fettered to her eye,
> The gods that wanton in the air
> Know no such liberty.

In writing an *Ode to Liberty* Collins may conceivably have been thinking of Lovelace's lines rather than Milton's, for the theme of *To Althea* is closer to Collins's subject in the ode. Though this

---

[12] But see *Poly-olbion,* Song XXIII, 147, for the same use of "navel," and cf. *Odyssey,* I, 50.

[13] Cf. *Ode to Liberty,* 11-12, with *Ode on the Morning of Christ's Nativity,* 65-70.

[14] It is so considered by J. M. Murry in his essay "The Poetry of William Collins" in *Countries of the Mind,* pp. 79-100, "To apply to Liberty, the Lady who shall rule the West, the phrase which Milton used of those who preferred the company of Amaryllis and Neaera to the last infirmity of noble mind. *Curiosa infelicitas!*" Of this passage Mr. Garrod, *Collins,* p. 90, cries: "Horrible! 'Were it not better done' not to meddle with Milton at all than so to use him?"

possibility accounts for the appearance of the phrase, it does not soften the infelicity of the image.

The influence of Milton on Collins is, then, of signal importance. Milton was his ideal poet. He saw the pastoral scene as Milton had observed it. His fondness for the traditions of folklore, his portrayal of the remote and the antiquarian were colored by Milton's view of them. Collins appropriated and modified the verse forms Milton had used in *L'Allegro, Il Penseroso,* the *Ode on the Morning of Christ's Nativity,* and the translation of the "Pyrrha Ode." He copied many a Miltonic image and personification, sometimes fusing the borrowed image with his own imaginative concept as he did so successfully in the odes to *Evening* and *On the Poetical Character.* Collins must have known Milton by heart so thoroughly that he cannot always have been conscious that the word or phrase he chose was first Milton's. He knew not only the familiar minor poems, but he was acquainted with such relatively slight pieces as *At a Solemn Musick* and the paraphrase of Psalm CXXXVI. He knew thoroughly *Paradise Lost* and *Paradise Regained.* From all of Milton's poems he culled images and wove them into his own imaginative scheme. He tried, sometimes too closely, to follow Milton's idiom. In every sense his trembling feet pursued the guiding steps of his master.

III

POPE AND DRYDEN

ALEXANDER POPE died in 1744, two years before the *Odes Descriptive and Allegoric* appeared, two years after the publication of the *Persian Eclogues,* and shortly after the *Epistle to Hanmer* was printed. The date of Pope's death marks a transition in Collins's poetry, for at about that time he turned from imitating Pope to following in the footsteps of Milton. Collins must have seen Pope when he visited Winchester School. At any rate he read carefully the works of the greatest living poet of his day, and began by copying the manner of Pope, the representative of an older tradition, before he turned to the imitation of Milton, whom his own generation set up as the model and ideal poet. In the poems Collins wrote in the heroic couplet, the *Persian Eclogues* and the *Epistle to Hanmer,* the influence of Pope is most marked, but even in the odes themselves there are occasional indications that Collins continued somewhat in the tradition of Pope in spite of his stronger dependence on Milton.

The *Persian Eclogues,* Collins's earliest poetry, are closely modeled after the *Pastorals* of Pope in form, substance, and diction, but they show, too, the influence of *Windsor Forest,* which is also in the pastoral manner. There are four *Pastorals* of Pope as there are four of the *Persian Eclogues,* and both poets employ the heroic couplet. Moreover, the time element is similar in both groups of poems. The first of the *Persian Eclogues,* like Pope's *Spring,* takes place at morning; the second, like Pope's *Summer,* is set at noon; the third, like Pope's *Autumn,* suggests the evening time; the fourth, like Pope's *Winter,* occurs at night. Collins further imitates Pope's use of the four seasons by making the scene of each eclogue typical of some aspect of Persian topography. The first eclogue presents a valley near Bagdad; the second fittingly describes the desert; the third occurs in a forest; the fourth on a mountain in Circassia. The didactic element so

marked in *Eclogues I* and *II*, and evident to a lesser degree in
Eclogues III and *IV*, is in the manner of Pope. The ring of the
couplets throughout Collins's *Eclogues* suggests the balanced
and end-stopped lines of Pope, though there is often a graceful
and delicate music of Collins's own, particularly in *Eclogue III*.
For the rest, Collins imitates Pope's diction more than his
imagery, although some of the didactic passages are obviously
drawn from Pope. The *Eclogues* show more consistently the
influence of Pope than any of the later poems of Collins. A
number of passages echo the imagery of one of the *Pastorals*
or of *Windsor Forest*. Line 61 of the *First Eclogue:*

> Cold is her Breast Like Flow'rs that drink the Dew,

echoes a couplet in Pope's *Second Pastoral*, 31-2:

> Once I was skill'd in ev'ry herb that grew
> And every plant that drinks the morning dew.

Again the sentiment in lines 49-50 of the eclogue:

> The balmy Shrub, for ye shall love our Shore,
> By *Ind'* excell'd or *Araby* no more,

is suggested by *Windsor Forest*, 29-30:

> Let India boast her plants, nor envy we
> The weeping amber, or the balmy tree.

Moreover Selim's useful lesson for the fair and young, admon-
ishing the Persian Dames to cultivate each softer virtue and each
tender passion, "the lov'd Perfections of a Female Mind," rather
than to trust "beauty's feeble Ray," lines 20-42, seems copied
after the grave Clarissa's advice in *The Rape of the Lock*, V,
9-34, which also recommends virtue as a necessary complement
to beauty.

The *Second Eclogue*, the lament of Hassan, the camel driver,
that he has preferred gold and silver and "far-fatiguing Trade"
to peace and love, is again drawn from Pope, at least in its didactic element. The germ of the whole eclogue as well as its
moral comes from the *First Epistle of the First Book of Horace
—To Bolingbroke*, 69-80:

To either India see the merchant fly,
Scared at the spectre of pale poverty!
See him, with pains of body, pangs of soul,
Burn through the tropic, freeze beneath the pole.
Wilt thou do nothing for a nobler end,
Nothing, to make philosophy thy friend? . . .
Here Wisdom calls: "Seek virtue first, be bold!
As gold to silver, virtue is to gold."[1]

And at least part of the imagery of the eclogue owes something to a suggestion in the *Third Pastoral*. Lines 55-8 of the eclogue:

By Hunger rous'd, he scours the groaning Plain,
Gaunt Wolves and sullen Tygers in his Train:
Before them Death with Shrieks directs their Way,
Fills the wild Yell, and leads them to their Prey,

resemble lines 85-9 of Pope's pastoral:

I know thee, Love! on foreign Mountains bred,
Wolves gave thee suck and savage Tigers fed.
Thou wert from Aetna's burning entrails torn,
Got by fierce whirlwinds, and in thunder born.

Again line 66 of the eclogue:

From LUST of Wealth, and DREAD of DEATH secure;

is taken almost directly from *Epistle to Robert, Earl of Oxford,* 26:

The LUST of lucre and the DREAD of DEATH.

In the *Third* and *Fourth Eclogues* also there are occasional direct suggestions of Pope. Lines 3 and 4 of the *Third Eclogue:*

While Ev'ning Dews enrich the glitt'ring Glade,
And the tall Forests cast a longer Shade,

closely resemble the *Third Pastoral,* 99-100:

When falling dews with spangles deck'd the glade
And the low sun had lengthen'd every shade.

And in spirit and sentiment, at least, lines 37-50 of the eclogue resemble the famous passage in the *Second Pastoral,* 71-85, set

[1] Compare the passage particularly with 31-48 of *Eclogue II*. Pope expresses a similar sentiment in the *Sixth Epistle of the First Book of Horace—To Mr. Murray,* 69 ff.

to music by Handel. In the *Fourth Eclogue* there are also suggestions of Pope. The description of the midnight hour, 5-6:

> What Time the Moon had hung her Lamp on high,
> And past in Radiance, thro' the cloudless Sky:

suggests the line in the *Fourth Pastoral,* 5:

> The moon, serene in glory, mounts the sky,

although Collins's phrasing is Miltonic. A similar echo occurs
in line 30 of the *Eclogue:*

> And leave to ruffian Bands THEIR FLEECY CARE,

which resembles the *First Pastoral,* 19:

> Poured o'er the whitening vale THEIR FLEECY CARE.[2]

though the phrase is of common occurrence. Moreover, line 56
of the eclogue:

> Their Eyes' BLUE LANGUISH, and their golden Hair!

recasts a line from Pope's *Iliad,* XVIII, 50:

> And the BLUE LANGUISH of soft Alia's eye.

For the rest, the diction of the eclogues is characteristic of the
pastoral manner of Pope. "Murmuring," "springs," "verdant,"
"fragrant," "balmy," "breeze," "green," "bowers," "whisper-
ing," "groves," "shades," "sweets," "glade," "vales," "gales,"
"fountains," occur frequently and characteristically both in the
pastorals and in the eclogues. Collins's manner, then, in the
eclogues was thoroughly imitative and Pope was his most significant model.

The *Epistle to Hanmer* is, in a sense, Collins's *Essay on Criticism,* and while in substance it owes more to Dryden's *Essay of
Dramatic Poesy* and to Spence's *Dialogues on the Odyssey* than
to Pope's *Essay on Criticism,* it is done in the manner of Pope,
in couplets that resemble Pope's rather than Dryden's in cadence.
There are several suggestions of Pope in the poem. The account
of the dramatist's power to rouse the spectator's feeling for the

---

[2] Collins also uses "whitening." See *Eclogue IV,* 49. As a possible parallel
cf. 35-38 of the eclogue with *An Essay on Criticism,* 534 ff.

tragic scene he witnesses, 33-8, 87-104, echoes the sentiment of the *Prologue to the Tragedy of Cato*. Again, though the device is more or less conventional, the passage describing the progress of drama from earliest Greece to the time of Shakespeare, lines 31-85 of the *Epistle*, seems modeled after the passage in *An Essay on Criticism*, 643-744, which traces the history of criticism from Athens and Rome to England in the time of Queen Anne. The power of the dramatist over the emotions of the spectator, lines 37-8 of the epistle:

> Line after Line, our pitying Eyes o'erflow,
> Trace the sad Tale, and own another's Woe,

suggested again in 90-105, shows that already Collins is following Pope's distinction between the "poet" and the "man of rhymes," a concept he was to develop more fully in his *Ode on the Poetical Character*. The first line of the passage is, moreover, an echo of *Eloisa to Abelard*, 35. Pope's definition of the Poet in the *Epistle to Augustus*, 341-7, is in the spirit and sentiment of the passages in Collins's poem:

> 'Tis he, who gives my breast a thousand pains,
> Can make me feel each passion that he feigns;
> Enrage, compose, with more than magic art,
> With pity and with terror tear my heart;
> And snatch me o'er the earth or thro' the air,
> To Thebes, to Athens, when he will, and where.

At least one echo of *The Rape of the Lock* also occurs in the poem. Lines 109-10 of the epistle describe:

> Where Swains contented own the quiet Scene,
> And twilight Fairies tread the CIRCLED GREEN.

The passage resembles closely *The Rape of the Lock*, I, 31-2:

> Of airy Elves by moonlight shadows seen,
> The silver token, and the CIRCLED GREEN.

Though the piece is in the metrical form and in the diction of Pope, there is not as much suggestion of his influence in the thought and imagery of the poem as one would expect.

In the volume of *Odes*, 1746, and in the later *Ode on the Death of Mr. Thomson*, there are occasional reminiscences of

Pope. But while the lines of the odes are frequently balanced and end-stopped as are Pope's couplets, Collins does not again employ the heroic measure. Nor does he, after the *Epistle to Hanmer,* follow Pope in didactic purpose. In only three of the odes, *The Manners, Ode to a Lady on the Death of Colonel Ross,* and *Ode Written at the Beginning of the Year 1746,* is the influence of Pope significantly felt. In the other odes there are, however, phrases or images that suggest Pope.

In *The Manners,* regarded as the earliest of the odes in point of composition, there are naturally suggestions of Pope, from whose influence the poet was then just turned by the stronger spell of Milton. There are four such reminiscences of Pope in *The Manners.* Strikingly enough, they are drawn largely from Pope's later works, the *Essay on Man* and *The Dunciad,* rather than from the *Pastorals, Windsor Forest,* or *An Essay on Criticism.* The sources are significant, too, in that while weighing his own possibilities for writing satire Collins should have remembered phrases from *The Dunciad,* and while expressing his hope of reading the native heart in man, he should have recalled the *Essay on Man.* Lines 13-14 of *The Manners:*

> Farewell the Porch whose Roof is seen,
> Arch'd with th' enlivening Olive's Green:

suggest *Dunciad* IV, 489-90:

> While through poetic scenes the genius roves,
> Or wanders wild in academic groves,

particularly in view of the idea expressed in the first twelve lines of *The Manners.* Again Collins's desire to learn from Nature, 29-30:

> And gazing oft her Mirror true,
> By turns each shifting Image view!

seems drawn from the *Essay on Man,* IV, 393:

> For wit's false mirror held up Nature's light.

Further Collins is echoing Pope's desire in the *Essay on Man,* I, 14, to

> catch the living manners as they rise

when he says in 41-2 of *The Manners:*

> Behold before her Musing Eyes,
> The countless *Manners* round her rise.

The passage immediately following, 43-4:

> While ever varying as they pass,
> To some *Contempt* applies her Glass:

is again drawn from the *Dunciad,* IV, 533-4:

> Kind self-conceit to some her glass applies,
> Which no one looks in with another's eyes.

It was but natural that Collins should recall Pope in dealing with the manners as in the same poem he recalled Le Sage when he was treating of humor.

The *Ode to a Lady on the Death of Colonel Ross* is modeled closely after Pope's *Elegy to the Memory of an Unfortunate Lady.* Both Pope's poem and Collins's are elegiac, both lament the death and burial of a friend in a foreign soil, and both describe a simple but hallowed grave. Both have a tone of tender and sympathetic melancholy. In imagery and sentiment, lines 13-24 of the *Ode to a Lady* bear the closest resemblance to the *Elegy to the Memory of an Unfortunate Lady:*

> By Rapid *Scheld's* descending Wave
> His Country's Vows shall bless the Grave,
>   Where'er the Youth is laid:
> That sacred Spot the Village Hind
> With ev'ry sweetest Turf shall bind,
>   And Peace protect the Shade.
>
> Blest Youth, regardful of thy Doom,
> Aërial Hands shall build thy Tomb,
>   With shadowy Trophies crown'd:
> Whilst *Honor* bath'd in Tears shall rove
> To sigh thy Name thro' ev'ry Grove,
>   And call his Heros round.

This passage represents a modification of lines 61-7 of Pope's *Elegy:*

> What though no sacred earth allow thee room,
> Nor hallowed dirge be muttered o'er thy tomb?

Yet shall thy grave with rising flowers be drest,
And the green turf lie lightly on thy breast:
There shall the morn her earliest tears bestow,
There the first roses of the year shall blow;
While Angels with their silver wings o'ershade
The ground, now sacred by thy reliques made.

The *Ode Written in the Beginning of the Year 1746,* itself modified from the *Ode to a Lady,* reflects the same source. The same passage must have suggested lines 2-6 of the *Ode Written in the Beginning of the Year 1746:*

When *Spring,* with dewy Fingers cold,
Returns to deck their hallow'd Mold,
She there shall dress a sweeter Sod,
Than *Fancy's* feet have ever Trod.

The first two lines of the second stanza:

By FAIRY HANDS their Knell is rung,
By FORMS unseen their Dirge is sung;

have the cadence and suggestion of lines 51-4 of Pope's *Elegy:*

By FOREIGN HANDS thy dying eyes were closed,
By FOREIGN HANDS thy decent limbs composed,
By FOREIGN HANDS thy humble grave adorned,
By strangers honoured, and by strangers mourned.

Collins undoubtedly had the sentiment and the substance of Pope's poem in his mind, but he has so condensed and crystallized it that one regards his treatment of the idea as finished and perfect in itself.

In the remaining poems the influence of Pope is relatively slight, but it is felt occasionally in a phrase or in a striking image. In the *Ode to Pity,* for example, lines 37-8:

There let me oft, retir'd by Day,
In Dreams of Passion melt away,

might have been a recollection of *Eloisa to Abelard,* 221-2:

To sounds of heavenly harps she dies away,
And melts in visions of eternal day.[3]

---

[3] Cf. *Ode to Fear,* 45: "Yet all the Thunders of the Scene are thine!" with Pope, *Prologue to a Play for Mr. Dennis,* 16: "And shook the stage with thunders all his own."

The concluding thought of the *Ode to Simplicity,* 51-3:

> I only seek to find thy temp'rate Vale:
> Where oft my Reed might sound
> To Maids and Shepherds round,

seems an echo of a passage in the *First Pastoral,* 11-12:

> O let my Muse her slender reed inquire,
> Till in your native shades you turn the lyre.

In the *Ode on the Poetical Character* there are three slight suggestions of Pope. The phrase "love-darting eye," 8, occurs in *Comus,* but is also found in the *Elegy to the Memory of an Unfortunate Lady,* 34. Again line 60:

> Its Gloomes embrown, its SPRINGS UNLOCK

while Miltonic in character, suggests *Windsor Forest,* 4:

> UNLOCK your SPRINGS, and open all your shades.

Finally lines 70-6, which express Collins's aspiration to follow in the footsteps of Milton, seem to echo *An Essay on Criticism,* 195-8:

> Oh may some spark of your celestial fire,
> The last, the meanest of your sons inspire,
> (That on weak wings, from far, pursues your flights;
> Glows while he reads, but trembles as he writes).

The idea is something of a commonplace in poetry, but it is significant that Pope is appealing to the triumphant bards of earlier days, as Collins is addressing his ideal poet, the Poetical Character.

Again in the *Ode to Liberty* one image comes directly from Pope and represents an interesting transposition of detail on Collins's part. Line 72 of the ode:

> Where *Orcas* HOWLS, his WOLFISH Mountains rounding;

is drawn directly from the *First Epistle of the Second Book of Horace—To Augustus,* 323-4:

> Loud as the WOLVES, on ORCAS' stormy steep,
> HOWL to the roarings of the northern deep.

In the *Ode to Evening,* too, Collins must have remembered one passage of *Eloisa to Abelard.* Lines 159-62:

> The DYING GALES that part upon the trees,
> The lakes that quiver to the curling breeze;
> No more these scenes my meditation aid,
> Or lull to rest the visionary maid,

are harmonious with Collins's own mood in the poem, and he weaves at least one suggestive phrase from Pope into his picture when he writes, 3-4:

> Like thy own solemn Springs,   •
> Thy Springs and DYING GALES.

And a passage from *Windsor Forest* may have colored the portrait of Chearfulness in *The Passions.* Lines 70-72 of *The Passions,* describing:

> ... A Nymph of healthiest Hue,
> Her BOW a-cross her Shoulder flung,
> HER BUSKINS GEM'D WITH MORNING DEW,

echo *Windsor Forest,* 169-70:

> Here arm'd with SILVER BOWS AT EARLY DAWN,
> Her BUSKIN'D virgins traced the DEWY lawn.

In the later poems, the *Ode on the Death of Mr. Thomson* and the *Dirge in Cymbeline,* there are several suggestions of Pope. Richmond and its environs, the scene of the *Ode on the Death of Mr. Thomson,* Pope had already described in his *Imitation of Spenser:*

> Ne Richmond's self, from whose tall front are ey'd,
> Vales, spires, meandering streams, and Windsor's towery pride.

Collins follows Pope in most of these details. The figure in lines 3-4 of the poem:

> The year's best sweets shall duteous rise
> To deck its Poet's sylvan grave![4]

---

[4] Compare as a possible source for the passage, *First Pastoral,* 99-100:
> The turf with rural dainties shall be crown'd,
> While opening blooms diffuse their sweets around.

is suggestive of Pope's phrasing, as are lines 17-18:

> And oft as Ease and Health retire
> To breezy lawn, or forest deep.

Stanza ten has the conventional atmosphere of the pastoral of Pope though it follows no definite passage. Finally in the *Song from Shakespeare's Cymbeline* there is a closer resemblance to the idiom of Pope. Lines 2-4:

> Soft maids and village hinds shall BRING
> Each op'ning sweet of EARLIEST BLOOM,
> And rifle all the BREATHING SPRING,

are drawn from lines 23-4 of Pope's *Messiah:*

> See Nature hastes her EARLIEST WREATHS to BRING,
> With all the incense of the BREATHING SPRING.

Collins turned to Pope first as his model in form and diction, in the *Persian Eclogues* and the *Epistle to Hanmer,* written while Pope was still alive. Although he had given his allegiance thoroughly to Milton by 1746, he did not entirely outgrow the influence of Pope. It persisted in the form of a continued regularity in verse-making, though he abandoned the couplet after 1743. Pope's influence colored his diction so that all through his writing there is an artificiality, not entirely the result of his Miltonic manner. Further he was constantly influenced by the pastoral tone of Pope. Besides this the *Elegy on the Death of an Unfortunate Lady* suggested to Collins the tone and something of the cadence of *Ode Written at the Beginning of the Year 1746,* and his reminiscence of his reading in Pope furnished an occasional image in the other odes.[5]

---

[5] Aside from "bold design," 180 (cf. *Essay on Criticism,* 136, "he checks the bold design,"), there is no direct evidence of the influence of Pope in the *Ode on the Popular Superstitions.* Pope was, however, interested in some of the eerie and supernatural aspects of a primitive people if one judge by a passage in *The Temple of Fame,* 100 ff., where he describes how Brachmans

> call'd th' unbodied shades
> To midnight banquets in the glimm'ring glades;
> Made visionary fabrics round them rise,
> And airy spectres skim before their eyes.

Pope, then, anticipated Collins in this sort of eerie detail. (See on Pope's Romanticism, Stevenson, S. W., "Romantic Tendencies in Pope," *ELH,* Sept. 1934, pp. 126-155.) For such "graveyard" atmosphere Collins turned to a contemporary poet, cf. *Pop. Super.,* 150-154, with Blair's *Grave,* 24-26.

Compared with his devotion to Milton and Pope Collins's allegiance to John Dryden was relatively slight. Only in two poems, the *Epistle to Hanmer* and *The Passions,* both works in Dryden's style, is Collins's debt to him significant. Collins first followed Dryden in the *Epistle to Hanmer,* which draws suggestions from two of Dryden's epistles in verse, that *To the Earl of Roscommon* and the *Epistle to Sir Godfrey Kneller.* Dryden's *To the Earl of Roscommon on his Excellent Essay of Translated Verse,* traces the progress of arts and infant science from Greece to Rome, shows its development in Italy and France and ends in Britain, 24-7:

> and Britain last
> In manly sweetness all the rest surpassed.
> The wit of Greece, the gravity of Rome,
> Appeared exalted in the British loom.

The *Epistle to Hanmer* traces a similar progress of the drama culminating in the plays of Shakespeare, 56-60:

> But Heav'n, still rising in its Works, decreed
> The perfect Boast of Time should last succeed.
> The beauteous Union must appear at length,
> Of *Tuscan* Fancy, and *Athenian* Strength.

The closest parallel in diction occurs in the passages describing the Renaissance. Dryden's account of:

> Italy reviving from the trance
> Of VANDAL, GOTH, and MONKISH Ignorance,

lines 15-16, is echoed in the *Epistle to Hanmer,* 35-6:

> As arts expired, resistless Dulness rose;
> GOTHS, PRIESTS, or VANDALS—all were learning's foes.[6]

A final point of similarity is that Dryden is praising the work of Roscommon as a translator, and Collins is commending Hanmer as an editor.

The *Epistle to Sir Godfrey Kneller* traces the progress of painting as Collins's verse-letter follows the development of tragedy. Lines 35-6:

[6] This is in the Dodsley version. But compare also *An Essay on Criticism,* 683-692.

> By slow degrees the godlike art advanced,
> As man grew polished, picture was enhanced,

resemble lines 29-30 of the *Epistle to Hanmer:*

> Each rising Art by slow Gradation moves,
> Toils builds on Toil, and Age on Age improves.

The idea is, however, something of a formula in "progress" poems. But the kinship of the arts of painting and drama and the suggestion that a painter might make the characters of the drama live through his art is common to both poems, although the idea was familiar enough to Collins from his reading of Spence.[7] It is reasonable, however, to suppose that Collins as a young student of Oxford should turn to Dryden as a model when he essayed a critical verse-letter of the sort in which Dryden excelled.[8]

The Passions, An Ode for Music with its mention of "Caecilia's mingled World of Sound" naturally suggests the two odes of Dryden, *A Song for Saint Cecilia's Day* and *Alexander's Feast.* Collins owes something to both of the odes, but neither in imaginative concept nor in verbal echo is *The Passions* as close to Dryden's odes as one might suspect. Perhaps the theme of Collins's ode is found in lines 16-24 of *A Song for Saint Cecilia's Day,* though it is typical of poems written for the occasion:

> What passion cannot Music raise and quell?
> When Jubal struck the chorded shell,
> His listening brethren stood around,
> And, wondering, on their faces fell
> To worship that celestial sound.
> Less than a god they thought there could not dwell
> Within the hollow of that shell
> That spoke so sweetly and so well. . . .

---

[7] Cf. *Epistle to Kneller,* 166-73, with *Epistle to Hanmer,* 119 ff.
[8] Cf. line 112 of the *Epistle to Hanmer:*
> And Spring diffusive decks th' enchanted isle,

with Dryden's *Prologue to the Tempest,* 17-18:
> The innocence and beauty, which did smile
> In Fletcher, grew on this enchanted isle.

The Passions thronged around the Magic Cell of Music are moved as are Jubal's brethren. Dryden next describes the passions which Music raises and quells; Collins tells how each Passion would prove his own "expressive Power" in music. The shell, the trumpet, the drum, the violin, the lyre, and, of course, the organ are instruments common to both poems; one might, however, anticipate some similarity here. But some of the Passions themselves must have been suggested to Collins from Dryden's poem. Fear and Anger are linked together in *The Passions* as they are in *A Song for Saint Cecilia's Day*—"shrill notes of anger and mortal alarms." "Despair" follows next in *The Passions* with "woeful measures"; in Dryden's *Ode* "the woes of hopeless lovers" are celebrated next in order. Jealousy, too, with her "veering song" seems inspired by the "jealous pangs and desperation" in Dryden's ode. But excepting "the doubling Drum" (*Passions*, 47) which echoes "the double double double beat Of the thundering drum" (*Song for Saint Cecilia's Day*, 28-9) there is no direct verbal parallel between the two poems.

Besides one reminiscence in diction ("flying fingers," *Passions*, 89; cf. *Alexander's Feast*, 22) there are several suggestions of *Alexander's Feast* in *The Passions*. The passage describing Revenge (*Passions*, 39-52) seems modeled after strophe 6 of Dryden's ode, in which Timotheus arouses Alexander to seek revenge for the "Grecian Ghosts" slain in battle and still unburied, though the resemblance is not close. Again the description of "Joy's ecstatic Trial" (*Passions*, 81-2) with its account of "Joy's viny crown" suggests the Bacchic procession of stanza 3 in *Alexander's Feast*. Finally each ode ends conventionally with a comparison between the music of "divine Caecilia" and that of Greece, though the conclusions drawn from the parallel differ.

To Dryden Collins apparently felt no such allegiance as Milton inspired in him. That may explain why he occasionally turned to him for a model yet followed him far less directly than he did Milton, or even Pope.

IV

THE ELIZABETHANS

THE SPACIOUS times of great Elizabeth attracted Collins as they did Lamb and Keats. First he was fascinated by the color and romance of a past age in history, for he was always an antiquarian at heart. Then, he apparently found in the literature of that day a wealth of words to his ear "antique." And, always moved by the drama, he turned much to Shakespeare— to the lyrics in the plays as well as to the more moving tragic scenes. The patriotic pride of Drayton, the historical and topographic lore of Camden, Drayton, and Spenser must have inspired him. He was, moreover, a collector of sixteenth century penny-pamphlets and black-letter books. In the *History of English Poetry*[1] Thomas Warton mentions that Collins showed him at Chichester shortly before his death a copy of Skelton's *Nigramansir,* "a very rare and valuable work." Warton further records in the same work (Section xli) that he saw in the dispersed library of Collins after his death "a thin folio of two sheets in black letter, containing a poem in the octave stanza entitled Fabyl's Ghoste, printed by John Rastell in the year 1533" as well as (Section lii) "a collection of comic short stories in prose, printed in the black letter under the year 1570."[2] And, a student of the glamorous Italian Renaissance, Collins found fresh delight in the translation of Fairfax which showed him how "th' heroic muse employ'd her Tasso's art." That he read widely in the literature of the period seems inevitable. Previous commentators have caught reminiscent suggestions of

---

[1] Section xxxiii, footnote.
[2] Mr. Garrod (*TLS,* 1929, p. 624) is inclined to believe that these titles are fabrications of Warton. But Mr. Blunden (*TLS,* 1929, p. 668) rightly assumes that they may well have been lost when the library was dispersed. Though Warton may be wrong about the date of *Fabyl's Ghoste* it is typical in substance of many a penny-pamphlet of Elizabeth's day. See for example such a pamphlet as *Ratsie's Ghost,* 1605, an account of the robberies and pranks of the noted highwayman, Gamaliel Ratsey.

Sidney's *Arcadia,* of Phineas Fletcher's *Purple Island,* of Hall's *Satires,* and of Jonson's plays,[3] while Collins himself alludes to the conversations of Drummond and Ben. Reminiscent echoes of Fletcher's lyrics color the *Ode to Evening,* and one cannot read the third of the *Persian Eclogues* without catching something of the flavor of Greene's and Peele's lyrics in praise of the quiet shepherd's life which is better than a kingly crown. Most significant sources of Collins's interest in the Elizabethans are the *Faerie Queene* of Spenser, the Fairfax translation of *Tasso,* and the plays of Shakespeare.

To Spenser and his *Faerie Queene* Collins makes two direct references. In the *Ode on the Poetical Character* he alludes to both the poet and his poem when he mentions:

> that gifted Bard,
> (Him whose School above the rest
> His Loveliest *Elfin* Queen has blest.)

Again in the *Ode on the Popular Superstitions* he calls the folktales of the highlands:

> Strange lays, whose power had charmed a SPENCER's ear.

In one poem, the *Ode on the Poetical Character,* he adapts his conceit from an incident in the *Faerie Queene* itself. The story of the magic girdle, told in *F.Q.* V, iv, and mentioned again in V, iii, 28, Collins retells in lines 5-16 of the ode:

> One, only One, unrival'd Fair,
> Might hope the magic Girdle wear,
> At Solemn Turney hung on high,
> The Wish of each love-darting Eye;
>
> Lo! to each other Nymph in turn applied,
>   As if, in Air unseen, some hov'ring Hand,

---

[3] On Collins's admiration for Jonson see the anecdote in *Dramatic Miscellanies,* Vol. II, p. 77, cited by Dyce:

That our poet admired Ben Jonson, we learn from Tom Davies (bookseller and would-be actor) who, speaking of the Epilogue to *Every Man out of His Humour,* at the presentation before Queen Elizabeth, observed, "Mr. Collins, the author of several justly esteemed poems, first pointed out to me the particular beauties of this occasional address." With lines 3-6 of the *Ode to Liberty* Mr. Garrod compares Jonson's *Vision of the Muses of his Friend Michael Drayton,* 66-9, another evidence of Jonsonian influence.

> Some chaste and Angel-Friend to Virgin-Fame,
>   With whisper'd Spell had burst the starting Band,
> It left unblest her loath'd dishonour'd Side;
>   Happier hopeless Fair, if never
>   Her baffled Hand with vain Endeavour
> Had touch'd that fatal Zone to her denied!

Collins does not "read aright" the story as Spenser gives it, however. Spenser describes the girdle in Stanza 3 of the canto:

> That girdle gave the vertue of chaste love,
> And wivehood true, to all that did it beare;
> But whosoever contrarie doth prove,
> Might not the same about her middle weare,
> But it would loose, or else asunder tear.

There is no indication in Spenser's account that the girdle was reserved for one "unrival'd Fair." Though it is hung on high at the tournament of the Knights of Maydenhead it is not then awarded to the rightful wearer. In stanzas 16-20 of the canto Spenser describes, as does Collins in lines 9-16 of the ode, how each of the ladies at the tournament tried to wear the Cest and failed. But in Spenser's account it fitted Amoret, although it was awarded to False Florimel, who could not wear it. Not until *F.Q.*, V, iii, when False Florimel vanishes, is the girdle restored to Florimel, to whom it originally belonged.[4] Collins, then, reports Spenser's incident inaccurately and changes Spenser's concept of the girdle to fit his own conceit of the Cest of Poetry. In describing the situation Collins employs a practice he frequently follows. Such words as "read aright," 2, (cf. *F.Q.*, III, iii, 16, 7); "elfin," 4; "unblest" (cf. *F.Q.*, IV, v, 18, 7); "loath'd," and "dishonour'd," 13; "Cest," 19, suggest the Spenserian original.

Since both Spenser and Collins were fond of personification, one would naturally expect that some of Collins's figures were drawn from Spenser. Yet there are relatively few examples, for Spenser's personified figures are usually more detailed and concretely pictorial than are Collins's. One is, however, reminded of the description of Shamefastness, *F.Q.*, IV, x, 50, 1-5, as he

---

[4] Collins's note identifies the "unrival'd Fair" as *"Florimel.* See *Spenser* Leg. 4th."

reads of "Chastity," the "wise suspicious Maid," of the first
Persian Eclogue. "Impatient Freedom," described in stanza 7
of the *Ode to a Lady,* has some resemblance to a figure in
Spenser:

> But lo where, sunk in deep Despair,
> Her Garments torn, her Bosom bare,
>   Impatient *Freedom* lies!
> Her matted Tresses madly spread,
> To ev'ry Sod, which wraps the Dead,
>   She turns her joyless Eyes.

The source of the passage might well be *F.Q.,* II, i, 13, 5-9:

> Where sate a gentle Lady all alone,
> With garments rent, and heare discheveled,
> Wringing her handes, and making piteous mone:
> Her swollen eyes were much disfigured,
> And her fair face with tears was fowly blubbered.

From *F.Q.,* III, xii, 12, Collins might have hit upon the idea
of describing Danger as part of the train of Fear in the *Ode to
Fear.* And for *The Passions,* in which the greatest number of
personified figures appear, Collins might have found hints in
Spenser for two of the Passions, Chearfulness and Hope. Chearfulness resembles Spenser's Belphoebe as she appears in *F.Q.,*
II, iii, 21-30. Hope Spenser describes in *F.Q.,* III, xii, 13, 1-5,
where she is part of the masque of Cupid:

> With him went Hope in rancke, a handsome Mayd,
> Of chearefull look and lovely to behold:
> In silken Samite she was light arayd,
> And her FAYRE LOCKES WERE WOVEN UP IN GOLD
> She always SMYLD. . . .

Spenser's picture furnishes Collins with the two descriptive details he employs in presenting Hope:

> And *Hope* enchanted SMIL'D, and wav'd Her GOLDEN HAIR.

Spenser's picture-making power, too, must sometimes have
given Collins a striking image. As early as the second of the
Persian Eclogues, 5-6, there is a trace of Spenser. Hassan, the
camel driver, carries

> A FAN of PAINTED FEATHERS in his Hand,
> To guard his shaded Face from scorching Sand.

One of the figures in the masque of Cupid in *F.Q.*, III, xii, 8, might have furnished Collins with the significant details in the passage:

> His garment nether was of silk nor say,
> But PAYNTED PLUMES in goodly order dight,
> Like as the SUNBURNT INDIANS do aray
> Their tawny bodies in their proudest plight. . . .
> And in his hand a WINDY FAN did beare,
> That in the ydle ayre he mov'd still here and theare.

A suggestion from Spenser also colored the *Ode to Peace*. Lines 16-18 of the ode:

> The *British* Lion, Goddess sweet,
> Lies stretch'd on Earth to Kiss thy Feet,
> And own thy holier Reign,

recall the description of Una and the Lion in *F.Q.*, I, iii, 6, lines 1-3:

> Instead thereof he kist her wearie feet,
> And lickt her lilly hands with fawning tong
> As he her wronged innocence did weet.

And although Collins did not remember that before the *Ode to Liberty* "any Poetical Use had hitherto been made" of the tradition, Spenser also describes the "blest Divorce" of England from France in *F.Q.*, II, x, 5, 5-9:

> Ne was it Island then, ne was it paysd
> Amid the ocean waves . . .
> But was all desolate, and of some thought
> By sea to have been from the Celticke Maynland brought.[5]

To the series of poetic impressions of evening which Collins recalls by reminiscent phrase in the *Ode to Evening* at least one from Spenser must be added. *F.Q.*, V, ix, 28, 4-6:

[5] The tradition is mentioned also in Camden's *Britannia*, in the eighteenth Song of the *Poly-olbion* (cf. his use of "watchet Weeds" in *The Manners* as another instance of acquaintance with the *Poly-olbion*, where the phrase occurs in *Song* 5, line 13), and in Thomson's *Liberty*.

But like a cloud . . .
That her brode-spreading wings did wyde unfold;
Whose skirts were bordered with bright sunny beames,

furnishes something of the diction and the imagery of lines
5-8 of the ode. In *The Passions,* too, the description of the haunt
of Melancholy, 57-68, especially in the line:

Through GLADES and GLOOMS the mingled Measure stole,

and in the image of her "wild sequester'd Seat" has the atmosphere of *F.Q.,* VI, v, 13, 5-7:

Farre in the forest, by a hollow GLADE,
Covered with mossie shrubs, which spredding brode
Did underneath them make a GLOOMY shade.

Though Collins wrote no imitations of Spenser as did Thomson
and Shenstone and though he never employed the Spenserian
stanza he apparently shared in the revival of interest in the *Faerie
Queene* which marked the first half of the century.[6]

Akin to his interest in the poetry of Spenser is Collins's enthusiasm for the colorful Fairfax translation of Tasso's *Ge-*

---

[6] There are in Collins, too, some verbal echoes of Spenser which, if not
so numerous as the reminiscences of Milton, are woven more subtly into his
verse. A comparison of some of the passages is, at least, suggestive:
Poetical Character, 2: "I READ ARIGHT that gifted Bard," cf. *F.Q.,* III,
iii, 16, 7: "Or whence it sprong, I CAN NOT READ ARIGHT"; *Poetical Character,* 46: "By whose the TARSEL'S Eyes were made," cf. *F.Q.,* III, lv, 49, 6:
"Having far off espied a TASSEL gent"; *Poetical Character,* 71: "My
TREMBLING FEET his guiding Steps pursue," cf. *Hymn . . . Heavenly Love,*
41: "Much less my TREMBLING VERSE . . . can hope it to rehearse"; *Mercy,*
14-15: "When he whom e'vn our Joys PROVOKE, The FIEND . . . "; cf.
Hymn in Honour of Love, 234: "PROVOKE the ire of damned FIENDS";
Liberty, 79: "And down the SHOULD'RING BILLOWS born," cf. *Ruins of
Rome,* xvi, 4: "Eftsoons of thousand BILLOWES SHOULDERED narre"; *Liberty,*
110: "In WARLIKE WEEDS, retir'd in Glory," cf. *F.Q.,* V, vi, 23, 6-7: ". . . not
to forgo Those WARLIKE WEEDES . . . "; *Liberty,* 72: "Where Orcas howls,
his WOLFISH Mountains rounding," cf. *Shepheardes Calendar,* Sept., 197: "This
WOLFISH sheepe would catchen his pray"; *Evening,* 9-10: "The weak-eyed
BAT . . . LEATHERN WING," cf. *F.Q.,* II, xii, 36, 6: "The LETHER-WINGED
BATT"; *Evening,* 49: "So long REGARDFUL of thy quiet Rule," cf. *F.Q.,* IV,
vii, 22, 4: "And evermore when with REGARDFULL sight"; *Evening,* 48:
"And RUDELY RENDS thy Robes," cf. *F.Q.,* VI, vi, 22, 6: "Him RUDELY
RENT and all to peeces tore"; *Manners,* 67-8: "Or him, whom Seine's blue
Nymphs deplore, In WATCHET WEEDS on Gallia's Shore," cf. *F.Q.,* III, iv,
91, 5: "Their WATCHET MANTLES frindgd with silver rownd." (cf. also
IV, xi, 27, 2); *Passions,* 63: "BUBBLING RUNNELS join'd the Sound," cf.
F.Q., III, iv, 33, 7: "Ne BUBLING ROUNDELL they behind them sent."

rusalemme Liberata. The translation had been reprinted in 1749, the year assigned to the *Ode on the Popular Superstitions* wherein Collins remembers Fairfax; at the same period he was writing the lost *Epistle to the Editor of Fairfax his Translation of Tasso.* A long passage, stanza XII of the *Ode on the Popular Superstitions,* celebrates Tasso's power in depicting scenes, which "daring to depart From sober truth, are still to nature true," and commends not only Tasso's art, but Fairfax's power as a translator. A comparison of Collins's passage with Fairfax is significant because it shows his ability to incorporate into his allusion the diction and flavor of the original. Lines 192-9 of the ode read:

> How have I trembled, when, at TANCRED's stroke
>   Its gushing blood the gaping cypress pour'd;
> When each live plant with mortal accents spoke,
>   And the wild blast up-heav'd the vanish'd sword!
> How have I sat, when pip'd the pensive wind,
>   To hear his harp, by British FAIRFAX strung.
> Prevailing poet, whose undoubting mind
>   Believ'd the magic wonders which he sung!

They allude to the events of Book XIII, stanzas xl-xlii, xli, and l of the translation, wherein Tancred, sent by Godfrey to the enchanted wood, is led through the magic of Ismeno to believe that the voice of the slain Clorinda speaks from within one of the trees of the forest. The lines, stanza xl, 2-6:

> And while he musèd on this uncouth writ,
>   Him thought he heard the softly whistling wind,
> His blasts amid the leaves and branches knit
>   And frame a sound like speech of human kind
> But full of sorrow grief and woe was it,

Collins suggests in the phrase, 196, "when pip'd the pensive wind." The central incident of the passage, stanzas xli-xlii:

> He drew his sword at last and gave the tree
>   A mighty blow, that made a gaping wound,
> Out of the rift red streams he trickling see
>   That all bebled the verdant plain around,
> His hair start up, yet once again stroke he,
>   He nould give over till the end be found

Of this adventure, when with plaint and moan
As from some hollow grave, he heard one groan.

"Enough, enough!" the voice lamenting said,
   "Tancred, thou hast me hurt, thou didst me drive
Out of the body of a noble maid,
   Who with me lived, whom late I kept on live,
And now within this woful cypress laid. . . ."

Collins suggests by echoing phrases from Fairfax, "Tancred's stroke" echoes "mighty blow"; "gaping wound," "Out of the rift red streams he trickling see," "Woful cypress," Collins concentrates into, 193, "Its gushing blood the gaping cypress pour'd." Line 194 of the ode:

When each live plant with mortal accents spoke,

is Collins's version of stanza l, 1-2:

. . . each tree through all that wood
Hath sense, hath life, hath speech like human kind.

Line 195, "And the wild blast up-heav'd the vanish'd sword!" is an almost verbal adaptation of stanza xlvi, 5-6:

A whirling wind his sword heaved up aloft,
   And through the forest bare it quite away.

Collins's general judgment of Tasso's art, lines 200-3:

Hence, at each sound, imagination glows;
   Hence his warm lay with softest sweetness flows:
Melting it flows, pure, num'rous, strong and clear,

is a highly sensitive and appropriate appreciation of such passages as those in Books XV and XVI of Tasso which describe the enchanting bowers of Armida. Yet in his assertion that Tasso "believ'd the magic wonders which he sung" he had apparently forgotten Tasso's invocation, I, ii, 6-7:

My verse ennoble and forgive the thing
If fictions light I mix with truth divine.

   In the earlier odes there are tantalizing hints that Collins had turned to Fairfax and was familiar with it before he praised the translation in the *Ode on the Popular Superstitions*. Lines 50-1 of the *Ode to Fear:*

> Or, in some hollow'd Seat,
> 'Gainst which the big Waves beat,

resembles a passage in III, vi, 5-6, a favorite simile in Tasso:

> as when one hears
> The hoarse sea waves roar, hollow rocks betwixt.

Three other phrases in Fairfax seem to resemble *The Passions*.
Book I, xiv, 8:

> And SHOOK his WINGS with rorie MAY-DEWS wet;

has been compared to *Passions*, 94,

> SHOOK thousand ODOURS from his DEWY WINGS.

But equally close parallels to phrases in the ode are found in
II, xi, 7, "the satyrs rough, the fauns and fairies wild" (cf.
Passions, 74-7) and in XII, lxxviii, 2, "a little RUNNEL tumbled
near the place" (cf. *Passions,* 63, "Bubbling RUNNELS join'd the
Sound").[7] The poet's fascination with the Renaissance, his love
of historical detail, and his appreciation of Tasso's art led
him to turn to the translation and occasionally to intersperse in
his odes old words which in Fairfax had helped to grace an
antique tale.

Shakespeare's influence on Collins is most marked early in
his poetical career although in the later *Ode on the Popular
Superstitions,* 176-82, he recalls Shakespeare's fascination with
the "wayward sisters" in *Macbeth* and perhaps the fairy lore
of *A Midsummer Night's Dream* as an admonition to Home
not to disdain the "homelier thoughts" of the rustic Highlanders. Shakespeare inspires Collins in three ways: first, Collins
recollects and describes scenes from the plays, associated perhaps with his own dramatic aspirations; secondly, he imitates
some of the lyrics in the plays; finally, he occasionally employs
words or phrases from Shakespeare as part of the diction of his
poetry. Instances of the recollection and description of scenes

---

[7] There are besides several verbal echoes of the translation in the diction
of the odes: "crisped locks," I, xliii, 1 (cf. *Manners,* 55, "crisped hair");
"up-bind," X, v, 7 (cf. *Peace,* 13); "up-piled," XIX, xxx, 3 (cf. *Poetical
Character,* 55); and "blust'ring winds," XIX, xix, 3, a favorite phrase in
Fairfax (cf. *Evening,* 33), are all found in Collins.

from the plays occur in the *Epistle to Sir Thomas Hanmer* and the *Ode on the Popular Superstitions*. In the *Epistle to Hanmer*, 93-4, Collins first recalls by allusion the historical trilogy *Henry IV*, 1, *Henry IV*, 2 and *Henry V*:

> There *Henry's* Trumpets spread their loud Alarms,
> And laurel'd Conquest waits her Hero's Arms.

The reference to the sad fate of "gentler Edward," 95, and the allusion to the "guilty King," 98, suggest *Richard III*, and the passage 101-5:

> When dreary Visions shall at last present
> Thy vengeful Image, in the midnight Tent:
> Thy Hand unseen[8] the secret Death shall bear;
> Blunt the weak Sword, and break th' oppressive Spear.

presents directly the incidents of *Richard III*, V, iii, 118-206. Less pointed allusion is made, in 106-10 of the *Epistle*, to *A Midsummer Night's Dream*, and lines 111-12 suggest *The Tempest*. A later passage, 123-32, describes the incidents of *Julius Caesar*, III, ii, 47-264, while lines 143-4 somewhat inaccurately present the events of *Coriolanus*, V, iii. It is curious that Collins here made no mention of the other great tragedies besides the two Roman plays. Perhaps his love of history and his fondness for the classics made him partial to them. In the *Ode on the Popular Superstitions*, 180-2, he turns by allusion to *Macbeth*, IV, i, appropriately enough, for the scene deals with the popular superstitions Collins is describing and is besides an instance of how a great poet may dare to depart from sober truth in treating a fanciful theme. One is, however, surprised in the *Ode to Fear* that no scenes from the plays of Shakespeare are described, in view of Collins's expressed desire to follow Shakespeare as a dramatic poet.

Two of Collins's lyrics, both written early in his career, *Song from Shakespeare's Cymbeline* and *Song. The Sentiments Borrowed from Shakespeare*, represent a more artistic adaptation of literary material. Both pieces are in Collins's best manner. They are finely phrased, delicate and fanciful in tone, and touched

---

[8] Here for the first time Collins employs a phrase which was to become a favorite.

with that note of gentle pity and pensive sadness so characteristic of the poet. One can but wish in reading them that Collins had oftener tried the simple lyric instead of the more ambitious ode. They have in them the best qualities of both the *Ode to Evening* and the *Ode Written in the Beginning of the Year 1746,* which they suggest in mood and imagery.

The *Song. The Sentiments Borrowed from Shakespeare,* is closest in manner to the pathetic little songs which Ophelia sings in *Hamlet,* IV, v. Each of her melancholy songs contributes some phrase to Collins's lyric. The mournful:

> He is dead and gone, lady,
>   He is dead and gone;
> At his head a grass-green turf;
>   At his heels a stone,

suggests to Collins the ominous bell-like quality of "Ye lowly hamlets, moan"; as well as specifically furnishing the image for:

> A dewy turf lies o'er his head,
>   And at his feet a stone.

Again Ophelia's song:

> White his shroud as the Mountain snow,—
>   Larded with sweet flowers;
> Which bewept to the grave did go
>   With TRUE-LOVE SHOWERS,

suggests to Collins the theme of sorrowing for a lost lover and specifically furnishes the image for:

> His shroud, which Death's cold damps destroy,
>   Of snow-white threads was made:

as well as being the source for:

> Ah me! How many a TRUE-LOVE SHOWER
>   Of kind remembrance fell!

There are other echoes of Ophelia's songs in the poem subtly varied by the poet:

> They bore him barefaced on the bier

becomes

> They bore him out at twilight hour.

Again

> And in his grave rain'd many a tear:—

is personalized into:

> Within his grave she dropp'd in grief.

The last of Ophelia's songs:

> And will he not come again?
>   No, no, he is dead:
>   Go to thy death bed:
> He never will come again . . .
>   He is gone, he is gone,
>   And we cast away moan:

inspires:

> But will he ne'er return, whose tongue
>   Could tune the rural lay?
> Ah, no! his bell of peace is rung,
>   His lips are cold as clay,

and furnishes the hint for the tragic conclusion of Collins's poem. Collins borrowed, too, the effectively sonorous "moan," which lends such appropriate tone-color to the poem. From the prose passages of Ophelia's speeches in the scene, Collins also drew several suggestions. Ophelia's "And there is pansies, that's for thoughts," and "I would give you some violets, but they withered all when my father died," Collins weaves into:

> Pale pansies o'er his corpse were placed,
>   Which, pluck'd before their time,
> Bestrew'd the boy, like him to waste
>   And wither in their prime.

And Ophelia's "but I cannot choose but weep, to think they should lay him i' the cold ground" suggests the grief of Lucy for her lover.

There is, however, some difference in tone between the songs in Shakespeare and Collins's adaptation of them. There is primarily a folk-quality in the songs of Ophelia. Collins's song is definitely pastoral in flavor, a rural lay. Moreover he has added some of his own favorite touches to the poem: the vale, the lowly hamlets, the bell of peace, and the twilight hour are all details of which he is fond. And the note of reserved tenderness which runs through the poem marks it as Collins's own. Though the sentiments be borrowed from Shakespeare, he has made it more truly his than did Chatterton, who was later to be touched by the same songs.

The *Song from Shakespeare's Cymbeline* "sung by Guiderus [sic] and Arviragus over Fidele, supposed to be dead" was inspired by the tender lyric in *Cymbeline,* IV, 2, "Fear no more the heat o' the sun."[9] Actually, however, the song of Collins suggests more closely the blank verse passages of the scene than the lyric itself. From the speeches of Guiderius and Arviragus, 216-30, come several of the phrases of Collins's dirge:

> *Gui.* If he be gone, he'll make his grave a bed;
>   WITH FEMALE FAIRIES WILL HIS TOMB BE HAUNTED,
>   And worms will not come to thee.
> *Arv.*   WITH FAIREST FLOWERS
>   Whilst summer lasts and I live here, Fidele,
>   I'll SWEETEN THY SAD GRAVE: thou shalt not lack
>   The FLOWER THAT'S LIKE THY FACE, pale primrose, nor
>   The azured harebell, like thy veins, no, nor
>   The leaf of eglantine, whom not to slander,
>   Outsweetened not thy breath: THE RUDDOCK WOULD,
>   WITH CHARITABLE BILL, . . . bring thee all this;
>   Yea, and FURR'D MOSS besides, when flowers are none,
>   To winter-ground thy corse.

Here are the hints for line 3:

> Each op'ning sweet, of earliest bloom,

and for line 11:

> The FEMALE FAYS shall HAUNT the green,

as well as the source for all of stanza four:

> The RED-BREAST oft at ev'ning hours
>   Shall kindly lend his little aid:

[9] "In Cymbeline he [Pope] has marked [with star as a *shining* passage] the lengthy series of elegiac laments in which Arviragus and Guiderius weep the supposed death of Imogen."—A. Warren, *Alexander Pope as Critic and Humanist,* p. 151. Did this star (*) attract Collins's attention to the passage and suggest the writing of "To fair Fidele's grassy tomb"? Mr. Garrod notes, however (*Collins,* p. 112 n), that Collins refers in the heading of the poem to "Theobald's *Edition of* SHAKESPEAR."

> With HOARY MOSS, and gather'd flow'rs,
> To deck the ground where thou art laid.[10]

A further passage in Belarius's speech, 284-5:

> The herbs that have on them cold dew o' the night
> Are strewings fit'st for graves, . . .

suggests line 12:

> And dress thy grave with pearly dew.

From the song itself come several suggestions for Collins's dirge.

> Fear no more the heat o' the sun,
> Nor the furious winter's rages. . . .

furnishes the motif for:

> When howling winds, and beating rain,
> In tempest shake the sylvan cell.

The concluding stanza:

> No exorciser harm thee!
> Nor no witchcraft charm thee!
> Ghost unlaid forbear thee!
> Nothing ill come near thee!

Collins echoes in:

> No wailing ghost shall dare appear
> To vex with shrieks this quiet grove:

and in:

> No wither'd witch shall here be seen,
> No goblins lead their nightly crew.

Again Collins's lyric differs in tone and effect from Shakespeare's. Shakespeare's is more universal in application. From Fidele's death comes the conclusion that:

> Golden lads and girls all must
> As chimney-sweepers, come to dust.

[10] Compare, however, Webster's *Dirge* (*White Devil,* V, iv, 102-11):
> Call for the robin-redbreast and the wren,
> Since o'er shady groves they hover,
> And with leaves and flowers do cover,
> The friendless bodies of unburied men.

In Shakespeare's song death is a quiet consummation, a relief from the fears, the hardships, and the thousand natural shocks that flesh is heir to. Collins's song is a tender though restrained tribute to fair Fidele. Again Collins's song is pastoral in tone, and it is colored by his favorite descriptive effects; the "ev'ning hours," the "howling winds, and beating rain," the "sylvan cell" all occur, as well, in the *Ode to Evening*. Collins's manner, too, is evident in the gentle pity of:

> The tender thought on thee shall dwell,

and of:

> Each lonely scene shall thee restore.

Yet, fine as it is, it lacks that quiet aloofness and calm detachment from life's tumult that marks Shakespeare's lyric. Nor does it have so fine a phrase as Shakespeare's "golden lads."[11]

---

[11] Perhaps a third lyric in the manner of Shakespeare is the work of Collins's pen. Mr. Iolo A. Williams and Mr. Garrod agree in attributing to Collins *A Song. Imitated from the Midsummer Night's Dream of Shakespeare,* printed anonymously in *Dodsley's Museum,* 1746, and later believed to be the work of Thomas Warton. It is modeled after the lullaby in *A Midsummer Night's Dream,* II, ii, 9-24. The song follows:

> Lo here, beneath this hallow'd Shade,
>   Within a Cowslip's Blossom deep,
> The lovely Queen of Elves is laid,
>   May nought disturb her balmy Sleep!
>
> Let not the Snake or baleful Toad
>   Approach the silent Mansion near,
> Or Newt profane the sweet abode,
>   Or Owl repeat her Orgies here!
>
> No Snail or Worm shall hither come
>   With noxious Filth her Bow'r to stain;
> Hence be the Beetle's sullen Hum,
>   And Spider's disembowl'd Train.
>
> The love-lorn Nightingale alone
>   Shall thro' *Titania's* Arbor stray,
> To sooth her Sleep with melting Moan,
>   And lull her with his sweetest Lay.

The imitation is done in Collins's manner. From Shakespeare's song are incorporated suggestive phrases and ideas: "Worm nor snail do no offense" is rendered "No Snail or Worm shall hither come." Following Shakespeare, too, the lyric mentions the snake, the baleful toad, the beetle, and the newt. As is Collins's usual practice the lyric incorporates some of its ideas from the passage in the play preceding Shakespeare's song. (Cf. *M.N.D.,* II, ii, 5, "the clamorous owl that nightly hoots" with line 8 of the song.) Some of

There are comparatively few verbal reminiscences of Shakespeare in the poems of Collins. Of these the largest number in a single poem occur in the *Ode to Evening*. A phrase in lines 9-10 of the ode:

> . . . save where the weak-ey'd Bat,
> With short shrill Shriek flits by on LEATHERN WING,

is drawn directly from *Midsummer Night's Dream*, II, i, 3:

> Some war with RERE-MICE for their LEATHERN WINGS.

Among other suggestive sources of lines 11-12 of the ode:

> Or where the BEETLE winds
> His small but sullen Horn,
> As oft he rises 'midst the twilight Path,
> Against the Pilgrim born in HEEDLESS HUM:

is *Macbeth*, III, ii, 40-3:

> Ere the bat hath flown
> His cloister'd flight, ere to black Hecate's summons
> The shard born BEETLE with his DROWSY HUMS
> Hath rung night's yawning peal.

Finally, "Vot'ress," 30, comes from *A Mid-Summer Night's Dream*, II, i, 163.[12]

---

the phrases in the lyric Collins is fond of using: "hallow'd shade," 1, "sullen Hum," 11, "melting Moan," 15. Moreover the cadence and the formula of stanza 3 resemble those of stanzas 2 and 3 of the *Song to Cymbeline*. "The Beetle's sullen Hum," 11, is suggestive of the *Ode to Evening*, "the Beetle winds His small but sullen Horn." And as Mr. Garrod suggests, *Collins*, p. 114, "the passage of Shakespeare which the poem professes to imitate is that from which Collins had twice elsewhere borrowed the expression 'leathern wing'." Mr. Williams makes a plausible case for attributing the poem to Collins in *Seven Eighteenth Century Bibliographies*, pp. 102-4, to which I am indebted for some of the details in this note. Mr. Williams originally claimed the song for Collins in the *London Mercury* for May, 1923.

[12] For the rest there are in the other poems of Collins a number of scattered parallels in diction, many of them, perhaps, purely accidental: "Russet Mantle," *Eclogue III*, 55 (*Hamlet*, I, i, 166); "LAP the BLOOD of Sorrow," *Fear*, 23 ("LAP their gentle BLOOD, *Richard III*, II, i, 115); "forceless," *Simplicity*, 39 (*Troilus & Cressida*, V, v, 40); "Gauds," *Simplicity*, 9, (*M.N.D.*, I, i, 33); "spher'd," *Poetical Character*, 66, (*Troilus & Cressida*, I, iii, 90; IV, v, 8); "Deathful," *Mercy*, 7, (2 *Henry VI*, III, ii, 404); "wolfish," *Liberty*, 72, (*Lear*, III, vii, 63); "Navel," *Liberty*, 90, (*Coriolanus*, III, i, 123); "pavilion'd," *Liberty*, 106 (*Henry V*, I, ii, 129); "consorted," *Liberty*, 111 (*Romeo & Juliet*, II, i, 31); "emblaze," *Liberty*, 124 (2 *Henry VI*, IV, x, 76); "crisped," *Manners*, 55, (*Merchant of Venice*, III, ii, 292);

One senses, too, the suggestion of Shakespeare's delicate dirge "Full fathom five thy father lies" in the fairy world of *Ode Written in the Beginning of the Year 1746*. And even in the clouded years at Chichester Collins's mind turned to Shakespeare and the magic world of *The Tempest*. Thomas Warton records in his *History of English Poetry*, section lx, that Collins had found in *Aurelio and Isabella* a source for *The Tempest*, a conclusion he had reached "with no less fidelity than judgment."[13]

"prattling," *Manners*, 24, (*Coriolanus*, II, i, 222); "swart," *Popular Superstitions*, 23 (of frequent occurrence); "bestrew," *Song. Sentiments*, 11 (*Tempest*, IV, i, 20). In general, however, the parallels in diction between Shakespeare and Collins are more difficult to isolate because it would appear that except in the lyrics and the *Ode to Evening* Collins made little conscious attempt to copy the Shakespearean phrase as he definitely did do with the poetry of Milton and of Spenser. They are frequently less definitive, too, because the words sometimes occur as well in Spenser and in Milton.

[13] On the same point see the comment in *Gentleman's Magazine*, XC, II, 590, (supplement to volume) "An Inquiry into the Progress of Anecdotal Literature."

V

CONTEMPORARY INFLUENCES

FOR ALL of his devotion to the poets of the past Collins was significantly influenced by his contemporaries. That he shared the critical concepts of poetry which flourished in his day has already been demonstrated. His admiration for Milton, his devotion to Spenser and to Shakespeare, even his imitation of Pope and Dryden, associate him directly with his contemporaries. All of the significant literary trends of his day influenced him. Previous commentators have found suggestions of the pastorals of Parnell in the *Persian Eclogues.* There is some reason to suppose that Lyttleton's *Progress of Love, in Four Eclogues,* 1732, was known to Collins—verses which, as Johnson says of them, "cant of shepherds and flocks, and crooks dressed with flowers."[1] Lyttleton's *Letters from a Persian in England to his Friend at Ispahan,* obviously in imitation of Montesquieu's *Lettres Persanes,* may conceivably have interested Collins in the East as a theme for his pastorals. But from the friends of his Winchester days, and his associates in London and in Thomson's circle at Richmond, he drew more specific suggestions.

To his intimate friend and Wykehamite schoolfellow, Joseph Warton, he owed a special debt. They had made their first literary venture together when at Winchester, they had planned to publish their odes together at the memorable meeting at the Guilford races, and as has been shown already, they shared the view that the poetry of their day lacked inspiration—a loss which could be remedied only by the fusion of Greek simplicity and Gothic fancy. Obviously there should be some reminiscences of Warton in the poetry of Collins; it is, in fact, remarkable that there are so few. For both poets deeply admired Milton, both imitated *L'Allegro* and *Il Penseroso* in verse-form and dic-

---

[1] *Lives,* III, 446.

tion, and both employed the unrhymed stanza of the "Pyrrha
Ode." Collins used it only in the *Ode to Evening;* Warton employed it three times: in a translation and imitation of Horace's
Ode xiii, Book III, *To a Fountain,* in an *Ode to Content,* and
in an *Ode on Shooting,* none of which has any resemblance in
substance or diction to the poems of Collins. Like Collins, Warton wrote an *Ode to Liberty* and an *Ode to Evening.* Again in
Warton's *Ode to Fancy* are enunciated some of the beliefs that
Collins expresses in the concluding lines of *The Passions.*

Except for the phrase describing

> peerless Rome
> Her high-tower'd head dash'd meanly to the ground,

there is no resemblance between Collins's *Ode to Liberty* and
Warton's. The two odes *To Evening* are closer, and since Warton's ode was written first, Collins's poem might have been
colored by his reading of Warton. Warton's epithet "meek-
eyed maiden," line 1, suggests Collins's "meekest Eve," line
42. The last stanza of Warton's ode:

> O modest Evening, oft let me appear
> A wandering votary in thy pensive train,
> List'ning to every wildly-warbling throat
> That fills with farewell notes the dark'ning plain,

perhaps suggested some phrases to Collins. "Modest Evening"
resembles "chaste Eve" and "modest Ear"; "wandering votary"
is like "calm Vot'ress"; "thy pensive train" becomes in Collins
"the pensive Pleasures Sweet"; "dark'ning plain" is transformed
to "dark'ning Vale." But for the "wildly-warbling throat" Collins has appropriately substituted a "soften'd Strain." Warton's
third stanza:

> The panting Dryads, that in day's fierce heat
> To inmost bowers and cooling caverns ran,
> Return to trip in wanton evening dance,

may have given the hint to Collins for:

> . . . at his warning Lamp
> The fragment *Hours,* and *Elves*
> Who slept in Buds the Day,
> And many a *Nymph* who wreaths her brow with Sedge,
> And sheds the fresh'ning Dew. . . .

Further, the "weary woodman" of Warton's poem corresponds with the "Pilgrim" in Collins, and "the hoarse hummings of unnumber'd flies" Collins suggests in the "heedless Hum" of the beetle. Again "twilight groves" in Warton is akin to "twilight Path" in Collins. Yet many of these resemblances might be considered commonplaces characteristic of any poem about evening. In spirit the two poems differ utterly. Warton's poem abounds in concrete imagery: "clamorous rooks," "stout ploughmen meet to wrestle on the green," "light skims the swallow." It has very little of the finer imaginative quality of Collin's poem.[2]

Warton may also have been responsible for suggesting some of the plan of the *Ode to Pity* and *The Passions* to Collins. According to the testimony of Thomas Warton in *The Reaper,* No. 26:

In the *Ode to Pity* the idea of a temple of Pity, of its situation, construction, and groups of painting with which its walls were decorated, was borrowed from a poem, now lost, entitled the temple of Pity, written by my brother, while he and Collins were schoolfellows at Winchester College.

Thomas Warton also mentions that his brother had written *The Assembly of the Passions,* also lost, before Collins wrote *The Passions.* In his *Memoirs of Dr. J. Warton,* p. 11, Wooll gives a sketch by Joseph Warton "laid out by him as a subject for verse at eighteen" which he says furnished Collins with his idea for *The Passions:*

The subjects of Reason having lately rebelled against him, he summons them to his court, that they may pay their obedience to him; whilst he sits on his throne, attended by the virtues, his handmaids. The first who made her appearance was Fear, with Superstition, a pale-faced, trembling virgin, who came from Gallia, and was ever

[2] The resemblances between Collins's *Passions* and Warton's *Ode to Fancy* are discussed in Part I, pp. 90-1. There is, however, a sharp verbal similarity between a passage in Warton's *Ode to Fancy* and the *Ode to Fear,* 10-12:

Warton:
> Where GIANT Terrour STALKS around,
> With sullen joy surveys the ground.

Collins:
> *Danger,* whose Limbs of GIANT Mold
> What Mortal Eye can fix'd behold?
> Who STALKS HIS ROUND, an hideous Form. . . .

present at earthquakes, fires, sieges, storms, and shuddered at everything she saw. Not so Anger, whose harbinger was Cruelty, with dishevelled hair; and whose charioteer, Revenge, drove wheels reeking with blood. He himself stood upright, brandishing a sword, and bearing a shield, on which was engraven Achilles dragging the carcass of Hector, with Priam and Andromache lamenting on the walls; round his girdle he ties the head of an enemy just slaughtered, and his chariot was drawn by tigers. Next came Joy, chanting a song, crowned with vine leaves, waving a rod in his hand, at whose touch everything smiled; he was attended by Mirth and Pleasure, two nymphs more light than Napaeans: he was the institutor of feasts and dances among shepherds at a vintage, at marriages and triumphs. Then came Sorrow, with a dead babe in her arms; she was often seen in charnels and by graves, listening to knells, or walking in the dead of night, and lamenting aloud; nor was she absent from dungeons and galley slaves. After her Courage, a young man riding a lion, that chafed with indignation, yet was forced to submit— not a fiercer roars in Egypt whilst the pyramids re-echo to his voice; naked, like an Englishman, blowing an horn, he was seen to attend Regulus to Carthage, Henry the Fifth to Agincourt, Moluc, Charles of Sweden, Kouli Khan, etc. He led Cowardice chained, who shuddered violently whenever he heard the horn, and would fain run away—so the beasts run when they hear the rattlesnake. Next came Emulation, with harp and sword; he followed a phantom of Fame that he might snatch the crown she wore; he was accompanied by a beautiful Amazon, called Hope, who, with one hand pointed to the heavens, and in the other held an optic which beautified and magnified every object to which it was directed. Pity led her old father Despair, who tore his grey locks, and could scarce move along for extreme misery; she nursed him with her own milk, and supported his steps, whilst bats and owls flew round his head. She frequents fields of battle, protects the slain, and staunches their wounds with her veil and hair. Next came Love, supported on each side by Friendship and Truth, but not blind, as the poets feign. Behind these came his enemies, Jealousy, who nursed a vulture to feed on his own heart, Hatred also, and Doubt shaking a dart behind Love, who, on his turning round, immediately vanished. Honour, twined round about with a snake, like Laocoon. Then Ambition in a chariot of gold, and white horses, whose trappings were adorned with jewels, led by Esteem and Flattery. Envy viewed him passing, and repined like a pard with a dart in his side. Contempt too, like a satyr, beheld, and pointed with his finger; but he too often reviled heaven, whence plagues, pestilences, wars, and famines. When these were all met, Reason (sitting grander than Solomon) on whom the man Justice, and the woman Temperance, attended, thus addressed them.

The resemblance of the sketch to *The Passions* is not particularly close. It is significant that the figures of Fear, Anger, Revenge, Joy "crowned with vine leaves," accompanied by Mirth, Hope, Pity, Despair and Jealousy are common to both.

Joseph Warton's brother, Thomas, had written little poetry before 1746, when Collins published the *Odes on Several Descriptive and Allegoric Subjects*. While both the *Pleasures of Melancholy*, 1745, and *Morning*, 1745, are in the Miltonic tradition of "pensive contemplation" popular at the time, there is no direct evidence that Collins was influenced by them, unless his figure of "pale Melancholy" in *The Passions* be colored by the earlier poem. Thomas Warton, however, also employed the unrhymed stanza of the "Pyrrha Ode" in two poems, translations of Horace, Book III, Ode xiii, and Book III, Ode xviii, respectively. The stanza form was, then, something of a trade-mark of the poetical school to which Collins belonged.

To his association with John Home in London he owed a more specific debt. Home may first have turned Collins's mind to the folk-lore and legend of Scotland. The tragedy of *Douglas* itself first suggested some of the imagery of the *Ode on the Popular Superstitions* to Collins. For *Douglas* celebrates how its young hero, reared a shepherd, heard the sounding tale of war's alarms[3] and offers an instance of how "hostile brothers met to prove each other's arms."[4] In addition several specific passages in the tragedy suggested images to Collins. The simile, Act I, 316-18:

> LIKE SOME ENTRANC'D AND VISIONARY SEER,
> On Earth thou stand'st, thy thoughts ascend to Heaven,

and the passage in Act IV, 51-5:

> Beneath a mountain's brow, the most remote
> And inaccessible by shepherds trod,
> In a deep cave dug by no mortal hand
> A hermit liv'd, . . .

become part of Collins's description of the "Wizzard Seer" of Sky in stanza IV of the ode. And the stirring account in Act III, 85-9:

[3] Cf. *Pop. Super.*, 49.
[4] Cf. *Pop. Super.*, 52.

> One stormy night, as I remember well,
> The wind and rain beat hard upon our roof;
> Red came the river down, and loud and oft
> The angry spirit of the river shrieked,

furnishes some of the atmosphere of stanza VII.

When Collins became part of Thomson's circle he was associated with David Mallet, whose *Amyntor and Theodora* also dealt with the folk-lore and legend of the North. *Amyntor and Theodora* also influenced the *Ode on the Popular Superstitions.* Mallet, following Martin Martin's *Voyage to St. Kilda* and *Description of the Western Islands of Scotland,* eulogizes the "blameless manners" of the islanders of St. Kilda, calling them "a race of people the most uncorrupted in their manners, and therefore the least unhappy in their lives of any, perhaps, on the face of the whole earth." Collins echoes this sentiment in stanza X of the ode. Both Collins's poem and Mallet's, following Martin, mention the migrations of the sea-fowl and the stormy coast of the islands. Both also deal with the phenomenon of "second sight." In *Amyntor and Theodora,* III, 514-542, the passage on "second sight" is oddly enough a panegyric on "Immortal William," the Duke of Cumberland, who is also celebrated in the interpolated stanzas of the 1788 London version of Collins's ode. Two passages at the beginning of *Amyntor and Theodora* show striking verbal resemblance to Collins. Lines 8-12 of canto I:

> Thrice happy land! tho freezing on the verge
> Of arctic skies; yet blameless still of arts
> That polish, to deprave, each softer clime.
> With simple nature, simple virtue blest
> Beyond Ambition's walk . . .

and lines 27-31 of the same canto:

> Firm in each sinew vigor's plyant spring,
> By Temperance brac'd to peril and to pain,
> Amid the flood they stem, or on the steep
> Of upright rocks their straining steps surmount
> For food or pastime,

suggest the phrasing of stanza X of the ode.

And Thomson himself was a more significant force in Collins's development as a poet than has generally been admitted. The poets were intimate friends during the last years of Thomson's life at Richmond. The *Ode on the Death of Mr. Thomson* is a touching tribute to the friendship, and the odes *To Liberty* and *On the Popular Superstitions of the Highlands of Scotland* are, to a degree, fruits of their literary acquaintance. And there are suggestive reminiscences of Thomson in some of the other poems.

As early as the *Persian Eclogues* Collins might have been influenced by Thomson. The descriptive background of the *Second Eclogue* set in the desert resembles more closely than anything else Thomson's description of the pilgrim smitten by the suffocating winds of the desert and overcome by the "wide glittering waste of burning sand" in *Summer, 961-79.* And as has been indicated previously, Thomson's concept of the Poetical Character was similar to that of Collins. But a more definite source of influence is evident in the antistrophe of the *Ode to Mercy.* Lines 14-22:

> When he whom ev'n our Joys provoke,
> The *Fiend of Nature* join'd his Yoke,
> And rush'd in Wrath to make our Isle his Prey;
> Thy Form, from out thy sweet Abode,
> O'ertook Him on his blasted Road,
> And stop'd his Wheels, and look'd his Rage away.
>
> I see recoil his sable Steeds,
> That bore Him swift to Salvage Deeds,
> Thy tender melting Eyes they own;

resemble *A Nuptial Song,* originally intended as part of Thomson's *Sophonisba,* 1730. In that song "gentle Venus" is invoked to stop the onslaught of the God of War and to soothe his wrath by her charms. Lines 23-38 are reasonably close to the lines in the *Ode to Mercy:*

> Come, thou delight of heaven and earth!
> To whom all creatures owe their birth;
> Oh, come! red-smiling, tender, come!
> And yet prevent our final doom.
> For long the furious god of war

Has crushed us with his iron car,
Has raged along our ruined plains,
Has cursed them with his cruel stains,
Has sunk our youth in endless sleep,
And made the widowed virgin weep.
Now let him feel thy wonted charms,
Oh, take him to thy twining arms!
And, while thy bosom heaves on his,
While deep he prints the humid kiss,
Ah, then! his stormy heart control,
And sigh thyself into his soul.

The *Ode to Evening* has more suggestive reminiscences of Thomson, particularly of *The Seasons*. They are not as verbally close to the poem as are many of the Miltonic echoes, but they suggest that Thomson was another of the poets who had sung of evening to whom Collins in his poem paid tribute. Though the diction is Miltonic, *Autumn,* 961, "The DEWY-SKIRTED CLOUDS imbibe the SUN" resembles "the bright hair'd SUN . . . whose CLOUDY SKIRTS . . . o'erhang his wavy Bed" of the *Ode to Evening*. Again *Summer,* 120-2:

>   . . . while round thy BEAMING CAR,
>   High-seen, the Seasons lead, in sprightly dance
>   Harmonious Knit, the ROSY-FINGERED HOURS. . .

recalls "the fragrant Hours" and "shadowy Car" of Evening. Further pictures in *The Seasons* resemble those of the *Ode to Evening*. If they show no more they reveal that the poetic eye of Thomson saw something of what Collins found congenial in nature. *Spring,* 952-4:

>   . . . and wood and LAWN,
>   And verdant field and DARKENING HEATH between,
>   And SPIRY TOWNS . . .

recall the "lone Heath," the "upland Fallows," and the "dim-discover'd Spires" of Collins's poem. Even closer in tone and mood is *Summer,* 1685-95:

>   . . . Evening yields
>   The world to night; not in her winter robe
>   Of massy Stygian woof, but loose arrayed
>   In mantle dun. A faint erroneous ray,
>   Glanced from the imperfect surfaces of things,

Flings half an image on the straining eye;
While wavering woods, and villages, and streams,
And rocks, and mountain-tops that long retained
The ascending gleam are all one swimming scene,
Uncertain if beheld.

Again *Winter,* 424-7:

Now, all amid the rigours of the year,
In the wild depth of winter, while without
The ceaseless winds blow ice, BE MY RETREAT . . .
A RURAL, SHELTERED, SOLITARY SCENE . . .

recalls:

Or if chill blust'ring Winds, or driving Rain
Prevent my willing Feet, BE MINE THE HUT
    That from the Mountain's Side,
    Views Wilds, and swelling Floods . . .

in its love of solitude and retirement even in inclement weather.
The resemblances may simply indicate that the two poets were
kindred spirits, for a passage in *Summer,* 1379-1443, almost
epitomizes Collins and his ode:

Now the soft hour
Of walking comes for him who lonely loves
To seek the distant hills, and there converse
With nature, there to harmonize his heart,
And in pathetic song to breathe around
The harmony to others.

In the *Ode to Liberty,* however, Collins most closely followed
Thomson. As Mrs. Barbauld noted long ago:[5] "The subject of
the poem is similar to that of THOMSON'S long, and to say
the truth, rather heavy composition, which bears the same title."
Collins's ode is, in fact, a concentrated and somewhat confused
version of Thomson's longer poem, *Liberty,* published in 1735-6.
Like Collins's ode, Thomson's poem traces the progress of Liberty from Greece to Rome and mentions its survival in the fragments of the Roman state. The Italian city republics, Florence,
Lombardy, Liguria, Genoa, and Venice are mentioned in both
poems, as is Switzerland. Both poets then trace the history of
Liberty in Britain from Druid days, and rejoice at the return

[5] *Critical Essay,* p. xxvii.

of Liberty to Britain, the final abode of the goddess. *Liberty* extends over five books, and is several thousand lines in length. The ode of Collins has but 144 lines. But there are many traces of Thomson in the imagery and diction of the ode. The account of Rome's decline and the image of the broken statue, lines 18-25 of the ode:

> How *Rome*, . . .
> With heaviest Sound, a Giant-statue fell,
> Push'd by a wild and artless Race,
> From off its wide ambitious Base,
> When Time his Northern Sons of Spoil awoke,
>   And all the blended Work of Strength and Grace,
>   With many a rude repeated Stroke,
> And many a barb'rous Yell, to thousand Fragments broke,

seems to be derived from *Liberty,* I, 17-20:

> While scattered wide around, awful, and hoar,
> Lies, a vast monument, once glorious Rome,
> The tomb of empire! ruins! that efface
> Whate'er of finished modern pomp can boast.[6]

Line 23 of the passage in Collins:

> And all the blended Work of STRENGTH and GRACE,

echoes *Liberty,* I, 102-3:

> All that to ROMAN STRENGTH the softer touch
> Of GRECIAN ART can join.

The phrase "WIDE AMBITIOUS BASE," line 21 of the ode, suggests *Liberty,* II, 246:

> Then stood untouched the SOLID BASE of Liberty.

Again the idea expressed in the first epode, lines 26-33 of the ode:

> Yet ev'n, where'er the least appear'd,
> Th' admiring World thy Hand rever'd;
> Still 'midst the scatter'd States around,
> Some Remnants of her Strength were found;
> They saw by what escap'd the Storm,
> How wond'rous rose her perfect Form;

---

[6] The figure is repeated in *Liberty,* III, 414-25.

> How in the great the labour'd Whole,
> Each mighty Master pour'd his Soul!

represents a concentration of a passage in *Liberty,* II, 291-7, describing the sculpture of Greece:

> Thy fair ideas, thy delightful forms,
> By love imagined, and the graces touched,
> The boast of well pleased nature, Sculpture seized,
> And bade them ever smile in Parian stone.
> Selecting beauty's choice, and that again
> Exalting, blending in a perfect whole,
> Thy workmen left even nature's self behind,

and suggests Collins's image of the "perfect Form," the "labour'd Whole" and the work of "mighty Masters." The rest of Collins's epode traces the progress of Liberty from the fall of Rome to its final arrival in Britain, following with reasonable closeness the scheme Thomson employs in the third part of *Liberty.* Part IV of *Liberty,* 391-450, describes how the Genius of the deep with storms and tempests sent the Goddess to Britain in Druid days. This is the probable model for the antistrophe of the *Ode to Liberty* with its account of the "wide wild storm" which brought about the "blest Divorce" of England from France. The traditional story of the separation of England from France is told in *Liberty,* IV, 460-5:

> For of old time, since first the rushing flood,
> Urged by Almighty power, this favoured isle
> Turned flashing from the continent aside,
> Indented shore to shore responsive still,
> Its guardian she . . .

and, moreover, in the passage is the suggestion for Collins's belief in lines 87-88 that since this "blest Divorce" Britain has been the peculiar home of Liberty.

In the second epode a number of Collins's ideas seem drawn directly from Thomson. A hint for lines 89-94 of the ode:

> Then too, 'tis said, an hoary Pile,
> 'Midst the green Navel of our Isle,
> Thy Shrine in some religious Wood,
> O Soul-enforcing Goddess stood!

comes from *Liberty,* IV, 626-30:

> Bold were those Britons, who, the careless sons
> Of nature roamed the forest-bounds, at once
> Their verdant city, high-embowering fane,
> And the gay circle of their woodland wars:

with its description of the Druids and its mention of the "high-embowering fane" (cf. *Ode to Liberty,* 98). Collins does not, like Thomson, proceed to trace how Britain rose "from Celtic might to present grandeur," but he does describe the restoration of the Temple of Liberty to Britain after its beauteous Model has been treasured in Heaven, and he seems indebted to *Liberty* for both of these ideas. For the belief that after the fane was destroyed:

> AMIDST THE BRIGHT PAVILION'D PLAINS,
> The beauteous *Model* still remains,

expressed in lines 97-112 of the ode, Collins undoubtedly turned to *Liberty,* III, 540-70, in which Liberty tells how she quitted earth during the wintry age when pride and fierceness alone dominated the world, and with arts and each good genius in her train soared to heaven. Lines 549-70 especially suggest the source of Collins's passage, describing as they do how in:

> . . . the BRIGHT REGIONS THERE OF PUREST DAY,
> Far other scenes and palaces arise
> Adorned profuse with other arts divine.

There are several passages in *Liberty* from which Collins apparently drew his image of the restored temple of Liberty, which closes the second epode of the *Ode to Liberty.* Lines 115-20 of the ode:

> How learn delighted, and amaz'd,
> What Hands unknown that FABRIC rais'd?
> Ev'n now before his favor'd Eyes,
> In GOTHIC PRIDE it seems to rise!
> Yet GRAECIA'S GRACEFUL ORDERS join,
> Majestic thro' the MIX'D DESIGN;

seem to be suggested primarily by *Liberty,* II, 387-90, a descriptive panegyric on the forms of Greek architecture ("*Graecia's* graceful Orders"):

> The whole so measured true, so lessened off
> By fine proportion, that the marble pile . . .
> . . . light as FABRICS looked
> THAT FROM THE MAGIC WAND AERIAL RISE.

The combination of Gothic and Grecian models, to Collins admirable, Thomson views with disapproval in *Liberty*, III, 507-11, a possible source of Collins's picture:

> . . . what sculpture raised
> To Trajan's glory following triumphs stole,
> And MIXED WITH GOTHIC FORMS (the chisel's shame)
> On that triumphal arch the FORMS OF GREECE.

But the closest suggestions of Collins's temple of Liberty in Thomson's poem occur in parts IV and V, where the Goddess describes the new shrine which she has raised in modern Britain. *Liberty*, IV, 1177-80:

> And now behold! exalted as the cope
> That swells immense o'er many-peopled earth,
> And like it free, my fabric stands complete,
> The palace of the laws. . .

and *Liberty*, V, 376-8:

> . . . laurelled science, arts, and public works,
> That lend my finished fabric comely PRIDE
> Grandeur and GRACE,

are especially suggestive of Collins. Finally Part V of *Liberty, The Prospect*, seems the source for the conclusion of the ode. In design and in suggestive imagery, then, Thomson's long poem furnished the principal source for Collins's ode.

For the *Ode on the Popular Superstitions of the Highlands of Scotland* Collins was also considerably indebted to Thomson. It was written at the time of their intimacy. Thomson was a Scot and already in *The Seasons* he had mentioned the people of St. Kilda and the Hebrides. And in the *Castle of Indolence*, I, xxx, written at the time when Collins was thinking of his ode, Thomson had described the folk-lore and superstitions of the Hebrid shepherds, in language closely suggestive of stanza IV of the *Ode on the Popular Superstitions:*

> As when a shepherd of the Hebrid Isles,
> Placed far amid the melancholy main,
> (Whether it be lone fancy him beguiles,
> Or that aerial beings sometimes deign
> To stand embodied to our senses plain,)
> Sees on the naked hill, or valley low,
> The whiles in ocean Phoebus dips his wain,
> A vast assembly moving to and fro;
> Then all at once in air dissolves the wondrous show.

But a number of passages in *The Seasons* indicate how much Collins found in Thomson to turn his fancy to the themes of the northern isles. The virtuous race of Kilda, described in stanza X of the ode, Thomson had mentioned in *Spring,* 955-8; and in *Autumn,* 862-78, he had described the migrations of the sea birds, the shepherd's sea-girt reign, and the hard life of the native, who gathers his "ovarious food," the eggs of the Solan Goose. A further passage, *Autumn,* 892-902, mentions the hardiness of the people of the northern isles, "a manly race Of unsubmitting spirit, wise, and brave" much as Collins describes them in the ode. Thomson and Collins both turned originally to Martin Martin, although it is significant that Thomson had preceded Collins in the treatment of the theme. But for two other passages in the ode Thomson seems to be Collins's closest source. Stanzas VI, VII, and VIII of the ode describe the terrors of the Will-o'-the-Wisp, the fate of the luckless swain trapped by the Water-Kaelpie, and the return of his lost spirit to his mourning wife. For the account of the Will-o'-the-Wisp and part of the account of the luckless swain Collins turned to *Autumn,* 1146-59, which describes the bewildered wanderer, who "decoyed by the fantastic blaze" sinks into a miry gulf, while his "pining wife" and "plaintive children" await his return. This he apparently supplemented by some details from the account in *Winter,* 276-321, of the disastered swain lost in the winter storm. Closest to Collins is the passage, *Winter,* 311-15:

> In vain for him the officious wife prepares
> The fire fair-blazing and the vestment warm;
> In vain his little children, peeping out
> Into the mingling storm, demand their sire

With tears of artless innocence. Alas!
Nor wife nor children more shall he behold,
Nor friends, nor sacred home.

This Collins renders in stanza VIII, 121-5:

For him, in vain, his anxious wife shall wait,
Or wander forth to meet him on his way;
For him, in vain, at to-fall of the day,
His babes shall linger at th' unclosing gate!
Ah, ne'er shall he return!

Finally, a passage in *Summer,* 1711-13, describing:

Those superstitious horrors that enslave
The fond sequacious herd, to mystic faith
And blind amazement prone . . .

Collins follows closely in stanza II of the ode, 26-30, where he
mentions the "herd" who fears the "elf-shot arrows" of those
"airy beings" which "awe th' untutor'd swain."

In a number of minor instances, then, Thomson apparently
suggested images or phrases to Collins and on at least two occasions, in the *Ode to Liberty* and the *Ode on the Popular Superstitions,* he definitely furnished an imaginative stimulus for the
theme of the poem itself.[7]

---

[7] In several instances there are parallels in diction between Collins and
Thomson. These may be accidental, for Milton was the avowed master of
both poets. Most striking examples are: *Liberty,* II, 98, "BOON NATURE,"
cf. *Manners,* 71, "O NATURE BOON"; *Liberty,* II, 139, "thymy," cf. *Simplicity,*
14; *Spring,* 517, "alleys green," cf. *Passions,* 77; *Autumn,* 134, "pillar'd,"
cf. *Ode to Liberty,* 76; *Autumn,* 962, "imbrown," cf. *Poetical Character,* 60;
Autumn, 950, "dun," cf. *Mr. Thomson,* 34; *Summer,* 945, "green delights,"
cf. *Persian Eclogues,* II, 25. With Thomson's description in *Spring,* 523-6:

. . . the river now
Dimpling along, the breezy ruffled lake,
The forest darkening round, the glittering spire.

compare the setting of the *Ode on the Death of Mr. Thomson.* With *Winter,*
610-16, compare *Manners,* 1-58; compare also *Spring,* 297-305, with *Fear,*
17-23. As possible instances of Collins's influence on Thomson see *Castle
of Indolence,* I, xlvi, 4-8 (cf. *Fear,* 10-15); *Ibid.,* I, xlix-l, the Mirror of
Vanity, (cf. *Manners,* 27-30); *Ibid.,* I, lvii-lix, possibly a description of
Collins (cf. the allusion to "boon nature," lvii, 9, drawn directly from *The
Manners* and the allusion to the *Ode to Evening* in lviii, 3-9).

VI

LITERATURE OF HISTORY AND TRAVEL

FROM THE FIRST, books of history and travel fascinated Collins. It is surely significant that in his first work, the *Persian Eclogues,* and in his last, the *Ode on the Popular Superstitions,* Collins's imagination should have been stimulated by the literature of travel. The poet himself was inclined to disparage the pastorals, calling them his "Irish Eclogues" as if to imply that the Persian element in them was but a slight veneer.[1] Yet the *Modern History* of "the ingenious Mr. Salmon" was a more significant stimulus to his imagination than the poet remembered. Even in the Preface, which describes in true romantic fashion how the manuscript came into the poet's hands, there are traces of the poet's reminiscence of Salmon. The paragraph:

There is an Elegancy and Wildness of Thought which recommends all their Compositions; and our Genius's are as much too cold for the Entertainment of such Sentiments, as our Climate is for their Fruits and Spices,

is especially illuminating. It reminds one of a comment made in a far different spirit by Lady Mary Wortley Montague when she sent a translation of some oriental poetry to Pope, April 1, 1717:

I cannot determine upon the whole how well I have succeeded in the translation, neither do I think our English proper to express such violence of passion which is very seldom felt among us.[2]

To Collins "Elegancy and Wildness of Thought" are evidences of true imagination. Here for the first time he regrets that lack of passion in the poetry of his day, which Lady Mary regarded as a commendable trait in the English. As he wrote the passage,

[1] Joseph Warton, *Pope's Works,* London, 1797, I, 64.
[2] *Letters from the Honorable Lady Mary Wortley Montague,* 1709-1762, Ed. R. Brimley Johnson, London, J. M. Dent, 1906, p. 123.

too, he must have remembered what he had read in Salmon about the poetry of the Persians:

There [sic] invention is fruitful and lively, their manner sweet, their temper amorous and their language has a softness proper for verse . . . the thoughts are noble and elevated, their expressions soft, and their terms always the most proper that can be hit upon.[3]

And in assigning the eclogues a fictitious date "probably in the Beginning of *Sha Sultan Hosseyn's* Reign, the Successor of *Sefi* or *Solyman* the Second," Collins must have remembered reading in *The Present State of Persia*, p. 406:

He was succeeded by his son Shaw Sefi the Second. . . . This prince changed his name and took that of Solyman, instead of Sefi . . . he died on the 29th of July, 1694, and was succeeded by his son Shaw Sultan Hossein.

In the eclogues themselves, moreover, Collins frequently draws upon Salmon for details which lend verisimilitude to his account. The *First Eclogue, Selim or the Shepherd's Moral,* is closer to the Persian custom than has been supposed. Selim (whose name occurs in the history) teaches somewhat in the manner of Pope "informing Morals" to the shepherd maids. While the moral taught is suspiciously Augustan, Collins must have found his hint for the theme in Salmon's account of the Persian poets:

According to the Persians—the antient philosophers in the east were all poets, and their wise lessons were delivered in verse, to render them the more amiable and venerable, and that the people might readily retain them in their memories. It is the same thing in effect at this day in Persia. The subject of their poems is generally some piece of morality, or philosophy.[4]

So Selim's "useful Lesson for the Fair and Young" has a Persian cast to it as well as an eighteenth century moral. Three other attempts at verisimilitude might be mentioned: the allusion to Balsora's pearls, line 30 of the poem, suggests the account of the pearl-fisheries at Bossora of which Collins had read

---

[3] Salmon, Thomas, *Modern History,* 1739, I, 398. Further page numbers refer to this edition.

[4] *Op. cit.,* I, 398.

in Salmon; the "balmy Shrub," 49, is mentioned in Salmon; and the "silken Veil" of Chastity, 62, is also a detail that Collins could have found in the history.

The *Second Eclogue, Hassan, or the Camel Driver,* owes something in detail to the same source. Salmon devotes considerable attention to the merchant caravans of camels which traverse Persia. Much of the local color of the piece is specifically taken from the poet's reading in his source. Particularly vivid are Salmon's descriptions of the hot winds which blow over the deserts and of the wild animals which haunt the countryside. Collins follows both of these accounts:

The hot winds which blow from the eastward over a long tract of sandy deserts are ready to suffocate them, and sometimes there happens a pestilential blast, which strikes the traveller dead in an instant. . . . But there is also a great deal to be ascribed to the nature of the soil, and the situation of the country, where the winds blow over large sandy deserts heated like an oven, and especially between the mountains, which reflect the heat from one side to the other. . . . In Hyrcania and Curdistan, the woody parts of the country, wild beasts abound, such as lions, tygers, leopards, wild-hogs, jackalls etc. . . . That part of the country which lyes upon the Caspian or Hyrcanian sea is full of serpents, toads, scorpions, and other venemous insects.[5]

Moreover, the choice of Schiraz as the city toward which the distraught Hassan should turn his thoughts is appropriate, although curiously enough "Schiraz' Walls," 14, do not exist:

The town is seated in a pleasant fertile valley, about twenty miles in length and six in breadth. . . . There are no walls about the place.

The *Third Eclogue, Abra, or the Georgian Sultana,* is indebted to Salmon both for theme and for descriptive detail. The story of great Abbas who found Abra tending her sheep near the forest, who wooed and won her, who bore her from the plain to the palace, yet frequently returned with her to enjoy the simple and carefree life of the shepherd is thoroughly pastoral in flavor. Yet Collins might well have found most of the basic details for his story in the story of Nour Mahal recounted by Salmon in *The Present State of Proper India,* pp. 242-4 in the

[5] *Op. cit.,* p. 368, p. 394.

history. The significant passages for Collins in the story are these:

His majesty, it seems, was walking on the terras, under which a fine river runs, when he saw a barge rowing under him wherein was a lady of a surprizing beauty sitting under a canopy: the emperor let the barge pass by, but sent immediately to enquire after her name and where her residence was.

In the story in Salmon, Nour Mahal was already married, but after her husband had met his death in the manner of Uriah the Hittite, she became empress:

But notwithstanding one of the greatest emperors of the East was captivated with her charms, and the empire was for some time governed by her nod, her parentage was but mean; and when she came from Persia, the place of her birth, with her husband he was no more than a camel driver. . . .

For the characteristics of the emperor, too, much of the story in Salmon might have contributed details:

No Prince, it seems, ever delighted more in laying aside his state, and conversing familiarly with his subjects; he frequently disguised himself and came into places of publick resort, where he would sit down and enter into merry disputes with the meanest of his subjects. . . . But this Emperor was not so entirely devoted to wine or women, as to lose the relish of a rural life; he frequently retired in the summer, into the Kingdom of Cachemire, the most northern part of his dominions which is looked upon in India as a terrestrial paradise, being exceeding temperate and beautiful, and abounding with all things that can render life desirable. . . . Here the Emperor built him an elegant palace, laid out delightful gardens, made canals and cascades, and imbellished it with a thousand beauties. The Sultaness took a particular delight in stocking the canals with tame fish, and many years after there were taken fish with gold rings, which this princess had fastened to some of her favourites.

There are, to be sure, some striking differences in detail between Collins's delicate pastoral theme and the story of the great Cha Selim, but there are similarities enough, too, to make it reasonable that Collins had strayed no further than the pages of Salmon to find it.[6]

[6] Other sources for the motif of the piece have been noted. Montégut cites *L'Histoire d'Alibée, Persan*, which was apparently the source of the Persian tale of Alibez, the shepherd lad of Cha-Abbas, who though raised

Two other slight details of local color in the eclogue are also drawn from Salmon. The first two lines describing *"Tefflis' Towers"* suggest Salmon's statement:

Teflis, as has been observed already, is the capital city of Georgia, but under the dominion of the Persians, and inhabited chiefly by Christians: insomuch that 'tis said, there is not one Mahometan mosque in the place, except that of the castle, though there are no less than 14 Christian churches.[7]

Further, lines 14-18, describing the flowers of Persia, "gay-motley'd Pinks and Sweet Junquils" which Abra wove into a chaplet, Collins admits in a note refer to this passage in Salmon:

In Media the fields produce tulips, anemonies and ranunculuses; about Isphahan and some other towns jonquils grow wild: they have also daffodils, lillies, violets and pinks in their season, and some flowers which last all the year round; but what they have the greatest quantity of are lilies and roses.[8]

The *Fourth Eclogue* describes the flight of the shepherds Agib and Secander before the invasions of Turk and Tartar, bewails the indolence of the Persian monarch, and laments the spoiling of the country. The whole historical background for the poem comes from chapter IV of the *Present State of Persia,* which details how the late Sophi, Shaw Sultan Hossein, chose to live an indolent, inactive life among his women in the harem and put himself in the hands of Mirewys, originally a Tartar. When the country was torn by the machinations of this favorite the Turk and Muscovite made the most of this condition and invaded the country. But the source for the immediate situation in the eclogue, the flight of the shepherds, seems to come directly from a passage in Salmon:

When the Persians are apprehensive of an invasion, their constant method is to withdraw all the people on the frontiers, and destroy the country in such a manner as the enemy shall find nothing to sub-

---

to high place in court kept "a sheep-hook, a pipe, and a shepherd's habit" to remind him of his early life. The tale appeared (Bronson notes) in *The Free Thinker* in 1719 and was reprinted in Nathan Drake's *Gleaner* in 1811. Dyce compares Cowley's *Country Life,* 17-22. An interesting modern variation of the motif appears in Beerbohm's *Zuleika Dobson,* ch. V.

[7] *Op. cit.,* I, 376.
[8] *Op. cit.,* I, 392.

sist on, not leaving so much as a spire of grass or a tree upon the
ground. But they give the husbandmen time to secure their grain,
fruits, and forage by burying them all. The army having thus destroyed the country for eight days journey together, they encamp
near it in separate bodies, and as they see occasion fall upon the
enemy and distress him in the march: sometimes on another in the
night time; and if they cannot by this means put a stop to his march,
they retire farther into the country, driving the people before them,
and destroying everything, as before; and by these means have they
defeated the greatest Turkish armies. When the enemy are retired,
every man returns to his lands again. . . .[9]

With this passage as a basis the poet's imagination has conjured
up a vivid picture of the horrors and cruelty of war which he
was later to feel in the odes—that fear of the horrible which
was always part of his imagination, coloring and making alive a
prosaic account in a prosaic history.

Collins had, then, in the eclogues leaned heavily on his source-
material. Yet he could not have found in Salmon the intense
horror and terror which is so marked in the *Second* and *Fourth
Eclogues,* nor could he have discovered there more than a hint
for the charming and almost Elizabethan quality of the *Third
Eclogue,* the delicate sweetness of which is all his own. In these
poems are already evident the finest qualities of the poet; already vividness of imagination and delicacy of touch are there.

A few years later Collins was to turn again to the history of
the ingenious Mr. Salmon. Most of the historical detail in the
epode of the *Ode to Liberty* is treated in Salmon. In the account
of the *Present State of Italy,* he might have found an account
of San Marino, renowned for its liberty, which led him to
mention it in lines 40-41:

They are esteem'd an honest well-meaning people, and according to
some of our modern travellers, live much more happy and contented
among their rocks and snows than any other Italians do in the most
fruitful valleys. Nothing, says Mr. Addison, can be a greater instance
of the natural love mankind have for LIBERTY, and of their aversion
to an arbitrary government, than to see such a savage mountain
cover'd with people, when the Campania of Rome (under a Monarch) in the same country, is destitute of inhabitants.[10]

[9] *Op. cit.,* I, 124.
[10] *Op. cit.,* II, 434.

There is in the same section of the history a reference to the Bucentaur (II, 368) to which Collins alludes in lines 43-4 of the ode, as well as an account of "sad Liguria." And undoubtedly the source for lines 52-6, describing "wild Helvetia":

> (Where, when the favor'd of thy Choice,
> The daring Archer heard thy Voice;
> Forth from his Eyrie rous'd in Dread,
> The rav'ning *Eagle* northward fled,)

is the account in the *Present State of Switzerland.* The William Tell story is there followed by this passage:

The Emperor Albert hearing of this defection, was about assembling an army to have reduced them to obedience; but being killed soon after as he passed the river Russ, these Cantons had a favourable opportunity of establishing themselves, while the Empire remain'd in confusion. About seven years after Archduke *Leopold,* the son of Albert, march'd into the Canton of Switz with twenty thousand men, threatening utter destruction to the confederated provinces. The Switzer's made little resistance, till the Austrian army was advanced into a narrow valley, between two mountains, from the tops of the hills, they put the Austrian cavalry in confusion; and at the same time attacking them in front with fifteen hundred men, they obtain'd a compleat victory, which they pursued with such diligence, that they drove the enemy entirely out of the country.[11]

And while the account of the tyrannies of the Duke of Alva and the refusal of Elizabeth to be queen of the Netherlands to which reference is made in lines 56-9 of the ode might have been suggested by Collins's reading in Sir William Temple's *Observations,* it is also told in Salmon, II, 149-55. A later passage in the same account apparently suggested to the poet the tradition regarding the stork, mentioned in line 57 of the ode and elaborated in the poet's note:

Here are all manner of tame fowls as in England; and of the wild, the stork, about the bigness of a heron, is the most remarkable, which builds on the tops of their chimneys in most of the towns and villages; and BY VIRTUE OF A NATIONAL SUPERSTITION IN THEIR FAVOUR, ARE NEVER DESTROY'D.[12]

[11] *Op. cit.,* II, 286-7.
[12] *Op. cit.,* II, 239. But cf. Browne, *Enquiries into Vulgar and Common Errors,* Book III, Chapter 27, 3:
"That Storks are to be found, and will only live, in Republikes or Free

Salmon, then, seems to have been the poet's historical *vade mecum,* the prosaic source of many an imaginative and colorful allusion.[13]

The ingenious use of his source book which Collins learned so early in writing the *Persian Eclogues* he shows with greater skill in his last significant poem, the *Ode on the Popular Superstitions of the Highlands of Scotland.* Though Thomson and Mallet may have turned his imagination to the islands west of Scotland, his reading of two travel books by Martin Martin, *A Description of the Western Islands of Scotland* and *A Voyage to St. Kilda,* furnished him with the specific information over which he was to cast the glamour of poetic fancy. As was his custom, Collins followed closely the material of his source, concentrating it into the language of poetry. At least half of the poem is colored by details gleaned from reading Martin. The description of the "fairy people" in stanza II of the poem illustrates the poet's method. Lines 22-5 of the ode:

States, is a petty conceit to advance the opinion of popular policies, and from Antipathies in Nature, to disparage Monarchican Government."
For a later use of the tradition see Tennyson, *The Talking Oak,* 53-6.
[13] Other sources of Collins's historical and traditional lore in the *Ode to Liberty* should here be mentioned briefly. First in significance is Camden's *Britannia,* p. 1, from which, as Mr. A. S. P. Woodhouse has shown (*Collins and the Poetic Imagination,* p. 113), much of the imagery of the antistrophe is derived. Further, as a source of the lines:

> *Mona,* once hid from those who search the Main,
> Where thousand Elfin Shapes abide,

and of the tradition (mentioned in Collins's note) "that a Mermaid, becoming ENAMOUR'D OF A YOUNG MAN of extraordinary Beauty . . . was receiv'd with a coldness" and "punish'd the whole Island, by covering it with a Mist," should be mentioned Waldron's *Description of the Isle of Man,* 1731, (*Pub. Manx Society,* Vol. XI). That book recounts (p. 7) how "a blue mist hanging continually over the land prevented the ships that passed by from having any suspicion there was an island." On p. 65 of the same book there is an account of "a very beautiful mermaid ENAMORED OF A YOUNG MAN who used to tend his sheep on these rocks." At first he encouraged her advances, but fearful that she had a design to draw him into the sea, he ran from her. In resentment she struck him with a stone and disappeared. The young man died a week afterward. It seems highly probable that Collins confused the two accounts. The usual tradition about the mist is that it was the work of a magician, Mannanan Mac-y, "who, by covering the isle with mists, prevented the access of foreigners," an account given again in Feltham's *Tour Through the Isle of Man in 1797-8* (*Pub. Manx Society,* VI, 104), showing that to be the more familiar and persistent version of the story.

> There each trim lass that skims the milky store
>   To the swart tribes their creamy bowl allots;
> By night they sip it round the cottage-door,
>   While airy minstrels warble jocund notes,

are drawn closely from two passages in Martin. The first describes the custom mentioned in lines 22-3:

They had an universal custom of pouring a cow's milk upon a little hill, or big stone, where the spirit called Browny was believed to lodge. This spirit always appeared in the shape of a tall man having very long brown hair. It is not long since every family of any considerable substance in those islands was haunted by a spirit they called Browny, which did several sorts of work; and this was the reason why they gave him offerings of the various products of the place: thus some when they churned their milk, or brewed, poured some milk and wort through the hole of a stone, called Browny's stone.[14]

A second discussion of the Brownies furnishes the suggestion for lines 24-5 of the ode:

A spirit, by the country people called Browny was frequently seen in all the most considerable families in the isles and north of Scotland. . . . The spirits used also to form sounds in the air resembling those of a harp, pipe, crowing of cock, and of the grinding of querns; and sometimes they have heard voices in the air by night singing Irish songs. . . .[15]

Stanza IV of the ode deals with the phenomenon of second sight which Martin discusses briefly in *A Voyage to St. Kilda* and at some length in the *Description of the Western Islands*. The stanza, lines 53-69 of the ode, reads:

> 'Tis thine to sing, how framing hideous spells
>   In SKY's lone isle the gifted wizzard seer,
> Lodged in the wintry cave with ————,   55
>   Or in the depth of Uist's dark forests dwells:
> How they, whose sight such dreary dreams engross,
>   With their own visions oft astonish'd droop,
> When o'er the wat'ry strath or quaggy moss
>   They see the gliding ghosts unbodied troop.   60
> Or if in sports, or on the festive green,
>   Their ———— glance some fated youth descry,

---

[14] *Description of the Western Islands of Scotland* in Pinkerton's *Voyages*, (1809), V, iii, 610. Further page references are to this edition.
[15] *Op. cit.*, p. 601.

Who, now perhaps in lusty vigour seen
    And rosy health, shall soon lamented die.
For them the viewless forms of air obey,   65
    Their bidding heed, and at their beck repair.
They know what spirit brews the stormful day,
    And heartless, oft like moody madness stare
To see the phantom train their secret work prepare.

Lines 53-6 of the passage describing the "hideous spells" of
the "gifted wizzard seer" might have been suggested by Collins's
reading about the "evil eye," which affects children and cattle,
and occasions frequent mischances and sometimes death,[16] or
more probably by his remembering "the account of one Roderick supposed to have had conversation with a familiar spirit"
detailed in the *Voyage to St. Kilda*,[17] though Roderick practiced
in St. Kilda and later retired to Sky. The rest of the account
follows the source more closely. Lines 57-60 of the poem, describing how those who have such dreary dreams "with their
own visions oft astonished droop," are drawn from the following
passage in Martin:

When a novice, or one that has lately obtained the second-sight, sees
a vision in the night-time without doors, and comes near a fire, he
presently falls into a swoon.[18]

Lines 61-4 of the ode seem inspired by such a story as the following, part of the account of second-sight:

Daniel Dow, above named, foretold the death of a young woman in
Minginnis, within less than twenty-four hours before the time; and
accordingly she died suddenly in the fields; though at the time of the
prediction she was in perfect health.[19]

The belief in lines 65-9 that persons gifted with second-sight
have some control over the elements suggests a passage in the
account of Roderick the imposter in the *Voyage to St. Kilda*:

[16] *Op. cit.*, p. 614.
[17] *Ibid.*, pp. 725-9.
[18] *Op. cit.*, p. 671.
[19] *Ibid.*, p. 676. A similar story is told about the prediction of a maiden's
death on p. 671. It is surprising that Collins made no use of the weird belief
on p. 670 concerning the vision of the person clothed in a shroud which
Rossetti employed so vividly in the *King's Tragedy*.

It hath been observed of him . . . that so often as he was employed by the steward to go to, or return from, Harries, they were always exposed to the greatest dangers by violent storms.[20]

The phrase "oft like moody madness stare," line 68 of the ode, is drawn from Martin's description:

At the sight of a vision, the eye-lids of the person are erected, and the eyes continue staring until the object vanishes.[21]

Stanzas IX and X of the ode also owe much to the two books of Martin. The mention of "those feath'ry tribes which spring From their rude rocks," is an allusion to Martin's several descriptions of the huge flocks of Solan geese and other water fowl which inhabit the rocky cliffs of these Hebrid isles. A specimen is Martin's statement in *A Voyage to St. Kilda:*

We put in under the hollow of an extraordinary high rock, to the north of this isle, which was all covered with a prodigious number of Solan geese hatching in their nests. The heavens were darkened by their flying over our heads. . . .

The reference in lines 142-5 of the ode to:

> that hoar pile which still its ruin shows:
> In whose small vaults a pigmy-folk is found,
> Whose bones the delver with his spade upthrows,
> And culls them, wond'ring, from the hallow'd ground,[22]

is to the ruins of a chapel of Saint Flannan on Island More, hallowed ground if the rites celebrated in approaching the altar be any sign.[23] A further passage describes the island of Pigmies, of which the narrator says:

There has been many small bones dug out of the ground here, resembling those of human kind more than any other.

Collins has combined the details of two passages in his treatment of them in the ode. The place mentioned in lines 146-7 of the ode

> where beneath the show'ry west
> The mighty Kings of three fair realms are laid;

[20] *Ibid.,* p. 729.
[21] *Ibid.,* p. 670.
[22] *Ibid.,* p. 701. See also pp. 664-5; pp. 709-12.
[23] *Ibid.,* p. 580.

is the church of St. Ouran on the island of Jona or Colmkil, also mentioned in *Macbeth,* I, ii, 61, as "Colme's inch." In his dedicatory letter to Prince George of Denmark, Martin says of the islands:

They can boast that they are honoured with the sepulchres of eight Kings of Norway, who at this day, with forty-eight Kings of Scotland, and four of Ireland lie entombed in the island of Jona; a place famed then for some peculiar sanctity.[24]

The account of the church and of the tombs is given again in the *Description of the Western Islands,* pp. 657-8.

For his panegyric on the simple but virtuous lives of Kilda's race in stanza X of the ode Collins was again drawing on Martin's *Voyage to St. Kilda.* Collins's mention of their "blameless manners," their sincere yet plain lives, their "sparing tem'prance," and his concluding apostrophe, lines 167-9:

> Thus blest in primal innocence they live,
>   Suffic'd and happy with that frugal fare
> Which tasteful toil and hourly danger give,

follows closely Martin's account in his Preface and his remarks near the close of the work:

The inhabitants of St. Kilda are much happier than the generality of mankind, being almost the only people in the world who feel the sweetness of true liberty: what the condition of the people in the golden age is feigned by the poets to be, that theirs really is, I mean, in innocence and simplicity, purity, mutual love and cordial friendship, free from solicitous cares and anxious covetousness; from envy, pride, and the consequences that attend them.[25]

The passage, lines 160-6 of the ode:

>   Of those whose lives are yet sincere and plain,
> Their bounded walks the rugged cliffs along,
>   And all their prospect but the wintry main.
> With sparing temp'rance, at the needful time,
>   They drain the sainted spring, or, hunger-prest,
> Along th' Atlantic rock undreading climb,
>   And of its eggs despoil the Solan's nest,

---

[24] *Op. cit.,* p. 572.
[25] *Op. cit.,* pp. 724-5.

represents Collins's concentration of several suggestive passages in Martin. On the climbing of the natives, their rocky prospect, and their despoiling the Solan's nest, a section in *A Description of the Western Islands* is most illuminating:

The inhabitants of St. Kilda excell all those I ever saw in climbing rocks. . . . This little commonwealth hath two ropes of about twenty four fathoms length each for climbing the rocks, which they do by turns; the ropes are secured all round with cows' hides salted for the use, and which preserves them from being cut by the edge of the rocks. By the assistance of these ropes they purchase a great number of eggs and fowls.[26]

Another passage in *A Voyage to Saint Kilda* supplements the first account, describing the rock Stack-ly, a haunt of the Solan goose:

One would think it next to impossible to climb this rock, which I expressed being very near it; but the inhabitants assured me it was practicable and to convince me of the truth of it, they bid me to look up near the top, where I perceived a stone pyramid-house, which the inhabitants built for lodging themselves in it in August . . . these are to land on this rock some days before the Solan geese take wing; if they neglect this piece of fore-sight, one windy day may disappoint them of five, six, or seven thousand Solan geese, which this rock affords yearly.[27]

A further passage testifies to the dexterity of the inhabitants in climbing to seemingly inaccessible places:

The inhabitants, I must tell you, run no small danger in quest of these fowls and eggs, in so much that I fear it would be thought an hyperbole to relate the inaccessibleness, steepness and height of those formidable rocks which they venture to climb. I myself have seen some of them climb up the corner of rock with their backs to it, making use only of their heels and elbows, without any other assistance and they have this way acquired a dexterity in climbing beyond any I ever yet saw: necessity has made them apply themselves to this, and custom has perfected them in it.[28]

Even to minor details which give a sense of verisimilitude Collins follows his source. His mention of "the sainted spring,"

[26] *Ibid.*, p. 667.
[27] *Op. cit.*, p. 707.
[28] *Ibid.*, p. 720.

164, is drawn from Martin's account of St. Kilder's well, from which the island is supposed to derive its name (p. 705). Line 170, "Hard is their shallow soil, and bleak and bare," almost paraphrases Martin's description (p. 705): "The whole island is one hard rock all thinly covered with black or brown earth, not above a foot, some places half a foot deep." Martin affirms, however, that the soil is fertile. And the phrase "show'ry west," 146, is a poetic statement of Martin's comment, p. 629, that "the south-west winds are observed to carry more rain with them than any other." Finally, Collins turns Martin's statement in *A Voyage to St. Kilda:*

There is no sort of Trees, no not the least Shrub grows here, nor ever a bee seen at any time,[29]

into what Mrs. Barbauld calls a "negative circumstance highly descriptive" when he writes, line 171, "Nor ever vernal bee was heard to murmur there!"[30]

This fascination with books of travel, from which Collins drew the stuff of his earliest poem and his latest, is a significant part of Collins's genius. While he did not write a *Rime of the Ancient Mariner* as a result of his reading in Salmon's *Modern History* and in Martin's voyages he did help to pave the way for that kind of poetic alchemy which was to produce the fanciful poems of remote and fascinating places that have immortalized Byron, Moore, and Coleridge.

---

[29] *Op. cit.,* p. 705.
[30] I find that I have been anticipated in my researches on *A Voyage to St. Kilda* by Mr. A. S. P. Woodhouse, "Collins and Martin Martin," *TLS,* 1928, p. 1011. The comments in my study were arrived at independently, but later checked with his findings. Especially significant is his conclusion that Collins purposely omitted the pleasant sides of Martin's picture in order to emphasize the romantic picture of primitive innocence. See also W. C. MacKenzie, "Collins and Martin Martin," *TLS,* 1929, p. 29, for a discussion of the "pigmy folk" and the site of the "hoar pile," Luckruban, or the Pigmies' Isle, at the butt of Lewis.

VII

TOOLS IN A POET'S WORKSHOP

THE HUNTING and listing of sources is at best a tentative business and does not always offer final and satisfactory proof that the poet's mind functioned as did that of the source-hunter. It bears, too, something of the stigma attached to the minute analysis of poetry. Perhaps analysis mis-shapes the beauteous forms of things, perhaps we murder to dissect. Yet it is justified in a study of a poet like Collins. For Collins's ideas were drawn largely from books, and he had not, as Mr. Garrod has observed, found an individual style of expression of his own. He was approaching that achievement in his *Ode on the Popular Superstitions,* yet that ode is fully as derivative and imitative in diction as the odes of 1746. Six years is a painfully short time to find one's own medium of expression. Even Keats longed for ten years. Were the pages which precede this section a mere listing of sources and a catalogue of verbal echoes, one might justly question if they are more than mere loads of learned lumber. But since they reveal something of Collins's mind to us, they may give us pause.

First in significance is the range of Collins's reading and the way in which he assimilated what he had read into the substance of his work. A book of travel like Martin's he culled for ideas and phrases and turned them into poetic form. A long poem like Thomson's *Liberty* he followed in outline and concentrated into a short ode. An image in Spenser he condensed from a Spenserian stanza to a line or two. Perhaps he had learned this faculty at the feet of Pope. At any rate, one wonders at the wealth of images, suggestive allusions, and stimulating pictures he has concentrated into such an ode as that *To Liberty.* He was truly loading every rift with ore; yet one sometimes feels that this very concentration is a defect. Until the *Ode on the Popular Supersti-*

tions Collins had not learned to be sufficiently diffuse with a wealth of material. On the other hand, *When Phoebe formed a Wanton Smile* and the *Ode Written in the Beginning of the Year 1746* are admirable instances of his power of condensation when his material is slight in content.

Secondly, one is struck by Collins's ability to suggest the language and imagery of his original without making his reminiscence mere copy-work. The passage on Tasso in the *Ode on the Popular Superstitions* is one case in point; the first section of the *Ode on the Poetical Character* dealing directly with an incident in Spenser is another.

One is further impressed by the poet's faculty of calling to mind through suggestive and allusive phrase the works of other poets who have approached the theme he is treating. Hence, in the *Ode to Evening* as he writes of evening he embroiders into his own picture phrases from Milton, from Shakespeare, from Spenser, from Pope, from Thomson, and from Warton. They are part of the beauty of his own poem, but they recall as well the poet who first phrased them. Again in the *Ode to Liberty* the theme is enhanced by the suggestions from *Comus* and *Lycidas,* both poems which have the fascination of remote and strange places. But rarely does one feel that the borrowed phrase intrudes. More often it is worked too subtly into the woof of the poem for that. For all of its suggestion of Pope and of Milton the *Ode Written in the Beginning of the Year 1746* is Collins's own. And the *Ode on the Poetical Character* is the more inspired for its Miltonic allusion. There are exceptions, however. The reference to *Lycidas* at the end of the *Ode to Liberty* is awkward, and nothing can save the image of the British Lion kissing the feet of Peace from infelicity, though it is drawn from the *Faerie Queene.*

Of the diction itself one must admit that it is formal and literary. In rare instances is it the language of men. But that is in itself significant. It shows how far Collins was part of the traditional school of poets that flourished in his day. His professed admiration for Milton and his friendship with Thomson and Joseph Warton, both imitators of the Miltonic manner, explain why so much of his diction echoes that of his master. Most remarkable, however, is the thoroughness with which Collins assimilated the phrases and the words of his model, and his art in combining them into something of an original result. The Spenserian "antique phrase" and the words drawn from Fairfax testify to Collins's place as a traditional poet. He was writing in a day when the cult of Spenser flourished. Yet Collins's use of the Spenserian phrase is less obtrusive and less artificial than that of most of the Spenserian imitators, less jarring than the appearance of such archaisms in *The Cotter's Saturday Night* or *Childe Harold's Pilgrimage*. And though there is more than a trace of Pope's manner in Collins—natural enough in a younger poet who has a renowned living writer for a model—one feels that Pope's best legacy to Collins was a love of polish and clean-cut form. The more conventional aspects of Pope's diction Collins was wise enough partially to outgrow. That he abandoned the heroic couplet for freer verse forms is significant evidence on this point, too, although one must admit that the regularity of Collins's lines even in the odes is marked to the end.

One final observation must be made. Collins was, as his sources show, an imitative poet even in his choice of theme. The *Persian Eclogues* are thoroughly conventional pastorals, and the *Epistle to Hanmer* is conceived after a familiar form, the verse epistle of Pope and Dryden. *The Manners* is a *L'Allegro* and *Il Penseroso* combined. *The Passions* is an ode for music in the manner of Dryden and Pope in their odes for Saint Cecilia's Day. The *Ode to Liberty* and the *Ode to Evening* are both on familiar contemporary themes. Even the *Ode on the Popular Superstitions,* a verse letter in form, is a composite of prospect and retrospect. It looks back over the literary material of folklore and it anticipates the development of interest in these themes with an enthusiasm of its own. One may conclude that Collins had not that strength of imagination required for a poet to strike out on new themes for himself. But he was young, and if he did not possess it neither did his age. The time was not ripe for a Coleridge or a Blake. To Collins's credit it must be said that imitative though he was, he made the later odes at least worthy of consideration with the work of his masters and in three cases, at least, he created masterpieces of his own. If Lowell be right, the *Ode on the Popular Superstitions* represents the germ of the whole romantic movement.

If source-hunting be not its own excuse for being, it is at least profitable to explore the creative processes of the poet, to try to enter his workshop, to understand his method of procedure, and perhaps to track him to his source more closely than a predecessor has done. When one has finished one understands a bit more intimately the intellect of the poet, perhaps one penetrates occasionally, too, into that region in which, in the poet's own words, the shadowy Tribes of Mind join in braided Dance.

PART III

COLLINS AND THE ROMANTIC MOVEMENT

I

THE RISE OF COLLINS'S LITERARY REPUTATION

WHEN THE odes of Collins appeared in 1746, they attracted so little notice that, according to Langhorne, the
poet "burnt the remaining copies" of the edition of a thousand
"with his own hands."[1] The extensive researches of Mr. Bronson,
supplemented materially by the more recent studies of Messrs.
H. O. White, Alan D. McKillop, and A. S. P. Woodhouse, have
presented ample evidence that Collins was noticed slightly in
his lifetime, that his fame developed as the century closed,
recognition of his power as a poet keeping pace with the growth
of romanticism. But nowhere has his gradual rise to a worthy
place among the English poets been fully traced. Collins exerted
a definite influence on romantic poetry in two ways: first, the
growing amount of critical comment on his life and genius ap-
pearing in contemporary magazines, together with the publication of new editions and biographies of the poet brought him
recognition; second, not only a host of versifiers but the major
poets who followed him made significant use of his verse.

The poet's rise to fame was slow at first, yet steady as the
century neared its close. Perhaps the first poet of importance to
notice him, outside of the Warton circle, was Gray, who in a
letter to Wharton dated December 27, 1746, shortly after the
odes were published, speaks of both Warton and Collins. In
Collins he recognizes "a fine fancy modelled upon the antique,
a bad ear, great variety of words and images, with no choice at
all." Of the two poets he says, "They both deserve to last some
years, but will not."[2] It is ironic enough, in view of the comment, that Gray's future fame was destined to be linked with that

---

[1] Langhorne, *Collins,* London, 1765, p. 31. But compare the justification
of Collins's publisher "who did all in his power to introduce Mr. Collins to
the notice of the public" in the *Monthly Review,* XXXII, 294.

[2] *Letters,* I, 153.

of the young poet to whom he had accorded faint praise. In the *Elegy Written in a Country Churchyard* Gray honored his contemporary poet by borrowing three suggestions from his poetry. The resemblance of the second stanza of the *Elegy* to Lines 9-14 of the *Ode to Evening* has frequently been noted. Further, the expression "woeful wan," line 107 of the *Elegy*, seems a reminiscent echo of line 25 of *The Passions*, "With WOEFUL Measures WAN Despair." And in the original manuscript of the *Elegy* the stanza:

> There scatter'd oft the earliest of ye Year
> By HANDS UNSEEN are frequent Vilets found
> The Robin [Redbreast][3] loves to build & warble there
> And little Footsteps lightly print the Ground,

contains suggestions of *Ode Written in the Beginning of the Year 1746*, 8, and of the *Dirge in Cymbeline*, 11-16, which had first appeared in 1744. The *Epistle to Hanmer* and the *Ode on the Poetical Character* may also have influenced Gray's *Progress of Poesy*.

Following Gray's reference, two allusions to Collins are made by Christopher Smart: once in *A New System of Castle Building*, ch. v., by Chimaericus Cantibrigiensis (a pseudonym for Smart), wherein Collins is mentioned with Fielding, Johnson, Armstrong, Akenside, Warton, and others as one of "a set of as clever men in the poetical way, nay, I may venture to say more so than ever were at any given time together";[4] and again in *History of the Birth and Adventures of Messrs. Inclination and Ability*.[5]

The next important allusion, the *Ode to Horror* "in the Allegoric, Descriptive, Alliterative, Epithelical, Fantastic, Hyperbolical, and Diabolical Style of our Modern Ode-Wrights and Monody-Mongers," which appeared in *The Student* in 1751[6] and was reprinted in the *Oxford Sausage*, 1764, is, as Mr. White

---

[3] Written above.
[4] In *The Student: an Oxford and Cambridge Miscellany*, Vol. II, No. 1, p. 7. I am indebted for this and several of the following references to Mr. H. O. White's notes on "Collins and His Contemporary Critics," *TLS*, 1922, p. 12, p. 23.
[5] In the *Midwife or Old Woman's Magazine*, 1751-3, Vol. II, p. 149.
[6] Vol. II, No. 8, pp. 313-5.

has shown, a satire on the poetic manner of Collins, Mason, and the Wartons. An incorrect allusion to Spenser's *Faerie Queene* in the form of an author's note, follows Collins's error in the *Ode on the Poetical Character.* A satirical footnote which ends "I don't remember that any poetical use has been made of this story" is an obvious gibe at Collins's inaccuracy in his author's note to the *Ode to Liberty,* where commenting on the possibility of "blest Divorce" of England from France, he ends with the statement, "I don't remember that any Poetical Use has hitherto been made of it." There are more direct suggestions of Collins in the *Ode* than Mr. White has noted. The title, "Allegoric, Descriptive, . . . Style," obviously suggests that of Collins's volume *Odes on Several Descriptive and Allegoric Subjects.* The "O Thou" formula, overdone in the *Ode to Horror* is a favorite with Collins. Moreover, suggestive reminiscences recall the *Ode to Evening, On the Poetical Character, To Liberty,* and the *Persian Eclogues.* The author of the *Ode to Horror* must have been thoroughly familiar with Collins's work to parody it so skilfully.[7]

Very early the concept of Collins as a neglected poet so popular in the later romantic period takes rise. An allusion in the *Gray's Inn Journal,* No. 62, Sat., December 23, 1753, complains that "a treatise on Cribbidge, or a calculation of the chances at Whist, is sure of being better received at present than the Odes of a Collins or any other performance of distinguished Genius."

---

[7] Four passages in the *Ode to Horror,* in addition to the one cited by Mr. White, echo the *Ode to Fear.* Line 2 of the *Ode to Horror,* "Of shadowy shapes thou black brow'd queen," echoes lines 1-2 of Collins's *Ode to Fear:*

> Thou, to whom the World unknown,
> With all its shadowy Shapes is shown.

Lines 9-10 suggest the mood of the *Ode to Evening* and in "meek" and "shuddering" echo the diction of the *Ode to Fear,* 53. Line 11, "strange forms and fiends of giant size" echoes the diction of the *Ode to Fear,* 10, 18. The invocation, 15, "Dark Pow'r," directly follows the invocation at the beginning of line 53 of the *Ode to Fear.* Line 34 of the *Ode to Horror,* "Teach me to breathe the solemn line" resembles "Teach me but once like Him to feel," 69 of the *Ode to Fear.* Mr. A. S. P. Woodhouse (*TLS,* 1929, pp. 62, 420) conjectures that Thomas Warton is the author of the *Ode to Horror.* (On this point see also P. Parker, *TLS,* 1929, p. 186.) In "Collins in the Eighteenth Century," *TLS,* 1930, p. 838, he suggests that the allusions before 1763 are largely by those with whom Collins might have had personal relationship, e.g., Smart and the Wartons.

Yet Collins was noticed in 1753 in Scotland (though Thomas Warton was responsible); *The Union, or Select Scots and English Poems,* printed at Edinburgh in that year for Archibald Munro and David Murray, contains the *Ode to Evening* and the *Ode on the Death of Mr. Thomson.* The collection was reprinted in London in 1759. His next champion is John Gilbert Cooper, his friend and fellow poet, to whom Collins had broached the project of the *Clarendon Review.* In his *Letters Concerning Taste,* 1755, Letter VII, pp. 47-50, Cooper mentions the *Ode to Evening,* and quotes lines 21-8, commenting that the scene "animated by proper Allegorical Personages, and colour'd highly with incidental Expression, warms the Breast with a sympathetic glow of retir'd thoughtfulness." But most significant is his comment in a footnote to the passage he has quoted:

See the "Collection of Odes" published a few years ago by Mr. William Collins, whose neglected Genius will hereafter be both an Honour and a Disgrace to our Nation.

In another letter, Letter XV, he asks, "Has Horace . . . any descriptive Ode equal to Collins's *Ode to Evening?*" Moreover, he honored his friend by echoing his phrasing in several poems.[8]

In January, 1757, the *Persian Eclogues* were issued as the *Oriental Eclogues.* They were noticed among the new books in the *Gentleman's Magazine* for that date. In the *Gentleman's Magazine* for February of the same year *Eclogue IV* was reprinted with the comment:

The following elegant Poem is one of four Oriental Eclogues, lately published by J. Payne in Pater-Noster-Row. As it cannot fail of be-

---

[8] Noted by Mr. White, *TLS,* 1922, p. 12. Mr. E. H. W. Meyerstein (*London Mercury,* December, 1924, pp. 169-74) also discusses Collins's indebtedness to Cooper. Mr. Meyerstein (*TLS,* 1935, p. 432) has recently discovered a tribute to Collins as a poet in the anonymous *Life and Memoirs of Mr. Ephraim Tristram Bates, commonly called Corporal Bates, a broken-hearted Soldier,* London, 1756: "I once read an Ode to the Memory of one Col. *Ross,* slain at the Battle of *Fontenoy:* and tho' I read it but once, can I ever forget it? One stanza is ever uppermost in my memory: [He quotes Stanza 5 of the Ode, hyphenating "fair-recording," which Collins writes "fair recording," and for "Sainted Rest" reading" Wanted Rest."] He was young, but old in Honour. May I have such a Bard when my debt to *Old England* is paid."

ing acceptable to our Readers, it may perhaps incline them to see the other three.[9]

In the *Monthly Review* for June of the same year they are praised for "images wild and local," harmonious versification, and appropriate thought. The reviewer concludes:

We are much mistaken, if in this little performance, we do not discover the elegance and the picturesque genius of the too much neglected author of Odes on Several Subjects, Descriptive and Allegorical.[10]

Goldsmith, actuated perhaps, as Mr. White suggests, by Cooper's remark or by that of the anonymous reviewer (who some commentators say was Goldsmith himself) mentions Collins in the *State of Polite Learning in Europe,* 1759:

The neglected author of the Persian Eclogues, which however inaccurate, excel any in our language, is still alive: happy if insensible of our neglect, not raging at our ingratitude.[11]

Goldsmith was to remember Collins again in one of the *Essays on the Study of Belles Lettres,* which appeared in the *British Magazine* from July, 1761, to January, 1763, when he wrote:

Milton's translation of Horace's *Ode to Pyrrha* is universally known and generally admired, in our opinion much above its merit. There is an ode extant without rhyme, addressed to Evening by the late Mr. Collins, much more beautiful.[12]

In 1761 Goldsmith printed an excerpt from the *Epistle to Hanmer* in *A Poetical Dictionary,* and in 1767 he included *Selim; or the Shepherd's Moral* in *The Beauties of English Poetry,* commenting in the Preface:

The following eclogues, written by Mr. Collins, are very pretty; the images, it must be owned, are not very local, for the pastoral subject could not well admit of it. The description of Asiatic Magnificence and Manners is a subject as yet unattempted amongst us, and I believe, capable of furnishing a great variety of poetical imagery.[13]

[9] *Gentleman's Magazine,* XXVII, 81.
[10] *Monthly Review,* XVI, 486-9.
[11] Goldsmith, *Works,* Bohn Standard Ed., 1886, III, 508.
[12] *Ibid.,* I, 384.
[13] *Op. cit.,* V, 158.

Finally in 1772 in *Threnodia Augustalis,* which Goldsmith himself terms "more properly . . . a compilation than a poem . . .," Goldsmith weaves into his verse three passages from Collins. Lines 120-127:

> And, oh! for this, while sculpture decks thy shrine,
> And art exhausts profusion round,
> The tribute of a tear be mine,
> A simple song, a sigh profound,
> Then faith SHALL COME—a PILGRIM GREY,
> To BLESS THE TOMB THAT WRAPS THY CLAY:
> And calm religion SHALL REPAIR
> To DWELL A WEEPING HERMIT THERE,

paraphrase lines 9-12 of the *Ode Written in the Beginning of the Year 1746.* Lines 216-21:

> Old Edward's sons, unknown to yield,
> Shall crowd from Crecy's laurell'd field,
>   To do thy memory right:
> For thine and Britain's wrongs they feel,
> Again they snatch the gleamy steel,
>   And wish th' avenging fight,

are an adaptation of stanza six of the *Ode on the Death of Colonel Ross;* and lines 246-9, 251:

> On the grave of Augusta these garlands be plac'd,
> WE'LL RIFLE THE SPRING OF ITS EARLIEST BLOOM,
> [Repeated in 251]
> And there shall the cowslip and primrose be cast,
> And the new blossom'd thorn shall whiten her tomb,

suggest the first stanza of the *Dirge in Cymbeline.*

But it is after Collins's death that references indicative of the growing interest in his verse are most evident.[14] After the appearance of the odes in 1746 some of them were reprinted in Dodsley's *Collection* in 1748, 1755, and in subsequent editions of that work,[15] and some of them also appeared in Dodsley's *Miscellany.* But besides a letter of Mrs. Anna Seward, "the Swan of Lichfield,"[16] which puts Collins with Mason as "much

---

[14] Three of the passages cited from Goldsmith were written after 1759.
[15] Except that of 1751, noted by Mr. Woodhouse, *TLS,* 1929, p. 838.
[16] *Poetical Works,* Ed. Walter Scott, 1810, p. lxxxiii.

greater poets than Butler or Shenstone," though not equal to
Gray in the lyric, no other significant notice of the poet comes
before the appearance of his odes in Fawkes and Woty's *Poetical
Calendar,* Nos. XI and XII, for November and December, 1763.
In the *Poetical Calendar* is also a brief life of the poet (which
inaccurately reports the date of his death as 1756) written, according to Mulso, by Hampton, Collins's schoolfellow, and a
"character" by Johnson introduced as "an account of Mr. Collins
by a gentleman deservedly eminent in the republic of letters, who
knew him intimately well." This sketch was reprinted in the
Gentleman's Magazine for January, 1764, and in the *Monthly
Review* for the same month. The reviewer in the *Monthly Review* comments on the reprint from the *Poetical Calendar:*

The features of the above portrait are certainly very strong, but to
us the character does not appear sufficiently explicit; of the genius
of Collins, in particular, the picture is very imperfect—, but the veil
which is drawn over the unhappy circumstances of his life is drawn
by the hand of humanity and there let it rest.[17]

Mulso apparently shared the reviewer's feeling, for he wrote
to Gilbert White from Thornhill, 2 April, 1764:

I have read Collins's Life. Not enough is said if it was right to say
anything at all: His Genius is not enough called forth to Light, to
whet ye Reader to buy one of his Works. As to Hampton, we had
always a Dislike to ye Man, tho ingenious, & his present Life does
not take off that Prevention.

An appreciation of his genius had already appeared, however,
in the same number of the *Monthly Review* for January; according to Sir Egerton Brydges[18] this eulogy was probably written by Langhorne. In August, 1764, over the signature "M,"
the *Scots Magazine* reprinted the eulogy substantially as it had
appeared in the *Monthly Review* earlier in the year. The comment of the reviewer (Langhorne?) is pertinent; for it shows
the beginning of a new interest in Collins, evidence that the
time was ripe for an edition of the poet. He asserts that the

[17] *Monthly Review,* XXX, 122.
[18] In his *Essay on the Genius and Poems of Collins.* See *Poetical Works of
Pope and Collins,* Boston, 1882, II, lx.

poems of Collins have been neglected, but adds "it shall not however, be our fault if they are neglected any longer." He continues:

If a luxuriance of imagination, a wild sublimity of fancy, and a felicity of expression so extraordinary that it might be supposed to be suggested by some superior power rather than to be the effect of human judgment, or capacity—if these are allowed to constitute the excellences of lyric poetry, the author of the Odes descriptive and allegorical will indisputably bear away the palm from all his competitors in that province of the Muse.

The conclusion of the review paints Collins as a neglected genius:

It is with peculiar pleasure that we do justice to a poet who was too great to be popular, and whose genius was neglected because it was above the common taste.[19]

In the January number of the *Monthly Review* also appeared two sonnets by Langhorne on Fancy and Wisdom which picture the "poor shade of Collins" and describe him as the

> Sweet Bard! belov'd by every muse in vain!
> With powers whose fineness wrought their own decay.[20]

Langhorne shortly took advantage of the popular interest in Collins which he had helped to create. The *Gentleman's Magazine* and the *Scots Magazine* for March, 1765, note among the new books Langhorne's edition of the poet, of which his *Observations on the Odes Descriptive and Allegorical* were a part.

Extreme as they may be in their adulation of the poet, Langhorne's *Observations* have some positive qualities as well. He saw early that Collins's genius was "perfectly capable of the grand and magnificent in description" and he observed rightly that Collins's "had skill to complain," that "he knew perfectly to exhibit such circumstances, peculiar to the objects, as awaken the influences of Pity." Yet he finds the *Ode on the Poetical Character* "so infinitely abstracted and replete with high enthusiasm, that it will find few readers capable of entering into the

---

[19] *Scots Magazine*, XXVI, 439-42; *Monthly Review*, XXX, 20-6.
[20] *Monthly Review*, XXX, 122-3. These sonnets were first noted by Alan D. McKillop, *Studies in Philology*, XX, 4-5.

spirit of it, of relishing its beauties." He enthusiastically declares *The Passions* "the finest ode in the English Language." Though skeptical of the place of the "blank ode" in English he declares of the *Ode to Evening:*

But whatever were the numbers, or the versification of this ode, the imagery and enthusiasm it contains could not fail of rendering it delightful.

He naïvely concludes his discussion of the poem:

It might be a sufficient encomium on this beautiful ode to observe that it has been particularly admired by a lady to whom Nature has given the most perfect principles of taste. She has not even complained of the want of rhyme in it, a circumstance by no means unfavorable to the cause of lyric blank verse; for surely, if a fair reader can endure an ode without bells and chimes, the masculine genius may dispense with them.

But most significant in the *Observations* is the concept of the poet that Langhorne builds up. He declares:

The genius of Collins was capable of every degree of excellence in lyric poetry, and perfectly qualified for that high province of the Muse. Possessed of a native ear for all the varieties of harmony and modulation, susceptible of the finest feelings of tenderness and humanity, but above all, carried away by that high enthusiasm, which gives to imagination its strongest colouring, he was, at once, capable of soothing the ear with the melody of his numbers, of influencing the passions by the force of his pathos, and of gratifying the fancy by the luxury of his description.

In his comment on *Eclogue IV* he says:

This ingenious man had not only a pencil to pourtray, but a heart to feel for the miseries of mankind; and it is with the utmost tenderness and humanity he enters into the narrative of Circassia's ruin, while he realizes the scene, and brings the present drama before us.

He recognizes in Collins a kinship in genius and enthusiasm with Milton, and in his notes on the *Ode to Pity* compares him to Otway:

There was a similitude in their genius and in their sufferings. There was a resemblance in the misfortunes and in the dissipation of their lives, and the circumstances of their deaths cannot be remembered without pain.

Coming as it did when the sentimental movement was at it
height both in England and in Scotland, the edition of Langhorne did much to turn public attention to Collins. As Mr
McKillop has observed,[21] early criticisms, following Langhorne
undoubtedly, presented him either as a feeble victim of extreme
sensibility or as a poet swept away by the strength of his imagination. Such a portrait had a powerful appeal to a generation which
read *Tristram Shandy* and *The Man of Feeling* and sighed over
Ossian. In an *Ode to the Lyric Muse* which appeared in the
Scots Magazine early in 1765, he is described as both a hapless
genius and an enthusiast.[22] Some verses in the same magazine
for October, 1766, include him among "the best Poetical Writers
of our country" and apostrophize him in this fashion:

> Poor Collins sang, but Nature could not bear—
> The wild bard fainted in his sister's arms,
> He sigh'd and died—pale Fancy dropt a Tear
> To see her son o'erpowered by her charms.[23]

Again in the *Scots Magazine* for September, 1773, in *Verses on
Some Late English Poets* he is portrayed in the sentimental manner:

> O Collins! nobly warm and wild,
> Fair Fancy's best beloved child!
> What mad ambitious thoughts could fire
> Thy mind to seize Apollo's lyre?
> Dids't thou not find those hands of thine
> Too rough to touch the chords divine?[24]

Langhorne's success shortly prompted other notices and editions of Collins. In 1765, soon after the appearance of Langhorne's edition, the *Verses Written on a Paper which contained
a Piece of Bride-Cake* were attributed to Collins in the *Gentleman's Magazine* for May. An article on Collins appeared in the
Supplement to the New and General Biographical Dictionary,
1768.[25] Langhorne's edition was popular enough to be reprinted

---

[21] *Studies in Philology*, XX, 3.
[22] *Scots Magazine*, XXVII, 101-2.
[23] *Ibid.*, XXVIII, 544.
[24] *Ibid.*, XXXV, 486.
[25] Noted by Mr. Woodhouse, *TLS*, 1930, p. 838.

in 1771, in 1776, and again in 1781. Other editions and print-
ings of the poems followed in short order, the most significant
of which are mentioned here. They appeared in Volume XLIII
of *British Poets,* 1773, with the *Elegies* of Hammond, printed
at Edinburgh for J. Balfour and W. Creech. Robert and Andrew
Foulis printed them at Glasgow in 1771 and reprinted the edition in 1777. Volume II of Pearch's *Collection of Poems,* 1775,
contains some of the poems of Collins. Further articles on Collins
appeared in Noorthhouck's *Historical and Classical Dictionary,*
1776, and in the second edition of the *Encyclopedia Britannica,*
1778. To this period, too, belongs Thomas Warton's tribute in
the *History of English Poetry,* 1774-1781, to his

lamented friend, Mr. William Collins, whose odes will be remembered while any taste for true poetry remains.

There is abundant evidence to substantiate Sir Egerton Brydges's
conclusion in his *Essay on the Genius and Poems of Collins:*

From the time of Langhorne's first edition Collins became a popular
poet . . . and as long as I can remember books, which goes back to
the year 1770, Collins's poems were almost universally on the lips
of readers of English poetry.

In 1779 the poems with Langhorne's *Observations* appeared
in Johnson's *Works of the English Poets, With Prefaces Biographical and Critical.* Collins's poems come last in volume
XLIX, preceded by Thomson's and Hammond's. The edition
is noted in the *Gentleman's Magazine,* XLIX, 600, under the
new books. Johnson's treatment of Collins was not noticed, however, until the *Lives of the Most Eminent English Poets with
Critical Observations* appeared in 1781. A correspondent to the
Gentleman's Magazine in March, 1780, writes:

Of Mr. W. Collins, a good account may be expected from Dr.
Johnson.[26]

In 1781, however, a reviewer in the *Monthly Review* comments
non-committally on Johnson's *Life of Collins:*

The next life that offers itself is that of Collin's: a writer whose im-
perfections and peculiarities are lost in the blaze of genius.[27]

---

[26] *Gentleman's Magazine,* L, 327.
[27] *Monthly Review,* LXV, 411.

Dr. Johnson's strictures on Collins's poetry are too well known to repeat in full, but one remembers the grudging praise in:

The grandeur of wildness, and the novelty of extravagance, were always desired by him, but not always attained. Yet, as diligence is never wholly lost, if his efforts sometimes caused harshness and obcurity, they likewise produced in happier moments sublimity and splendour. . . . His poems are the productions of a mind not deficient in fire, nor unfurnished with knowledge either of books or life, but somewhat obstructed in its progress by deviation in quest of mistaken beauties.[28]

Nor can one forget the harshness in the judgment:

He affected the obsolete when it was not worthy of revival; and he puts his words out of the common order, seeming to think, with some later candidates for fame, that not to write prose is certainly to write poetry. His lines commonly are of slow motion, clogged and impeded with clusters of consonants. As men are often esteemed who cannot be loved, so the poetry of Collins may sometimes extort praise when it gives little pleasure.[29]

Were it not better done to omit criticism entirely than so to treat one whom the critic yet remembered with tenderness? Yet it must be conceded that in his *Shakespeare* Johnson had given Collins's *Song from Shakespeare's Cymbeline* a place at the end of his comment of that play in honor of Collins's memory.[30]

But Collins was not then without his champions. Two letters to the *Gentleman's Magazine* for January, 1782, defend him. "Philo-Lyrister," hurt at the liberties Johnson has taken with "two of our most celebrated lyric poets," Collins and Gray, cries:

And let Dr. Johnson, with all his erudition, produce me another lyric ode equal to Collins on the Passions: indeed the frequent public recitals of this last-mentioned poem are a mark of its universally acknowledged excellence.[31]

The second correspondent, "H," comments discriminatingly on Gray's indebtedness to Collins's *Ode to Evening* in the *Elegy,*

---

[28] Johnson, *Lives,* III, 338.
[29] *Ibid.,* III, 341.
[30] Ed. G. B. Hill, VII, 358.
[31] *Gentleman's Magazine,* LII, 22.

speaks disparagingly of Langhorne's observations, and concludes:

. . . his four eclogues are mere trash; yet a part of his odes will, notwithstanding, command the admiration of mankind, as long as poetical genius or poetical taste shall remain in the world.[32]

Nor did Johnson's criticism affect the popularity of Collins. Bell's *Poets of Great Britain,* published at Edinburgh, 1781, vol. LXXXVIII, contains the *Poetical Works of William Collins.* Foulis' folio edition of 1787 appeared in Glasgow. And a review of John Scott's *Critical Essays on Some of the Poems of Several English Poets,* 1785, in the *Monthly Review* for January, 1787, shows that Collins had found yet another champion in John Scott:

Collins's *Oriental Eclogues* Mr. Scott endeavours to rescue from the disrepute into which they have lately fallen; he maintains, that they have all the requisites of a good poem, description, incident, sentiment, moral, and melody.[33]

He is again mentioned in the pages of the same review in January of the following year in the critique of *Imperfect Hints toward a New Edition of Shakespeare,* 1787,—in substance "an account of pictures, prints, and engravings, that relate to Shakespeare or have been taken from his plays." The reviewer writes:

It is remarkable that this plan of uniting the sister-arts of poetry and painting was first suggested by Mr. Collins, in his Epistle to Sir Thomas Hanmer. . . . The idea was worthy of a poet, and is now happily revived at a time when the artists of Britain possess fancy, taste, and execution.[34]

The rediscovery of the *Ode on the Popular Superstitions* and its appearance in the *Transactions of the Royal Society of Edinburgh* in 1788 may also have stimulated a second wave of en-

---

[32] *Gentleman's Magazine,* LII, 21.
[33] *Monthly Review,* LXXVII, 29. Scott says that the eclogues "were always till lately possessed of considerable reputation," attributing the change to the influence of Johnson's *Life* where Collins's own disparagement of them is mentioned. Since then, says Scott, "those who form their opinions not from their own reason, or their own feelings, have caught the hint, and circulated it."
[34] *Monthly Review,* LXXIX, 81.

thusiasm for the poet's work. The *Transactions* appeared near the end of March; they were noticed in the *London Chronicle* of April 1-3, 1788, and in the *European Magazine* for April, 1788. The *Scots Magazine* for April of that year reprints the *Transactions of the Royal Society of Edinburgh* and the ode with Mackenzie's stanzas added. They were also reprinted in the *Monthly Review* for the same month with the comment that the whole poem by "that excellent but unhappy genius, the late Mr. William Collins . . . deserves an attentive perusal."[35] An anonymous edition of the ode purporting to be a perfect copy came out shortly afterward, printed in London by J. Bell. The Preface explains:

A gentleman who, for the present, chooses not to publish his name, discovered last summer the following admirable Ode, among some old papers, in the concealed drawers of a bureau, left him, among other articles, by a relation.

The editor dedicated the work to the Wartons in a fulsome letter following the Preface. The edition was reviewed unfavorably and was received with considerable skepticism in the *English Review* for May, 1788, apparently the month of its publication. The *Monthly Review* for December was even more severely skeptical:

This is offered to the Public as a *perfect* copy of Mr. Collins's beautiful Ode. If it is, indeed, complete, it is to be lamented that the *evidence* of its authenticity is withheld from the public. Surely the gentleman, who found it in "the drawers of a bureau" should allow his name to be published and give us the satisfaction of knowing whether it was in the handwriting of Mr. Collins; which is certainly a material question. . . . The style does not seem to us to be in the manner of Collins.[36]

A second edition of the ode, however, appeared in 1789, and in a number of subsequent editions of the poet, including Chalmer's *English Poets,* 1810, and Swinburne's edition in Ward's *English Poets,* Vol. III. To 1788 belongs also the first appearance of *Song. The Sentiments Borrowed from Shakespeare,*

---

[35] *Monthly Review,* LXXIX, 532-7.
[36] *Monthly Review,* LXXIX, "Monthly Catalogue," p. 55.

which was twice printed during the year, first in the *Gentleman's Magazine* for February and later in the *Public Advertiser*.

Before the end of the century the poems were frequently published. Johnson's *English Poets,* reprinted in 1790, contained the *Ode on the Popular Superstitions.* Collins's poems appear in Volume IV of Anderson's *British Poets,* Edinburgh, 1794. *How Sleep the Brave,* the *Persian Eclogues,* and the *Ode on the Poetical Character* were included in Roach's *Beauties of the Poets of Great Britain,* 1794, and there were editions from Colchester, 1796,[37] from London, 1797 (with a prefatory essay by Mrs. Barbauld), and from London, 1798 (E. Harding). The inclusion of Collins's poems in such collections as those of Pearch, Bell, and Anderson, and the appearance of so considerable a number of collected editions before 1800 argue that Collins had taken his place among the English poets.

To these evidences of fame some minor testimonies should be added. A letter to the *Gentleman's Magazine* for December, 1789, dated December 16, at Chichester, proposes the project of erecting a monument to "that much neglected but admirable bard Collins." As originally planned, according to the letter, "his incomparable Ode on the Passions" was to furnish a design, "which is to be executed in the best manner by that ingenious artist Flaxman."[38]

The reverend Mr. Walker of Chichester[39] supported the project and he and Mr. William Hayley undertook to bring it to completion. Flaxman, then in Rome, was approached to do the sculpture and apparently the design from *The Passions* was suggested to him. Flaxman wrote to Hayley from Rome, July 4, 1792:

[37] *Reminiscences of Henry Crabb Robinson* (ed. Sadler, I, 13) for 1794 speaks of one Ben Strutt of Colchester:

"He published an edition of the poems of Collins, whom he praised and declared to be much superior to Gray. And I think (though I have lost the book) that it contains additional stanzas by himself to the Ode on Superstition [sic]."

[38] *Gentleman's Magazine,* LXVI, 1064.

[39] See excerpt from *Gentleman's Magazine* above and cf. also Hay, *History of Chichester,* p. 528, where an account of the monument is given.

I thus trouble you with your own thoughts for the Honored Bard, I am solicitous that my work may not degrade his memory and I disclaim profit on the present occasion, my first desire is to act with such caution respecting you, that you may not incur any additional expense in carr(iage) or custom-house duty, for which reason I have confined the price of those designs which I think likely the subscribers will choose between £60 and £70, the overplus I leave for the extra expences, among which I reckon the cutting the inscription which it would be impossible for me to have done here by an Italian, without the hazard of some enormous blunder which might ruin the work. . . .[40]

The letter concludes with the sculptor's recommendation for the cutting of the inscription and his directions for setting up the monument. With the letter he sent six designs, three of which have been lost. One of the extant sketches, numbered 2, a sketch for the whole monument, illustrates a passage from *The Passions,* the whole surmounting an inscription, "And Hope enchanted smiled and wav'd her golden Hair." Another sketch gives an alternate frieze illustrating a passage earlier in the ode. The third sketch was entitled "Music and Painting placing a Garland on the altar of Pity." These designs were rejected in favor of another, the principal motif of which is the medallion of the poet reading the Bible, following Johnson's story in the *Lives.* Of this motif Flaxman submitted three designs ranging in price from £225 to £90, one with an elaborate frieze, a second with a smaller frieze, and a third with no frieze. The third and cheapest design was chosen and after several modifications was finished. Flaxman wrote:

I have attended to your own words that the poet was found reading the Bible in his last illness, which situation I like much better than the action of pointing. . . . I think I have succeeded, it has pleased all who have seen it in Rome.[41]

Its final appearance is well described in the *Gentleman's Magazine* for December, 1824, in *A Compendium of County History —Sussex:*

[40] The letter of Flaxman to Hayley and the details of the designs for the monument are drawn from Constable, W. G., *John Flaxman,* London, 1927, pp. 42-5. Plates XII, XIV, and XV of that book picture some of the designs described in the text.
[41] Cited by Mr. Blunden, *Poems of William Collins,* p. 35.

In the nave is a neat tablet by Flaxman to the unfortunate poet Collins who was born and died in this city. He is represented as just recovered from one of those fits of phrenzy to which he was subject, and in a calm and reclining posture, seeking refuge from his misfortunes in the gospel, while his lyre and one of his poems lie neglected on the ground. Above are the figures of Love and Pity entwined in each other's arms.[42]

His epitaph, the work of Hayley and Sargeant, perpetuates the sentimental tradition of the poet:

YE! WHO THE MERITS OF THE DEAD REVERE,
WHO HOLD MISFORTVNE SACRED, GENIVS DEAR,
REGARD THIS TOMB! WHERE COLLINS, HAPLESS NAME!
SOLICITS KINDNESS, WITH A DOVBLE CLAIM:
THO' NATURE GAVE HIM, AND THO, SCIENCE TAVGHT
THE FIRE OF FANCY, AND THE REACH OF THOVGHT,
SEVERELY DOOM'D TO PENVRY'S EXTREME,
HE PASS'D IN MADD'NING PAIN LIFE'S FEVERISH DREAM;
WHILE RAYS OF GENIVS ONLY SERV'D TO SHEW
THE THICK'NING HORROR, AND EXALT HIS WOE.
YE WALLS THAT ECHOED TO HIS FRANTIC MOAN,
GVARD THE DVE RECORD OF THIS GRATEFVL STONE!
STRANGERS TO HIM, ENAMOVR'D OF HIS LAYS,
THIS FOND MEMORIAL OF HIS TALENTS RAISE;
FOR THIS THE ASHES OF A BARD REQVIRE,
WHO TOVCH'D THE TENDEREST NOTES OF PITY'S LYRE:
WHO IOIN'D PVRE FAITH TO STRONG POETIC POWERS,
WHO IN REVIVING REASON'S LVCID HOVRS,
SOVGHT ON ONE BOOK HIS TROVBLED MIND TO REST,
AND RIGHTLY DEEM'D THE BOOK OF GOD THE BEST.

The bas-relief and epitaph together cover a large marble slab, which is affixed to a pier in the north aisle of the nave. The monument was completed in 1795. It is twice mentioned in the *Gentleman's Magazine* for that year; in the September number its completion is recorded and the inscription on the monument is noted, the date of the poet's death being inaccurately stated as 1756:

---

[42] *Gentleman's Magazine*, CXXXVI, 502. Other accounts of the monument are given in *History of the County of Sussex*, London, 1935, III, 145; in Hay's *History of Chichester*, p. 528; and in Hirsfield, T. W., *History, Antiquities and Topography of the County of Sussex*, London, 1835, II, 13.

This monument was erected, by a voluntary
subscription,
in honour of WILLIAM COLLINS,
who was born in this city MDCCXXI.
and died in a house adjoining to the cloisters
of this church MDCCLVI.[43]

The *Scots Magazine* for February, 1799, prints the "Inscription upon the Monument lately erected in Chichester Cathedral to the memory of the Unfortunate Collins. By Messrs. Sargent and Hayley."

An examination of contemporary critical magazines in the first third of the new century reveals even more clearly the secure position which Collins held as a poet of renown all through the romantic period and well into the reign of Victoria. They are no more than indicative of a general tendency. The *Gentleman's Magazine,* always closely linked with Collins's fame and, in a sense, the organ of contemporary tastes in literature, is full of allusions to him. A critic in the January number for 1793, in *Thoughts on Poetry Especially Modern with Criticism on Several Poets* gives a penetrating criticism on *The Passions:*

Next therefore, to the Alexander's Feast, and in some respects superior, is Collins's noble Ode to the Passions, which, whether we consider the originality and magnificence of the design of the whole, and its parts, or its imagery, its sentiments, its expressions, and its versification, has ever appeared to me one of the happiest efforts of human poetry. . . . From his almost constant adherence to allegory, it is a subject of great regret that even he seems sometimes to have mistaken the form for the soul.[44]

In November, 1795, one Nuncuniensis seeks an explanation of a line in *The Passions,* calling Collins "a poet of so much merit."[45] In November, 1798, appears a Latin version of *To a Lady Weeping,* signed "Marcius." In September, 1803, there is a Latin version of Collins's *Dirge in Cymbeline,* signed "L." The July number for 1812 reviews Disraeli's *Calamaties of Authors* and comments on the author's belief that Collins "sacrificed

[43] See *Gentleman's Magazine,* LXXVIII, 741, 902.
[44] *Gentleman's Magazine,* LXXIII, 12-14.
[45] *Ibid.,* LXXVIII, 1091.

his reason and his happiness to his imagination." Again in
January, 1819, in *Remarks on the Signs of Inns* the "exquisite
dirge by Collins," the *Song from Shakespeare's Cymbeline,* is
quoted. Again in June, 1819, in *A Visit to Corscombe, Seat of
the Celebrated Mr. Hollis* occurs:

> Collins's lines rushed on my fancy;
>> "See the fairy valleys fade,
>> Dun Night now veils the solemn view."[46]

In *Saeculomastix; or the Lash of the Age we live in,* which appeared in the July, 1820, number, Collins is mentioned and compared to Pope:

> Let Gray, let Collins from the field retire,
> Let partial love withdraw her Goldsmith's lyre . . .
> And Fancy's self no later strain can show,
> Soul-thrilling Heloise to match thy woe. . . .[47]

Again in the review of Fosbroke's *Sketches of Ross and Archen-
field,* in the number for January, 1822, two stanzas of an interesting parody on *The Passions* are given:

At the end of the General History Mr. F. has given a facetious
parody by himself of Collins's *Ode to the Passions,* and has entitled
the parody, "The Last Thirty Years." It is a mere *Jeu d'esprit.* We
shall give two stanzas for the amusement of our readers:

> "But oh! how alter'd was its marching tone,
> When Government, a nymph of brawny hue,
> With Habeas Corpus o'er her shoulder flung,
> And Volunteers in buskins gemmed with dew,
> Blew an inspiring air, that inn and pothouse rung,
> The Soldier's call, to tippling idlers known;
> The Cyprian fair, and their dram-drinking queen,
> Peeping from forth our alleys green;
> Pipe-clay'd Militia-men* rejoic'd to hear,
> And six-foot tailors grasped the sergeant's spear.
> Last came Finance's dubious trial,
> He with the income-tax advancing;
> First to the yellow Gold his hand address'd;
> But soon he saw the Bank-Restriction viol
> Whose more prolific notes he loved the best;

---

[46] *Gentleman's Magazine,* CXXV, 512.
[47] *Ibid.,* CXXVI, 53.

> They would have thought, who heard the strain,
> They saw in Lombard Street the Bankers mad,
> All bills discounting, whether good or bad;
> To rising Stock perpetual dancing;
> While, as his flying fingers kiss'd the strings,
> Pitt and the Bank framed a fantastic round;
> Loose were her tresses seen, her zone unbound.
> And he amidst his frolic play,
> As if he would one time or other pay,
> Exchequer bills shook from his paper wings."

* Alluding to the old Trained Bands of the London Citizens.[48]

Collins had, then, in the period from 1790 until 1825 become a familiar poet, imitated, quoted, and parodied. In such critical magazines as *The Quarterly* and *Blackwood's* he was frequently mentioned; with few exceptions he is spoken of as a poet whose literary position is established. There is, too, some evidence of his influence on contemporary literary tastes and fashions. In the *Quarterly Review* for September, 1812, a critic, commenting on Disraeli's *Calamities of Authors,* speaks of

Collins, now not undeservedly one of our most popular poets, whose poems find their way into every selection and are printed in every possible form.[49]

Two years later, in October, 1814, a reviewer, writing on Chalmers's *English Poets,* speaks of the fame that has come to

Collins, whose exquisite odes, after lying for years neglected in the bookseller's warehouse, have become the storehouse from which manufacturing poets extract epithets to debase and misapply them.[50]

A reviewer of *Hayley's Life and Writings* in the *Quarterly Review* for March, 1825, complains that in his own day "the truer lyric strain and higher poetical qualities of Collins obtained no notice." Later in the same year an essayist writing on *Sacred Poetry* says that in the mid-eighteenth century hardly a single specimen of sacred poetry "excepting, perhaps, Gray's Elegy, and possibly some of the most perfect of Collins's poems" has obtained any celebrity.[51] Two years later (the year of Dyce's

---

[48] *Gentleman's Magazine,* CXXXI, 112, 113.
[49] *Quarterly Review,* VIII, 112.
[50] *Quarterly Review,* XII, 89.
[51] *Ibid.,* XXXII, 231.

edition) in the reviews of *Dr. Sayer's Works* Collins is praised.
Of the "Pyrrha stanza" of the *Ode to Evening* the critic writes:

Collins saw what could be made of it, and few poems have been more
frequently imitated than the *"Ode to Evening,"* to which he has so
finely and beautifully applied its slow and solemn movement. This
has been the only successful attempt at introducing an unrhymed lyric
measure in English poetry.[52]

In a later article on *Translations of Pindar,* 1834, the *Ode to
Evening* is highly praised:

And, in our judgment, Collins's rhymeless *Ode to Evening* is not
surpassed for musical effect in any language of Europe.[53]

By reviewers in *Blackwood's Magazine* Collins was even more
enthusiastically received, particularly in the years between 1825
and 1840, perhaps because of the influence of Dyce's edition of
1827. Though one reviewer in 1825 questioned "whether it is
at all likely that Collins ever will be a popular author with
more than a very small circle of highly refined readers,"[54] the
poet was treated enthusiastically in every article that mentioned
him in the next ten years. In a review of *Keble's Christian Year,*
June, 1830, he is mentioned:

Even Collins, pure, sweet, and ethereal—though his song commerces
with the skies, and though a wide and melancholy beauty from his
own spirit passes upon all the forms of nature and of life that he
touches—though there might seem to be a perfect inspiration in his
poetry, yet does he not rather give to nature than receive from
her. . . .[55]

In April of the same year he is commemorated in one of a
series of *Poetical Portraits* by *A Modern Pythagorean:*

> Waked into mimic life,
>   The Passions round him throng,
>   While the loud "Spartan fife"
>   Thrills through his startling song.[56]

---

[52] *Quarterly Review,* XXXV, 211-2. In an earlier review of *Dr. Sayer's
Works,* XXXV, 193, the lyric poems of Collins and Gray are said to "have
become equally popular," and Collins's odes are called "the effusions of an
ardent poetical spirit."
[53] *Quarterly Review,* XLIII, 25.
[54] *Blackwood's Magazine,* May, 1825, XVII, 509.
[55] *Ibid.,* XXVII, 833.
[56] *Ibid.,* XXVII, 632.

He is discussed again in *An Hour's Talk about Poetry* in September, 1831:

Among the honoured, Collins was a poet, and his name was Fine Ear. But feeling his own weakness, he took refuge in abstractions—and hid himself in the shadowy twilight which they afford. Filmy visions floated before his half-shut eye—and they were beautiful; but unsubstantial all, and owning remotest kindred with the flesh and blood creatures of this our living world.

Though the reviewer disparages the Highland Ode and calls *The Passions* "but a poor performance" because it calls no spirits from the vasty deep, he concludes:

But he had a soul finely strung to the obscure pathetic—and it often yields melancholy murmurs by moonlight "when the high woods are still," which spell-like sadden the imagination making the night pensive.[57]

Another encomium of the poet appears in the review of *Coleridge's Poetical Works* in October, 1839:

. . . his odes are all exquisitely beautiful—except his *Ode to Freedom*, and it is sublime. Let us call it, then, and contradict ourselves, the only truly great ode in the English language.[58]

Perhaps the most generous estimate of all closes the account. The same critic in *Our Pocket Companions* in January, 1839, devotes fourteen pages to the appreciative analysis of Collins's verse. First examining Dr. Johnson's strictures on the odes he writes:

Read the *Ode to Liberty*—lustrous in its learning—and you will be almost disposed to think the doctor a dolt.

Further in justification of Collins he says:

The diction and the versification of Collins are exquisite—a more musical ear and soul were never given to any one of the Muse's sons

He praises the *Ode to Evening:*

So perfect is its music that the ear never misses the rhyme—the sou forgets that there is such an artifice as rhyme; and the imagination is so gradually filled to overflowing, that it feels but not thinks of the

---

[57] *Blackwood's Magazine*, XXX, 482.
[58] *Ibid.*, XXXVI, 533.

beauty of the medium through which its visions arise—the lucid and transparent veil of inspired words.

Of the *Ode to Liberty* his praise is ecstatic. He cries:

Here is the noblest ode in our language. . . . Let no man presume to soliloquize a comment on that ode.

And so moved is he by the *Ode on the Popular Superstitions* that he is resolved "next summer to visit Iona again—and for the first time St. Kilda."[59]

Neglected in his lifetime, sentimentalized as a hapless and unappreciated bard by the readers of the 1760's, popularized by the edition of Langhorne, Collins slowly achieved a modest yet just renown by the end of the century. In the early years of the nineteenth century his place was secure and his fame established, and by the time of Dyce's edition in 1827, he was appreciated and evaluated more justly. He had put his trust in good verses, and in time he achieved a modest fame for which he had scarcely dared to hope.

[59] *Blackwood's Magazine,* XLV, 130-44.

II

COLLINS AND THE POETS OF THE EIGHTEENTH CENTURY

MORE SIGNIFICANT proof of Collins's importance is his influence on the poets of the last half of the century[1] and well on into the next. Most numerous are the imitations of the *Ode to Evening*. Though Mr. Garrod[2] notes only two instances, a number of commentators have added to the list of unrhymed lyrics inspired by Collins's ode. Mr. Woodhouse, Mr. Havens, Mr. White and others have listed well over a hundred instances of the form, significant among them Clare's *To Autumn*, Shelley's *To Harriet*, Keble's *Tuesday before Easter*, to which should be added Leigh Hunt's *To Friendship In the Manner of Collins's Ode to Evening*[3] and Fitz-Greene

---

[1] A second minor source of influence is evident in the number of musical settings of Collins's poems. Besides Hayes' setting of *The Passions*, Mr. Bronson has noted a setting of the *Ode to Evening*, 1785 (*Collins*, pp xxxi-ii). To these Mr. Woodhouse (*TLS*, 1930, p. 838) has added an imposing supplementary list, showing ten settings of the *Song from Cymbeline*, one of *The Passions* besides that of Hayes, three of *How Sleep the Brave* two settings of the *Ode to Evening*, and one each of the odes *To Mercy, To Fear, On the Death of Mr. Thomson*, as well as one setting of *Eclogue II* To these should be added some interesting later settings. In Ritson's *Select Collection of English Songs*, 3 v., second edition by T. Park, 1813, London appear "How sleep the brave," set as a glee (III, 293), and "To Fair Fidele's Grassy Tomb," composed as a glee for four voices, by Mrs. Park, set by Dr. Arne (III, 293). In the *Musical Magazine*, London, n.d., occurs a setting of *How Sleep the Brave* as a duet. Some American settings of later date should also be noted. *How Sleep the Brave* was turned into a Requiem "performed by the Utica Musical Academy at the Public Ceremonies in Memory of William Henry Harrison and respectfully dedicated to the Mayor and Common Council of Utica, by Geo. Dutton," Utica, N.Y., 1841. It was again set to music as a soldier's dirge "Composed for the Funeral Services of Gen. Frederick W. Lander, Salem, Mass., March 8th, 1862. Music by H. K. Oliver." (Both of these settings are preserved in the Drexel Collection of the New York City Public Library.) In *Fifty English Songs and Ballads* by J. W. Jeudwine, N.Y., 1906, the *Dirge in Cymbeline* in Arne's setting is arranged for high voice. Only three stanzas of the dirge are given.

[2] *Collins*, p. 72.

[3] *Juvenilia*, 1801, p. 113. On this point see "Review of Garrod, *Poetry of Collins*," *TLS*, 1929, p. 95; Ronald Bailey, "William Collins," *TLS*, 1929

Halleck's *Field of the Grounded Arms,* 1831. But aside from the powerful appeal of the *Ode to Evening* the poetry of Collins inspired the greater romantic figures from 1770 to 1832, an influence which is more than "the scant and shadowy harvest" which Mr. Bronson[4] proclaims it to be. It is felt in Chatterton in the *African Eclogues* particularly in a passage like the following, which suggests Collins's *Third Eclogue:*

> On Tiber's banks where scarlet jasmines bloom,
> And purple aloes shed a rich perfume;
> Where, when the sun is melting in his heat,
> The reeking tigers find a cool retreat;
> Bask in the sedges, lose the sultry beam,
> And wanton with their shadows in the stream.[5]

The manner of Collins is felt in Chatterton's *Elegy* in such phrases as "when dusky contemplation veils the scene" or "the thick'ning veil of evening's drawn," remotely in *Ode to Miss Hayland* in which Evening is personified, and again more positively in *Clifton.* The personification in *To Mr. Holland* reminds one of Collins, though it is equally suggestive of Gray:

> Black Anger's sudden rise, extatic pain;
> Tormenting Jealousy's self-cank'ring sting;
> Consuming Envy, with her yelling train;
> Fraud closely shrouded with the turtle's wing.

In the *Elegy on the Death of Mr. Phillips* the idiom of Collins is most marked. Such touches as:

> Oft AS THE FILMY VEIL OF EVENING DREW
> The THICK'NING SHADE upon the vivid green,

the description of the forest "glimmering from afar," the picture of "pale rugged Winter" and his train, the account of Peace "gentlest, softest of the virtues," who spreads "his silver pinions wet with dewy tears," and the passage:

> Then would we wander through this DARKEN'D VALE,

bear the stamp of Collins.

---

p. 295; H. O. White, "William Collins," *TLS,* 1929, p. 315; A. S. P. Woodhouse, "Imitations of the *Ode to Evening,*" *TLS,* 1929, p. 436. To these should be added Havens, R. D., *Influence of Milton,* pp. 560-5, pp. 682-4.

[4] *Collins,* p. lvii.

[5] As Mr. Blunden points out, Chatterton's "Let me like midnight Cats, or Collins sing" refers to Emanuel Collins of Bristol, not to William Collins.

And, as a commentator in the *Gentleman's Magazine* for December, 1781, long ago noticed, there is a parallelism between the poems of Rowley and Collins. He writes:

In the Tournament, a chorus of minstrels opens with the following beautiful and nervous lines:

> When Battayle, mesthynge wythe new
> quickenn'd gore,
> Bendynge with spoiles his bloddie
> droppynge hedde
>
> Pleasure, dauncyng fromm her wode,
> Wreathedd wythe flowres of eglentine,
> From his vysage washedd the bloude,
> Hylte his swerd and gaberdyne.
>
> With lyne and eyne shee swotelie hymn
> dydd view,
> His spryte didd chaunge untoe
> anodherr hue,
> Hys armes, ne spoyles, mote anie
> thoughts emploie.

These lines, he states, resemble the *Ode to Mercy*. Again the lines:

> Whanne Dacya's sonnes, whose hayres of
> bloodredde hue
> Lyche kynge cuppes brastynge wythe
> the mornynge due,

resemble the *Ode to Liberty,* he points out. It is only fair to conclude that Collins influenced Chatterton, for "Rowley" could not have been known to Collins.[6]

To Cowper Collins was unknown until 1784. In a letter to Mr. Unwin, March 21, 1784, he writes, after reading Johnson's *Lives of the Poets:*

In all the number I observe but one man (A POET OF NO GREAT FAME,—OF WHOM I DID NOT KNOW THAT HE EXISTED TILL I FOUND HIM THERE) seems to have had the slightest tincture of religion; and he was hardly in his senses. His name was Collins. He sunk into a state of melancholy and died young.

[6] See *Gentleman's Magazine,* LI, 622-3.

This is not surprising in view of his admission in a letter to Joseph Hill, November 23, 1783:

English Poetry, I never touch, being pretty much addicted to the writing of it, and knowing that much intercourse with those gentlemen betrays one unavoidably into a habit of imitation, which I hate and despise.

Yet as Henry Mackenzie observed[7] there is a considerable similarity of character and situation between Collins and Cowper. In his only mention of Collins, Cowper was drawn to him by that misery which

> still delights to trace
> Misfortune in another's case.

If he had read Collins when he wrote *The Task,* 1786, perhaps he remembered the *Ode to Evening* when he described:

> Hedge-row beauties numberless, square tow'r,
> Tall spire, from which the sound of cheerful bells
> Just undulates upon the list'ning ear,
> Groves, heaths, and smoking villages remote. . . .[8]

Robert Burns came slightly under the spell of the poet also. A letter to an anonymous Ayrshire lady[9] indicates that he had read the poems, possibly in one of the Glasgow or Edinburgh

---

[7] *Anecdotes and Egotisms,* ed. H. W. Thompson, London, 1927, p. 165. Mackenzie's other comments on Collins are significant and suggestive. In the comparison with Cowper, though admitting that "Collins is abstract (sometimes bordering on obscurity and his figures so bold as scarcely to be understood), drawing from his imagination independently of actual things," he concedes that Collins is "in *expression* . . . infinitely more rich and poetical." Again in reviewing the poetry of the age following Pope (*Ibid.,* p. 158) he calls Collins "the most allegorical and ideal of all poets," adding, "The enthusiasm of his admirers was equal to his own; but he was *caviare to the million,* and except his *Ode to the Passions,* whose pictures spoke to the eye as well as to the mind, little of his poetry was quoted, or lived in the memory of the bulk of readers." In *A Vision of Vanity* he speaks of the power

> That taught a Collins' raptured eye to gaze
> Full on her fires, and drink their fiercest blaze.

Moreover, we owe to Mackenzie a reference to his composition of stanzas to the *Ode on the Popular Superstitions* which filled up "a chasm that had somehow been made in it." (*Anecdotes and Egotisms,* p. 166).

[8] Compare also the description of Evening "with matron-step slow-moving" bringing peace to her "votary calm," *The Task,* IV, 243-266.

[9] Letter #76, To Margaret Chalmers (?) in Ferguson's *Letters of Robert Burns,* Oxford, 1931, I, 65.

editions, for the Scotch had been among the first to appreciate Collins. His letter to Dr. John Moore, London, dated 17 January, 1787, speaks of Collins as a poet who described the heart, one of those who persuade Burns that he should not be "vain enough to hope for distinguished poetic fame." In a letter to the Earl of Buchan, September, 1791, answering his request that Burns write a poem in honor of Thomson, Burns writes:

Your lordship hints at an Ode for the occasion; but who would write after Collins? I read over his verses to the memory of Thomson and despaired.

Yet he did write an *Address to the Shade of Thomson* in the manner of Collins, the last stanza of which particularly echoes the spirit of the *Ode on the Death of Mr. Thomson:*

> So long, sweet Poet of the year!
>   Shall bloom the wreath thou well hast won;
> While Scotia with exulting tear,
>   Proclaims that Thomson is her son.

The spirit of the same poem is felt in *Elegy on Stella,* which echoes some of the phrasing of Collins's ode:

> At the last limits of our isle,
> Wash'd by the western wave,
> Touch'd by thy fate, a thoughtful bard
>   Sits lonely by thy grave.
>
> The tears of pity which he sheds,
> He asks not to receive;
> Let but his poor remains be laid,
>   Obscurely in the grave.
>
> His grief-worn heart, with truest joy,
> Shall meet the welcome shock,
> His AIRY HARP shall lie unstrung,
>   And silent as the rock.

And the elegiac strain of the *Dirge in Cymbeline,* perhaps flavored with the melancholy of Ossian, touches the *Lament of Mary, Queen of Scots:*

> And, in the narrow house of death,
> Let Winter round me rave;
> AND THE NEXT FLOW'RS THAT DECK THE SPRING,
> BLOOM ON MY PEACEFUL GRAVE.

Perhaps the tender pity in Collins most endeared him to a greater poet, himself touched by the melancholy and sympathy that Collins felt but could not express so well.

Blake, too, in those years before he found the poetical style of the *Songs of Innocence,* the *Songs of Experience,* and the later prophetic books, came to know Collins and to try his hand in Collins's manner. Several of the *Poetical Sketches,* 1783, show traces of the *Odes on Several Descriptive and Allegoric Subjects.* The unrhymed lyrics *To Spring, To Summer, To Autumn, To Winter,* and *To the Evening Star* in diction frequently suggest Collins. It is possible, too, that the division into stanzas in four of these poems was suggested to Blake by the form of the *Ode to Evening* although it is not that which Collins employs.[10] But in general concept and in suggestive phrase the influence of Collins is present. Spring, like Collins's Evening, is a shadowy form blended with those parts of Nature touched by her influence. Such phrases as: "dewy locks," 1; "bright pavilions," 7, "deck her forth with thy fair fingers," 13, "modest tresses," 16, are reminiscent of Collins's manner; in *To Autumn,* 10, "modest Eve" suggests Collins again; in *To Winter,* the "iron car," 4, and the picture of "the monster . . . driv'n yelling to his caves," 16, are in the idiom of Collins. But *To the Evening Star* shows the closest resemblance to the *Ode to Evening,* though it is seen through Blake's imaginative eye. Line 2:

> NOW, WHILST the SUN rests on the mountains . . .

has the ring of

> WHILE NOW the bright hair'd SUN
> Sits in yon western Tent. . . .

Especially reminiscent is the passage, 5-10:

[10] See Woodhouse, *TLS,* 1929, p. 436, and Damon, S. F., *William Blake,* Boston, 1924, p. 253.

> . . . and while thou drawest the
> Blue curtains of the sky, scatter thy silver dew
> On every flower that shuts its sweet eyes
> In timely sleep. Let thy west wind sleep on
> The lake; speak silence with thy glimmering eyes,
> And wash the dusk with silver.

The last line:

> Protect them with THINE INFLUENCE,

is suggested by:

> THY gentlest INFLUENCE own

of Collins's ode. Blake's love of shadowy and visionary forms—the side of his genius closest to that of Collins—turned him at this early stage to a poet with whom he had imaginative kinship. And even when in the *Prophetic Books* he had developed his own power in a thoroughly original way he perhaps remembered Collins when he wrote in *Tiriel,* 179:

> When evening drew her solemn curtain

or in *Europe—a Prophecy,* 13:

> And fold the SHEETY waters as a mantle round my limbs.

In the verse of William L. Bowles, himself the early inspiration of Coleridge, the strain of Collins is heard. Bowles shared Collins's love of evening, his mild and quiet melancholy, and his fondness for the enchantment of distance. There are many suggestions of Collins in Bowles. He writes often of evening, and his own appreciation of its spell is colored by his memory of Collins. In *Tynemouth Priory,* 6-8:

> . . . and now the beam
> Of evening smiles on the gray battlement
> And yon forsaken tower that time has rent:—

the picture suggests Collins. It is clearer in the sonnet *To Evening:*

> Evening! as slow thy placid shades descend,
> VEILING WITH GENTLEST HUSH THE LANDSCAPE still,
> The lonely battlement, the farthest hill
> And wood . . .

> . . . and watch the tints that
> O'ER THY BED
> HANG LOVELY; oft to musing Fancy's eye
> Presenting FAIRY VALES, . . .

In the *Sonnet to the River Cherwell*, 14, "Eve's last hush"
closes the silent scene; in *On Mr. Howard's Account of Lazaret-
to*, 21, "Evening's lingering gleam" is mentioned. In the *Sylph
of Summer*, 382-93, a passage again suggests the *Ode to
Evening:*

> . . . distant hills,
> . . . in refracted light, hang beautiful
> BENEATH THE GOLD CAR OF EVE, ere yet
> THE DAYLIGHT LINGERING FADES.

The "simple bell" which Collins associated with evening's sway
is also a part of Bowles's evening scene. *Lockwell*, 8-9, describes
the time:

> Where o'er the pensive scene, at Evening's close,
> The distant bell was heard. . . .

And the *Legend of St. Cecilia and the Angel* begins:

> 'Twas when, O MEEKEST EVE! thy shadows dim
> Were slowly stealing round,
> With more impassioned sound
> Divine Cecilia sang her vesper hymn.

By *The Passions* Bowles was sufficiently impressed to write
Hope, an Allegorical Sketch to which he prefixed a motto from
Collins's poem. In development Bowles's ode resembles Col-
lins's, particularly in the lines describing Melancholy:

> But now such sounds with mellow sweetness stole,
> As lapped in dreams of bliss her slow-consenting soul.

And the passage in the *Sorrows of Switzerland*, 167-9, describing:

> She whose green buskins swept the frosts of morn,
> Who walked the high wood with her bugle horn

reminds one of Chearfulness in *The Passions*. Again a passage
in *Monody written at Matlock*, 101-3:

> Songs of conquest pealing round the CAR
> Of hard Ambition, of the FIEND OF WAR,
> SATED WITH SLAUGHTER. . . ,

suggests the *Ode to Mercy*. In diction, too, Bowles echoes Collins. Instances are: *On a Beautiful Landscape*, 3, "and MINGLED MURMURS of tumultous life"; the *Grave of Howard*, 125-6:

> If ever fortune thy loved footsteps leads
> To the wild Neiper's banks and WHISPERING REEDS . . .;

St. Michael's Mount, 59, "And such is he, who clad in WATCHET WEEDS"; the *Visionary Boy*, 88, "Arrayed in coloured BREDE, with semblances more fair,' and 179, "The MINGLED MEASURE swells in air, and dies"; and in line 215:

> And airy spirits touch thy lovely harp at eve,

the tone of Collins is felt. The soft strains of Bowles which were to soothe the young Coleridge were first touched by the softened strains of the poet of evening.

The same mood of tender pensiveness which endeared Collins to Bowles accounts for his appeal to female lovers of sentiment near the end of the century, Mrs. Anne Radcliffe and Charlotte Smith among others. In the *Mysteries of Udolpho* and the *Romance of the Forest* especially is the influence evident. In the chapter headings—brief quotations from the poets—three in the *Mysteries of Udolpho* and five in the *Romance of the Forest* are taken from poems of Collins. The sentimental lyrics interspersed in the prose itself are full of suggestions of Collins in mood and diction. One instance in *The Sea Nymphs* (*Mysteries of Udolpho*) suggests *The Passions:*

> Then from the air spirits obey,
> My potent voice they love so well,
> And on the clouds paint visions gay,
> WHILE STRAINS MORE SWEET AT DISTANCE SWELL.

The stanzas of *Hamet the Camel-Driver* show the influence of *Eclogue II* and *Eclogue IV* of the *Persian Eclogues*. The *Song of the Evening Hour* is full of suggestive echoes of Collins's ode. Instances are:

> Where'er I move a tranquil pleasure reigns:
>   O'er all the scene the dusky tints I send,
> That FORESTS WILD and MOUNTAINS, stretching plains
>   And PEOPLED TOWNS, in soft confusion blend.
>
> Wide o'er the world I waft the freshening wind,
>   Low breathing through the woods and TWILIGHT VALE,
> In whispers soft that woo the pensive mind
>   Of him who loves my lonely steps to part.

Equally suggestive are the lines:

> His tender OATEN REED I watch to hear. . . .

and:

> I wake the FAIRY ELVES, WHO SHUN THE LIGHT;
> When from their BLOSSOM'D BEDS they slily peep,
> And spy MY PALE STAR leading on the night.

The lines *To Melancholy* with their mention of "Evening's dying gale," "this lovely hour" and especially the following verses recall not only the *Ode to Evening* but the *Ode on the Death of Mr. Thomson* as well:

> Lead to the mountain's dusky head,
> Where, far below, in shade profound,
> Wide forests, plains, and hamlets spread,
> And sad the chimes of vesper sound.
> Or guide me where the DASHING OAR
> Just breaks the stillness of the vale,
> As slow it tracks the winding shore,
> To meet the ocean's distant sail.

Once, too, Collins is mentioned in the text of the book:

Then the *lucciola,* the fire-fly of Tuscany was seen to flash its sudden sparks among the foliage, while the *cicala,* with its shrill note, became more clamorous than ever during the noon-day heat, loving best the hour when the English beetle with less offensive sound,

>   . . . winds
> His small but sullen horn,
> As oft he rises 'midst the twilight path,
> Against the pilgrim born in heedless hum.[11]

---

[11] There are also suggestions of Collins in the lyrics called the *First Hour of Morning, To a Sea Nymph, The Mariner,* the *Butterfly to His Love, Shipwreck, To Autumn,* and *To the Bat.*

In the *Romance of the Forest* Collins's manner is evident in several of the lyrics, *Sonnet to the Lily, Song of a Spirit, Titania to Her Lover,* and *Morning on the Seashore* in particular. The little poem *To Night* is most thoroughly characteristic of the Collins strain:

> Now evening fades, her pensive step retires
> And night leads on the dews and SHADOWY HOURS.
>
> But chief I love thee, when thy LUCID CAR
> Sheds through the MISTY MOUNTAINS FROM AFAR,
> The nearer forest, and the valley's stream:
>
> THEN LET ME STAND AMIDST THY GLOOM PROFOUND
> ON SOME WILD WOODY STEEP, and hear the breeze
> That swells in mournful melody around,
> And faintly dies upon the distant trees.

And in *A Journey made in the Summer of 1794 through Holland and the Western Frontier of Germany* Mrs. Radcliffe again remembered Collins. She writes upon a trip to the town of Xanten:

It was a fine evening in June, and the rich lights, thrown among the forest glades, with the solitary calmness of the scene, and the sereneness of the air, filled with scents from the woods, were circumstances which persuaded to such tranquil rapture as Collins must have felt when he had the happiness to address to Evening—
        "For when thy folding star, arising shews . . ."

She quotes this and the following stanza of the ode.[12] Again at Goodesburg she pays tribute to the poet and his poem:

It was a still and beautiful evening, in which no shade remained of the thunder clouds, that passed in the day. To the west, under the glow of sun-set, the landscape melted into the horizon in tints so soft, so clear, so delicately roseate as Claude only could have painted. Viewed, as we then saw it, beyond a deep and dark arch of the ruin, its effect was enchanting; it was to the eye, what the finest strains of Paisiello are to the heart, or the poetry of Collins is to the fancy—all tender, sweet, elegant and glowing.
    From the other side of the hill the character of the view is different . . . the little plain of Goodesburg appears reposing amidst wild and awful mountains. These were now melancholy and silent; the last rays were fading from their many points, and the obscurity of

[12] Radcliffe, *Journey in the Summer of 1794,* London, 1795, pp. 88-9.

twilight began to spread over them. We seemed to have found
the spot, for which Collins wished:

> "Now let me rove some wild and heathy scene,
> Or find some ruin 'midst its dreary dells,
>   Whose walls more awful nod
>   By thy religious gleams."
>
> ODE TO EVENING.[13]

Charlotte Smith, too, wrote of Collins and in his mood; her
association with Sussex and the Arun was a bond of kinship. In
her volume of *Elegiac Sonnets and other Poems,* which had
gone through its eighth edition by 1797, there are references to
her admiration for Collins and evidences of her knowledge of
his odes. She speaks in his idiom in *On the Departure of the
Nightingale* when she writes:

> With cautious step, the love-lorn youth shall glide
>   Thro' the lone brake that shades thy mossy rest;
> And shepherd girls from eyes profane shall hide
>   The gentle bird, who sings of pity best.

In her sonnet *To Friendship* she borrows a phrase from the
Ode to Pity when she writes:

> Tis Thine, O Nymph! with "BALMY HANDS TO BIND"
> The wounds inflicted in misfortune's storm.

And in her second sonnet *To the River Arun* she mentions the

> Wilds!—whose lorn echoes learned the deeper tone
> Of Collins' powerful shell!

Again in the sonnet *On Leaving a Part of Sussex* she epitomizes
him:

> . . . while in Fancy's ear
> As in the evening wind thy murmurs swell,
> The Enthusiast of the Lyre who wandered here
> Seems yet to strike his visionary shell,
> Of power to call forth Pity's tenderest tear,
> Or wake wild frenzy from her hideous cell!

In the *Ode to Despair* and *A Descriptive Ode* one finds pale
copies of the *Ode to Fear.* There was in Collins the tender
sensibility so dear to the female novelist and poet of the closing
years of the century.

[13] *Ibid.,* pp. 138-9.

III

COLLINS'S INFLUENCE AT THE TURN OF THE CENTURY

IN THE LAST years of the century, too, Collins made his first appeal to Wordsworth, Coleridge, and Southey, young and significant poets of the new romantic generation. In the works of all three poets there is definite evidence of his influence, a force which they were never to outgrow. At various times in his career Wordsworth spoke favorably of Collins. He showed considerable interest in Dyce's edition of the poet, and Dyce apparently consulted him on several points. He was particularly concerned with the Highland Ode and definitely repudiated the version in Bell's copy (the 1788 anonymous edition). He writes January 12, 1827:

You are at perfect liberty to declare that you have rejected Bell's copy in consequence of my opinion of it; and I feel much satisfaction in being the instrument of rescuing the memory of Collins from this disgrace.[1]

He speaks again of the ode in a letter to Dyce, October 29, 1828,[2] remarking that "it was circulated through the English newspapers, in which I remember to have read it with great pleasure upon its first appearance," and noting further the source of some of the imagery, he says:

By the bye, I am almost sure that that very agreeable line,
        "Nor ever vernal tree was heard to murmur"
is from Warton's account of St. Hilda.

Knight has evidently misread "tree" for "bee," "Warton" for "Martin," and "Hilda" for "Kilda"; Wordsworth is referring to *A Voyage to St. Kilda,* with which he was familiar, for he mentions the *Voyage among the Western Isles* at the head of

[1] Knight, *Letters,* II, 358.
[2] *Ibid.,* III, 420.

poem XXXIV in the *Itinerary Poems of 1833.* On three occasions he gives a favorable opinion of Collins as a poet. He
says in the letter to Dyce, January 12, 1827:

These three writers, Thomson, Collins, and Dyer had more poetic
imagination than any of their contemporaries unless we reckon Chatterton as of that age.

Again in his letter of October 29, 1828, he calls Collins

An author who from the melancholy circumstances of his life, particularly the latter part of it, has a peculiar claim upon such attention
as you [Dyce] have bestowed upon him and his works.

In his *Essay Supplementary to the Preface,* 1815, he comments
on Collins's neglect in his lifetime and his subsequent fame:

When Thomson died, Collins breathed forth his regrets in an Elegiac
Poem, in which he pronounces a poetical curse upon him who should
regard with insensibility the place where the poet's remains were de-
posited. The poems of the mourner himself have now passed through
innumerable editions, and are universally known; but if, when
Collins died, the same kind of imprecation had been pronounced by
a surviving admirer, small is the number whom it would not have
comprehended. The notice which his poems attained during his lifetime was so small and of course the sale so insignificant, that not
long before his death he deemed it right to repay the bookseller the
sum which he had advanced for them, and threw the edition into the
fire.

He also commented critically on the *Ode to Evening.* In a letter
to Dyce, May, 1830, he writes:

A word or two about Collins. You know what importance I attach
to following strictly the last copy of the text of an author; and I do
not blame you for printing in the *Ode to Evening* "brawling" spring;
but surely the epithet is most unsuitable to the time, the very worst,
I think, that could have been chosen.[3]

When Wordsworth wrote his first poetry Collins was one of
the eighteenth century poets to whom he turned. *Lines Written*

---

[3] Knight, II, 419. Wordsworth was indirectly responsible for Crabb Robinson's expression of opinion about Collins. From Wordsworth's criticism of
"brown hamlet" in Mrs. Barbauld's *Ode to Content* Crabb Robinson dissents:
"for evening harmonizes with content, and the brown hamlet is the evening
hamlet. Collins has with exquisite beauty described the coming on of evening:
'And hamlets brown and dim discovered spires'." (*Reminiscences,* ed. Sadler,
I, 13).

While Sailing in a Boat at Evening and *Remembrance of Collins* are tributes to him, both suggestive of the *Ode on the Death of Mr. Thomson*. There are slight reminiscences of Collins in both *An Evening Walk* and *Descriptive Sketches*. Line 235 of *An Evening Walk* echoes Wordsworth's favorite line from *The Passions:*

> Yet hears her song "by distance made more sweet."

which he was later to remember in *Personal Talk,* II, 24-5, when he wrote:

> . . . sweetest melodies
> Are those that are BY DISTANCE MADE
> MORE SWEET.

Lines 280-1 of *An Evening Walk* (1820 version) recall the *Ode to Evening:*

> Or clock that blind against the wanderer born
> Drops at his feet and stills his DRONING HORN,

as do lines 291-4:

> Like Una shining on her gloomy way,
> The half-seen form of Twilight roams astray;
> Shedding through paly loop-holes mild and small,
> Gleams that upon the lake's still bosom fall.[4]

Line 372 echoes the *Ode on the Death of Mr. Thomson:*

> The boat's first motion—made with DASHING OAR.

Other instances from *An Evening Walk* are: "EVE'S MILD HOUR invites my steps abroad," 89; "the hound, the horse's tread, and MELLOW HORN, 245; "heard by calm lakes as peeps the FOLDING STAR;" 280.

Three times in his later poetry he was to remember the poet of evening. *Miscellaneous Sonnet,* XXI (Part II) begins:

> Hail Twilight, sovereign of one peaceful hour!

and especially in

> At thy MEEK BIDDING, SHADOWY POWER!

---

[4] Cf. *Descriptive Sketches,* 115:
> That glimmer hoar in eve's last light descried
> Dim from the twilight water's shaggy side.

uggests Collins. Sonnet XXXV, *Gordale,* begins in the manner and idiom of Collins:

> At early dawn, or rather when the air
> Glimmers with fading light and SHADOWY EVE
> Is busiest to confer and to bereave,
> Then, PENSIVE VOTARY, let thy feet repair
> To Gordale chasm . . . .

And in *Miscellaneous Sonnets,* Part II, VI, *June, 1820,* he
pays tribute both to Thomson and to Collins:

> For I have heard the quire of Richmond hill
> Chanting with indefatigable bill,
> Strains that recalled to mind a distant day;
> When, haply under shade of that same wood,
> And scarcely conscious of the DASHING OARS
> Plied steadily between those willowy shores,
> The sweet-souled poet of the Season stood—.

Collins, then, exercised a slight but definite influence on the
poetry of Wordsworth who remembered him with pleasure.
Upon the young Coleridge, the poet of "tumid ode and
turgid stanza," Collins cast even a stronger spell. Coleridge
admits his early admiration long afterwards in the *Preface to the
Edition of 1832:*

The poems produced before the author's twenty-fourth year, devoted as he was to the "soft strains" of Bowles, HAVE MORE IN COM-
MON WITH THE PASSIONATE LYRICS OF COLLINS and the picturesque
wildness of the pretended Ossian, than with the well-turned senti-
mentality of that Muse which the overgrateful poet has represented
as his earliest inspirer.

He preferred Collins to Gray[5] and thought he had the greater
genius.[6] He found part of his pleasure in Collins's poetry because it was but generally and not perfectly understood.[7] He
was particularly impressed by the *Ode on the Poetical Character,*
on which he twice comments. Writing to Thelwall, December
17, 1796, he confesses:

Now Collins's *Ode on the Poetical Character*—that part of it, I should

---

[5] *Biographia Literaria,* ed. Everyman, p. 10.
[6] *Table Talk,* April 21, 1811, ed. H. Ashe, p. 301.
[7] *Anima Poetae,* p. 4.

say, beginning with "The band (as fairy legends say) Was wove on
that creating day,"—has . . . whirled *me* along with greater agitation
of enthusiasm than any the most *impassioned* scene in Schiller or
Shakespeare, using the "impassioned" in its confined sense, for writing
in which the human passions of pity, fear, anger, revenge, jealousy,
or love are brought into view with their workings.[8]

Again he comments in the *Preface to the Second Edition of
the Poems:*

A poem that abounds in allusions, like the "Bard" of Gray, or one
that impersonates high and abstract truths, like Collins's "Ode on the
Poetical Character," claims not to be popular—but should be acquitted
of obscurity. The deficiency is in the Reader. But this is a charge
which every poet, whose imagination is warm and rapid, must expect
from his *contemporaries.* Milton did not escape it; and it was adduced
with virulence against Gray and Collins. We now hear no more of
it: not that their poems are better understood at present than they
were at their first publication; but their fame is established; and
a critic would accuse himself of frigidity or inattention who should
profess not to understand them.

It is further suggestive that he had planned an edition of Collins
and Gray; the project is twice mentioned in his *Note Book.*[9]

The early poems of Coleridge abound in suggestions of
Collins—his diction, his personification, and his imagery. Two
passages in *Dura Navis* recall the *Ode to Fear.* The picture of
Vengeance, 39-40:

> Whilst Vengeance drunk with human blood stands by
> And smiling fires each heart and arms each hand,

and the passage, 49-55:

> With trembling hands the lot I see thee draw
> Which shall, or sentence thee a victim drear,
> To that ghaunt Plague which savage knows no law,
> Or, deep thy dagger in the friendly heart,

---

[8] *Letters,* ed. E. H. Coleridge, I, 196.

[9] Folio 21a, *Archiv,* XCVII, 1896, p. 352; fol. 25a, p. 354. To Coleridge
too, we owe a slight bit of evidence concerning Collins's influence on the continent, a problem upon which Mr. Woodhouse has touched (*TLS,* 1930,
838). Coleridge records of Klopstock (*Satyrane's Letters,* Ed. Everyman,
301): "An Englishman had presented him with the Odes of Collins, which
he had read with pleasure." Herder, however, asserted "the infinite superiority
of Klopstock's Odes to all that Gray and Collins had ever written." (*
Crabb Robinson, *Diary and Reminiscences,* Ed. Sadler, I, 73.)

Whilst each strong passion agitates thy breast,
Though oft with Horror back I see thee start,
Lo! Hunger *drives* thee to th' inhuman heart,

have Collins's tone. The epithet "meek-eyed Peace," 59, is also from Collins, though it was first Milton's.

The *Monody on the Death of Chatterton,* 1790, echoes Collins in its praise of Otway, 20, "Whom Pity's self had taught to sing." Its description of "Poverty of Giant Mien," 48, recalls the *Ode to Fear,* and the imprecation, 86-7, is again in the manner of the *Ode to Fear:*

Grant me, like thee, the lyre to sound,
Like thee, with fire divine to glow.

A Wish, 1792, is an unrhymed lyric, the first stanza of which faintly suggests the *Ode to Evening. Ode, April, 1792,* is like Collins throughout, but the conclusion, 31-40 particularly, suggests the *Ode to Mercy:*

Then cease, thy frantic Tumults cease,
    Ambition, sire of War!
Nor o'er the mangled Corse of Peace
    Urge on thy scythed Car.
And oh! that Reason's voice might swell
Wish whisper'd Airs and holy spell
    To rouse thy gentler Sense,
As bending o'er the chilly bloom
The Morning wakes its soft Perfume
    With breezy Influence.

The *Song of the Pixies,* 1796, is peculiarly in Collins's vein. In describing the fairy-folk of Devonshire, it deals with those "airy beings" whom Collins delighted to present. Stanza V is full of echoes of the *Ode to Evening:*

When EVENING'S DUSKY CAR
Crown'd with her DEWY STAR
Steals o'er the fading sky in shadowy flight;
    On leaves of aspen trees
    We tremble to the breeze
Veil'd from the grosser ken of mortal sight.
    Or, haply, at the visionary hour,
Along our wildly-bower'd sequestered walk,

> We listen to the enamour'd rustic's talk
> Or guide of soul-subduing power
> The glance that from the half-confessing eye
> Darts the fond question or the soft reply.

Equally suggestive of Collins are "the parting gleam" of day on Otter's Stream, 67, and the band of "sombre hours," 76-7, attendant upon Night. The picture of the train of virtues which accompany the Faery Queen of the Pixies, 96-100, is typical of Collins's personifications:

> Graceful Ease in artless stole,
> And white-robed Purity of soul,
> With Honour's softer mien;
> Mirth of the loosely-flowing hair,
> And meek-eyed Pity eloquently fair,
> Whose tearful cheeks are lovely to the view,
> As snow-drop wet with dew.

The personification, diction, and manner of Collins are evident in a number of the other early poems to a lesser degree. *An Effusion at Evening*, 1792, mentions the "shadowy pleasures," 7, and echoes the *Ode to Evening* in lines 57-8:

> No more shall deck THY PENSIVE PLEASURES SWEET
> With wreaths of sober hue my evening seat.

The same strain runs indefinably through *Lines on an Autumnal Evening*. *Translation of Wrangham's Hendecasyllabi* mentions "white-robed Truth," 1, and "meek-eyed Pity," 5. *Pantisocracy*, 8, speaks of the "wizard passions" in Collins's phrase. The figures of "Heart-fretting Fear, with pallid look aghast" and its mingled forms of Misery, 11-18, suggest again the *Ode to Fear*. In two of the *Sonnets on Eminent Characters* there are echoes of *The Passions*. In *To William Godwin*, 7-8, Coleridge quotes directly:

> Thy steady eye has shot its glances keen—
> And bade th' All-lovely "scenes at distance hail."

In *To Robert Southey*, 6-7, he echoes lines 93-4 of the same ode:

> Waked by the Song doth HOPE-born FANCY fling
> RICH SHOWERS OF DEWY FRAGRANCE FROM HER WING.

Lines Written at Shurton Bars, 1795, 29-30, mentions the viewless influence of "Meek Evening," and *To the Author of Poems,*
1795, 41, speaks of "Eve's mild gleam." The revised *Monody
on the Death of Chatterton* mentions the "wizard passions,"
147, "sober eve," 152, and "young-eyed Poesy," 154, all in
Collins's characteristic idiom. *To a Young Friend,* 1796, 55, borrows "fancy-blest" from the *Ode to Liberty.* The influence of
Collins is, then, abundantly evident in many of the poems between 1790 and 1796, a time at which the young Wordsworth
was also turning to him.

In one significant instance Coleridge was to remember Collins after this date. The familiarity with *The Passions* so evident
in the earlier poems was to manifest itself in the strange dream
vision of *Kubla Khan.* The passage in Collins, 64-6:

> Thro' Glades and Glooms the MINGLED MEASURE stole,
> Or o'er some HAUNTED Stream with fond Delay,
>   Round an HOLY Calm diffusing,

was transmuted into:

> A savage place! as HOLY and enchanted
> As e'er beneath a waning moon was HAUNTED
> By woman wailing for her demon lover!

and was remembered again in:

> Where was heard the MINGLED MEASURE
> From the fountains and the caves.[10]

Perhaps, too, Coleridge remembered the fragment the *Bell of
Arragon.* The lines:

> The bell of Arragon, they say,
> Spontaneous speaks the fatal day,

and

> Whatever dark aërial power,
> Commissioned, haunts the gloomy tower,

suggest a passage in *Christabel,* lines 198-201:

---

[10] See on this point J. L. Lowes, the *Road to Xanadu,* p. 399, p. 400, and
E. Blunden, *TLS,* 1929, p. 592. Mr. Blunden also suggests that the scenery
of the *Ode on the Poetical Character* (probably in the antistrophe) colors
that of *Kubla Khan.*

> I have heard the gray-haired friar tell
> How on her death-bed she did say,
> That she should hear the castle-bell
> Strike twelve upon my wedding-day.

It is not surprising to find Coleridge so drawn to Collins. In their love of folk-lore, in their magic of word music, in their love of scholarship and erudite lore as well as in their indolence and indecision, they were akin. In Coleridge we may find a hint of what Collins would have been had his genius fully flowered.

Southey, too, was a devotee of Collins. Had he written nothing else his enthusiastic appreciation in the *Life of Cowper* would reveal his admiration:

That he [Cowper] should never before have heard of Collins, shows how little Collins had been heard of in his life-time; and that Cowper in his knowledge of contemporary literature, was now awakening, as it were, from a sleep of twenty years. In the course of those years Collins's Odes, which were utterly negected on their first appearance, had obtained their due estimation. But it should also be remembered, that in the course of one generation these poems, without any adventitious aid to bring them into notice, were acknowledged to be the best of their kind in the language. Silently and imperceptibly they had risen by their own buoyancy, and their power was felt by every reader who had any true poetic feeling.[11]

In his *General Preface,* 10 May 1837, he pays another tribute to the poet:

Everyone who has an ear for metre and a heart for poetry must have felt how perfectly the metre of Collins's *Ode to Evening* is in accordance with the imagery and the feeling.

His own admiration for the poet led him to attempt a number of unrhymed lyrics in the stanza form of the *Ode to Evening* or in variations on that form. *To Hymen* is in the form, and stanza six suggests the diction of Collins's ode in:

> And many a virtue come
> To join thy happy train.

Other instances are: *Written on the First of January, To Recovery* (in which the epithet "nymph adored" suggests Collins),

---

[11] *Bohn Lib.,* I, 321.

he *Death of Wallace, Ebb Tide,* and *Song of the Chikkashah
Widow. To Horror* is a poor and melodramatic *Ode to Fear.* In
To Contemplation the influence of the *Ode to Evening* is par-
:icularly strong, especially in the lines:

> Or LEAD ME WHERE, amid the TRANQUIL VALE,
> The broken streamlet flows in silver light;
>   And I will linger where the gale
>   O'er the banks of violets sighs,
> Listening to its SOFTENED SOUNDS arise,
> And hearken the DULL BEETLE'S DROWSY FLIGHT.

It is felt again in:

> Thee, meekest Power! I love to meet,
>   As oft with solitary pace,
> The ruined abbey's hallowed rounds I trace.

Stanza 2 of *Translation of a Greek Ode on Astronomy* bears
a striking resemblance to a passage in the *Ode on the Poetical
Character:*

> For then to the celestial palaces
> Urania leads,—Urania, she
>   The goddess who alone
>   Stands by the blazing throne,
> Effulgent with the light of Deity;
> Whom Wisdom, the creatrix, by his side
> Placed on the heights of yonder sky,
> And smiling with ambrosial love, unlocked
> The depths of Nature to her piercing eye,
> Angelic myriads struck their harps around;
>   And, with triumphant song,
>   The host of stars, a beauteous throng,
>   Around the ever-living Mind
> In jubilee their mystic dance begun;
>   When at thy leaping forth, O Sun!
>   The Morning started in affright,
> Astonished at thy birth, her child of Light!

And in *Vision of Judgment,* Canto I, the spell of the *Ode to
Evening* is again felt:

Derwent returning yet from eve a glassy reflection,
Where his expanded breast, then still and smooth as a mirror
Under the woods reposed . . .

Pensive I stood, and alone; the hour and the scene had subdued me . .
Then as I stood, the bell, which awhile from its warning had rested,
Sent forth its note again, toll, toll, through the silence of evening.

Of the thirty-five thousand lines of verse which Southey esti-
mated he had written by December, 1793, a generous share must
have come from the inspiration of Collins.

Mr. Bronson[12] has said that Scott like Wordsworth found
his inspiration elsewhere than in the pages of Collins. Yet
Scott, too, robust in nature as he was, turned occasionally to
the pages of the delicate and less fortunate poet with whom
he felt a kinship. Scott's tribute to Collins in the *Bride of Trier-
main* is a commentary at once on the poet's genius and on his
reputation:

> For Lucy loves (like Collins, ill-starred name,
> Whose lay's requital was that tardy fame,
> Who bound no laurel round his living head,
> Should hang it o'er his monument when dead)
> For Lucy loves to tread enchanted strand,
> And thread, like him, the maze of fairy land;
> Of golden battlements to view the gleam,
> And slumber soft by some Elysian stream.

The *Ode on the Popular Superstitions* naturally attracted
Scott early, for here Collins had touched on a theme which
Scott was to develop in the *Lady of the Lake* and the *Lord of
the Isles*. In the *Minstrelsy of the Scottish Border* Scott included
three supplemental stanzas to Collins's ode by his "valued
friend," William Erskine, Esq., Advocate, which had already
appeared in the *Edinburgh Magazine,* for April, 1788, the
year in which the poem was found. Scott's comment that the
stanzas are "worthy of the SUBLIME ORIGINAL" shows his own
feeling for the poem. His motto to *Glenfinlas, or Lord Ronald's
Coronach,* which originally appeared in Monk Lewis's *Tales of
Wonder,* comes from the *Ode on the Popular Superstitions,*
65-9; in the poem itself Moy, the prophetic seer from Columb's
isle, who has the power of second-sight, suggests the influence
of Collins. Lines 33-6 embroider a superstition that Collins
had neglected:

[12] *Collins,* p. lvii.

> For there [in Columb's isle] 'tis said, in mystic mood,
> High converse with the dead they hold
> And oft espy the fated shroud,
> That shall the future corpse enfold.

Three times in the notes to the *Minstrelsy* Scott mentions Collins. In the *Introduction to the Tale of Tamlane*[13] Scott associates lines 58-9, 62-3 of the *Ode to Fear* (which he quotes inaccurately and apparently from memory) with St. John's Eve, in his mind the thrice-hallowed eve of Collins's poem. Again in his comment on Leyden's *Mermaid*[14] he refers to Collins's *Ode to Liberty*, 82, and the poet's note about the scorned mermaid who cast a mist over the Isle of Man. And in his notes on the *Gray Brother,* alluding to "classic Hawthornden" he quotes line 212 of the *Ode on the Popular Superstitions* as it appeared in the *Transactions of the Royal Society* copy: "The traveller now looks in vain for the leafy bower:

> Where Jonson sate in Drummond's SOCIAL shade."

There are also occasional suggestions in the historical romances that Scott remembered some of the other odes as well as the *Ode on the Popular Superstitions*. In the *Lay of the Last Minstrel,* I, xii, 4:

> Till to her bidding she could bow
> THE VIEWLESS FORMS OF AIR

echoes lines 65-6 of the *Ode on the Popular Superstitions,* a passage which Scott had already used as the motto to *Glenfinlas.* It is suggested again in *Lady of the Lake,* I, xxx:

> While VIEWLESS MINSTRELS TOUCH THE STRING,
> 'Tis thus our charmed rhymes we sing.

And in *Soldier Rest* Scott must have remembered *Ode Written in the Beginning of the Year 1746* when he wrote:

> In our isle's enchanted hall,
> HANDS UNSEEN THY COUCH ARE STREWING,
> FAIRY STRAINS OF MUSIC FALL.

In the *Lord of the Isles* his allusion to the Seer of Skye and to "Iona's piles,"

[13] Ed. Crowell, p. 299.
[14] *Op. cit.,* p. 651.

Where rest from mortal coil the Mighty of the Isles,

suggests Collins as much as Martin Martin. And twice he echoes *The Passions.* In *Rokeby,* V, xvii, Rokeby's maid prays:

> Here to renew the STRAINS she loved,
> AT DISTANCE HEARD and well approved,

—a suggestion of *The Passions,* 60. In the *Vision of Don Roderick,* LXII:

> Or may I give adventurous fancy scope,
> And stretch a bold hand to the awful veil
> That hides futurity from anxious HOPE,
> BIDDING BEYOND IT SCENES OF GLORY HAIL,

echoes "AND BAD THE LOVELY SCENES AT DISTANCE HAIL," line 32 of *The Passions.* In the Waverley novels Scott found very little occasion to remember Collins. He did, however, twice choose a motto at the head of a chapter from Collins's verse. The heading for Chapter IV of *The Monastery* comes from lines 58-9 and 61-2 of the *Ode to Fear,* rendered inaccurately. Chapter XI of *Peveril of the Peak* employs line 82 of the *Ode to Liberty* as its motto. In the introductory epistle to the *Fortunes of Nigel* he quotes two lines of the *Ode on the Popular Superstitions,* 68-9, as part of a discussion of the phenomenon of second sight or "deuteroscopy" as Scott calls it. In all three allusions it is evident that Collins's love of folk-lore most attracted Scott.

The evidence of Collins's direct influence on Scott is slight, but it reveals that Scott was familiar with a poet who had anticipated him in celebrating the glamor and fascination of the Highlands of Scotland.

IV

COLLINS AND THE YOUNGER ROMANTICS

To the younger group of romantic poets Collins also
appealed; Keats was particularly influenced by him, and
to a lesser degree Byron and Shelley. Byron mentions him
several times. Collins is to him an instance in point of a belief
that poets are frequently mad, though they rarely go mad. He
mentions the notion in a letter to Miss Milbanke, November
10, 1813:[1]

They say poets never or rarely go *mad*. Cowper and Collins are instances to the contrary (but Cowper was no poet).

He makes the same point again in a letter to Leigh Hunt, November, 1818,[2] here citing Collins's madness as an instance that:

An addiction to poetry is very generally the result of "an uneasy
mind in an uneasy body."

Collins he mentions with Johnson, Gray, and Burns as a
victim of "hypochondriacism," which in his case was the prelude to a more awful malady.[3] Twice he comments on the *Persian Eclogues*. In the diary for January 11, 1821[4] he takes issue
with Campbell's statement[5] that "no just reader" cares any more
about Collins's failure to secure verisimilitude in the eclogues
"than about the authenticity of the tale of Troy." Byron retorts:
" 'Tis false! we do care about the authenticity of the tale of
Troy." In the letter to Tom Moore prefixed to *The Giaour* he
mentions the eclogues again:

It is said among those friends, I trust truly, that you are engaged
in the composition of a poem whose scene will be laid in the East;
none can do those scenes so much justice. The wrongs of your own

[1] *Letters,* III, 405.
[2] *Letters,* ed. E. H. Coleridge, III, 247.
[3] Byron-Bowles Controversy III, *Letters,* V, 578.
[4] *Letters,* V, 165.
[5] *Specimens of the British Poets,* ed. 1819, V, 311.

country, the magnificent and fiery spirit of her sons, the beauty and
and feeling of her daughters may there be found; and Collins when
he denominated his Oriental, his Irish Eclogues, was not aware how
true, at least, was a part of his parallel.[6]

Yet the *Persian Eclogues* influenced Byron not at all. He was,
however, touched by two of Collins's poems—the *Ode Written
in the Beginning of the Year 1746* and the *Ode on the Death
of Mr. Thomson.* The first impressed him early and he frequently quoted part of it or wrote in phrases suggestive of it. Its
influence is present in *Epitaph on a Beloved Friend,* 17-18:

> Affliction's semblance bends not o'er thy tomb,
> Affliction's self deplores thy youthful doom.

Again in *A Fragment,* 8-9, he writes:

> My epitaph shall be my name alone,
> If that with Honour fail to crown my clay.

In *English Bards and Scotch Reviewers,* 809-11, he pays tribute
to Burns in Collins's phrase:

> What! must deserted Poesy still weep
> Where her last hopes with pious Cowper sleep?
> Unless, perchance, from her cold bier she turns,
> TO DECK THE TURF THAT WRAPS her minstrel Burns.

In *Childe Harold,* I, xlii, 2, he cries of the dead on Talavera's
plain:

> There shall they rot, Ambition's honoured fools!
> Yes, Honour DECKS THE TURF THAT WRAPS THEIR CLAY!

He echoes the phrase again in *Childe Harold,* IV, lx, 6. And
in *Hebrew Melodies,* "Oh snatch'd away in beauty's bloom"
seems reminiscent of the same poem in such lines as:

> But on THY TURF shall roses rear
> Their leaves, the EARLIEST OF THE YEAR . . . .

Again in *Don Juan,* II, 109, 1-5, there is a remembrance of
Collins:

> When Nero perish'd by the justest doom,
> Which ever the destroyer yet destroy'd . . .
> Some HANDS UNSEEN STREW'D FLOWERS UPON HIS TOMB.

[6] *Works,* Ed. E. H. Coleridge, III, 224.

The *Ode on the Death of Mr. Thomson* impressed him equally. In *Lines Written on a Blank Leaf of "Pleasures of Memory,"* 7, he recalls the poem when he writes:

> And "Memory" O'ER HER DRUID'S TOMB,
> Shall weep that AUGHT OF THEE CAN DIE.

Stanza 75 of *Oscar of Alva* suggests stanza seven of Collins's ode:

> Lo! see'st thou not a LONELY TOMB,
> Which rises o'er a warrior dead?
> IT GLIMMERS THROUGH THE TWILIGHT GLOOM.

And the passage in *Childe Harold,* III, lxxxvi, 7-8:

> on the ear
> Drops the light drip of the SUSPENDED OAR

seems an echo of line 15 of the *Ode on the Death of Mr. Thomson:*

> And oft SUSPEND THE DASHING OAR.[7]

It is significant that Byron, who sought a soldier's grave, should have been most deeply touched by one of the finest tributes to the heroic dead.

One is, however, surprised to find so little trace of Collins in the poetry of Shelley, to whom in tenderness, in sensitiveness, and in love of the world of fancy he is so much akin. Only the *Ode to Evening,* which in spirit and substance is closest to Shelley's nature, and the *Ode Written in the Beginning of the Year 1746* seem to have impressed him. *Stanzas, April 1814* echoes both poems. Line 2:

> Rapid clouds have drunk THE LAST PALE BEAM OF EVEN

suggests the first, and line 14:

> The BLOOMS OF DEWY SPRING shall gleam beneath
> Thy feet . . .

draws a phrase from the second.

A Summer-Evening Churchyard, Lechlade, Gloucestershire, September 1815, 3-4, transmutes an image from the *Ode to Evening* into a creation of Shelley's own fancy:

---

[7] Lines 14-18 of *To a Knot of Ungenerous Critics* may be an echo of *The Manners,* 38-44.

> And pallid Evening twines its beaming hair
> In duskier braids around the languid eyes of Day.

Again in *Boat on the Serchio*, 24, "the beetle forgot to wind
his horn" recalls the *Ode to Evening*. Collins's "brede ethereal"
fascinated Shelley. He writes in *Alastor*, 336-8:

> Twilight, ascending slowly from the East,
> Entwined in duskier wreaths her BRAIDED locks
> O'er the fair front and radiant eyes of day . . . .

It occurs again in the *Daemon of the World*, 193-6:

> Thou must have marked the BRAIDED WEBS of gold
>   That without motion hang
>   Over the sinking sphere.

And Collins's picture of Evening's "gradual dusky Veil" may
have suggested to Shelley the image in *Prometheus Unbound*,
IV, 211-2:

> the hills and woods
> Distinctly seen through that DUSKY aery VEIL.

A similar picture is drawn in the *Triumph of Life*, 31-3:

> . . . the scene came through
> As clear as, when A VEIL OF LIGHT IS DRAWN
> O'ER EVENING HILLS, THEY GLIMMER . . . .

The suggestions of Collins in Shelley are slight, but they seem
definite. Yet one is surprised to find no evidence that Shelley
was touched by the glorious *Ode on the Poetical Character*, which
in spirit and enthusiasm and myth-making faculty must have
struck a responsive chord in his sensitive nature.

Keats, however, shows a deeper interest in Collins than does
Shelley. Perhaps Collins's passion for Greek form touched him;
perhaps, a lover of finely-molded phrase himself, he found a
kindred spirit in Collins. There are traces of Collins in *Endym
ion,* and in *Sleep and Poetry,* and one might suspect that Hunt
himself an enthusiastic admirer of Collins, had introduced the
poet's work to his young friend. In 1818 Keats was attending
Hazlitt's lectures and heard that critic's enthusiastic defense of

Collins.[8] It is plausible to suppose that this lecture rekindled his interest in Collins, for in the *Odes* and *Hyperion* there are slight but significant evidences of the spell of Collins.

The reminiscences in the early works are slight, but suggestive. Lines 134-5 of *Sleep and Poetry:*

> And now I see them on the GREEN-HILL'S SIDE
> IN BREEZY rest . . .

suggest an image and phrase from the *Ode on the Death of Mr. Thomson:* "breezy lawn," 18, and "Now waft me from the green hill's side," 31. *Endymion,* II, 832-5:

> And then the forest fold it in a dream
> To a sleeping lake, WHOSE COOL AND LEVEL GLEAM
> A POET CAUGHT as he was journeying
> To Phoebus' shrine;[9]

shows an appreciative reading of the *Ode to Evening. Endymion,* III, 891-2:

> Then LOVE took WING, and FROM HIS PINIONS SHED
> ON ALL THE MULTITUDE A NECTAROUS DEW

echoes *The Passions,* 90-4, where Love

> As if he would the charming Air repay,
> SHOOK THOUSAND ODOURS FROM HIS DEWY WINGS,

a passage to which Keats was to return in the *Ode on a Grecian Urn.* Again *Endymion,* IV, 394-9, suggests the imagery of the *Ode to Evening* and perhaps the *Ode on the Popular Superstitions:*

> Or from old Skiddaw's top, where fog conceals
> His rugged forehead in a mantle pale,
> With an eye-guess towards some pleasant vale
> Descry a favourite hamlet faint and far.

And *Endymion,* IV, 970-1:

> Wan as primroses gather'd at midnight
> By CHILLY FINGER'D SPRING.

---

[8] Letter to George and Thomas Keats, 21 February 1818, *Works,* Ed. H. B. Forman, 1901, IV, 80.
[9] On this point see Saito, Takeshi, "Collins and Keats," *TLS,* 1930, p. 99.

weaves in a phrase from the *Ode Written in the Beginning of the Year 1746*.[10] But these are mere hints and suggestions of Collins's phrase. In the *Odes* and in *Hyperion* the influence of Collins is stronger and becomes part of the imaginative plan of the poems, an indication that in writing odes which in the main show a fine harmony of classical restraint and romantic fancy, Keats turned to an earlier poet who in his degree had achieved a similar harmony. The *Ode to Apollo* suggests Collins in many ways: in its theme it has some of the exalted tone of the *Ode on the Poetical Character;* it glorifies Milton, Shakespeare, Spenser, and Tasso, favorite poets of Collins. One stanza of it suggests the theme of *The Passions:*

> Thou biddest Shakespeare wave his hand,
>   And quickly forward spring
>   The Passions—a terrific band—
>   And each vibrates the string
>   That with its tyrant temper best accords,
> While from their Master's lips pour forth the inspiring words.

The stanza in praise of Tasso suggests Collins's encomium in stanza XII of the *Ode on the Popular Superstitions:*

>   Next thy Tasso's ardent numbers
>   Float along the pleased air,
>   Calling youth from idle slumbers,
>   Rousing them from Pleasure's lair:—
>   Then o'er the strings his fingers gently move,
>   And melt the soul to pity and to love.

In the final stanza, lines 45-6 catch the spirit of the *Ode to Evening* when they describe:

>   The dying tones that fill the air,
>   And charm the ear of evening fair.

The *Ode on a Grecian Urn,* breathing the spirit of Tempe and the dales of Arcady, turns back to the pastoral setting of *The*

---

[10] Perhaps, as Mr. Blunden suggests, lines 5-6 of *The Manners:*
>   No more my Sail that Deep Explores,
>   No more I Search those magic Shores,

furnishes the germ for a fine image in *On First Looking into Chapman's Homer*—"Western Islands," "realms of gold," and the "demesne" of Homer.

Passions—in ancient Greece "when music heavenly Maid was young." The fine line, "In Notes by Distance made more sweet," which fascinated Wordsworth and Coleridge and Campbell, Keats weaves into its ultimate form when he writes:

> Heard melodies are sweet, but those unheard
> Are sweeter.

The spirited image in stanza III:

> And, happy melodist, unwearied,
>   For ever piping songs forever new;

in fact, the mood of the whole passage goes back to the description of "Joy's ecstatic Trial" in *The Passions,* 85-6:

> They would have thought who heard the Strain,
> They saw in TEMPE'S VALE her native Maids,
> Amidst the FESTAL SOUNDING SHADES,
> To SOME UNWEARIED MINSTREL DANCING . . .

and "brede," 41, is Collins's word—the "Brede ethereal" of the *Ode to Evening.* And perhaps Keats remembered the opening lines of the *Ode to Pity:*

> O Thou, the FRIEND OF MAN assign'd,
> With balmy Hands his Wounds to bind,
> And charm his frantic WOE:

when he wrote, lines 47-8 of the ode:

> Thou shalt remain, in midst of other WOE
> Than ours, A FRIEND TO MAN . . . .

But in harmonious balance between restraint and emotion Keats's ode transcends his original. Mr. Blunden[11] has already pointed out that in the *Ode to Psyche* there is a suggestion of the *Ode to Pity.* Lines 50-1 of the *Ode to Psyche:*

> Yes, I will be thy priest, and BUILD A FANE
>   IN SOME UNTRODDEN REGION OF MY MIND,

surely recalls 25-7 of the *Ode to Pity:*

> Come, *Pity,* come by Fancy's aid,
> Ev'n NOW MY THOUGHTS, relenting Maid,
>   Thy TEMPLE'S PRIDE design.

[11] Collins, p. 167; *TLS,* 1929, p. 592.

Further, the concluding stanza of the *Ode to Pity,* 37-9:

> There let me oft, retir'd by Day,
> In DREAMS OF PASSION MELT AWAY,
> Allow'd with Thee to dwell,

is not far from the concluding passage of the *Ode to Psyche:*

> And there shall be for thee all soft delight
> That SHADOWY THOUGHT can win.

And again in the *Ode to Melancholy* Keats remembered Collins when, describing the "Sovran Shrine" of Melancholy, he wrote:

> His soul shall taste the sadness of his might,
> And be among her CLOUDY TROPHIES HUNG,

which echoes the *Ode on the Death of Col. Ross,* 20-1:

> Aërial hands shall build thy Tomb,
> With SHADOWY TROPHIES crown'd.

In the *Ode to Autumn,* however, the suggestion of Collins is strongest. Like Collins, Keats describes the time by detailing the aspects of nature touched by the power of the goddess— the richness of imagery in Keats is appropriate to Autumn, the presiding spirit, as the softness of Collins's picture is harmonious with the mild and genial influence of Evening. The shadowy form of Autumn "sitting careless on a granary floor," her hair "soft lifted by the winnowing wind," has all that harmony between the real world and the imaginative that Collins has felt in his poem. True, Keats's picture is the more colorful and the richer, but that is because the color and richness are appropriate to the mood of the season. Yet the richness, the languidness, and the soft melancholy of Autumn, the season, are made the more effective by attributing those qualities to the presiding spirit, Autumn, the Goddess, just as Collins imparts to Evening, the Goddess, the reserve, the composure, and the soft pensiveness of the evening hour. The two poems are akin, yet each is in the best manner of its author; each is in itself a masterpiece.[12]

---

[12] The relationship of the two poems was long ago pointed out by Bronson, *Collins,* p. xlviii. It is also discussed in E. Blunden's "Nature in English

Once again after the *Odes*, Keats was to remember Collins and the *Ode to Evening* when he described in *Hyperion*, II, 35-6:

> . . . a forlorn moor,
> When THE CHILL RAIN BEGINS AT SHUT OF EVE.

Both poets were possessed of the romantic spirit and the classical love of form; if Nature was more lavish in her gifts to Keats, she gave him as well the admiration for a kindred spirit whose softened strain touched him and stimulated him.[13]

To the other less gifted poets and essayists of the day Collins also appealed. Leigh Hunt's *Autobiography* reveals that in his early years he, too, was touched by the spell of Collins. In recollecting his schooldays he records his passionate admiration for the poet:[14]

In those times, Cooke's edition of the British poets came up. I got an old volume of Spenser; and I fell passionately in love with Collins and Gray.

He confesses later:[15]

My favourites, out of school hours, were Spenser, Collins, Gray, and the Arabian Nights.

He rejoiced that he might buy as much Collins and Gray as he pleased[16] and he tells an amusing anecdote of how the *Ode on the Death of Mr. Thomson* influenced him and his school-fellow, Barnes:

On the same principle of making invocations as loud as possible, and at the same time of fulfilling the prophecy of a poet, and also for the

---

Literature," *London Magazine,* 1921, p. 42, and is mentioned in M. Dela-mare's "L'Originalité de Collins," *Revue Anglo-Americaine,* 1932-3, p. 28, where the date of Mr. Blunden's article is erroneously given as 1821.

[13] Mr. E. De Selincourt in his edition of the *Poems of John Keats,* London, 1912, (Third Edition), pp. 583-4, and in his glossary, cites as words common to both poets: "pillared," "laurelled," "honied," "curtained," "shouldered," "paly," "elf," "pebbled," though he admits that they are found elsewhere and that "Collins's love of Spenser and Milton would continually recall to Keats the language and tone of his two greatest masters." To the list might be added, with similar qualifications, "sphered," "viewless," and "beamy."

[14] Ed. Ingpen, 1903, I, 86.

[15] *Ibid.,* I, 88.

[16] *Ibid.,* I, 92.

purpose of indulging ourselves with an echo, we used to lie upon our oars at Richmond, and call, in the most vociferous manner, upon the spirit of Thomson to "rest." It was more like "perturbing" his spirit than laying it.

The allusion is, of course, to stanza IV of the *Ode:*[17]

> Remembrance oft shall haunt the shore
> When Thames in summer wreaths is drest,
>   And oft suspend the dashing oar
>   To bid his gentle spirit rest.

Hunt admits, too, that in his *Juvenilia* he "wrote 'odes' because Collins and Gray had written them."[18] The *Juvenilia* frequently suggest Collins's influence. In *Christ's Hospital* he is called "Collins, bard sublime;" in *To Honour* he is

> enraptured Collins . . .
> As Fancy wild her reeds among.

To Eliza. Imitated from the Spanish, is very obviously in imitation of Collins:

> And when thou wav'st thy AIRY WING,
> No CHILLING RAINS shall patter there;
> No DRIVING HAIL deform thy spring;
> Go, sigh my sorrows, gentle air.

Written at the Time of the War in Switzerland patently copies the *Ode Written in the Beginning of the Year 1746* in such lines as:

> Oft before the DEWY SPRING
> Sadly smiles, is FREEDOM SEEN
> WEEPING, fresh-blown flow'rs to bring,
> AND DECK EACH CORSE WITH HONOURS GREEN!

And in *To Friendship. In the Manner of Collins' Ode to Evening* Hunt employs the unrhymed stanza and perhaps echoes Collins in:

> O lovely maid, if aught my humble lay
> Avail to move thy gen'rous pitying breast
>   Whose rugged numbers oft
>   Have HAILED THY GENIAL REIGN.

---

[17] *Ibid.,* I, 117.
[18] *Op. cit.,* I, 120.

In the *Poetical Register* for the same year appeared the *Shade of Collins, an Ode,* also by Hunt. He twice mentions Collins in the *Feast of the Poets.* In lines 13-14 he writes:

> There was Collins, 'tis true, had a good deal to say,
> But the rogue had no industry,—neither had Gray.

Lines 505-6 in the 1814 edition speak of those poets

> Whom Fancy has crowned with one twig of the bay,
> From old father Chaucer to Collins and Gray.

Hunt speaks of Collins again in his review of the poems of Keats in *The Examiner,* No. 492, Sunday, June 1, 1817, p. 485:

Even the poets [of Pope's age] who gave evidences meanwhile of a TRUER POETICAL FACULTY, Gray, Thomson, Akenside, AND COLLINS HIMSELF, were content with a great deal of second-hand workmanship,

—an indication that his early attitude of admiration persisted, though tempered with maturer criticism.

Two of Hunt's later poems bear the stamp of Collins. Lines 9-10 of *An Unfinished Poem in Heroic Couplets:*

> To mark o'er all how Twilight's shadowy hand
> Came with its gentle blessing on the land

suggest the *Ode to Evening.* And a dirge, ascribed to Hunt in *Chambers' Cyclopedia of English Literature* (1844, 1860, 1870, 1892), is shot through with echoes of the *Ode Written in the Beginning of the Year 1746:*

> BLEST IS THE TURF, serenely blest,
> Where throbbing hearts may SINK TO REST,
> Where life's long journey turns to sleep,
> Nor ever PILGRIM wakes to weep.
> A tear for long departed hours,
> Is all that feeling hearts request
> To hush their weary thoughts to rest.
> There shall no vain ambition come,
> To lure them from their quiet home:
> Nor sorrow lift, with heart-strings riven,
> The meek imploring eye to heaven;
> Nor sad remembrance stoop to shed
> His wrinkles on the slumberer's head,

> And never, never love REPAIR,
> To breathe his idle whispers THERE.

Thomas Campbell included a selection from the poetry of Collins in his *Specimens of the British Poets*, 1819.[19] His introductory essay reveals his enthusiasm for Collins. He does not hesitate to compare Collins with the young Milton, when he writes of the *Persian Eclogues* and the odes:

Those works will abide comparison with whatever Milton wrote under the age of thirty. If they have rather less exuberant wealth of genius, they exhibit more exquisite touches of pathos. Like Milton he leads us into the haunted ground of imagination; like him, he has the rich economy of expression haloed with thought, which by single or few words often hint entire pictures to the imagination.

He praises Collins's eclogues which he feels are marked by "a touching interest and a picturesque novelty" lacking in the pastoral eclogue "which is insipid in all other English hands." He mentions the appeal of the *Ode to Evening* and speaks of the "unbounded popularity" of *The Passions*. His final criticism of Collins's imagination is stimulating and penetrating:

His genius loved to breathe rather in the preternatural and ideal element of poetry, than in the atmosphere of imitation, which lies closest to real life; and his notions of poetical excellence, whatever vows he might address to the manners, were still tending to the vast, the undefinable, and the abstract.

In Campbell's poetry, too, the Collins strain is felt. A hymn, "Where Jordan hushed his waters still," suggests the *Ode to Mercy:*

> See, Mercy, from her golden well,
>   Pours a glad stream to them that mourn;
> Behold, she binds with tender care,
>   The bleeding bosom of despair.

The *Pleasures of Hope* is full of reminiscent echoes of Collins, who had already celebrated Hope in *The Passions*. The famous line, "'Tis distance lends enchantment to the view," and the couplet, 11-12:

> Thus, from afar each DIM-DISCOVERED scene
> More pleasing seems than all the past hath been

[19] *Specimens of the British Poets,* V, 311 ff.

suggest two images in *The Passions:* line 60, "In Notes by Distance made more sweet" and lines 31-2:

> Still it whisper'd promis'd Pleasure,
> And bad the lovely Scenes at Distance hail!

"Dim-discovered," moreover, comes directly from the *Ode to Evening,* 37. Another couplet, 35-6:

> When Murder BARED HER ARM, and Rampant War
> Yoked the red dragons of her IRON CAR[20]

echoes phrases from the *Ode to Fear* and the *Ode to Peace.* A fourth passage, lines 241-4, suggests a mood peculiar to Collins —the elegiac mood of his *Ode on the Death of Mr. Thomson:*

> Wilt thou, sweet mourner! at my stone appear,
> And soothe my parted spirit LINGERING NEAR?
> Or wilt thou come, AT EVENING HOUR TO SHED,
> The tears of memory o'er my narrow bed.

Typical of Collins, too, is the couplet, 635-6:

> In vain, to soothe, the solitary shade,
> AERIAL NOTES in MINGLING MEASURE played;

which echoes a phrase from *The Passions.* And again, lines 1001-2:

> Can FANCY'S FAIRY HANDS NO VEIL CREATE
> To hide the sad realities of Fate?

recreate a favorite image of Collins.

In the shorter lyrics of Campbell there are echoes of the favorite *Ode Written in the Beginning of the Year 1746.* In *Gilderoy:*

> Then will I seek the dreary mound,
> That WRAPS thy mouldering CLAY

catches the tone of it, as do the lines in the *Ode to Burns:*

> Still may the grateful PILGRIM stop,
> To BLESS THE SPOT that holds thy dust.

The tone is heard again in *Hallowed Ground:*

> What hallows ground where heroes sleep?
> 'Tis not the sculptured piles you keep!

---

[20] Cf. also lines 397-8.

> In dews that heavens far distant weep,
>   Their turf may bloom;
> Or Genii twine beneath the deep
>   Their coral tomb.

In the poetry of Thomas Moore, too, there are occasional faint traces of Collins. The *Elegiac Stanzas* beginning:

> When wearied wretches sink to sleep,
> How heavenly soft their slumbers lie!

suggests the *Ode Written at the Beginning of the Year 1746,* as do the lines in *To—1801:*

> To keep this semblance fresh in bloom,
> My heart shall be its lasting tomb,
> And memory with embalming care,
> Shall keep it fresh and fadeless there.

In *Melologue* a passage suggests the same ode when Moore writes:

> What muse shall mourn the breathless brave,
> In sweetest dirge at Memory's shrine?
> What harp shall sigh o'er Freedom's grave?

And in a section of *Rhymes on the Road,* Extract XIV, there is a suggestion of the *Ode to Evening* in such lines as:

> I felt the veil of sleep serene
> Come o'er the memory of each scene,
> As twilight o'er the landscape falls . . .

or in:

>   the haze
> Of evening to some sunny view,
> Softening such charms as it displays
> And veiling others in that hue,
> Which fancy only can see through.

Nor should one forget that to the essayists Collins also appealed. In a letter to Coleridge, June 13, 1796, Lamb coupled him with Milton in "Sublimity," and in a letter of December 10, 1796, he alters two lines of the *Ode on the Poetical Character* when he writes:

The tender cast of soul, sombred with melancholy and subsiding recollections is favorable to the Sonnet or the Elegy, but from

"The sainted growing woof
The teasing troubles keep aloof."

The music of poesy may charm for awhile the importunate teasing cares of life; but the teased and troubled man is not in a disposition to make that music.

And perhaps Lamb's beautiful *Old Familiar Faces,* an unrhymed lyric, harks back to the unrhymed lyric of Collins, the *Ode to Evening.*

To Hazlitt we owe the fine tribute to Collins in the sixth lecture on the English Poets, 1818. He is thoroughly appreciative of the poet's genius when he writes:[21]

Collins . . . had perhaps less general power of mind than Young; but he had that genuine inspiration, which alone can give birth to the highest efforts of poetry. . . . He is the only one of the minor poets of whom, if he had lived, it cannot be said that he might not have done the greatest things. The germ is there. He is sometimes affected, unmeaning, and obscure; but he also catches rich glimpses of the bowers of Paradise, and has lofty aspirations after the highest seats of the Muses. With a great deal of tinsel and splendid patchwork, he has not been able to hide the solid sterling ore of genius. In his best works there is an Attic simplicity, a pathos and fervour of the imagination. . . .

After lamenting Collins's melancholy madness and deploring the neglect of his poetry during his lifetime, Hazlitt comments directly on his poetry:

The proofs of his capacity are, his Ode on Evening, his Ode on the Passions (particularly the fine personification of Hope), his Ode to Fear, the Dirge in *Cymbeline,* the Lines on Thomson's Grave, and his *Eclogues,* parts of which are admirable. But perhaps his Ode on the Poetical Character is the best of all. A rich distilled perfume emanates from it like the breath of genius; a golden cloud envelopes it; a honeyed paste of poetic diction encrusts it, like the candied coat of the auricula. His Ode to Evening shows equal genius in the images and versification. The sounds steal slowly over the ear, like the gradual coming on of evening itself.

His quotation of the *Ode to Evening* in full ends the commentary, but he adds in the beginning of his remarks on Gray:

[21] *Lectures on English Poets,* Oxford, 1924, pp. 178-80.

I should conceive that Collins had a much greater poetical genius than Gray, he had more of that fine madness which is inseparable from it, of its turbid effervescence, of all that pushes it to the verge of agony or rapture.

The comment, in Hazlitt's most glamorous prose style, does justice to both the Attic simplicity and the imaginative power of the poet and is a fine critical tribute to him. In the light of such a tribute so allusive an author as Hazlitt must have remembered Collins among other poets whose lines he wove into the texture of his essays. He writes in *On Poetry in General:*

It is the perfect coincidence of the image and the words with the feeling we have and of which we cannot get rid in any other way, that gives an instant satisfaction. . . . When Collins makes Danger, with "limbs of giant mould,"

"Throw him on the steep of some loose hanging rock asleep;"

the passion . . . of terror is perfectly satisfied.

In the fine discussion of "Mr. Coleridge" in the *Spirit of the Age* occurs the passage:

Next he was engaged with Hartley's TRIBES OF MIND "ethereal braid, thought-woven,"—

which suggests both the *Ode on the Poetical Character* and the *Ode to Evening.* Later in the same essay he writes:

. . . he bathed his heart in beauty . . . and WEDDED WITH TRUTH IN PLATO'S SHADE—

an incorrect reminiscence of *The Manners.* A reference to the second of the *Persian Eclogues* comes at the close of the essay:

"His words were hollow, but they pleased the ear" of his friends of the Lake School, who turned back disgusted and panic-struck from the dry desert of unpopularity, like Hassan the camel-driver,

"And curs'd the hour, and curs'd the luckless day,
When first from Shiraz' walls they bent their way."

They are safely enclosed there. But Mr. Coleridge did not enter with them; pitching his tent upon the barren waste without, and having no abiding place nor city of refuge.

And on at least two occasions he remembered the fine description of Hope in *The Passions.* In *On the Feeling of Immortality in Youth* he writes:

As in setting out on a delightful journey, we strain our eager gaze
forward—
> "Bidding the lovely scenes at distance hail,"

and see no end to the landscape, new objects presenting themselves
as we advance; so, in the commencement of life, we set no bounds
to our inclinations, nor to the unrestricted opportunities of gratifying
them.

He uses the same passage appropriately enough in the essay
on *Why Distant Objects Please*. He closes *A Farewell to Essay
Writing* with the last line of the *Ode on the Poetical Character*:

I have learned to set a grateful value on the past, and am content to
wind up the account of what is personal only to myself . . . with an
act of easy oblivion,
> "And curtain close such scene from every future view."

The few examples from his most familiar essays are not the
sum of his slight borrowing from Collins, but they do show
that Collins was one of the poets to whom he delighted to allude,
a poet familiar in literary circles.[22]

In those poets like Keble and Clare who spanned the transition period between romanticism and the Victorian era, the spell
of Collins is still strong. The *Christian Year*, itself the work of
a gentle and sensitive spirit, shows the influence of the earlier
poet. It is first evident in Keble's choice of stanza forms: *Third
Sunday in Advent, Christmas Day, Sexagesima Sunday, Third
Sunday in Lent*, and *Second Sunday after Easter* are in the stanza
form of the *Ode to Simplicity; Tuesday before Easter* is in the
unrhymed stanza of the *Ode to Evening*. The quiet mood of
the *Ode to Evening* is felt in *Evening* in such lines as:

> In darkness and in weariness
> The traveller on his way must press,
> No gleam to watch on tree or tower,
> Whiling away the lonesome hour.

---

[22] To DeQuincey, too, Collins was a significant figure. In his Diary, *aet.*
17, Collins is listed with Shakespeare, Spenser, Milton, Thomson, Chatterton,
Wordsworth, and Coleridge (among others) as one of the twelve best poets
of all time. Again he writes, "From my youth up I have revered [the elder
poets] . . . Spenser—Shakespeare—Milton—Thomson (partially)—and Collins were the companions of my childhood." (See Eaton, H. A., *Thomas De-
Quincy—a Biography*. Oxford University Press, 1936, p. 93, p. 114.)

There are echoes of Collins's diction in *Second Sunday after Easter* when Keble writes of "a bright and breezy lake." In the *Sixth Sunday after Epiphany* in the lines:

> Dearer than ever past noon-day
> That twilight gleam to her though faint and far away,

the *Ode to Evening* is recalled. In *Third Sunday in Lent* there is a direct quotation from the *Ode to Liberty* in:

> The olive-wreath, the ivied wand,
> "The sword in myrtles drest."

Moreover, the opening lines of *Second Sunday after Easter* are Collins-like in spirit:

> O for a sculptor's hand,
> That thou might'st take thy stand,
> Thy wild hair floating on the eastern breeze,
> Thy tranc'd yet open gaze
> Fix'd on the desert haze
> As one who deep in heaven some airy pageant sees.

In the poems of the peasant-poet Clare, too, there are frequent echoes of Collins. In *Cooper's Hill* the touch of Collins is mingled with that of John Dyer and John Denham. The spell of the *Ode to Evening* is felt in *Solitude* with its use of such phrases as: "eve's warning bell," "fallows bare and brown," "Even's hour," "lonely heath," "glimmering streamlets." In *Summer Images,* too, there are traces of Collins in such phrases as:

> Or fields, WHERE BEE-FLY GREETS
> The ear with MELLOW HORN,

or in:

> But now the evening curdles dark and grey,
>   Changing her WATCHET hue for sombre weed,
> And moping owls, to close the lids of day,
>   On drowsy wing proceed,

where the influence of Gray is also present. And again the mood of the *Ode to Evening* is felt in:

> How sweet the soothing calmness that distills
> O'er the heart's every sense its opiate dews,

In MEEK-EYED MOODS and ever balmy trills!
   That softens and subdues,
With gentle Quiet's bland and sober train,
   Which dreamy eve renews
   In many a mellow strain!

The same mood, blended with the richness of Keats's *Ode to Autumn,* is felt in Clare's *To Autumn,* written in the unrhymed stanza of the *Ode to Evening.* Clare hails the shadowy figure of Autumn as Collins welcomed Evening—the tone of pensive solitude is common to both poems, Clare's more deeply touched by his sadness in thinking that Autumn must soon pass. Clare's Goddess of Autumn, like Collins's calm votaress, touches the landscape with her spell, but in Clare the picture is more definite and more rustic when he describes

Meadow pools, born wide by lawless floods,
   Where water-lilies spread their oily leaves,
      On which, as wont, the fly oft battens in the sun,

or when he pictures

Ploughed lands, their [sic] travelled with half-hungry sheep,
   Pastures traced deep with cows,
   Where small birds seek for seed.

Collins's musing pilgrim is transformed in Clare to the "cowboy" with "plashy step and clouted shoon." But in the imaginative portrait of Autumn:

Syren of sullen moods and fading hues. . . .
Sweet Vision, with the wild disheveled hair,
And raiment shadowy of each wind's embrace,

the kinship of Clare to Collins is most evident.

V

CONCLUSION

THE FAME and influence of Collins during the romantic
period was, then, steady and significant. To the poets who
followed him he was deemed worthy of imitation and enthusiastic interest. After the edition of Langhorne in 1765 his
place as a poet was established. Burns, Chatterton, and Blake
did him the honor of imitating his verse. Bowles, himself a
stimulating influence on the young poets who were maturing in
the closing years of the century, owed something of his own
poetic idiom to Collins. Young poets especially found in Collins
an ideal or standard of verse to emulate. In their early work
Wordsworth, Coleridge, Byron, Shelley, Keats, Southey, and
Hunt, among others, paid him tribute and tried to express themselves in his imagery and diction. It is a fair tribute to his work,
and a fair criticism of it, too, that young poets tried their hand in
his style before they had found one of their own. It is further
significant that they recognized the genuinely imaginative quality
of his verse and placed him above most of his contemporaries.
That they should have remembered him when their own poetic
styles had matured testifies to the enduring influence of his verse.
Collins's poetry did not rouse a host of imitators with such
sweeping force as Sidney's *Astrophel and Stella* stimulated the
writing of sonnets in Elizabeth's day, but quietly and unob-
trusively his influence was felt—a quiet and unobtrusive triumph
in keeping with the softened strain of his own verse. That he
should have appealed to many poetic natures so diverse from
his own is a hint of his own unfulfilled possibilities, for each
poet who remembered him chose from his work the elements
closest to his own nature. To Wordsworth the spell of the
Ode to Evening was strongest. To Byron the *Ode Written in
the Beginning of the Year 1746* appealed most; to Scott the

Ode on the Popular Superstitions and the passages in the other
odes which concerned folk-lore were significant. To Keats his
Greek qualities and his mythological figures were most stimulating. It is significant, too, that minor poets, possessed of some
of Collins's own "sensibility,"—poets like Mrs. Radcliffe,
Campbell, Moore, and Keble—should have found a kindred
spirit in him.

Nor did his influence die out in English verse with the coming
of the Reform Bill. Tennyson speaks of him, Arnold mentions
him, Swinburne writes enthusiastically of his poetry, and a
sensitive minor poet, William Watson, pays him kindly tribute
in *Wordsworth's Grave* when he writes:

> From dewy pastures, uplands sweet with thyme,
>   A virgin breeze freshened the jaded day.
> It wafted Collins' lovely vesper chime,
>   It breathed abroad the frugal notes of Gray.

Nor in our own day is his poetry forgotten. Allan Tate has
written an *Ode to Fear, Variation on a Theme by Collins,* and
Mr. E. H. W. Meyerstein's recently published volume of *New
Odes* includes one "To Collins." And in a small village in the
Adirondacks, far from the spot where Collins composed the *Ode
Written in the Beginning of the Year 1746,* his influence is
still present. A recent book on *The Adirondacks* describes the
burial of a veteran of the World War on a bitterly cold December day in 1921:

Despite a bitterly cold wind that lashed the slow moving cortège, sixty
uniformed World War veterans of the Central Adirondacks . . .
followed the caisson to Stephen's last resting place on a wooded
knoll. . . . On his modest headstone these words were inscribed:

> How sleep the brave who sink to rest
> By all their country's wishes blest.[1]

"That," as Coleridge said of Thomson's *Seasons,* "is true fame."

[1] Grady, Joseph F., *The Adirondacks,* Journal and Courier Press, Little
Falls, N.Y., 1933, pp. 313-14.

APPENDIX

VERBAL ECHOES OF MILTON IN THE POETRY OF COLLINS

THE LIST following includes all examples of direct or close parallels in the poetry of Collins to passages in Milton. In cases where the parallel is not given in full the borrowings are merely verbal with no direct suggestion that Collins had the specific passage of Milton in mind. Poems are listed in chronological order when it is known.

Sonnet. When Phoebe formed a wanton smile:

   7. 'teeming'—cf. *Comus,* 175.
   8. 'fabled'—cf. *P.L.,* IX, 30.

Song. The Sentiments borrowed from Shakespeare:

   2. 'lowland HAMLETS'—cf. *All.,* 92, 'upland HAMLETS.'
   3. 'dewy'—cf. *P.L.,* V, 56. A favorite of Collins;
      cf. *Pity,* 13; *Ode 1746,* 3; *et. al.*
   5. 'damps'—cf. *P.L.,* X, 848; *Comus,* 640; *P.R.,* IV, 406.
  11. 'bestrew'—cf. *P.L.,* I, 311; IV, 631.

Persian Eclogues
  Eclogue I:

  14. 'The radiant Morn resum'd her ORIENT Pride.'
     cf. *P.L.,* VI, 524:
       'Now, when fair Morn ORIENT in Heaven appeared.'
27–34. Compare in sentiment to *P.R.,* II, 220-48.
  45. With Truth she wedded in the SECRET GROVE,'
     cf. *Pen.,* 28-9:
      '. . . in SECRET shades
      Of woody Ida's inmost GROVES.'
  49. 'Balmy'—cf. *P.L.,* IV, 159; V, 23; *Comus,* 991.
  50. 'Ind'—cf. *P.L.,* II, 2; *Comus,* 606.
51–68. The train of Modesty is reminiscent of the trains of Melancholy and Mirth in the companion poems. Note especially the use of the Miltonic formula in 'Come . . . to lead the train.'

61–82. 'Cold is her Breast, LIKE FLOW'RS THAT DRINK THE DEW,
A SILKEN VEIL conceals her from the View.'
cf. *Samson Agonistes,* 728-30:
'LIKE A FAIR FLOWER surcharged with DEW, she weeps, . . .
Wetting the borders of her SILKEN VEIL.'

65. 'Desponding Meekness with her DOWN-CAST Eyes,'
cf. *Pen.,* 43:
'With a sad laden DOWNWARD CAST.'

Eclogue II:

1. 'In silent Horror o'er the BOUNDLESS WASTE'
cf. *P.L.,* III, 423-4:
'. . . a BOUNDLESS continent
Dark, WASTE, and wild.'

4. 'Scrip'—cf. *Comus,* 626.

6. 'To guard his shaded Face from SCORCHING sand.'
cf. *P.L.,* X, 691:
'Avoided pinching cold and SCORCHING heat.'

7. 'sultry'—cf. *Lycidas,* 28.

12. 'strook'—cf. *P.L.,* II, 165; *Nativity Ode,* 95; *et. al.*

15–16. 'Ah! little thought I of the blasting Wind,
The Thirst or PINCHING Hunger that I find.'
cf. *P.L.,* X, 691:
'Avoided PINCHING cold and scorching heat.'

15. 'blasting'—*P.L.,* IV, 928; *All.,* 49.

24. 'mitigate'—cf. *P.L.,* I, 558.

32. 'far-fatiguing'—not found in Milton, but cf. 'Far-beaming,'
Nativity Ode, 9.

33. 'Store' (noun)—a favorite word of both Milton and Collins.
See e.g. *The Passion,* 44. For other instances in Collins see:
Simplicity, 13; *Pop. Super.,* 22, 173, *et. al.*

55. 'scours'—cf. *P.L.,* II, 633.

56. 'sullen'—a favorite word in both poets; cf. *P.R.,* I, 500;
Pen., 76; *et. al.* For other instances in Collins see: *Liberty,*
5; *Passions,* 26; *Mr. Thomson,* 29; *et. al.*

57. 'Before them Death with SHRIEKS directs their Way'
cf. *All.,* 4:
' 'Mongst horrid shapes and SHRIEKS and sights unholy.'

63. 'swoln'—cf. *Lycidas,* 126.

67. 'tempt' = try—cf. *P.L.,* IX, 281.

67. 'unfelt'—cf. *P.L.,* VII, 475.

Eclogue III:

    6. 'BREATHING Maize'—cf. *Arcades*, 32, 'BREATHING roses.'
       See also in Collins: *Hanmer*, 126; *Liberty*, 135; *Evening*,
       42; *et. al.*

    7. 'amidst'—of frequent occurrence in both poets; cf. *P.L.*, I,
       791; II, 263, 896, *et al.* Other instances in Collins are:
       Pity, 17; *Mercy*, 7; *Liberty*, 28, 105; *Evening*, 13; *Pas-*
       sions, 87.

   12. 'Mead'—cf. *All.*, 90.

   13. 'LIVE-LONG Hours'—cf. *All.*, 99, 'the LIVELONG daylight.'

   14. 'Till late at silent EVE she PENN'D the FOLD,'
       cf. *P.L.*, II, 185:
         'Watching where shepherds PEN their FLOCKS at EVE.'

   15. 'DEEP in the GROVE beneath the SECRET SHADE'
       cf. *Pen.*, 28-9:
         '. . . in SECRET SHADES
       Of woody Ida's INMOST GROVE.'

18–19. 'The VIOLET-BLUE, that on the Moss-bank grows;
       ALL-SWEET TO SENSE, the flaunting ROSE was there' . . .
       cf. *All.*, 21-2:
       'There, on beds of VIOLETS BLUE,
       And FRESH-BLOWN ROSES washed in dew . . .'

   19. 'All-sweet'—not found in Milton, but cf. 'all-cheering,' *P.L.*,
       III, 581; 'all-bounteous,' *P.L.*, V, 640.

   19. 'FLAUNTING Rose'—cf. *Comus*, 545, 'FLAUNTING Honey-
       suckle.'

   48. 'all-rural'—a compound in the Miltonic manner. cf. 'all-
       sweet.'

   55. 'low-roof'd'—cf. *P.R.*, IV, 273.

   57. 'russet'—cf. *All.*, 71.

Eclogue IV:

    3. 'awful Midnight''—cf. *All.*, 2, 'blackest midnight.'

 5– 6. Cf. *P.L.*, IV, 607-9.

   19. 'Yon RAGGED Cliff, whose dang'rous Path we try'd'
       cf. *All.*, 9-10:
         'There under ebon shades and low-browed rocks
         AS RAGGED as thy locks . . .'

   27. 'Yon CITRON GROVE'—cf. *P.L.*, V, 22, 'how blows the CIT-
       RON GROVE.'

39. 'sultry'—cf. *Lycidas*, 28.
52. 'But Ruin spreads her BALEFUL Fires AROUND.'
    cf. *P.L.*, I, 56:
    'ROUND he throws his BALEFUL eyes . . .'
53. 'spicy'—cf. *P.L.*, VIII, 517.
70. 'inur'd'—cf. *P.R.*, I, 339; *P.R.*, IV, 139; *Comus*, 735.

Epistle to Sir Thomas Hanmer:

34. 'unfriendly'—cf. *P.R.*, II, 413, 'unfriended.'
55. 'nicely'—cf. *P.R.*, IV, 377.
57. 'Mold' (noun)—a favorite in Milton as in Collins; cf. *P.L.*,
    V, 321. For other uses of the word in Collins, cf.: *Ode,
    1746*, 4; *Fear*, 10; *Liberty*, 123.
66. 'unrival'd'—cf. *P.L.*, III, 68.
90. 'vengeful'—cf. *P.L.*, I, 148; *et. al.*
91. 'unseen'—a favorite word of both poets; cf. *P.L.*, II, 659; IV,
    130; *All.*, 57; *et. al.* Other instances in Collins are: *Ode,
    1746*, 8; *Poet. Char.*, 10; *et. al.*
93– 6. 'Where'er we turn, by FANCY charm'd, we find
    Some sweet ILLUSION of the CHEATED MIND.
    Oft, WILD OF WING, she calls the Soul to ROVE
    With humbler Nature, in the rural Grove.''
        cf. *P.L.*, VIII, 188-92:
        'But apt the MIND or FANCIE is to ROAVE
        UNCHECKT, and of her ROAVING is no end; . . .'
        and *Comus*, 155:
        'Of power to CHEAT the eye with blear ILLUSION.'
100. 'decks'—cf. *P.L.*, IV, 710; V, 189, 379; *Comus*, 120, 717.
112. 'breathing'—see above, *Eclogues*, III, 6.
125. 'insatiate'—cf. *P.L.*, IX, 536.
126. 'destin'd'—frequent in Milton; cf. *P.L.*, X, 646; XII, 233;
    Lycidas, 20; *et. al.*

Song from Shakespeare's Cymbeline:

1. 'grassy'—cf. *P.L.*, V, 391; VII, 463; XI, 324, 433; *et. al.*
2. 'hinds'—a favorite in both Collins and Milton; cf. *Comus,*
   174. Other instances in Collins are: *Col. Ross*, 16; *Pop.
   Super.*, 44.
6. 'shrieks'—cf. *All.*, 4; *Nativity Ode*, 178; *et. al.* The word is a
   particular favorite of Collins; cf. *Eclogue* IV, 57; *Evening*, 10; *et. al.*

7. 'quiet grove'—a favorite with Collins. See above in *Persian Eclogues*, I, 45; III, 15; IV, 27; IV, 53; in *Epistle to Hanmer*, 96.

9. 'wither'd'—cf. *P.L.*, XI, 540.

10. 'nightly' = happening by night—cf. *P.L.*, IX, 22; *Nativity Ode*, 179; *All.*, 48; *Pen.*, 84.

10. 'crew'—common in Milton; cf. *Comus*, 653; *P.L.*, I, 51, 477, 688, 751; *et. al.*

17. 'howling winds'—cf. *Pen.*, 126, 'rocking winds.'

18. 'sylvan cell'—cf. *P.L.*, V, 377, 'sylvan lodge.' See also Milton's use of 'cell' in *Nativity Ode*, 180; *All.*, 5; *Pen.*, 169; *Comus*, 387. The word is frequent in Collins. See also: *Pity*, 21; *Manners*, 37; *et. al.*

22. 'duly'—cf. *All.*, 106.

Odes Descriptive and Allegoric: for 'allegoric,' cf. *P.R.*, IV, 390.

Ode to Pity:

1. 'assign'd'—cf. *P.L.*, VI, 817; *P.L.*, IX, 231; X, 926; *Samson Agonistes*, 1116, 1217.

2. 'balmy'—see *Persian Eclogues*, I, 49.

5. 'waste' (verb)—cf. *P.L.*, XI, 567; II, 502; *et. al.*

5. 'destin'd'—see *Epistle to Hanmer*, 126.

8. 'frame' (verb)—cf. *P.L.*, V, 460.

9. 'Rite'—cf. *Comus*, 125; *Samson Agonistes*, 1320, 1378.

11. 'sky-worn'—a compound in the manner of Milton; cf. 'sky-tinctured,' *P.L.*, V, 285.

11. 'Thy SKY-WORN ROBES of tend'rest Blue'
      cf. *Comus*, 83:
         'My SKIE ROBES spun out of Iris Wooff'

12. 'dewy'—see *Song. Sentiments Borrowed from Shakespeare*, 3.

13. 'wherefore'—cf. *P.L.*, I, 264; II, 159, 450; *et. al.*

13–15. 'But wherefore need I wander wide
      To old Ilissus' distant Side,
         Deserted Stream, and mute?'
      Contrast with *P.R.*, IV, 249-250:
         '. . . there Ilissus rolls
         His whispering stream.'

17. 'midst'—see *Persian Eclogues*, III, 7.

20. 'infant' (adj.)—cf. *P.L.*, II, 664; *P.R.*, II, 78.

21. 'Cell'—see *Song. Cymbeline*, 18.
32. 'involving'—cf. *Samson Agonistes*, 304.
33. 'prevail'—cf. *P.L.*, IX, 873; X, 40, 258.
34. 'BUSKIN'D MUSE'—cf. *Pen.*, 102, 'BUSKINED Stage.'
35. 'prompt' (verb)—cf. *P.L.*, IX, 854.
36. 'disastrous'—cf. *P.L.*, I, 597.
37– 9. cf. *All.*, 135-43. See discussion of the influence of *L'Allegro* and *Il Penseroso*, pp. 131-5 of the text.
40. 'There waste the mournful Lamp of Night,'
      cf. *Pen.*, 85:
         'Or let my lamp at midnight hour'
40. 'waste' (verb)—cf. *Pity*, 5.
40. 'mournful'—cf. *P.L.*, I, 244.
42. 'Shell'—cf. *Comus*, 231.

Ode to Fear:

2. 'shadowy'—cf. *All.*, 108; P.R., IV, 399; *et. al.*
3. 'unreal'—cf. *P.L.*, X, 481.
7. 'hurried'—cf. *P.L.*, V, 778.
8. 'disorder'd'—cf. *P.L.*, VI, 696.
12. 'stalks' (verb)—cf. *Samson Agonistes*, 1245.
12. 'Round'—cf. *All.*, 54.
12. 'hideous'—cf. *P.L.*, V, 1107.
14. 'Steep' (noun)—cf. *P.L.*, II, 948; IV, 680; *Comus*, 139; *Lycidas*, 52.
17. 'prompt' (verb)—cf. *Pity*, 35.
17. 'accurs'd'—cf. *P.L.*, II, 1025; IV, 691; *et. al.*
18. 'Fiends'—common in Milton.
21. 'Lifts her RED ARM, expos'd and bare:"
      cf. *P.L.*, II, 174:
         'Arm again his RED RIGHT ARM to plague us.'
22. 'Brood' (noun)—cf. *P.L.*, I, 576; *Samson Agonistes*, 1247.
24. 'ghastly'—cf. *P.L.*, VI, 368; XI, 481.
24– 5. Compare with the structural formulæ of *L'Allegro* and *Il Penseroso*.
26. 'partial'—cf. *P.L.*, II, 552.
27. 'addrest'—cf. *P.L.*, IX, 496.
28. 'awful'—cf. *P.L.*, I, 753; IV, 347, 960; *et. al.*
29. 'Amazement'—cf. *P.L.*, II, 758; *P.R.*, I, 107.
30. 'invok'd'—cf. *P.L.*, XI, 492, 590, 591; *Comus*, 854; *et. al.*
31. 'disdain'd'—cf. *P.L.*, IV, 180; VI, 798; *et. al.*

34. 'grace' (verb)—cf. *Comus*, 24.
35. 'a-while'—cf. *Comus*, 551; *Samson Agonistes*, 115; *P.L.*, II, 567, 918; *et. al.*
35. 'rove'—see *Epistle to Hanmer*, 95.
36. 'dreary'—cf. *P.L.*, I, 180; II, 618.
36. 'trace' (verb)—cf. *P.L.*, XI, 329.
37. 'share' (verb)—cf. *Sonnet*, XV, 14.
37. 'baleful'—cf. *P.L.*, II, 576; *Comus*, 255.
37. 'Grove'—see above, *Eclogues*, I, 45.
38. 'wrapt'—cf. *Nativity Ode*, 31.
38. 'cloudy' = gloomy—cf. *P.L.*, VI, 450.
43. 'with'ring'—see *Song. Cymbeline*, 9. See also *Liberty*, 75; *Passions*, 43.
44. 'mingled'—cf. *Comus*, 994. See also in Collins: *Simplicity*, 15; *Passions*, 64.
48. 'haunted Cell'—cf. *All.*, 5, 'uncouth cell.'
50. 'hollow'd'—cf. *P.L.*, VI, 574.
50– 2. cf. *Il Penseroso*, 74 fol.
53. 'shudd'ring'—cf. *Comus*, 802; *P.L.*, II, 611.
53. 'MEEK SUBMITTED Thought'—cf. *P.L.*, IV, 494, 'MEEK SUBMISSION.'
55. 'awak'ning'—cf. *P.L.*, V, 672.
56. 'blasted'—cf. *P.L.*, X, 412.
58. 'o'eraw'd'—a compound in the Miltonic manner; cf. 'o'ergrown,' 'o'er-weary,' 'o'erpower'; *et. al.*
59. 'thrice-hallow'd'—a compound in the Miltonic manner; cf. 'thrice happy,' 'thrice fugitive.'
60– 3. 'When GHOSTS, as Cottage-Maids believe,
       THEIR PEBBLED BEDS PERMITTED LEAVE,
       And GOBBLINS haunt from FIRE, or FEN,
           Or MINE, or FLOOD, the WALKS of Men.'
           cf. *Comus*, 432-6:
               'Some say no evil thing that WALKS by night
               In fog, or FIRE, by lake or moorish FEN,
               Blew meager Hag, or STUBBORN UNLAID GHOST
               THAT BREAKS HIS MAGICK CHAINS AT CURFEW TIME
               No GOBLIN or swart faery of the MINE. . . .'
           cf. also *Pen.*, 93-4:
               'And of those demons that are found
               In FIRE, air, FLOOD, or UNDERGROUND.

71. 'Meed'—cf. *Lycidas,* 14, 84.
70– 1. Follows the concluding formula of *L'Allegro* and *Il Penseroso.*

Ode to Simplicity:

8. 'disdain'st'—see *Fear,* 31.
9. 'Gauds'—cf. *Nativity Ode,* 33; *Pen.,* 6; *Comus,* 841, 'gaudy.'
9. 'pageant WEEDS'—cf. *P.R.,* I, 314; *et. al.,* 'rural WEEDS.'
9. 'trailing PALL'—cf. *Pen.,* 98, 'scepter'd PALL.'
10. 'DECENT Maid'—cf. *Pen.,* 36, 'DECENT shoulders.'
11. 'Attic Robe'—cf. *Pen.,* 33, 'robe of darkest grain.'
11. 'array'd'—cf. *P.L.,* IV, 596; VI, 13; X, 233; *et. al.*
12. 'chaste'—cf. *P.L.,* IV, 761; XI, 12; *Comus,* 146, 442, 450; *et. al.*
12. 'unboastful'—a compound in the Miltonic manner; cf. 'unbeheld,' 'unbenighted.'
13. 'honey'd'—cf. *Pen.,* 142.
13. 'Store' (noun)—see *Eclogues,* II, 33.
15. 'Blooms'—cf. *P.L.,* V, 25; *Samson Agonistes,* 1576; *et. al.*
15. 'mingled'—see *Fear,* 44.
15. 'Murmurs'—cf. *P.R.,* IV, 248; *P.L.,* VII, 68; *et. al.* A favorite word in Collins as in Milton. See also: *Passions,* 68; *Poet. Char.,* 48.
13–15. 'By all the honey'd Store
On Hybla's Thymy Shore,
By all her Blooms and mingled Murmurs dear,'
cf. *P.R.,* 247-8:
'There, flowery hill, Hymettus, with the sound
Of bees' industrious murmur, oft invites
To studious musing . . .'
16. 'By Her, whose LOVE-LORN Woe'
cf. *Comus,* 224:
'the LOVE-LORN Nightingale'
18. 'Sooth'd sweetly SAD ELECTRA'S POET'S ear'
cf. *Sonnet,* VIII, 12-13:
'the repeated air
Of SAD ELECTRA'S POET. . . .'
21. 'warbled' (adj.)—cf. *P.L.,* II, 242; *Comus,* 854.
21. 'Retreat' (noun)—cf. *P.L.,* II, 317.
22. 'enamel'd'—cf. *P.L.,* IV, 149; IX, 525; *Lycidas,* 139; *All.,* 84.
24. 'equal' (adj.)—frequent in Milton; cf. *P.L.,* IV, 296; *et. al.*

24. 'allure' (verb)—frequent in Milton; cf. *P.L.*, III, 573; *et. al.*
24. 'future' (adj.)—frequent in Milton; cf. *P.L.*, II, 222; *et. al.*
27. 'sober'—cf. *Comus*, 263.
27. 'infuse'—cf. *P.L.*, IX, 836.
29. 'cull'—cf. *Comus*, 255; *Vacation Exercise*, 21.
30. 'range' (verb = arrange)—cf. *P.L.*, VII, 426.
30. 'ordered'—cf. *Passion*, 49.
33. 'Laureate'—cf. *Lycidas*, 151.
34. 'staid' = lingered—cf. *P.R.*, II, 326; *P.L.*, II, 1010; *et. al.*
36. 'alter'd'—cf. *P.L.*, XI, 1132.
37. 'IN HALL OF BOW'R'—cf. *Comus*, 45, "IN HALL OF BOW'R.'
42. 'servile'—frequent in Milton; cf. *Samson Agonistes*, 5, 574; *et. al.*
48. 'MEETING SOUL'—cf. *All.*, 138, 'Such as the MEETING SOUL may pierce.'
51. 'temp'rate'—cf. *P.R.*, III, 160.

Ode on the Poetical Character (for the influence of whole passages in Milton, see the discussion, pp. 141-4 of the text.)

1. 'light Regard'—cf. *P.L.*, IV, 877, 'with stern regard'; *P.R.*, III, 216, 'meek regard.'
2. 'aright'—frequent in Milton; cf. *P.L.*, VI, 470; X, 156; XI, 578; *et. al.*
5. 'unrival'd'—cf. *P.L.*, III, 68.
7. 'AT SOLEMN TURNEY HUNG on high,'
   cf. *Pen.*, 117-18:
   'In sage and SOLEMN tunes have sung,
   Of TURNEYS and of trophies HUNG.'
8. 'LOVE-DARTING EYE'—cf. *Comus*, 753, 'LOVE-DARTING EYES.'
10. 'unseen'—see *Epistle to Hanmer*, 91.
10. 'hov'ring'—cf. *Comus*, 214.
11. 'chaste'—see *Simplicity*, 12.
11. 'Angel-Friend'—cf. *P.L.*, V, 328, 'angel-guest'; *At a Solemn Music*, 11, 'angel-trumpet.'
12. 'whisper'd Spell'—cf. *Nativity Ode*, 179, 'breathed spell.'
13. 'unblest'—cf. *Psalm* V, 14; *P.L.*, X, 988; *Comus*, 907; *et. al.*
13. 'loath'd'—cf. *P.L.*, XII, 178.
15. 'baffled'—cf. *Samson Agonistes*, 1237.
15. 'Endeavour' (noun)—cf. *Sonnet*, XIV, 5.
16. 'Zone'—cf. *P.R.*, II, 214.

19. 'amplest'—cf. *Samson Agonistes,* 1011.
20. 'God-like'—frequent in Milton; cf. *P.L.,* II, 306; VI, 301;
    P.R., III, 21; *et. al.*
20. 'assigns'—cf. *P.L.,* VI, 817; IX, 231; X, 926; *et. al.*
21. 'gird'—common in Milton; cf. *P.L.,* IX, 1096; *P.R.,* I, 120;
    P.L., VI, 714; et. al.
21. 'blest'—common in Milton; cf. *P.L.,* III, 149; VI, 184;
    Comus, 329; *et. al.*
21. 'prophetic'—cf. *Pen.,* 174; *et. al.*
21. 'Loins'—cf. *P.L.,* IX, 1096, 'girded on our loins.'
22. 'gaze' (verb)—frequent in Milton; cf. *P.L.,* III, 613; *P.R.,*
    I, 414; *et. al.*
22. 'unmix'd'—cf. *P.L.,* VI, 742.
23. 'wove'—cf. *P.L.,* IV, 348.
24. 'creating Day'—cf. *P.L.,* IX, 556, 'Creation-day.'
28. 'Main' = Sea—cf. *Comus,* 28; or *P.R.,* IV, 457.
32. 'SAPHIRE THRONE'—cf. *P.L.,* VI, 758, 'a SAPPHIRE THRONE.'
33. 'the whiles'—cf. 'the while,' *P.L.,* II, 731; VII, 248; *et. al.*
33. 'vaulted'—cf. *P.L.,* I, 298; VI, 214.
34. 'seraphic WIRES'—cf. *Vacation Exercise,* 38, 'golden WIRES';
    et. al. 'Seraphic' occurs in *P.L.,* I, 539.
35. 'sublimest'—frequent in Milton; cf. *P.L.,* X, 1014.
37. 'VEILING CLOUD'—cf. *P.L.,* IX, 425, 'Eve . . . VEILED in a
    CLOUD of fragrance,' or better: *P.L.,* XI, 229, 'Yonder
    blazing CLOUD that VEILS the hill.'
37. 'rich-haired'—a compound in the Miltonic manner; cf. *P.R.,*
    II, 352, 'rich-clad.'
41. 'dang'rous'—cf. *P.L.,* II, 107, 342; *et. al.*
41. 'aloof'—cf. *P.L.,* I, 380; *P.R.,* I, 313; *Samson Agonistes,*
    135, 1611.
42. 'sainted'—cf. *Comus,* 11.
42. 'Woof'—cf. *Comus,* 84.
43. 'Ecstatic'—cf. *Passion,* 42.
44. 'List'ning the DEEP applauding THUNDER.'
        cf. *Psalm* LXXXI, 29-30 (Milton's paraphrase):
          'I answered thee in THUNDER DEEP,
          With clouds encompass'd round.'
45. 'sunny'—cf. *P.L.,* III, 625.
45. 'Vest'—cf. *P.L.,* XI, 241.
45. 'array'd'—cf. *P.L.,* IV, 596; VI, 13; X, 223.

47. 'shad'wy'—see *Fear*, 2.
48. 'braided'—cf. *P.L.*, IV, 349.
48. 'Murmurs'—see *Simplicity*, 15.
50. 'ambrosial'—frequent in Milton; cf. *P.L.*, II, 245; III, 135; VI, 475; *et. al.*
52. 'presuming'—cf. *P.L.*, VII, 13, 'earthly sight if it presume.'
52. 'avow'—cf. *Samson Agonistes*, 1151.
53. 'Rapture'—cf. *P.L.*, IX, 1082; *et. al.*
54. 'hallow'd'—cf. *P.L.*, III, 116.
54. 'design'd'—cf. *P.L.*, X, 277; *et. al.*
52–62. cf. *P.L.*, IV, 132-149. See text, p. 143.
55. 'up-pil'd'—a compound in the Miltonic manner; cf. 'up-tear,' 'up-lock,' 'uprear'; *et. al.*
56. 'rude'—cf. *Comus*, 352.
56. 'access'—cf. *P.L.*, I, 761; II, 130; IV, 137; *et. al.*
56. 'PROSPECT'—cf. *P.L.*, III, 548: 'a PROSPECT wide and various.'
57. 'TANGLED round the Jealous Steep'
     cf. *Nativity Ode*, 188:
          'The Nymphs in twilight shade of TANGLED thickets mourn.'
57. 'jealous'—cf. *All.*, 6.
57. 'Steep'—*Fear*, 14.
58. 'o'erbrow'—a compound in the Miltonic manner; cf. 'o'erspread,' 'o'ershadow'; *et. al.*
60. 'Gloomes'—cf. *P.L.*, X, 848; *Pen.*, 80; *et. al.*
60. 'embrown'—cf. *P.L.*, IV, 246.
60. 'UNLOCK'—cf. *P.L.*, II, 852; *Comus*, 852-3, 'She can UNLOCK the clasping charm.'
61. 'ambitious'—cf. *P.L.*, I, 41; II, 34; *et al.*
63–67. cf. *Pen.*, 60-65; *P.L.*, IV, 680-8. See text, pp. 134-5.
64. 'fancied'—cf. *Sonnet*, XXIII, 10.
65. 'Ethereal'—frequent in Milton; cf. *P.L.*, I, 45, 285; II, 139; *et. al.*
66. 'nigh'—frequent in Milton; cf. *P.L.*, VI, 533; *P.L.*, VIII, 564; *et. al.*
66. 'SPHER'D'—cf. *P.L.*, VII, 247, 'SPHERED in a radiant cloud.'
67. 'TRUMP'—cf. *Nativity Ode*, 156, 'The wakeful TRUMP.'
68–71. With Collins's farewell to Waller's myrtle shades compare Milton's avowed purpose as he states it in *At a Vacation Exercise*, 19-23.

75. 'o'erturn'd'—a Miltonic compound; cf. 'o'erbrow' above.
75. 'Bow'rs'—common in Milton; cf. *All.*, 87; *P.L.*, IV, 246, 205; V, 230; VIII, 305; *et. al.*
76. 'CURTAIN'D CLOSE'—cf. *Comus*, 554, 'CLOSE-CURTAINED.'

Ode Written in the beginning of the Year 1746:

3. 'dewy'—see *Song. Sentiments from Shakespeare*, 3.
4. 'Returns to deck their HALLOW'D MOLD,'
   cf. *P.L.*, V, 321:
   'Adam, earth's HALLOWED MOULD.'
4. 'deck'—see above, *Epistle to Hanmer*, 100.
9. 'There Honour comes, a PILGRIM GREY,'
   cf. *P.R.*, IV, 427:
   'With PILGRIM steps in amice GREY.'
10. 'Turf'—cf. *P.L.*, V, 391; XI, 324; *Comus*, 280.
10. 'wrap'—cf. *Nativity Ode*, 31.
11. 'awhile'—see *Fear*, 35.
11. 'repair'—cf. *P.L.*, X, 1087, 1099; *et. al.*

Ode to Mercy:

2. 'awful'—see *Fear*, 28.
3. 'sky-born'—a compound in the Miltonic manner; cf. 'sky-tinctured,' *P.L.*, V, 285.
5. 'fatal' = deadly, ruinous—cf. *P.L.*, II, 712, 786; *P.R.*, I, 441; *et. al.*
7. 'amidst'—see *Eclogues*, III, 7.
7. 'deathful'—cf. *Samson Agonistes*, 1513.
8. 'Godlike'—frequent in Milton; cf. *P.L.*, XII, 427; *P.R.*, I, 188, 386; *et. al.*
11. 'loaded'—cf. *Samson Agonistes*, 149.
12. 'Genius'—cf. *Nativity Ode*, 186; *et. al.*
13. 'decks'—see *Epistle to Hanmer*, 100.
14-19. cf. *P.L.*, IV, 970 fol. See text, pp. 139-40.
14. 'provoke'—cf. *Samson Agonistes*, 237, 643; *et. al.*
15. 'Fiend'—frequent in Milton; but compare especially *P.L.*, IV, 1013.
15. 'Yoke' (noun)—frequent in Milton; cf. *P.R.*, II, 48, or (more in the sense of the passage) *Pen.*, 59.
17. 'Abode' (noun)—cf. *P.L.*, III, 734; *P.L.*, IV, 939; *et. al.*
18. 'o'ertook'—a compound in the Miltonic manner; cf. 'o'erweary,' 'o'erwatch.'
18. 'blasted'—see *Fear*, 56.

19. 'And stop'd his WHEELS'—cf. *P.L.,* IV, 975, 'draws't his triumphant WHEELS."

20. 'recoil'—cf. *P.L.,* IV, 17, 'like a devilish engine back RECOIL.'

20. 'sable'—cf. *Comus,* 221.

20. 'Steeds'—frequent in Milton; cf. *P.L.,* IX, 35; IV, 858; *et. al.*

22. 'melting'—cf. *All.,* 142.

24. 'Where Justice BARS her IRON Tow'r'—cf. *P.L.,* IV, 897-898, 'let him surer BARR his IRON gates . . .'

25. 'roseate'—cf. *P.L.,* V, 646.

25. 'Bow'r'—see *Simplicity,* 37.

Ode to Liberty (for a full discussion of the sources and the use made of them see text, pp. 148-53):

3. 'divinely'—frequent in Milton; cf. *P.L.,* X, 67; *et. al.*

3. 'spreading'—cf. *Comus,* 84.

4. 'vernal'—cf. *P.L.,* III, 43; *Lycidas,* 141.

5. 'sullen'—see *Eclogue* II, 56.

3–5. 'Whose LOCKS . . . Like Vernal HYACINTHS'
    cf. *P.L.,* IV, 300:
        'HYACINTIN LOCKS'

5. 'shedding'—of flowers; cf. *Lycidas,* 149, 'bid amaranthus all his beauty shed.'

7. 'Fancy-blest'—a compound in the Miltonic manner.

8. 'drest'—cf. *Sonnet,* XIV, 11.

9. 'a-while'—see *Fear,* 35.

10. 'seal' (verb)—cf. *P.L.,* X, 637.

10. 'renown'd'—cf. *P.R.,* IV, 46; *P.L.,* III, 465; *et. al.*

11. 'revealing'—frequent in Milton; cf. *Samson Agonistes,* 50, 383, 491; *et. al.*

12. 'prompted'—cf. *P.R.,* I, 12.

14. 'court' (verb)—cf. *Pyrrha Ode,* 2; *Samson Agonistes,* 719.

15. 'Shell'—see *Pity,* 42.

15. 'misguided'—cf. *Samson Agonistes,* 912.

16. 'mindful'—a word in the Miltonic manner.

21. 'ambitious'—see *Poet. Char.,* 61.

24. 'RUDE' = destructive—cf. *Pen.,* 136, 'the RUDE ax.'

25. 'barb'rous'—cf. *P.R.,* IV, 86.

28. ' 'midst'—see *Eclogue* III, 7.

32. 'labour'd'—cf. *On Shakespeare,* 2; *Comus,* 291.

38. 'Relick'—in Milton 'relique'; cf. *P.L.,* III, 491.

39. 'jealous'—see *Poet. Char.*, 57.
42. cf. *Lycidas*, 17.
42. 'ennobling'—cf. *P.L.*, IX, 992; *Pen.*, 102; *Samson Agonistes*, 1491.
43. 'deck'd'—see *Epistle to Hanmer*, 100.
44. 'pearly'—cf. *P.L.*, V, 430.
45. 'green-hair'd'—a compound in the Miltonic manner; cf. 'green-eyed.'
47. 'LYDIAN Measure'—cf. *All.*, 136, 'soft LYDIAN airs.'
50. 'Haunts' (noun)—cf. *P.L.*, VII, 330; *et. al.*
52. 'favor'd'—cf. *P.R.*, II, 91.
54. 'Eyrie'—cf. *P.L.*, VII, 424.
56. 'Meads'—cf. *All.*, 90.
58. 'Those whom the ROD of Alva BRUIS'D'
    cf. *P.L.*, V, 887-8:
    '. . . An Iron ROD to BRUISE and break Thy disobedience.'
62. 'Spell'—see *Poet. Char.*, 12.
63. 'Nymph'—frequent in Milton; cf. *Comus*, 54; *All.*, 25; *et. al.*
64. 'The MEASURE VAST of Thought'—cf. *P.L.*, I, 177, the VAST IMMEASURABLE Abyss.'
65. 'Wizzard'—cf. *Comus*, 482. A favorite in Collins. See also: *Manners*, 11; *Pop. Super.*, 54.
66. 'antique'—cf. *All.*, 128.
67. 'adverse'—cf. *P.L.*, X, 289.
67. 'Strand'—cf. *Comus*, 876.
68. 'sublime'—frequent in Milton; cf. *P.L.*, II, 528; *et. al.*
68. 'hoary'—cf. *P.L.*, II, 891, or *Comus*, 871.
69. 'unwet'—a compound in the Miltonic manner; cf. 'unsmooth,' 'unsleeping,' 'unshed'; *et. al.*
70. 'banded'—cf. *P.L.*, VI, 85. See text, pp. 149-50.
74. 'confounding'—cf. *P.L.*, II, 996; *P.L.*, IV, 871.
75. 'with'ring'—see *Fear*, 43.
75. 'GIANT SONS'—cf. *P.L.*, I, 778, GIANT SONS.'
75. 'uncouth'—frequent in Milton; cf. *P.L.*, II, 407; *P.L.*, X, 475; *All.*, 5.
76– 9. Compare as sources: *P.R.*, IV, 455; *P.L.*, X, 664-7. See text, pp. 150-1.
76. 'pillar'd'—cf. *P.R.*, IV, 455; *Comus*, 598.
77. 'inward'—cf. *P.L.*, IV, 861.
78. 'dread' (adj.)—frequent in Milton; cf. *P.L.*, I, 589; *P.L.*, II, 16, 510; *et. al.*

79. 'should'ring'—cf. *P.R.*, II, 462.
80–84. Compare as source, *Comus*, 21-3. See text, p. 151.
  80. 'Train'—see *Eclogues*, I, 51-68.
  82. 'Main'—see *Poet. Char.*, 28.
  84. 'West'ring'—cf. *Lycidas*, 74.
  84. 'check' (verb)—cf. *P.L.*, III, 732; *P.L.*, V, 214; *Comus*, 761.
  89. 'Pile'—cf. *P.L.*, I, 722; *P.L.*, II, 591.
  90. ' 'Midst the green NAVEL of our Isle'
     cf. *Comus*, 52:
       'the NAVEL of this hideous wood.'
  91. 'religious'—cf. *Pen.*, 160.
  92. 'soul-enforcing'—a compound in the Miltonic manner.
  93. 'painted'—cf. *P.L.*, VII, 434.
  94. 'wont' (verb)—frequent in Milton; cf. *P.L.*, I, 764; *P.L.*, V, 32; *et. al.*
  94. 'celestial'—frequent in Milton; cf. *P.L.*, I, 245, 658; II, 15; *et. al.*
  95. 'trace' (verb)—see *Fear*, 36.
  96. 'backward'—cf. *Comus*, 817.
  97. 'fiery-tressed'—compound in the Miltonic manner; cf. 'golden-tressed.'
  98. 'o'erturn'd'—see above, *Poet. Char.*, 75.
  99. 'Heav'n-left'—compound in the Miltonic manner.
101. 'infuse'—cf. *P.L.*, IX, 836.
103. 'braided'—cf. *P.L.*, II ,1026; X, 473.
104. 'paving'—cf. *P.L.*, II, 1026; X, 473.
104. 'light-embroider'd'—a compound in the Miltonic manner.
105. 'amidst'—see *Eclogues*, III, 7.
105. 'Amidst the bright PAVILION'D Plains,'
    cf. *P.L.*, XI, 215:
      'The field PAVILIONED with his guardians bright.'
106. 'beauteous'—cf. *P.L.*, IV, 697; VI, 481; *et. al.*
110. 'warlike WEEDS'—cf. *All.*, 120, 'WEEDS of peace.'
110. 'retir'd'—frequent in Milton; cf. *P.L.*, II, 557; IV, 532; *et. al.*
111 'consorted'—cf. *Pen.*, 145; *Nativity Ode*, 132.
112. 'Triumphs'—common in Milton; cf. *P.L.*, I, 123; III, 338; X, 186, 572; *et. al.*
112. 'String'—*Pen.*, 106; *All.*, 87; *et. al.*
113. 'unfold' = reveal—cf. *Comus*, 786; *et. al.*

116. 'Fabric'—cf. *P.L.*, I, 710.
117. 'favor'd'—cf. *P.R.*, II, 91.
121. 'secret' (adj.)—cf. *Nativity Ode*, 28; *Pen.*, 28; *et. al.*
122. 'SPHERE-FOUND Gem'—cf. *University Carrier*, II, 5-6:
   'Made of SPHEAR-METAL, never to decay
   Untill his revolution was at stay.'
123. 'Mold'—see above, *Epistle to Hanmer*, 57.
124. 'emblaze'—cf. *Comus*, 73.
128. 'engrav'd'—cf. *P.L.*, I, 716.
128. 'Rage' = desire—cf. *Samson Agonistes*, 836.
128. 'prophetic'—cf. *Pen.*, 174.
129. 'Laureate'—cf. *Lycidas*, 151.
130. 'inmost Altar'—cf. *P.L.*, IV, 738, 'inmost bower'; cf. also
  Pen., 29.
131. 'blissful'—cf. *Comus*, 1010; *P.L.*, I, 5; *et. al.*
135. 'breathing'—see *Eclogues*, III, 6.
139. 'enamour'd'—cf. *P.L.*, II, 765; IV, 169; *et. al.*
140. 'Play with the TANGLES of her HAIR.'
  cf. *Lycidas*, 68-9:
   'To sport with Amaryllis in the shade,
   Or with the TANGLES of Neaera's HAIR.'
  See on this point, text, p. 152.

Ode to a Lady on the Death of Colonel Ross:

1– 6. cf. *Nativity Ode*, 186-7. See text, p. 138.
 5. 'unseemly'—cf. *Samson Agonistes*, 690, 1451.
 6. 'chearful'—cf. *P.L.*, V, 123; XI, 543.
 7. 'musing Pity'—cf. *Comus*, 386, 'musing meditation.'
 16. 'Hind'—see *Song, Cymbeline*, 2.
 17. 'Turf'—see *Ode*, 1746, 10.
 17. 'bind' = wreathe, encircle—cf. *P.L.*, III, 361.
 19. 'Doom' = fate, lot—cf. *Sonnet*, I, 10.
 20. 'Aërial'—cf. *P.L.*, V, 548; *Comus*, 3.
 21. 'shadowy'—see *Fear*, 2.
 21. 'Trophies'—cf. *P.R.*, IV, 37; *Pen.*, 118; *et. al.*
 21. 'crown'd'—cf. *P.L.*, IV, 262; *P.L.*, V, 260; *et. al.*
 22. 'whilst'—cf. *Lycidas*, 154.
 22. 'bath'd'—cf. *Comus*, 812.
 22. 'rove'—see *Epistle to Hanmer*, 95.

23. 'Grove'—see *Eclogue* I, 45.
25. 'WARLIKE Dead'—cf. *P.L.*, IV, 902, 'the WARLIKE Angel.'
26. 'recording'—cf. *Samson Agonistes*, 984.
27. 'sainted'—see *Poet. Char.*, 42.
30. 'blooming Guest'—cf. *Comus*, 289, 'Of manly prime, or youthful bloom.'
31. 'unknown'—cf. *P.L.*, III, 496; *P.L.*, VII, 75; *P.L.*, IX, 905.
32. 'fix'd Delight'—cf. *P.L.*, I, 97, 560; 'fixed mind'; *et. al.*
35. 'gleamy'—an adjective in the Miltonic manner; cf. 'glassy,' 'gloomy.'
36. 'avenging'—cf. *P.L.*, VI, 278; *P.L.*, VII, 184.
41. 'wraps'—see *Ode, 1746*, 10.
42. 'joyless'—cf. *P.L.*, IV, 766.
48. 'sated'—cf. *P.L.*, IX, 598; *Comus*, 714.
50. 'impart'—cf. *P.R.*, II, 397.
54. 'insulting'—cf. *P.L.*, IV, 926.
55. 'courts't'—see *Liberty*, 14.

Ode to Evening: (for a full discussion of the Miltonic influence in the poem cf. text pp. 144-8):

1. 'If ought of OATEN STOP, or PASTORAL SONG,'
   cf. *Comus*, 345:
         'Or sound of PASTORAL REED with OATEN STOPS'
1. 'If ought'—cf. *Pen.*, 116; 'And IF OUGHT else, great Bards beside,'
2. 'modest'—cf. *P.L.*, IV, 310.
2. 'chaste'—see *Simplicity*, 12.
3. 'solemn'—cf. *P.L.*, VII, 395.
4. 'dying GALES'—cf. *Pyrrha Ode*, 11, 'flattering GALES.'
5. 'BRIGHT-HAIR'D Sun'—cf. *Pen.*, 23: 'BRIGHT-HAIRED Vesta.'
6. 'YON WESTERN TENT'—cf. *P.L.*, XI, 205, 'YON WESTERN TENT.'
6. 'Tent'—cf. *P.L.*, V, 291.
6. 'CLOUDY'—cf. *P.L.*, VII, 360, 'CLOUDY shrine'; *P.L.*, VII, 248, 'CLOUDY tabernacle,' which best fit into the spirit of the line.
6. 'cloudy SKIRTS'—cf. *P.L.*, V, 187, 'till the sun paint your fleecy SKIRTS'; *P.L.*, XI, 882, 'the fluid SKIRTS of that same watery cloud.'
7. 'Brede'—in Milton 'braid'; cf. *Comus*, 862.

7. 'ethereal'—cf. *P.L.*, III, 716; V, 267; *et. al.*

7. 'wove'—cf. *P.L.*, IV, 348, 'wove . . . his braided train.'

8. 'o'erhang'—a compound in the Miltonic manner; cf. 'o'er-flow,' 'o'erleap.'

8. 'wavy Bed,' and the passage 5-8—cf. *Nativity Ode*, 228-30:
> 'So when the Sun in BED,
> Curtain'd with cloudy red,
> Pillows his chin upon an Orient WAVE . . .'

Milton's picture is, of course, a morning scene.

10. 'Shriek'—see *Eclogues*, II, 57.

11–12. 'Or where the BEETLE WINDS
His small but SULLEN HORN,'
> cf. *Lycidas*, 28:
> > 'What time the gray-fly WINDS her sultry HORN.'

'Sullen' occurs frequently in both poets. See above.

13. ' 'midst'—see *Eclogue* III, 7.

15. 'compos'd'—cf. *P.L.*, VI, 469; *P.L.*, XII, 596; *et. al.*

16. 'breathe' = to speak in verse—cf. *Comus*, 245.

16. 'soften'd'—cf. *Passions*, 46.

16. 'soften'd STRAIN'—cf. *Nativity Ode*, 16, 'solemn STRAIN.'

17. 'NUMBERS'—cf. *P.L.*, III, 38, 'harmonious NUMBERS.'

17. 'darkning VALE'—cf. *P.R.*, I, 304, 'shady VALE.'

18. 'unseemly'—cf. *Samson Agonistes*, 690, 1451.

18. 'suit' (verb)—cf. *P.L.*, VIII, 388.

19. 'hail' (verb)—cf. *Samson Agonistes*, 354.

21. 'For when THY FOLDING STAR arising shews'
> cf. *Comus*, 93:
> > 'The STAR that bids the shepherd FOLD.'

22. 'paly CIRCLET'—cf. *P.L.*, V, 169, 'bright CIRCLET.'

22. 'warning LAMP'—cf. *Nativity Ode*, 242; 'Handmaid LAMP';
and for the spirit of 21-2, cf.:
> 'And bid haste the evening Starr
> On his Hill top, to light the bridal LAMP.'

23. 'fragrant'—cf. *P.L.*, IV, 645, 695; *et. al.*

25. 'And many a Nymph who wreaths her Brows with SEDGE,'
> cf. *Lycidas*, 105:
> > 'with bonnet SEDGE.'

26. 'sheds' (verb)—cf. *P.L.*, IV, 501.

27. 'Pensive'—cf. *Pen.*, 31.

28. 'shadowy CAR'—cf. *Nativity Ode*, 241, 'polished CAR.'

29. 'calm Vot'ress'—cf. in spirit *Comus*, 188-9:
>   'When the gray-hooded EEV'N
>   Like a sad VOTARIST in Palmer's Weed,'

30. 'some time-hallow'd Pile'—cf. *P.R.*, IV, 547; cf. *To Shake-speare*, 2:
>   'the labour of an age in piled stone.'

30. 'cheers'—cf. *P.R.*, IV, 433.

31. 'UP-LAND Fallows'—cf. *All.*, 92, 'UPLAND Hamlets.'

31. 'FALLOWS GREY'—cf. *All.*, 72, 'Russet lawns and FALLOWS GREY.'

33. 'chill BLUST'RING WINDS—cf. *P.L.*, II, 286, 'the sound of BLUSTERING WINDS.'

34. 'Forbid'—cf. *P.L.*, V, 61; *Comus*, 269; *et. al.*

34. 'WILLING FEET'—cf. *P.L.*, III, 73, 'WILLING FEET.'

36. 'Floods'—cf. *P.L.*, IV, 231; VI, 830; VII, 57, 295; *et. al.*

37. 'HAMLETS brown'—cf. *All.*, 92, 'upland HAMLETS.'

37. 'dim-discover'd'—a compound in the Miltonic manner.

39. 'dewy'—see *Song. Sentiments from Shakespeare*, 3.

40. 'gradual'—cf. *P.L.*, V, 483.

40. 'dusky'—cf. *P.L.*, II, 488; V, 186; *et. al.*

40. 'Veil'—see *Fear*, 38.

41. 'wont' (verb)—see *Liberty*, 94.

42. 'bathe'—see *Col. Ross*, 22.

42. 'breathing'—see *Eclogues*, III, 6.

42. 'Tresses'—cf. *P.L.*, IX, 841; *et. al.*, especially *Comus*, 929.

43. 'sport' (verb)—cf. *Lycidas*, 68; *P.L.*, VIII, 405.

45. 'sallow'—cf. *Comus*, 709.

46. 'yelling'—cf. *P.R.*, IV, 923.

47. 'affrights' (verb)—cf. *Nativity Ode*, 194; *Comus*, 148.

47. 'Train'—see *Eclogue* I, 51-68.

48. 'rends'—cf. *P.L.*, X, 700.

49. 'Shed' (noun)—cf. *Comus*, 323.

49. 'SYLVAN Shed'—cf. *P.L.*, V, 377, 'SYLVAN Lodge.'

Ode to Peace:

1– 6. Compare with *Nativity Ode*, 44-52. See text, pp. 138-9.

1. 'Turtles'—cf. *Nativity Ode*, 50, 'with TURTLE wing.'

5. 'bent' (verb)—cf. *P.L.*, I, 681; *P.L.*, II, 354, 373; *et. al.*

5. 'iron' (adj.)—cf. *P.L.*, II, 327.

5. 'Car'—see *Evening*, 28.
7. 'rude'—see *Poetical Character*, 56.
7. 'TYRANNIC Sway'—cf. *P.R.*, I, 219, 'TYRANNIC Power.'
7. 'Sway' (noun)—cf. *P.R.*, III, 160, 'temperate SWAY.'
9. 'sullen'—see *Eclogues*, II, 56.
10. 'TURNING SPHERES'—cf. *Nativity Ode*, 48, 'down through the TURNING SPHERE.'
11. 'partial'—cf. *P.L.*, II, 552.
13. 'upbind'—a compound in the Miltonic manner; cf. 'up-sprung.'
15. 'beamy'—an adjective in the Miltonic manner.
19. 'court' (verb)—see *Liberty*, 14.
20. 'grace' (verb)—see *Fear*, 34.
21. 'warlike'—see above, *Liberty*, 110.

The Manners: (the structural resemblance of the poem to *L'Allegro* and *Il Penseroso* is discussed in the text, p. 133) :

1. 'Ken'—cf. *P.L.*, III, 622; *P.L.*, XI, 379.
1. 'design'd'—cf. *Samson Agonistes*, 801, where the word is used in the sense of 'intended.'
2. 'dim-discover'd'—a compound in the Miltonic manner.
2. 'Tracts'—cf. *P.L.*, VI, 76, 'many a TRACT of Heaven.'
5. 'Deep' (noun)—cf. *P.L.*, VII, 413; *Comus*, 23, 733; *Lycidas*, 50.
7. 'What REGIONS part the WORLD OF SOUL,'
   cf. *Il Penseroso*, 90:
     'WHAT worlds or what VAST REGIONS hold
     THE IMMORTAL MIND that hath forsook
     Her mansion in this fleshly nook;'
7. 'part' (verb)—cf. *P.L.*, II, 660; *P.L.*, I, 420.
9. 'round' (verb)—cf. *P.L.*, X, 684; *P.R.*, I, 365.
10. 'impart'—cf. *P.R.*, I, 417; III, 124. The word occurs also in *Manners*, 25.
11. 'wizzard' (adj.)—see *Liberty*, 65.
11. 'giant' (adj.)—see *Liberty*, 75.
13–14. cf. *P.R.*, IV, 245-6.
15–16. 'Where Science, PRANK'D in tissued Vest,
     By REASON, Pride, and Fancy DREST,'
       cf. *Comus*, 759:
         'Obtruding false rules PRANCKT in REASON'S GARB.'

15. 'tissued'—cf. *Nativity Ode,* 146.
15. 'Vest'—see *Poet. Char.,* 45.
17. 'trim array'd'—cf. *Nativity Ode,* 33, 'gaudy trim'; *Comus,* 120, 'decked with daisies trim.'
19. 'uncheated'—a Miltonic compound.
20. 'invite'—cf. *All.,* 92.
21. 'ampler'—cf. *P.L.,* IX, 876.
22. 'Life's WIDE PROSPECTS . . . '
     cf. *P.L.,* V, 88:
         "the Earth . . . a PROSPECT WIDE and various.'
23. 'mingling'—cf. *Comus,* 994.
23. 'Converse' (noun)—cf. *P.L.,* VIII, 409; *P.L.,* IX, 247, 909.
30. 'shifting'—cf. *P.L.,* IX, 515.
31. 'meddling'—cf. *Comus,* 846.
31. 'officious'—cf. *P.R.,* II, 302; *P.L.,* IX, 104.
33. 'alluring'—cf. *P.L.,* III, 573; XI, 718; *et. al.*
34. 'To dream in her enchanted School';
     cf. *All,* 129-30:
         'Such sights as youthful poets dream,
         On summer eves by haunted stream.'
37– 8. 'Retiring hence to thoughtful CELL,
         As Fancy breathes her potent SPELL'
     cf. *Pen.,* 169-ff.
         'Find out the peaceful hermitage,
         The hairy gown, and mossy CELL
         Where I may sit and rightly SPELL . . . '
38. 'potent Spell'—cf. *Comus,* 255, 'potent herbs.'
40. 'In PAGEANT QUAINT, in motley MASK'
     cf. *Allegro,* 128:
         'With MASK and ANTIQUE PAGEANTRY.'
40. 'quaint'—cf. *Comus,* 157, 'my QUAINT HABITS.'
45. 'white rob'd'—cf. *Death of a Fair Infant,* 54.
50. 'The COMIC SOCK that binds thy Feet!'
     cf. *All.,* 132:
         'If Jonson's LEARNED SOCK be on.'
52. 'favor'd' (adj.)—cf. *P.R.,* II, 91.
53. 'ME too midst thy BAND ADMIT,'
     cf. *Allegro,* 38:
         'Mirth, ADMIT me of thy CREW.'
54. 'young-eyed'—a compound in the Miltonic manner.

54. 'healthful'—cf. *P.L.*, XI, 523.
55. 'crispèd'—cf. *P.L.*, IV, 237.
58. 'In LAUGHTER loos'd attends thy SIDE!'
    cf. *All.*, 32:
      'LAUGHTER holding both his SIDES.'
60. 'Love-inwoven'—a compound in the Miltonic manner; cf. 'love-darting.'
71. 'NATURE BOON'—cf. *P.L.*, IV, 242, 'NATURE BOON.'
72. 'prompted'—See *Fear*, 17; *Pity*, 35.
76. 'oft-turn'd'—a Miltonic compound; cf. 'oft-invocated.'
78. 'rove'—see *Epistle to Hanmer*, 95.
78. 'Scene-full'—a compound in the Miltonic manner.

The Passions, an Ode for Music:

4. 'Shell'—see *Pity*, 42.
7. 'glowing'—cf. *P.L.*, V, 10.
16. 'prove'—cf. *P.L.*, IX, 616; *P.R.*, I, 370.
19. 'back recoil'd'—cf. *Comus*, 593, "But Evil on itself shall BACK RECOIL'; see also, *P.L.*, VI, 194; *P.R.*, II, 759.
22. 'secret Stings'—cf. *P.R.*, I, 466, 'inly stung.'
23. 'rude'—see *Poet. Char.*, 56.
25. 'woful'—cf. *P.L.*, X, 984; *Lycidas*, 166.
25. 'wan'—cf. *Sonnet*, XIII, 6.
26. 'sullen'—see *Eclogues*, II, 56.
26. 'Low SULLEN Sounds his Grief beguil'd'
    cf. *Pen.*, 76:
      'Swinging slow with SULLEN roar.'
27. 'MINGLED Air"—cf. *Comus*, 994. Collins employs the word three times in the poem; see line 64, 'MINGLED Measure,' and line 114, 'MINGLED World.'
37. 'Close' (noun)—cf. *Nativity Ode*, 100; *Comus*, 548.
37. 'responsive'—cf. *P.L.*, IV, 683.
43. 'with'ring'—see *Fear*, 43.
44. 'dread'—see *Liberty*, 78.
45. 'prophetic'—see *Poetical Character*, 21.
51. 'unalter'd'—cf. *P.R.*, I, 493.
53. 'Numbers'—see *Evening*, 17.
55. 'veering'—cf. *P.L.*, IX, 315.
56. 'courted'—see *Liberty*, 14.
57–68. With the description of 'Pale Melancholy' compare the Melancholy of *Il Penseroso*.

57– 8. 'With Eyes up-rais'd, as one inspir'd'
   cf. *Pen.*, 39-40:
      'And looks commercing with the skies,
      Thy rapt Soul sitting in thine eyes':
59–61. 'And from her wild sequester'd Seat,
   In Notes by Distance made more sweet,
   Pour'd thro' the mellow Horn her pensive Soul':
      cf. *Comus*, 386-8:
         '. . . musing meditation most affects
         The pensive secrecy of desert cell
         Far from the cheerful haunt of men.'
   64. 'Glades'—cf. *P.L.*, IV, 231; *Pen.*, 27; *Comus*, 79, 532.
   64. 'Glooms'—cf. *Nativity Ode*, 77.
   66. 'Or o'er some HAUNTED STREAM'—cf. *All.*, 130, 'HAUNTED STREAM.'
   66. 'diffusing'—cf. *P.L.*, IV, 818; VII, 265; IX, 852.
   68. 'hollow Murmurs'—cf. *Nativity Ode*, 178, 'hollow shriek.'
70– 2. '. . . Chearfulness, a Nymph of healthiest Hue,
   Her Bow a-cross her shoulder flung . . .
   Blew an inspiring Air, that Dale and Thicket rung . . .'
      cf. *Comus*, 422-3:
         'And like a quiver'd Nymph with Arrows keen
         May trace huge Forests, and unharbour'd Heath.'
   72. 'Buskins'—cf. *Pen.*, 102.
   72. 'gem'd'—cf. *P.L.*, VII, 325.
74– 6. 'The Hunter's Call to FAUN and DRYAD known!
   The Oak-crown'd SISTERS, and their chast-eye'd QUEEN,
   SATYRS and sylvan Boys were seen . . .'
      cf. *Lycidas*, 34-5:
         'Rough SATYRS danc'd, and FAUNS with clov'n heel,
         From the glad sound would not be absent long.'
   75. 'Oak-crown'd' and 'chast-eye'd'—compounds in the Miltonic manner.
   76. 'sylvan'—see *Song, Cymbeline*, 18.
   77. 'ALLEYS GREEN'—cf. *Comus*, 311, 'Each lane and every ALLEY GREEN,'
   80. 'ecstatic'—see *Poet. Char.*, 43.
   82. 'lively'—cf. *All.*, 49.
   83. 'Viol'—cf. *Passion*, 28.
   83. 'brisk'—cf. *Comus*, 671.
   84. 'entrancing'—cf. *Comus*, 1005.

87. 'amidst'—see *Eclogue* III, 7.
87. 'sounding' (adj.)—cf. *P.L.*, I, 668; *Lycidas*, 154.
88. 'unwearied'—cf. *P.L.*, VI, 404; *P.L.*, VII, 522
89. 'KISS'd the Strings'—cf. *Nativity Ode*, 65, 'smoothly the waters KISSED.'
90. 'fram'd'—cf. *P.L.*, XII, 249.
90. 'a gay FANTASTIC ROUND,'
    cf. *All.*, 34:
        'On the light FANTASTIC TOE.'
        cf. also *Comus*, 143-5, from which, in fact, the whole spirit of lines 82-94 seems derived:
    'Come, knit hands, and beat the ground,
In a light FANTASTIC ROUND.'
91. 'Tresses'—see *Evening*, 42.
91. 'Zone'—see *Poet. Char.*, 16.
92. 'And He amidst his FROLIC PLAY'
    cf. *All.*, 18-19:
        'The FROLIC wind that breathes the spring,
        Zephyr with Aurora PLAYING.'
93. 'charming' (adj.)—cf. *P.L.*, III, 368; *Comus*, 476; *et. al.*
93– 4. 'As if he would the charming Air repay,
SHOOK thousand Odours from his DEWY WINGS.'
    cf. *P.L.*, V, 285-7:
        '. . . Like Maia's son he stood,
        And SHOOK his PLUMES that heav'nly fragrance fill'd
        The circuit wide.'
    cf. also as a source of the passage, *P.L.*, IV, 156-9. Bronson, following Dyce, suggests also *P.R.*, II, 362-5; Pope's *Eloisa to Abelard*, 218, and (with more plausibility) Fairfax's *Tasso*, I, 14: "And SHOOK HIS WINGS with roarie MAY-DEWS wet' as sources of the passage.
95. 'O Music, SPHERE-DESCENDED MAID,'
    cf. *At a Solemn Music*, 1-2:
        'Blest pair of Sirens, pledges of Heav'ns joy,
        SPHEAR-BORN harmonious Sisters, Voice and Verse . . .'
    See especially in this connection line 108,
        'thy recording Sister.'
100. 'all-commanding'—cf. *Psalm* CXXXVI, 25.
101. 'mimic' (adj.)—cf. *P.L.*, V, 110.
107. 'God-like'—see *Mercy*, 8.
118. 'confirm'—cf. *P.L.*, I, 663.

Ode on the Death of Mr. Thomson:

2. 'winds' (verb)—cf. *P.L.*, IV, 545.
2. 'stealing'—cf. *P.L.*, XI, 847; *Arcades*, 31.
3. 'Sweets'—cf. *P.L.*, V, 296: 'those odorous SWEETS.'
3. 'duteous'—cf. *P.L.*, IX, 521.
4. 'deck' (verb)—see above, *Epistle to Hanmer*, 100.
4. 'sylvan'—see *Song, Cymbeline*, 18.
5. 'whisp'ring'—cf. *All.*, 116; *P.R.*, IV, 250.
7. 'airy'—cf. *P.L.*, II, 536.
10. 'swell' (verb)—cf. *Comus*, 732.
18. 'breezy LAWN'—cf. *All.*, 71, 'russet LAWN.'
26. 'glimm'ring'—cf. *Pen.*, 27; *P.L.*, III, 429.
29. 'lorn'—cf. 'love-lorn', *Comus*, 234.
29. 'sullen'—see *Eclogue* II, 56.
30. 'SEDGE-crowned Sisters'—cf. *Lycidas*, 104, 'Bonnet SEDGE.'
31. 'waft'—cf. *Lycidas*, 164.
34. 'DUN NIGHT has veil'd the solemn View!'
    cf. *P.L.*, III, 71-2:
       '. . . NIGHT
       In the DUN Air sublime. . . .'
41– 2. 'Long, long, thy STONE and POINTED CLAY
    Shall melt the musing Briton's Eyes,'
    cf. *On Shakespeare*, 1-4:
       'What needs my Shakespear for his honour'd Bones,
       The labour of an age in piled STONES,
       Or that his hallow'd reliques should be hid
       Under a STAR-Y POINTING Pyramid?'

Ode on the Popular Superstitions of the Highlands of Scotland
(A discussion of the specific influence of *L'Allegro* and
Il Penseroso and *Lycidas* on the ode is given in the text, pp.
136-8. In the following analysis only the lines in the Transactions version are examined, though I have followed here
Mr. Blunden's line numbering, which includes the additions
of the 1788 London edition. I have added to the discussion
of this ode a brief analysis why, on the grounds of diction
alone, the additions can hardly be considered the work of
Collins.)

5. 'unmindful'—cf. *P.L.*, XI, 611; *Comus*, 9.
5. 'cordial'—cf. *P.L.*, V, 12.

6. 'endear'd'—cf. *Samson Agonistes*, 796.
9. 'regardless'—cf. *P.L.*, XII, 47.
14. 'prompt'—See *Fear*, 35.
17. 'genial'—cf. *Samson Agonistes*, 594.
18. 'DORIC QUILL'—cf. *Lycidas*, 188-9:
    'He touch'd the tender stops of various QUILLS,
    With eager thought warbling his DORICK lay.'
21. 'mead'—see above, *Eclogues*, III, 12; cf. also *Liberty*, 56.
22. 'trim' (adj.)—cf. *All.*, 75; *Pen.*, 50.
22. 'store' (noun)—see *Eclogue* II, 33.
23. 'SWART tribes'—cf. *Comus*, 436, 'SWART Faery,' a passage to
    which Collins had already turned in the *Ode to Fear*.
23. 'creamy bowls'—cf. *All.*, 106, 'to earn his CREAM-BOWL duly
    set.'
23. 'allots'—cf. *P.R.*, II, 123.
25. 'airy'—see *Mr. Thomson*, 7; see also line 30 of this ode.
25. 'JOCUND notes'—cf. *All.*, 94, 'JOCUND rebecks'; cf. also *P.L.*,
    I, 786-7.
28. 'foregoes'—cf. *Samson Agonistes*, 1483.
29. 'heart-smit'—cf. *P.L.*, XI, 264, 'heart-strook.'
30. 'swain'—cf. *Comus*, 84, 951, 634; *Lycidas*, 92, 113, 186;
    et. al.
42. 'uncouth'—see *Liberty*, 75.
42. 'vest'—see *Poet. Char.*, 45.
43. 'fantastic'—see *Passions*, 90.
44. 'hind'—see *Song, Cymbeline*, 2.
45. 'choral'—cf. *P.L.*, V, 162.
47. 'choicest'—cf. *P.R.*, IV, 329; *Samson Agonistes*, 633, 1654;
    et. al.
47. 'And STREW'D with CHOICEST herbs his scented grave;'
    cf. *Lycidas*, 151 (and the passage preceding) :
    'To STREW the Laureat Herse where *Lycid* lies.'
49. 'SOUNDING tale'—cf. *Lycidas*, 154: 'SOUNDING Seas.' See also
    P.L., I, 668.
51. 'sturdy'—cf. *P.R.*, IV, 417.
51. 'swarms' (noun)—cf. *Samson Agonistes*, 192.
52. 'prove' (verb) = try—cf. *P.L.*, II, 369.
53. 'framing'—cf. *P.L.*, V, 460.
53. 'hideous'—see *Fear*, 12.

53. 'spells'—see *Poet. Char.,* 12.
54. 'gifted wizzard seer'—cf. *Samson Agonistes,* 36, 'heaven-gifted.'
54. 'wizzard' (adj.)—see *Liberty,* 65.
57. 'dreary'—see *Fear,* 36.
57. 'engross'—cf. *P.L.,* V, 775.
60. 'They see the GLIDING GHOSTS UNBODIED TROOP.'
     cf. *Nativity Ode,* 233:
         'The FLOCKING SHADOWS pale TROOP to the infernal jail.'
62. 'descry'—cf. *P.L.,* I, 290; *P.L.,* II, 636; *et. al.*
63. 'lusty'—cf. *Nativity Ode,* 36.
64. 'rosy'—cf. *P.L.,* V, 1; VI, 3; *et. al.*
65. 'viewless'—cf. *P.L.,* III, 518.
66. 'beck'—cf. *P.R.,* II, 238.
66. 'repair'—cf. *P.L.,* X, 1087, 1099.
95. 'dell'—cf. *Comus,* 312.
95. 'espied'—cf. *P.L.,* IV, 477.
96. 'glimmering'—see *Mr. Thomson,* 26.
96. 'maze'—cf. *P.R.,* II, 246.
96. 'cheer'—see *Evening,* 30.
96. 'excursive' = journeying—cf. *P.L.,* VIII, 231, 'excursion.'
99. 'lurking'—cf. *P.L.,* IX, 1172.
99. 'unrustling'—cf. such Miltonic compounds as 'unhallowed,' 'unbenighted.'
100. 'mirk'—cf. *P.L.,* X, 250.
100. 'WILY monster'—cf. *P.L.,* IX, 91, 'WILY snake.'
101. 'steed'—see *Mercy,* 20.
102. 'And frequent ROUND him ROLLS his SULLEN EYES.'
      cf. *P.L.,* I, 56:
          '. . . ROUND he THROWS his BALEFUL EYES . . .'
104. 'unblest'—cf. *Comus,* 907; *et. al.*
105. 'dank'—cf. *P.L.,* IV, 177; *Comus,* 891.
106. 'smoking HAMLET'—cf. *All.,* 92, 'upland HAMLET.'
110. 'WHELMING flood'—cf. *Lycidas,* 157, 'WHELMING tide.'
112. 'meditate'—cf. *Lycidas,* 66.
112. 'wish'd'—cf. *Comus,* 594, 950.
113. 'SOME dim HILL'—cf. *All.,* 55, 'SOME hoar HILL.'
113. 'uprising' (verbal adj.)—cf. *P.L.,* V, 139.

114. 'grim'—cf. *Comus*, 694.
114. 'grisly'—cf. *P.L.*, II, 704.
115. 'clad'—see *P.L.*, I, 410; IV, 289, 599; *et. al.*
116. 'wat'ry'—cf. *Lycidas*, 12; *et. al.* See also line 129 of the ode.
116. 'surge'—cf. *P.L.*, X, 417; *P.L.*, I, 173.
117. 'swelling' (verb)—cf. *Comus*, 732.
118. 'And DOWN THE WAVES he floats a pale and breathless corse.'
    cf. *Lycidas*, 62-3:
        'His goary visage DOWN THE STREAM was sent,
        Down the swift Hebrus to the Lesbian shore.'
    See also *Lycidas*, 12.
124. 'unclosing'—a Miltonism.
126. 'travell'd'—cf. *P.L.*, III, 501.
129. 'moist'—cf. *Comus*, 918.
130. 'shuddering'—cf. *Comus*, 802.
136. 'While I lie WELTERING on the osier'd shore.'
    cf. *Lycidas*, 13:
        '. . . and WELTER to the parching wind.'
139. 'wasting'—cf. *P.R.*, II, 256.
144. 'bounded'—cf. *P.L.*, III, 432, 539; *et. al.*
144. 'rugged cliffs'—cf. *Psalm* CXIV, 17.
145. 'prospect'—see *Poet. Char.*, 56.
145. 'main'—see *Poet. Char.*, 28.
147. 'drain' (verb)—cf. *P.R.*, II, 346.
147. 'sainted'—see *Poet. Char.*, 42.
147. 'hunger-prest'—cf. *P.R.*, II, 416, 'hunger-bit.'
148. 'undreading'—cf. *P.L.*, X, 595, 'undreaded.'
149. 'despoil'—cf. *Samson Agonistes*, 539.
151. 'suffic'd'—cf. *P.R.*, II, 276.
154. 'vernal'—see *Liberty*, 4.
155. 'unbounded'—cf. *P.L.*, IV, 60.
156. 'feathery'—cf. *Comus*, 347.
157. 'rude'—see *Poet. Char.*, 56.
157. 'skirting'—cf. *P.L.*, VI, 80.
158. 'MOIST marge'—cf. *P.L.*, V, 422, 'MOIST continent.'
158 'each cold Hebrid isle"—cf. *Lycidas*, 156, 'the stormy Hebrides.'
142. 'hoar pile'—see *Evening*, 30.
161. 'upthrows'—cf. in Milton 'upsend,' 'upspring,' 'uptear.'
162. 'culls'—see *Simplicity*, 29.

162. 'hallow'd'—see *Poet. Char.*, 54.
163. 'SHOWERY west'—cf. *P.L.*, VI, 759, 'SHOWERY arch.'
168. 'rifted'—cf. *Comus*, 518.
168. 'YAWNING cells'—cf. *P.L.*, X, 635, 'YAWNING Grave.'
168. 'cells'—see *Manners*, 37-8.
168. 'unfold'—cf. *P.L.*, IV, 381; *P.L.*, X, 635.
169. 'stalk' (verb)—cf. *P.L.*, IV, 402; *Samson Agonistes*, 1245.
170. 'pageant robes'—cf. *Simplicity* above. See 183 of the ode.
170. 'sheeny'—cf. *Death of a Fair Infant*, 48.
171. 'twilight'—cf. *Nativity Ode*, 188; *Pen.*, 133; *Comus*, 844.
171. 'aerial'—see *Col. Ross*, 20.
179. 'drest'—see *Liberty*, 8.
181. 'afflicted'—cf. *P.L.*, I, 186; IV, 939.
181. 'aghast'—cf. *Nativity Ode*, 160; *P.L.*, II, 616; *et. al.*
182. 'shadowy'—see *Fear*, 2.
184. 'quit'—cf. *P.R.*, III, 241.
188. 'suit'—cf. *P.L.*, VIII, 388.
194 'gaping'—cf. *P.L.*, II, 440, 'wide-gaping.'
196. 'upheav'd'—cf. *P.L.*, VII, 236, 471.
197. '. . . where PIP'D the pensive WIND'
    cf. *Pen.*, 126:
        'While rocking WINDS are PIPING loud.'
199. 'prevailing'—cf. *Samson Agonistes*, 661, 869.
199. 'undoubting'—a typical Miltonism.
208. 'SMOOTH Annan'—cf. *Comus*, 825, 'SMOOTH Severn.'
211. 'SPREADING broom'—cf. *P.L.*, X, 1067, 'SPREADING trees.'
212. 'stretching heaths'—cf. *P.L.*, II, 1003.
214. 'dress'—see line 179.

Stanzas Written on a Paper which Contained a Piece of Bride-Cake:

  1. 'curious'—cf. *P.R.*, I, 319.
  2. 'profane' (adj.)—cf. *Samson Agonistes*, 1362.
  2. 'hallow'd'—see *Poet. Char.*, 54.
  3. 'forbear' (verb)—cf. *P.L.*, II, 736.
  5. 'relick'—see *Liberty*, 38.
 10. 'nice'—cf. *P.L.*, VIII, 399.
 13. 'WITH ROSY HAND'—cf. *P.L.*, VI, 3, 'WITH ROSY HAND.'
 13. 'spicy'—see *Eclogue* IV, 53.
 16. 'ambrosial'—cf. *P.L.*, IV, 219; *Comus*, 16; *et. al.*

17. 'ambiguous'—cf. *P.L.*, V, 703; VI, 568; *et. al.*
18. 'unalter'd'—cf. *P.R.*, I, 493.
19–20. 'RELUCTANT pride, and AMOROUS FAINT CONSENT,
    And meeting ardours, and exulting youth,'
        cf. *P.L.*, IV, 310-11:
            'Yielded with coy submission, modest pride,
            And SWEET RELUCTANT AMOROUS DELAY.'
32. 'raven' (adj.)—cf. *Comus*, 251.

A number of minor borrowings of word or phrase Collins drew from Spenser, from Fairfax's *Tasso*, from Shakespeare, from Pope, and from Thomson. These are neither so numerous nor so convincing as the suggestions drawn from Milton, partly because many words included in the list of Miltonic words are also the common property of Shakespeare and the Elizabethans. With few exceptions the parallels between Collins and Thomson are found in Milton as well. These borrowings are noted in footnotes at the appropriate places in Part II.

The only part of Collins's poetry not examined in the preceding pages is the section of the *Ode on the Popular Superstitions* which appeared in the anonymous London edition of 1788. Bronson has already proved convincingly that the stanzas are not the work of Collins. A study of the Miltonic diction in these stanzas seems to substantiate his contention. In the twenty-five lines interpolated less than ten words are suggestively Miltonic—notably "welkin," "fell" (adj.), "swain," "dank," "mirky," "fen," and "brake." This is a painfully small proportion in a poem so thoroughly Miltonic as this one; certainly fewer words in these lines suggest Milton than in any corresponding number of lines in the rest of the poem. In the other additions the Miltonic diction is equally slight. "Sedgy," in the completion of line 107, suggests Milton, as do "sheen" in the interpolated line 177, and "awful" in interpolated line 213, but the rest of the lines in which these words occur are foreign in spirit to both Collins and Milton. Aside from consideration of the diction it seems incredible that between the inspired and poetic passages on "second sight" and the death of the "luckless swain," Collins could have dropped to such redundant and prosaic passages as:

Oft have they seen FATE give the FATAL blow

In the FIRST year of the FIRST George's reign

Ah HOMELY swains! your HOMEWARD steps ne'er lose.

Nor at that stage in his poetic career would Collins have padded out such a line as:

The Seer, in Sky, shriek'd as the blood DID FLOW

Moreover, except for the allusions to "Preston's fight" and "Pale, red Culloden," and the praise of "Illustrious William," who had by the time Collins was writing somewhat outlived his popularity, the ideas in the passage seem drawn from what precedes and follows them with none too skilful connection. Surely the allusions themselves are in bad taste in a poem celebrating the folkways of the Highlanders who had sympathized with the Pretender.

INDEX

INDEX

Addison, Joseph, 43n, 91n, 95n, 205.
Aeschylus, 1, 22.
Akenside, Mark, *Pleasures of the Imagination,* 92, 95n, 222, 279.
Alcaeus, 74, 105, 119.
Aldine Collins, 4n, 5, 6n, 7n, 8; on election to New College, 9; 12, 16n, 24n.
Anderson, *British Poets,* 235.
Aristogiton, 74, 77n.
Aristotle, *Poetics,* 16, 17, 22, 35, 37, 38, 81, 114, 122, 122n.
Armstrong, Doctor, 14, 21, 222.
Arne, Dr. Thomas, 244n.
Arnold, Matthew, *Thyrsis,* 56; *Balder Dead,* 61n; 289.
Ascham, Roger, 10.
Aurelio and Isabella, 184.

Bailey, Ronald, 244n.
Balfour, J., printer, 231.
Balmerino, 66, 71.
Barbauld, Mrs. Lætitia, 35, 39, 40, 68, 79, 82, 101n, 115, 193, 213, 235; her *Ode to Content,* 257n.
Barnes, schoolfellow to Hunt, 277.
Barrett, *Guide to Chichester,* 22n.
Barrow, John (Thomas), 23, 23n, 24n.
Barrowby, Doctor, 14.
Beattie, James, *The Minstrel,* 56.
Beauties of English Poetry, 225-6.
Beerbohm, Max, *Zuleika Dobson,* 204n.
Belden, H. M., 100n.
Bell, *Poets of Great Britain,* 53n, 68, 233; anonymous edition of *Ode on the Popular Superstitions,* 234, 256.
Beloe, *The Sexagenarian,* 7n.
Bernbaum, Ernest, 73n.
Bible, Exodus, 102n; *Proverbs,* 100.
Biographia Britannica, 19, 22, 114.
Blackwood's Magazine, 240, 241; *Translations of Pindar,* 241, 242; *Our Pocket Companions,* 242; *An Hour's Talk about Poetry,* 242, 243.
Blair, *The Grave,* 164n.

Blake, William, *To the Muses,* 85, 113, 216; influence of Collins on *Poetical Sketches,* 249-50, 288.
Bloxam, *Register of Magdalen College,* 9.
Blunden, Edmund, 12, 13, 20n, 22n, 27n, 36n, 39, 50n, 73n, 81, 82, 95n, 96n, 101n, 103; *Poems of Collins* quoted, 145; 148, 168n, 236, 245n, 263n, 274n, 275, 276-7n, 317.
Boswell, James, *Life of Samuel Johnson,* quoted, 27-8.
Bourke, Margaret, 52n.
Bowles, William L., influence of Collins on, 250-2, 259.
British Magazine, 225.
Bronson, W. C., 5, 6n, 36n, 42, 69n, 73n, 101n, 148, 148n, 204, 221, 244n, 245, 266, 276n, 316, 322.
Brontë, Emily, 79.
Browne, Sir Thomas, *Enquiries into Vulgar and Common Errors,* quoted, 206-7n.
Browning, Robert, 80, 83, 101.
Brydges, Sir Egerton, 227, 231.
Buchan, Earl of, 248.
Bundy, Miss, 13, 16n, 17, 20, 42.
Burnet, Nell, 13.
Burns, Robert, 3, 43n; *Cotter's Saturday Night,* 61n, 216; *Address to the Deil,* 65; *Address to the Shade of Thomson,* 248; *Elegy on Stella,* 248; *Lament of Mary Queen of Scots,* 248; influence of Collins on, 248-9; 269, 270, 288.
Burton, Dr. John, Collins's teacher at Winchester, 5n.
Bute, Lord, 23n.
Butler, Samuel (?), 227.
Byron, George Gordon, Lord, *Letters and Journals,* 36n, 74, 213; *Childe Harold's Pilgrimage,* 216; on Collins's madness, 269; on the *Persian Eclogues,* 269-70; influence of Collins on, 270-1; 288.

Callimachus, 119.
Callistratus, 119.

to Dodsley's *Museum,* 20; interest
in Martin Martin through Thomson and Mallet, 21; friendship
with Thomson at Castle Inn,
20-1; introduces Joseph Warton to
Thomson, 21; writes *Ode on the
Death of Mr. Thomson,* 21; re-
ceives bequest from Colonel Martin, 22; acquaintance with John
Home, 22-3; writes *Epistle to Editor of Fairfax,* 23; composes *Ode
on the Popular Superstitions,* 23;
mentions *Clarendon Review,* 24;
letter to William Hayes, 24-5;
projects *Ode on the Music of the
Grecian Theater,* 25; *The Passions*
performed at Oxford and Winchester, 24-5; Collins's madness begins, 25; travels to France and to
Bath, 26; confined in a madhouse,
26; last meeting with Johnson, 26;
retires with sister to Chichester,
26; visited by the Wartons at
Chichester, 27; shows fragment of
The Bell of Arragon, 27; visits
Oxford in melancholy circumstances, 27-8; finds source of *The
Tempest,* 29; continues *Review of
the Advancement of Learning,* 29;
reprints *Persian Eclogues* as *Oriental Eclogues,* 29; visited by William Smith of Chichester, 29;
anecdotes concerning his last years,
29-30; his death, 30; tastes in
reading, 32-3; interest in drama,
33; fascination with pageantry, 34;
suggestions of stage in odes, 36-7;
influence of *Poetics* on, 37-8; skill
at painting, 38; pictorial qualities
in odes, 39-40; influence of Spence
on, 41; influence of sculpture
on, 41-2; interest in music, 42-4;
interest in nature, 45-58; pastoral element in descriptions of
nature, 46-7; portrayal of imaginative and symbolic in nature, 53-
5; topographical interest in nature,
55-6; fondness for wildness and
magnificence in nature, 56-7; his
treatment of humble man, 58-
65; aloofness of studies of humble man, 58-62; humble man in
the *Ode on the Popular Superstitions,* 60-2; fascination with the
Druids, 62n-63n; sympathetic interest in folk-lore, 63-5; interest

in contemporary events, 66-78; his
love, 67, 67n; blending of classical
and romantic in odes, 77-8; reticence in dealing with emotion, 79-
80; on death, 79; feels need of
describing emotion more deeply,
80; seeks power to feel, 80-3;
achievements and shortcomings in
expression of feeling, 83-4; feeling
concerning the poetry of his day,
85 *seq.;* theory of poetry shared
with Joseph Warton, 85-7, 89-91;
concept of poet and his function,
96 *seq.;* concept of poetic imagination, 85 *seq.;* criticism of the
poetry of his day, 85 *seq.;* concept
of Fancy, 97-105; considers simplicity an adjunct to Fancy, 106;
descriptive and allegoric qualities
in poetry of, 107-13; his personified figures, 107-12; personification of minor figures in odes, 112-
13; tragedy of his slight ac-
complishment, 114; Thomson's description in *Castle of Indolence*
applicable to, 114; his achievement, 114-5; influence of Homer
on, 119-20; debt to Pindar, 120-2;
debt to Greek tragedy, 122-4; influence of Virgil on, 124-6; influence of Horace on, 126-7; use of
Miltonic verse forms, 130-1; influence of *L'Allegro* and *Il Penseroso*
on, 131-5; influence of *Comus* and
Lycidas on, 135-8; influence of
Nativity Ode on, 138-9; Miltonic
image and idiom, in *Ode on the
Poetical Character,* 140-4, in *Ode
to Evening,* 144-8, in *Ode to Liberty,* 148-53; influence of Pope,
on *Persian Eclogues,* 154-7, on
Epistle to Hanmer, 157-8, on *Odes
Descriptive and Allegoric,* 158-65;
influence of Dryden's verse epistles
on, 165-6; influence of Dryden's
odes on, 166-7; collector of Elizabethan books, 168; influence of
Spenser on, 169-73; use of Fairfax's *Tasso,* 173-6; influence of
Shakespeare on, 176-84, on his
lyrics, 177-83; contemporary influences on *Persian Eclogues,* 185;
debt to Joseph Warton's verse,
185-9; debt to Thomas Warton's
verse, 189; influence of Home's
Douglas on, 189-90; influence of